New Economic Patterns in Czechoslovakia

PRAEGER SPECIAL STUDIES IN
INTERNATIONAL ECONOMICS AND DEVELOPMENT

New Economic Patterns in Czechoslovakia

IMPACT OF GROWTH, PLANNING, AND THE MARKET

George R. Feiwel

FREDERICK A. PRAEGER, Publishers
New York · Washington · London

The purpose of the Praeger Special Studies is to make specialized research monographs in U.S. and international economics and politics available to the academic, business, and government communities. For further information, write to the Special Projects Division, Frederick A. Praeger, Publishers, 111 Fourth Avenue, New York, N.Y. 10003.

FREDERICK A. PRAEGER, PUBLISHERS
111 Fourth Avenue, New York, N.Y. 10003, U.S.A.
5, Cromwell Place, London S.W. 7, England

Published in the United States of America in 1968
by Frederick A. Praeger, Inc., Publishers

Library of Congress Catalog Card Number: 68-28474

Printed in the United States of America

To

FRED ZINNEMANN

truly "A Man for All Seasons"

as a token of gratitude

PREFACE

This study is an outgrowth of my research on the sources of growth and retrogression and on the changes in working arrangements of the East European economies on which the Soviet mode of development and the planning system were imposed after World War II. The various countries that came within the Soviet orbit of power differed, *inter alia*, in their stage of economic development and in their degree of involvement in and dependence on foreign trade. A study of the various cases furnishes an opportunity of investigating the performance and the merit of the Soviet economic model under varied economic conditions.

In the 1960's a new dimension--the recognition of what has come to be known as the various roads to socialism or the so-called alternate models of the functioning of the socialist economy--has been added. This offers an opportunity of studying, of observing, and of assessing the working of the economies under modified institutional arrangements. The Yugoslav case aside, it is probably true that so far the differences in actual functioning are significant, but not as pronounced as is usually professed. In analyzing the alterations in working arrangements, one of the main difficulties lies in distinguishing and identifying the changes that were actually introduced and those that are still the "music of the future." Although almost all are for some blending of the plan and the market, it is not at all clear what would be the optimum combinations of the plan and the market at the different stages of development.

It is quite clear that industrially advanced and sophisticated economies, heavily dependent on the international division of labor, cannot do without exposure to and effective participation in foreign trade and without the stimulus, rewards, penalties, compelling pressures, and effort-releasing effect of competition and of the market.

The Czechoslovak experience--the case of the inverse economic miracle--offers an insight into the retrogressive effects of the Soviet model imposed on a relatively mature industrial economy where the sources of extensive growth were gradually exhausted. A genuine attempt was made in Czechoslovakia to implement consequential changes in economic arrangements and to seek in the eradication of inefficiencies a palpable source of sustained economic growth. An examination of the Czechoslovak case points to the requirements of integrated, consistent, and concerted economic refurbishing. It unequivocally demonstrates not only the interdependence of the economic system: growth strategy, planning, value parameters, economic incentives, etc.; but it clearly shows the consequences that follow from a flagrant violation of the requirements of economic efficiency. Furthermore, it emphasizes the interlinking of planning techniques and the institutional arena within which the system operates. Coefficients of economic choice aside, without a fundamental overhaul of the vertical planning pyramid, market-type decentralization is hardly workable. Above all it unmistakably shows that dramatic changes in the economy's working arrangements are intertwined with the political system, and their success to a large measure hinges on concomitant political liberalization. Contrariwise a retrogression in economic liberalization may be expected with a political setback.

This is not to say that the retardation in economic performance is not one of the primary or perhaps the decisive factor in precipitating economic reforms. Their content, direction, and rapidity of implementation largely depend on the severity of the revealed economic crisis (by itself a function of the stage of economic development achieved). The inability to cope with dislocations by the proven and expedient methods of the traditional system and the threat of popular discontent if economic ills should adversely affect the living standards force the leadership to take a hard look at economic realities. As I have suggested in a paper on the plan and the market, read at the December, 1967, session of the American Association for the Advancement of Science, as a corollary to the theory of cyclical development in the traditional socialist economy, one could envisage a theory of cyclical economic reforms.

As this study was nearing completion, with the original target to evaluate in this volume the changes until the end of 1967, one of the main impediments to reform implementation was removed--Antonin Novotny lost his seat of power and Czechoslovakia embarked on a new course of momentous changes. I have always been a firm believer in the division of labor and it is not without great hesitation that I took on the task of analyzing political events, but I increasingly became convinced that the underlying political currents are of cardinal importance for the success of the reform.

ACKNOWLEDGMENTS

I am at a loss for words to express adequately my appreciation to all those who have left their imprint on this book.

I am beholden to Professor Abram Bergson, Director of Harvard University's Russian Research Center, for his incessant encouragement and good and friendly advice and for giving me the opportunity of benefiting from the superb facilities of the Center. The Conference on Eastern European Economies, organized by Professors Abram Bergson and Simon Kuznets, sponsored by the Social Science Research Council, and held in Cambridge, Mass., in May, 1967, was helpful in providing the opportunity to exchange views, particularly with Professors Miloslav Bernesek, Vaclav Holesovsky, Jan Michal, and George J. Staller. Professor Bergson kindly invited me to present the results of my research to his Seminar on Comparative Economics at Harvard University in September, 1967, where I benefited from the comments of the participants, particularly Professors Bergson, Joseph S. Berliner, Leonard Kirsch, and Leon Smolinski.

It is always a pleasant task to acknowledge my indebtedness to Professor Alexander Erlich. I have also profited from discussions of some of the aspects of this study with Professor John Michael Montias. Dr. Alfred Zauberman rendered his authoritative and moral support to my analysis of the changes of planning techniques. It was good to debate some of the points raised with Professor Alec Nove. Discussions with Professor Gregory Grossman, especially on the thorny issue of the plan and the market, were helpful as always. I would also like to express my appreciation to Professor

Adam Ulam for his good advice. I hope that the many Czechoslovak economists and government officials who have rendered a helping hand will not take it amiss if I thank them collectively.

I must record here again a debt of gratitude to my former teachers at McGill University, especially Professors Donald E. Armstrong and Earl F. Beach. Sincere appreciation is due to my colleagues and graduate students for their interest in my work and for the atmosphere of good companionship. Thanks are due to the University of Tennessee and Deans Arthur E. Warner and Allen H. Keally for support. The assistance of the University of Tennessee Library has proven invaluable, as always; I cannot but mention here the help of Professors Olive H. Branch and Sarah B. Holland. It is also a pleasure to acknowledge the support of the American Council of Learned Societies.

All those mentioned must be absolved of any responsibility for the arguments presented or the errors committed. While I shoulder all the blame, all credit goes to my wife.

Knoxville, Tennessee George R. Feiwel

CONTENTS

Page

PREFACE vii

ACKNOWLEDGMENTS xi

LIST OF TABLES xv

LIST OF CHARTS xxi

ABBREVIATIONS xxiii

1 MAIN CURRENTS IN ECONOMIC DEVELOPMENT 1

Adoption of Soviet Growth Strategy 4
Assessment of Growth Performance 56

2 THE FUNCTIONING OF THE ECONOMY 82

Adoption of the Traditional System 82
The Anatomy of the Planning System 89
The 1958-59 Reform and Its Aftermath 103

3 IN SEARCH OF MARKET SOCIALISM 129

Plan and Market: Erosion of Old Myths 129
The Draft Principles of the New System 146
Plan and Market: Debate on Reform Implementation 150

4 BLUEPRINT FOR THE NEW PATTERNS 187

The Implementation Schedule 187
Administrative Reorganization 189
Experiments 195

		Page
5	THE INCIPIENT PHASE	219
	Plan and Performance	219
	Guidelines for Reform	232
	The 1966 Version of the New System	237
	Performance in 1966	256
6	PRELUDE TO THE 1967 CHANGES	274
	The Price Revision	274
	Regulations for 1967 Changes	288
	Investments in the New System	306
	Aspects of Foreign Trade Policy	317
7	THE FALTERING WINDS OF ECONOMIC CHANGE	319
	The Lessons of 1967: Effects of Price Revision	319
	New Policies and Their Efficacy	329
	Results and Prospects	358
8	EPILOGUE	405
	A Background of the Struggle for Political and Social Reform	405
	The Writers' Revolt	412
	A Power Struggle	422
	The Changing of the Guard	427
	Democracy in the Czechoslovak Setting	431
	Pressure Groups and Loyal Opposition	445
	Purges and Rehabilitations	451
	On Federation	453
	The Action Program	457
	Aspects of New Economic Arrangements	465
	Foreign Relations	472
	Another Step Forward	489
	Internal Opposition	493
POSTSCRIPT		501
ABBREVIATIONS USED IN NOTES		505
NOTES		511
ABOUT THE AUTHOR		591

LIST OF TABLES

Table		Page
1	Ownership Share in Creation of National Income, 1948 and 1953	5
2	Composition of Exports and Imports, 1937 and 1953	8
3	Shifts in the Contribution to National Income by Sectors, 1957-61	9
4	GNP at Factor Cost by Sector of Origin, 1948-56	10
5	Relative Industrial Production in Eastern Europe, 1955-63	11
6	Official Index of Industrial Output, 1937-66	12
7	Rate of Growth of Net Industrial Output, 1950-65	13
8	Official Index of Industrial Output (1948=100) by Branches, 1949-57	14
9	Staller's Value-Added Index of Output (1948=100), 1948-59	16
10	National Income, Investments, and Ratio of Investments to National Income Produced, 1948-65	17
11	Fixed Investment by Main Sectors of the Economy, 1951-65	18

Table		Page
12	Annual Ratio of Gross Fixed Investment to National Income and Changes in the Distribution of Gross Fixed Investment by Sector, 1949-58	19
13	Growth of State Investments in Principal Branches of Industry, 1952-59	20
14	Alton-Ernst Recomputation of the Size and Distribution of Gross Fixed Investment, 1950-63	21
15	Share of Invididual Industrial Branches in Gross Production and Fixed Assets, 1950-60	23
16	Fixed Assets of Industrial Enterprises, 1948-65	24
17	Age Structure of Machinery in Industry, 1957-65	24
18	Age of Foundry Equipment in Different Industries	25
19	Manpower in Czechoslovakia, 1948-65	26
20	Percentage Share of Employment in the National Economy, 1948-63	26
21	Distribution Pattern of Industrial Employment, 1948-57	28
22	Growth of Employment in Industrial Branches, 1950-64	29
23	Share of Exports in Gross Output of Principal Branches of Industry, 1955-65	32
24	Some Czechoslovak Imports from and Exports to the U.S.S.R., 1945-70	34

Table		Page
25	Commodity Composition of Imports from and Exports to the U.S.S.R., 1948-65	35
26	Principal Imports from and Exports to the U.S.S.R., 1961-65	36
27	Trade Turnover with the U.S.S.R., Socialist, and Capitalist Countries, 1945-66	37
28	Export and Import Prices as Percentages of EFTA Prices, 1964	43
29	Commodity Composition of Czechoslovak Trade with CMEA Members, 1953-60	46
30	Regional Distribution of Foreign Trade, 1955-65	50-51
31	Exports and Imports by Types of Goods, 1955-65	52
32	Annual Growth Rates of National Income and Fixed Investment in Eastern Europe, 1950-65	56
33	Growth of National Income in Selected Countries, 1950-65	57
34	Growth of GNP in Selected East and West European Countries, Prewar to 1964	58
35	Factors Propelling and Constraining Economic Growth, 1951-64	64
36	Estimates of Growth of Aggregate Productivity per Composite of Labor and Capital, 1951-64	65
37	Potential and Recorded Growth Rates, 1951-64	66

Table		Page
38	Goldmann's Calculation of the Growth Rates of Gross National Income, 1950-65	70
39	Increase in Stocks, Unfinished Construction, and Accumulation, 1956-64	76
40	Index of Changes in Labor Productivity and Fixed Assets in Industry, 1950-62	77
41	Centrally Planned Output, 1953-59	114
42	Variations in Output of Selected Branches and Products in 1963 Compared to 1962	137
43	Distribution of EPU's by Number of Employees and by Branches of Industry	191
44	Distribution of EPU's by Annual Industrial Gross Output	192
45	Extent of 1965 Experiments	198
46	Composition of Above-Plan GY at Kablo, January 1, to June 30, 1965	202
47	Allotments to and Expenditures from the Workers' and Premium Funds in Experimenting Enterprises, January 1, to June 30, 1965	207
48	Share of Individual Price Categories in Marketable Output of Experimenting Enterprises	209
49	Inventories in Experimenting Enterprises in Slovakia, First Quarter, 1965	210
50	Savings at Ton Factory, First Quarter, 1965	212

Table		Page
51	Plan Fulfillment in the Chemical Industry, First Quarter, 1965	213
52	Results of Experimenting Enterprises in Fuels, Chemical, Machine-Building, and Consumer Goods Industries, First Three Quarters, 1965	215
53	Distribution of GY (Profit) by Experimenting Enterprises of the Fuels, Chemical, Machine-Building, and Consumer Goods Industries, First Three Quarters, 1965	216
54	Planned Changes in Industrial Factor Inputs and Output, 1965-70	230
55	Planned Changes in Gross Industrial Output by Main Branches, 1965-70	231
56	Obligatory and Informative Plan Indexes, 1964-70	234
57	Wholesale Price Index, 1966	249
58	Growth of Gross Output in Industry in 1966 over 1965	258
59	Production of Some Industrial Goods in 1966	259
60	Investment in 1966	262
61	Composition of Exports and Imports, 1965-66	267
62	GY in 1966	270
63	Wholesale Price Increases in Main Branches of Industry in 1967	321
64	Profitability in the First Quarter, 1967	324

Table		Page
65	Budget Subsidies for Investments in 1967	330
66	Market Situation in 1967: Crude Relationship Between Supply and Demand	339
67	Average Shares of Premiums in Wages at the Technoplast Plant (Chropyne), 1966-70	347
68	Basic and Variable Shares of Average Income, 1966-67	348
69	Wage Differentiation, 1966-67	349
70	Earnings and Profit-Sharing Differentials in Industry, 1967	350
71	Criteria and Points for Profit-Sharing Premium Distribution at Technoplast, 1967	350
72	Distribution of Profit-Sharing, 1967	351
73	Index of the Growth of Investments, 1955-67	362
74	Volume, Structure, and Index of Production, 1966-67	364
75	Original and Revised Plan Targets of Growth for Slovakia, 1968-70	382

LIST OF CHARTS

Chart		Page
1	Potential and Recorded Growth Rates of National Income, 1951-65	67
2	Indexes Specified by the Government for the FYP and the Annual Plans, January 1, 1959	110-111
3	Indexes Provided by the Ministry for EPU's in the FYP and in the Annual Plans, January 1, 1959	112-113
4	Creation and Distribution of GY, 1966	238
5	Profit in the 1967 Wholesale Prices	281
6	Formation and Distribution of GY in 1967	292

ABBREVIATIONS

AP	Action Program
CAS	Czechoslovak Academy of Sciences
CC	Central Committee
CCTU	Central Council of Trade Unions
CM	Council of Ministers
CMEA	Council for Mutual Economic Assistance
CPC	Communist Party of Czechoslovakia
CSB	Czechoslovak State Bank
CWU	Czechoslovak Writers' Union
EC	Economic Council
EEC	European Economic Community
EFTA	European Free Trade Association
e.i.n.	Enterprise incentive normative
EPU	Economic production unit
FYP	Five year plan
GNP	Gross national product
GY	Gross income
kcs.	Czechoslovak crown
MCI	Ministry of Culture and Information

ME	Ministry of Education
MF	Ministry of Finance
NA	National Assembly
NF	National Front
p.i.n.	Personal incentive normative
SCFPW	State Commission for Finance, Prices, and Wages
SCOM	State Commission for Organization and Management
SCT	State Commission for Technology
SOP	State Planning Office
SPC	State Planning Commission
SPO	State Price Office
SSO	State Statistical Office
SWU	Slovak Writers' Union

New Economic Patterns in Czechoslovakia

CHAPTER 1 MAIN CURRENTS IN ECONOMIC DEVELOPMENT

Before World War II, Czechoslovakia was an advanced European economy and the most industrialized of the Slavic countries. Together with East Germany, it was the most industrialized country among those that, after World War II, came within the Soviet orbit of power.

When the Austro-Hungarian Empire was broken up in 1918, the newly created independent Czechoslovak Republic--consisting of less than 25 per cent of the Empire's territory, with a little over a quarter of its population--inherited the largest share of the Empire's resources. The Republic comprised the main Austro-Hungarian coal basin, the largest two industrial regions, the timber-rich area of Slovakia, the Moravian and Bohemian sugar beet plantations, and a large part of the richest agricultural area. The area embraced by Czechoslovakia had formerly contributed to the Empire the following shares of total output: sugar, 92 per cent; chemical products, 75 per cent; metals, 60 per cent; china, 100 per cent; glass, 92 per cent; cotton textiles, 75 per cent; woolen textiles, 80 per cent; leather, 70 per cent; footwear, 75 per cent; and paper, 65 per cent.[1]

Within the Republic, industry was located predominantly in the Czech lands: Bohemia, Silesia, and Moravia; Slovakia was mainly agricultural and had made little progress toward industrialization before World War II. One of the problems inherited by Czechoslovakia from Austro-Hungary was that of national minorities.[2] The union of Czechs and Slovaks was not altogether devoid of tensions which, as we shall see, have continued to the present. One of the more irksome problems was, and still is, the Slovak claim to industrialization.[3]

According to the 1930 census, Czechoslovak industry employed about 35 per cent of the economically active population; manpower was about equally distributed between consumer and producer goods production. About the same percentage was engaged in agriculture.

There was a tendency for concentration in industry.[4] For example, six large concerns produced the bulk of the output of heavy industry. There were specialized marketing organizations for selling abroad. Special organizations (e.g., the Czechoslovak Cloth Convention) managed wages and prices among the different firms. Extensive concentration and coordination sprung from the need to cater to foreign markets, involving extensive studies of foreign demand and of comparative advantages. This tradition of coordinated economic activity was partly responsible for the Czechoslovak responsiveness to economic planning immediately after World War II.[5]

Constrained by a narrow domestic raw materials and fuels base and by a limited domestic market, Czechoslovak industry depended heavily on intensive and aggressive world-wide trade. The bulk of trade was conducted with other European countries, and Germany was the principal trading partner. Czechoslovak industry was relatively less devastated by World War I than that of Germany and that of some parts of Western Europe. For a number of years Czechoslovak industry thrived on the high demand for manufactured goods in these countries. Later a vigorous effort was made to redirect the pattern and direction of trade, chiefly in response to the industrialization drive in Southeast Europe, to the powerful and effective German economic offensive, and to the rising tide of protectionism.

The high technical standards, sophistication, and superior quality of Czechoslovak products earned them respect on the world market. Among Czechoslovakia's chief exports were china, glassware, furniture, sugar, machinery, and textiles. In the interwar period, about 60 per cent of total industrial production was destined for foreign markets.[6] Czechoslovakia relied heavily on imported raw materials (cotton, wool, iron ore, nonferrous metals, and chemicals), fuels (coal and crude oil), semifabricates (chiefly for the textile and leather industries), foodstuffs, and agricultural products.[7]

Immediately after World War I, Czechoslovakia was forced to depend on foreign capital from France, Great Britain, and the United States to see it through the first difficult years. But borrowing abroad was cautious; there was a good deal of compunction about tieing the Czechoslovak economy to financial crises abroad. The adverse repercussions of the Great Depression in Czechoslovakia brought in their wake considerable animosity and mistrust. These feelings might have been partly responsible for the proclivity to reorient the Czechoslovak outlook toward the East at the end of World War II.[8]

World War II took a heavy toll of light industry, which in the immediate prewar period had not done as well as the other industries in recovering from the depression and which had been on the low priority list of the occupying German forces. Whereas the capacity of heavy industry was expanded in order to increase Germany's war potential, the stock of capital in light industry deteriorated during the war. On the whole, Czechoslovakia did not suffer great war damages, at least in comparison with Poland.[9] However, after the war, the expulsion of German workers particularly complicated the reactivation of the textile industry. The great issue at that time was whether to concentrate on heavy industry and to predominantly reorient foreign trade to the East or to reconstruct the consumer goods industries and to mainly rely on trade with the West. The vast resources required to modernize the consumer goods industries, the decline of Germany and the opportunity to take her place as a principal exporter of capital goods, the promise of East European markets due both to war devastation and to the upsurge of industrialization in the area, and the insecurity of postwar trade developments--all were among the factors that were stressed in favor of concentrating on heavy industry and of directing trade toward the East.[10] At least these were the arguments publicly announced, presumably, irrespective of political bias. Later, of course, the emphasis on heavy industry was attuned to the adoption of a Soviet-type growth strategy.

ADOPTION OF SOVIET GROWTH STRATEGY

Nationalization proceeded in two main stages.[11] Public ownership was extended by a series of nationalization decrees in October, 1945. As a result of the diversity of legal regulations and the application of loosely defined criteria, such as "national interest" or "size" (number of employees or technical capacity), the extent of nationalization differed widely in various industries. Some key industries (such as mining, iron, steel, and electric power) were almost entirely nationalized. In general, all industrial enterprises employing more than 150 to 500 persons were to be nationalized. Within a year after the 1945 decrees, 62 per cent of employees in Czech lands were working in the nationalized sector. About half of the financial institutions and one third of land came under state ownership.

The second stage of nationalization occurred after the February coup of 1948 and the consolidation of Communist power. The new Communist regime took immediate steps to vastly extend state ownership. The new nationalization law called for state take-over of all enterprises employing more than fifty people. Certain sectors were nationalized entirely irrespective of the number of employees. Private enterprise was cut to about a quarter of its previous strength and its share in industry dropped to 5.1 per cent.[12] By 1949, for all intents and purposes, the state had achieved complete direct control over the "commanding posts" of the economy and had virtually extinguished the private sector. These changes marked the end of

Table 1

OWNERSHIP SHARE IN CREATION OF NATIONAL INCOME, 1948 AND 1953
(At current prices, percentages)

Types of ownership	1948	1953
Socialist sector	66	90
state enterprises	63	84
cooperatives	3	6
Private plots of cooperative farmers	1	2
Private sector	33	8
Total national income	100	100

Source: SR 1962, p.26.

the interesting postwar experiment with a mixed economy. Indicative or indirect planning by guidance, with enterprises enjoying a large degree of autonomy; the competition of private entrepreneurship; planning implemented by, and largely subjected to, economic levers; and a partly operative market mechanism--all these were replaced by the imperative, direct, comprehensive, all embracing, administrative planning of the Soviet type.[13]

In agriculture the collectivization drive began in earnest in 1948 and was sharply accelerated in the 1950-53 period. By mid-1953 the state and cooperative sectors represented 53 per cent of total arable land and the cooperative sector alone accounted for 44 per cent. In 1956 there was a renewed collectivization drive which shifted 30 per cent of arable land into the cooperative sector by January 1, 1957. In 1958, Slovakia became the target for a resurgence of collectivization. The collectivized area in Slovakia rose from 42 per cent at the end of 1957 to 55 per cent at the end of 1958. By the end of 1959 only 16 per cent of arable land in Czechoslovakia was privately owned, of which a bulk consisted of farms of two hectares and less. By 1960 87.4 per cent of agricultural land was in the state-owned and cooperative sectors, and collectivization was virtually completed.[14]

The period after the Communist take-over was marked by a concentrated effort to force and accelerate the growth of selected branches of the economy, creating tensions and sectoral imbalances (chain of disequilibria),[15] depleting reserves, and postponing development of the nonpriority sectors. To overcome disproportions, production often was increased at almost any cost through a stop-gap redistribution of producer goods and labor. Such a "solution" caused disproportions in other branches and sectors; thus the disproportions were not alleviated, but simply moved from one sector to another and from one branch of industry to another. These pronounced imbalances accompanied the struggle for immediate maximum economic growth rates, which were considered as panacea for all economic ills. Consistency in balancing the quantitative proportions in economic plans was the planners' major preoccupation; no plan was subjected to the test of economic efficiency.[16]

Having secured the commanding posts, planners obtained enhanced discretionary powers to predetermine the proportions to be maintained. But a planner could hardly be guided by the "law of planned proportional development," for it had no operational significance: It provided no guidance on the correct proportions; it did not specify the degree of determinateness; and it afforded no criteria for determining the proportions. Obviously, development of the whole depends on the proportional development of its parts. What was lacking was a specification of proportions: i.e., in what proportions to each other should the various sectors of the economy develop? No guidelines were offered to reduce these proportions to quantitative relationships.[17]

There were many grave economic problems confronting Czechoslovakia at the threshold of the 1950's. Among them were:

1) A severe drought in 1947 that contributed

to the adverse agricultural performance, which fell short of anticipated results by about 50 per cent, aggravating the problem of feeding the population and of supplying agricultural raw materials to industry. The starting point in planning agricultural output in the Two-Year Plan (1947-48) was the substantial improvement in crops in the 1945-46 season. However, by 1947 the grain harvest amounted only to 81 per cent, the potato crop to 52 per cent, and the sugar beet crop to 58 per cent of the preceding year's crops. Moreover, there was a more substantial drop in grain deliveries than in the grain harvest, attributed to increased consumption by agricultural producers. Livestock production, which had also increased in 1946, suffered a severe setback in 1947 due to shortages of fodder.[18]

2) Nationalization had not yet made deep inroads in wholesale and retail trade. By 1948 the nationalized sector accounted for only about 5 per cent of total turnover.[19] Apparently the prevailing shortages were aggravated by private trade, speculation, and hoarding.

3) One of the weakest sectors was construction. Besides a crippling shortage of labor and materials, there were difficulties of an administrative nature. The housing construction target of the Two-Year Plan fell by the wayside; it was met by only 44.7 per cent. The bottlenecks in construction materials, the starting of an excessive number of projects, the delays in completion, and other similar "plagues" that were to haunt Czechoslovak planners for many years to come--all these loomed large on the horizon of the Two-Year Plan. Similarly the quality of industrial output was generally below prewar standards.[20]

4) As a result of both foreign and domestic developments, crucial changes took place in the structure and geographical distribution of Czechoslovak foreign trade.[21] Prior to 1948 the nationalized sector accounted for a little over 50 per cent of exports. The large volume of exports from the private sector was apparently instrumental

in significant foreign currency leakages (estimated by the National Bank at 2.5 billion Czechoslovak crowns [kcs.] in 1947).[22] An almost complete turnabout of trade from West to East took place in the years 1948-53, marking the new Soviet-oriented industrialization drive. Whereas in 1948, about 60 per cent of the volume of Czechoslovak foreign trade was with the so-called capitalist countries, in 1950, 55.5 per cent of the volume of foreign trade was with the socialist bloc, and 44.5 per cent with the capitalist countries. The respective figures for 1953 became 77.1 and 22.9 per cent; for 1955, 70 and 30 per cent; and for 1958, 71.8 and 28.2 per cent.[23]

Table 2

COMPOSITION OF EXPORTS AND IMPORTS, 1937 AND 1953

Products	Exports (percentage of total)		Imports (percentage of total)	
	1937	1953	1937	1953
Machinery and equipment	6.4	42.4	9.8	14.1
Raw materials and fuels	47.0	36.8	68.0	54.2
Manufactured consumer goods	36.8	12.2	5.9	1.5
Foodstuffs	9.8	8.6	16.3	30.2

Source: Ekonomicheskoye razvitie Chekhoslovakii (translated from the Czech) (Moscow: 1959), p. 190.

Table 2 indicates the change in the structure of foreign trade. Czechoslovakia was an exporter chiefly of manufactured finished products. But the composition of trade changed markedly after World War II. Whereas before the war manufactured consumer goods (mainly textiles, clothing, and leather goods) played an important role among exports, machinery and equipment assumed a crucial role in the postwar years. At the same time, in exports the share of raw materials and fuels declined sharply. Imports of foodstuffs increased and aggravated significantly the balance of payments. The export of machinery and equipment was restrained by the domestic demand for investments that accompanied the industrialization upsurge; however, these exports had to be reintensified because of the growing problems in the balance of payments.

The basic transformation of the economy after 1948 was reflected in the considerably increased share and altered structure of industry and the diminished share of agriculture in the economy.

Table 3

SHIFTS IN THE CONTRIBUTION TO NATIONAL INCOME BY SECTORS, 1957-61
(At current prices, percentages rounded)

Sectors	1937	1948	1955	1956	1960	1961
Agriculture	23	22	16	16	16	14
Industry[a]	53	59	64	64	63	65
Construction	6	7	10	12	10	10
Freight and transport	5	4	3	3	4	4
Trade and catering	12	8	6	4	6	6

[a]Includes handicrafts

Sources: Nicolas Spulber, in Vratislav Busek and Nicolas Spulber (eds.), Czechoslovakia (New York: Frederick A. Praeger, Inc., 1956), p. 235; SR 1966, p. 125; and SA 1963, p. 29.

Alfred Zauberman's calculations indicated that although in prewar Czechoslovakia, the contribution of agriculture was about 23 per cent and that of industry and construction about 53 per cent, in 1961 the respective contributions were 14 and 74 per cent. Zauberman emphasized the rough nature of his calculations, because "there is no adequate way of separating contribution of handicrafts."[24]

Thad Alton's team in the Columbia University's Project on National Income in East Central Europe recalculated the gross national product (GNP) at factor cost by sector of origin.[25] This group estimated the contributions to be as shown in Table 4.

Table 4

GNP AT FACTOR COST BY SECTOR OF ORIGIN, 1948-56
(Rounded)

Sectors	1948	1955	1956
Agriculture	20	17	17
Industry	38	38	38
Construction	4	8	9
Transportation	11	10	10
Trade and banking	8	8	8
Housing	5	9	9
Government	10	8	8

Source: Thad Paul Alton *et al*., *Czechoslovak National Income and Product 1947-1948 and 1955-1956* (New York: Columbia University Press, 1962), p. 60.

On the basis of Alton's team's fundings, Maurice Ernst reported that in Czechoslovakia in 1960 the percentage of GNP at factor cost was 52 per cent in industry and construction, 15 per cent in agriculture and forestry, and 33 per cent in services (transportation, communications, trade, housing, personal services, and government direct services). The advancement of industrialization could be gauged by the percentage composition of the increase of GNP during the period 1951-64: Industry's share was 68 per cent, agriculture's share diminished by 2 per cent, and the share of services was 34 per cent.[26] The relative strength of Czechoslovak industry among the East European countries is shown in Table 5.

Table 5

RELATIVE INDUSTRIAL PRODUCTION IN EASTERN EUROPE, 1955-63
(U.S.S.R. = 100)

	Pryor-Staller estimate		Other per capita estimates			
	Total output 1955	Per capita output 1955	Soviet 1958	Polish 1963	Czechoslovak 1961	Hungarian 1958
Czech-oslovakia	9.5	143	132	147	136	130
Bulgaria	1.4	37	40	61	30	39
East Germany	13.0	142	129	167	133	130
Hungary	4.6	91	62	89	60	59
Poland	10.3	74	76	83	75	75
Rumania	4.3	49	50	89	52	50
Yugoslavia	3.4	38	-	-	-	-
U.S.S.R.	100.0	100	100	100	100	100

Source: Frederic L. Pryor and George J. Staller, EP, No. 1, 1966, p. 6.

According to official statistics, 1948 industrial output was doubled by 1954, tripled by 1958, and quadrupled by 1963. The performance is still more impressive when 1937 is used as a base. The structural changes in the economy could be gauged from a comparison of the index of growth of industrial production of producer and consumer goods, as illustrated in Tables 6 and 7. The orientation to producer goods was reflected also in the breakdown of the official index of the growth of industrial production by branches, as shown in Table 8.

Primary preoccupation was with forcing the growth of heavy industry--particularly machine-building, metallurgy, and the chemical industries.[27]

Table 6

OFFICIAL INDEX OF INDUSTRIAL OUTPUT, 1937-66

Year	Industrial output	Industrial output	Producer goods	Consumer goods
1937	100			
1948	108	100	100	100
1949	124	114	-	-
1950	143	132	132	131
1951	163	150	156	144
1952	192	177	194	160
1953	210	193	219	166
1954	219	202	229	174
1955	243	224	249	197
1956	266	245	276	212
1957	293	270	304	234
1958	326	300	340	259
1959	361	333	383	280
1960	403	372	434	307
1961	439	405	473	333
1962	467	430	507	348
1963	463	427	502	348
1964	482	444	527	357
1965	520	480	576	378
1966	559	515	624	400

Sources: SA 1965, pp. 53-54; SR 1966, pp. 28-29; and SA 1966, p. 49.

Expansion of the fuels base promoted the growth of manufacturing and the steady increase in steel production furthered the expansion of the machine-building and metal-working industries. The growth of the consumer-oriented industries trailed behind that of the producer goods industries. The importance of textile,garment, leather, footwear, and foodstuffs industries decreased considerably.

The official index was computed on the basis of the gross value of industrial output at constant wholesale prices (net of turnover tax). This measure is particularly biased because, *inter alia*, it is especially vulnerable to multiple

Table 7

RATE OF GROWTH OF NET INDUSTRIAL OUTPUT, 1950-65
(Annual increments, per cent)

Year	Annual rate of growth		
	Industrial output	Producer goods	Consumer goods
1950	14.5	16.0	15.0
1951	14.7	18.0	9.2
1952	16.7	24.2	11.2
1953	8.7	12.3	4.4
1954	4.0	3.7	5.4
1955	11.5	8.8	13.1
1956	9.5	10.9	8.1
1957	9.4	9.9	10.2
1958	10.3	11.5	10.9
1959	10.8	13.2	7.6
1960	11.9	13.0	9.9
1961	8.9	9.2	8.3
1962	6.2	7.3	4.7
1963	- 0.6	- 1.5	0.0
1964	4.1	5.5	2.7
1965	7.9	8.6	6.7

Source: Josef Goldmann and Karel Kouba, Hospodarsky rust v CSSR (Prague: 1967), p. 36.

counting and sensitive to changes in the recorded stages of production; also, it is affected by the pricing of new products.[28] In Czechoslovakia, it is generally accepted that the official index is inflated.[29]

In 1957 the Czechoslovak State Statistical Office produced a net output series, calculating industry's contribution to national income ("material production"). The index (1948=100) recorded 285 for 1961 (238 for 1959 and 185 for 1956) as compared to the official gross value index of 405 in 1961.[30] Accepting the U.N.'s tentative estimate (which shows that in 1948 the net value of Czechoslovak output was 3 per cent above the 1937 level), we find that Zauberman's

Table 8

OFFICIAL INDEX OF INDUSTRIAL OUTPUT (1948=100) BY BRANCHES, 1949-57

Branches	1949	1950	1951	1952	1953	1954	1955	1956	1957
Machine-building	122	156	202	267	323	336	368	419	463
Chemicals	118	141	169	207	237	244	287	325	369
Rubber	130	136	157	202	226	247	276	349	397
Iron and steel	106	117	134	174	203	201	221	247	267
Building materials	120	128	147	174	196	222	251	287	333
Mining and fuels	103	109	113	126	133	142	151	162	180
Electric power generation	109	124	138	156	165	183	207	234	252
Fuel-processing	113	117	130	150	153	160	173	186	218
Mining	102	111	127	138	140	148	153	164	187
Woodworking	119	144	176	215	210	223	248	266	288
Paper	108	121	133	144	152	161	169	178	190
Printing	96	115	122	118	125	136	144	149	156
China and ceramics	107	121	125	139	127	134	152	172	192
Glass	104	114	121	124	121	133	152	166	186
Textiles	115	125	131	141	139	150	171	175	192
Clothing	126	166	188	208	199	174	204	192	216
Footwear and leather	106	114	119	124	119	124	138	140	167
Food (provisions)	121	150	161	175	183	188	199	211	228
Total industry	114	132	150	177	193	202	224	245	270
Producer goods	114	133	157	195	219	227	247	274	301
Consumer goods	114	131	143	159	166	175	198	214	236

Source: Ekonomicheskoye razvitie Chekhoslovakii, p. 32.

recomputation of industrial growth from 1937 to 1962 indicates that industrial output trebled rather than quintupled as shown by the official index.[31] The dynamics of the growth of industrial output were scrupulously recalculated by George J. Staller, as illustrated in Table 9. In his recomputation of the index, Staller selected 1948 as the weight and comparison base period, because, inter alia, the information on the structure of "industry proper" and of "manufacturing crafts" was better than that in any postwar period, the economy had recuperated from war losses, and market forces were more operative than during any other period thereafter. The value-added index recomputed by Staller shows that the results were not as impressive as claimed, but still respectable by international standards. His findings clearly indicate the rapid shift toward the producer goods industries, with machine-building and metal-working reaching a prominent place by 1959. Staller noted that in view of the top priority accorded by planners to industry, it was noteworthy that Czechoslovakia did not record a faster tempo of growth than the countries of the European Economic Community.[32]

The Alton-Ernst recomputed index of growth of industrial output (1955=100) shows prewar as 69, 1950 as 80, 1960 as 155, and 1964 as 167.[33] The uneven pace of growth is indicated by the average annual percentage increases of 4.6 per cent for 1951-55, of 9.1 per cent for 1956-60, of 1.9 per cent for 1961-64, and of 5.4 per cent for 1951-64.[34]

Structural changes in the national economy during the period immediately after World War II were primarily propelled by investments and assignment of the labor force to priority branches. An inordinately high increase in capital stock reflected, inter alia, the aim to compensate partly for some of the flagrant built-in inefficiencies. Generally, the rate of growth of investments was faster than the growth rate of national income, with the tendency for the share of investments in national income to increase, with a

Table 9

STALLER'S VALUE-ADDED INDEX OF OUTPUT (1948=100), 1948-59

Industries	Relative weights	1949	1950	1951	1952	1953	1954	1955	1956	1957	1958	1959	1948-1959[a]
b	4.07	110.2	123.5	137.0	154.8	164.5	181.1	199.8	220.8	235.8	261.1	291.2	10.2
c	6.45	102.9	110.2	113.3	128.5	131.2	141.4	147.3	161.6	180.4	200.5	202.3	6.6
d	3.17	119.4	118.0	140.2	171.8	165.8	180.2	199.5	206.4	242.5	272.0	294.6	10.3
e	8.35	108.8	122.8	135.1	153.6	176.4	179.3	198.0	215.7	234.7	246.4	262.3	9.2
f	23.91	114.5	133.0	147.5	159.1	173.1	177.1	207.3	220.2	251.3	288.2	334.9	11.6
g	4.56	109.8	134.0	135.6	163.6	171.8	196.3	242.0	279.5	307.5	338.6	362.0	12.4
h	5.51	107.5	129.4	146.4	170.9	166.3	177.1	196.9	204.9	205.4	214.6	220.0	7.5
i	4.39	109.9	121.6	123.2	119.1	119.7	122.3	125.5	129.2	133.7	148.7	159.0	4.3
j	7.14	99.8	106.5	105.7	116.0	116.9	138.9	163.5	187.2	214.8	243.3	279.5	9.8
k	16.11	116.1	126.4	126.9	130.2	124.8	116.6	134.0	131.3	140.9	150.9	162.9	4.5
l	6.45	103.7	108.5	94.5	93.2	88.4	90.9	93.7	100.0	115.2	125.6	133.5	2.7
m	9.89	109.4	119.1	122.6	122.1	119.0	122.4	125.9	134.1	144.1	149.2	153.2	4.0
n	100.00	110.6	123.3	129.7	140.3	144.7	150.5	169.2	180.6	199.5	220.0	241.8	8.4
o	51.08	109.0	125.6	138.5	155.2	164.0	169.4	191.4	208.4	232.7	258.8	288.8	10.1
p	48.92	112.2	120.9	120.5	124.9	124.6	130.7	146.1	151.5	164.8	179.5	192.7	6.1

a - Average rate of increase (per cent), b - Power-generating, c - Mining of fuels, d - Fuel-processing, e - Smelting, f - Machinery and metal-working, g - Chemicals, h - Wood-working, i - Paper and printing, j - Ceramics and glass, k - Textile and clothing, l - Leather and rubber, m - Provisions, n - Total industry, o - Producer goods, p - Consumer goods.

Source: George J. Staller, AER, June, 1962, p.389

Table 10

NATIONAL INCOME, INVESTMENTS, AND RATIO OF INVESTMENTS TO NATIONAL INCOME PRODUCED, 1948-65

Year	National income[a]	Index	Investment[a]	Index	National income[b]	Investment[b]	Rate of increase of investments	Share of investments in national income[c]
1948	70.2	100	8.9	100	59.3	8.6	-	14.5
1949					74.4	12.9	50.5	17.3
1950	85.0	121	14.3	160	85.4	16.1	24.5	18.8
1951	93.1	133	17.3	194	102.6	20.9	30.2	20.4
1952	103.1	147	20.5	229	115.9	23.7	13.3	20.5
1953	109.7	156	21.2	238	128.8	24.3	2.4	18.8
1954	113.6	162	20.8	233	122.9	23.5	-3.3	19.1
1955	125.3	178	22.4	251	133.7	25.1	7.2	18.8
1956	131.9	188	25.4	285	133.1	28.6	13.9	21.5
1957	141.5	202	27.8	311	140.9	31.4	9.6	22.3
1958	153.2	218	31.6	353	149.2	34.3	9.2	23.0
1959	162.9	232	37.7	422	152.0	38.2	11.4	25.1
1960	176.0	251	42.4	475	163.0	43.0	12.5	26.4
1961	173.0	268	45.5	509	172.0	46.1	7.3	26.8
1962	175.4	272	44.3	495	175.4	44.3	-4.0	25.2
1963	171.6	266	39.4	441	172.9	39.4	-11.0	22.8
1964	172.6	267	39.7	493	169.7	40.5	2.7	23.9
1965	179.0	277	42.8	529	173.5	42.8	5.8	24.7

[a]In billion of kcs.; until 1960 at constant 1955 prices; from 1960 at constant 1960 prices.
[b]In billion of kcs. at current prices.
[c]Percentage - at current prices.

Sources: SR 1966, pp.24-25; Oldrich Kyn, The Czechoslovak Economy From 1953-1965 (mimeographed; no date), p. 4; EBE, Vol. 18, No. 1, p. 61; SA 1968, pp. 29 and 43; and SP, No. 8, 1967, p. 264; EC, No. 4, 1966; and Josef Goldmann and Karel Kouba, Hospodarsky rust v CSSR (Prague: 1967), p. 68.

corresponding decline of the rate of growth of national income, as illustrated in Table 10. For example, for the period 1949-58 the reported average annual rate of increase of national income was 8 per cent, the rate of growth of gross fixed investments was 11.3 per cent, and the share of gross fixed investment in national income was 28.2 per cent. For the period 1949-53 the respective rates were reported as 9, 14.7, and 27.1 per cent. For the period 1953-58 the respective rates were reported as 7.2, 8.8, and 29 per cent.[35]

Table 11

FIXED INVESTMENT BY MAIN SECTORS OF THE ECONOMY, 1951-65

Period	Total Investment [a]	Percentage distribution			
		Industry and construction	Agriculture	Transport & trade	Nonproductive sectors
1951-55	102.3	43.2	11.3	14.6	30.9
1956-60	165.0	43.2	16.3	13.3	27.2
1961-65	220.0	47.0	15.4	13.7	23.9

[a]At constant prices - billion kcs.

Source: EBE, Vol. 18, No. 1, 1966, p. 41.

Determination of the share of investment in national income encounters intricate and often insurmountable measurement problems. Among them are: the distorting price weights, the underpricing of capital goods, the pricing of new products, and the divergent movements of prices of investment and consumer goods (dual price system).[36] Differences in conceptual framework in measuring national product, particularly in the sphere of "nonmaterial services," make comparisons with Western statistical measurement difficult.[37] For example, according to the U.N.'s estimate, the share of gross fixed investment in Czechoslovak national (material) product was 27.2 per cent in 1953, if computed in

Table 12

ANNUAL RATIO OF GROSS FIXED INVESTMENT TO NATIONAL INCOME AND CHANGES IN THE DISTRIBUTION OF GROSS FIXED INVESTMENT BY SECTOR, 1949-58
(In 1949 prices)

	1949	1950	1951	1952	1953	1954	1955	1956	1957	1958
Annual ratio of gross fixed investment to national income	22.1	24.1	26.5	28.5	27.2	25.6	25.0	28.8	29.5	29.3
Changes in distribution										
Heavy industry and construction	42.8	43.7	42.7	44.4	38.4	38.1	34.7	32.8	33.4	37.8
Light industry, agriculture and trade	15.0	16.5	17.7	15.8	17.0	19.3	22.6	23.2	23.1	25.6
Transport and communications	14.7	13.2	13.7	13.6	14.8	12.3	10.7	9.3	10.2	10.1
Housing	16.1	14.8	13.1	13.6	14.3	18.5	20.1	22.7	21.6	15.8
Miscellaneous non-productive sectors	11.3	11.7	12.8	12.5	15.4	11.7	11.9	11.9	11.7	10.7

Source: WES 1959, Chapter 3, pp. 114 and 122.

Table 13

GROWTH OF STATE INVESTMENTS IN PRINCIPAL BRANCHES OF INDUSTRY, 1952-59
(1948=100)

	1952	1953	1956	1958	1959
Total industry	219	192	221	301	367
Electric power	159	166	292	274	274
Fuel mining	151	178	264	393	382
Ferrous metallurgy	456	371	262	420	650
Mining and processing of nonferrous metals	600	944	1433	539	598
Machine-building	287	222	190	316	382
Chemicals	223	204	120	221	225
Building materials	561	462	656	1049	1500
Textiles	127	74	120	184	229
Clothing	88	38	63	129	238
Food processing	172	124	175	215	250

Sources: SR 1959, p. 111; SR 1960, p. 108; and Artur Bodnar, Gospodarka europejskich krajow socjalistycznych (Warsaw: 1962), p. 123.

1949 prices, or 16.9 in 1953 prices.[38] The percentage of gross fixed investment in national income in 1957 was 29.5 per cent in 1949 prices, 18.3 per cent in 1953 prices, 20.6 per cent in 1957 prices, and 28.6 per cent in 1957 prices (excluding turnover tax).[39] According to Zauberman's recalculations, the share of capital formation as a percentage of GNP (Western method) was 44 per cent in 1953 and 36 per cent in 1956.[40] Results obtained by Alton's team show that in 1955 and 1956 the share of gross investment in GNP at current market prices was about 24 per cent and 30 per cent, respectively, and at factor cost it was about 34 and 39 per cent, respectively.[41] Boris P. Pesek's independent recalculations show that the share of gross investment in GNP in current prices was about 19 per cent in 1955 and about 21 per cent in 1956.[42]

The accelerated industrialization drive was accompanied by the channeling of over 40 per cent of all investments to industry during the period 1948-59. Thus industry's fixed capital grew by over 80 per cent during the period in question, whereas the investments for the economy as a whole increased by about 50 per cent.[43] According to official statistics, during 1949-63 investments absorbed about 475 billion kcs. (in 1963 prices) of which about 42 per cent went to industry, 14 per cent to agriculture, 11 per cent to transportation and communications, and 27 per cent to services.[44] The share of investment channeled to

Table 14

ALTON-ERNST RECOMPUTATION OF THE SIZE AND DISTRIBUTION OF GROSS FIXED INVESTMENT, 1950-63

Years	Percentage of GNP at factor cost in constant prices				Distribution of percentages of total investment at constant market prices		
	Total	Industry and construction	Agriculture	Services	Industry	Agriculture	Services
1950-54	23.5	10.6	2.3	10.6	45	10	45
1955-59	27.3	11.4	4.3	11.6	42	16	42
1960-63	27.7	12.9	4.4	10.4	46	16	38

Source: Maurice Ernst, in U.S. Congress, Joint Economic Committee, New Directions for the Soviet Economy (Washington: GPO, 1966), p. 890 .

industry was generally much higher than in Western Europe, whereas that allocated to services was much lower.[45]

The development pattern pursued featured concentration of investment outlays in branches with a high capital-output ratio and a long process of gestation (e.g., the fuels, power, and metallurgy industries). Whereas the share of fixed capital of these branches in industry as a whole rose from 35 per cent in 1948 to 44.5 per cent in 1963, their share in gross industrial output remained virtually stagnant. The high priority accorded to industry was accompanied by neglect of other sectors of the economy, particularly of services.[46] Statistics on the structural changes in the stock of fixed assets of industrial enterprises as at the end of 1948 and 1965 show that priority branches (power, fuels, metallurgy, machine-building, and chemicals) claimed the bulk of investments and that the underprivileged consumer goods industries suffered a decline of their stock of capital, as illustrated in Table 15. The measures of the average effectiveness of fixed assets could only bear out that electricity, fuels, mining, and metallurgy were the branches absorbing the lion's share of the growth of fixed assets, but demonstrating the slowest rate of increase in their effectiveness, which was, moreover, the lowest in comparison with other branches.[47]

While the stock of capital increased rapidly, the existing stock of machinery and equipment aged and dilapidated.[48] The over-all stock of fixed capital was increased predominantly by expanding new production facilities in heavy industry. Less than 2 per cent of the total "value" of the stock of machinery was retired between 1949 and 1964. Maintenance of fixed assets was neglected.[49] There was a continuous increase of antiquated machinery. Analysis of about half of the total stock of plant and equipment at the beginning of 1960 disclosed that 52 per cent of the stock was over ten years old, 27 per cent was over twenty years old, 13 per cent was over thirty years old, and 6 per cent was over forty years old. The distribution of the assets is interesting for it points out that the older ones were concentrated in consumer goods industries.[50]

Table 15

SHARE OF INDIVIDUAL INDUSTRIAL BRANCHES IN GROSS PRODUCTION AND FIXED ASSETS, 1950-60

Branches of industry	Stock of capital structure in percentages			Gross production structure in percentages		
	1950	1955	1960	1950	1955	1960
All industry	100.000	100.000	100.000	100.000	100.000	100.000
Power generation	10.482	12.257	12.807	2.887	2.888	3.027
Fuels and coal	14.146	13.426	14.985	8.848	7.608	7.083
Metallurgy and ore mining	10.427	13.666	15.251	8.950	10.002	9.947
Machine-building	18.148	18.534	18.892	20.134	28.361	33.849
Chemicals and rubber	3.572	5.675	6.516	4.064	5.058	6.294
Building materials	3.721	4.019	5.060	2.257	2.435	3.185
Woodworking	2.138	2.209	1.938	3.946	4.097	3.536
Cellulose and paper	2.369	2.316	2.475	1.994	1.678	1.432
China, glass, and ceramics	2.403	1.923	1.575	1.890	1.509	1.572
Textiles	12.857	9.961	7.328	10.673	8.799	7.330
Clothing	0.652	0.591	0.385	3.258	2.418	2.154
Leather and footwear	2.068	1.564	1.350	3.152	2.308	2.275
Printing	0.860	0.703	0.622	1.069	0.820	0.659
Foodstuffs	15.914	12.807	10.376	26.562	21.229	16.917
Other branches	0.245	0.422	0.440	0.314	0.788	0.714

Source: Zdenek Srein and Zdenek Tlusty, PE, No. 3, 1963, p. 189.

Table 16

FIXED ASSETS OF INDUSTRIAL ENTERPRISES, 1948-65
(As at end of year, in 1955 prices)

Industries	Billions kcs.			Index		
	1948	1958	1965	1948	1958	1965
Total	88.7	156.6	258.1	100.0	100.0	100.0
Electricity	9.0	19.8	32.8	10.2	12.6	12.7
Fuels	13.1	23.2	40.6	14.8	14.8	15.7
Metals	8.9	23.0	45.3	10.0	14.7	17.5
Machinery	15.7	29.5	50.6	17.6	18.8	19.6
Chemicals	2.6	9.8	18.7	2.9	6.3	7.3
Building materials	3.3	6.6	13.4	3.8	4.2	5.2
Woodworking	1.7	3.2	4.6	2.0	2.1	1.8
Paper	2.1	3.9	5.8	2.4	2.5	2.3
Glass and china	2.2	2.7	3.9	2.5	1.7	1.5
Textile and clothing	12.5	13.6	15.8	14.1	8.7	6.1
Leather and footwear	1.9	2.2	3.0	2.2	1.4	1.2
Printing	0.8	1.0	1.3	0.9	0.7	0.5
Foodstuffs	14.7	17.3	21.4	16.6	11.1	8.3
Others	0.2	0.7	0.9	0.2	0.4	0.3

Source: Vladimir Nachtigal, CEP, No. 8, 1967, p. 119.

Table 17

AGE STRUCTURE OF MACHINERY IN INDUSTRY, 1957-65
(Percentages at end of year)

Year	Over 10 years	Under 10 years
1957	25.5	74.5
1958	25.1	74.9
1959	25.1	74.9
1960	25.6	74.4
1961	26.0	74.0
1962	27.1	72.9
1963	27.1	72.9
1964	27.3	72.7
1965	26.4	73.6

Source: Vladimir Nachtigal, CEP, No. 8, 1967, p. 121.

Table 18

AGE OF FOUNDRY EQUIPMENT IN DIFFERENT INDUSTRIES

Branches	Age of equipment in percentage				
	To 5 Years	5.0-9.9	10.0-19.9	20.0-29.9	30.0 & up
All foundry equipment	28.7	23.9	29.2	10.7	7.5
Fuel and power	21.2	18.1	52.0	6.3	2.4
Metallurgy and ore mining	20.9	30.4	27.1	9.2	12.4
Chemical	30.3	27.0	29.2	12.4	1.1
Heavy machinery	26.8	24.8	29.8	11.1	7.5
General machinery	30.5	23.1	29.5	10.1	6.8
Construction	42.6	29.0	23.1	4.1	1.2
Consumer goods	25.7	20.1	32.9	12.8	4.5
Foodstuffs	33.4	8.9	40.0	13.3	4.4
Transportation and communications	35.8	6.4	32.1	15.4	10.3
Producer cooperatives	41.7	1.7	26.3	18.9	11.4
Local industry	42.6	14.5	21.6	16.6	4.7

Source: Jaroslav Ceska, Statistika, No. 4, 1964, p. 187.

The adopted growth strategy was also reflected in the high rise of employment and redirection of labor to the priority branches of industry. Employment in other sectors increased only slightly or recorded some decline, as illustrated in Tables 19 and 20. The industrial sector registered the highest increase in employment (39.2 per cent) between 1950 and 1964. The increase of employment in the producer goods branches (53.5 per cent) was much faster than the increase in the consumer goods branches, with considerable transfers of the labor force from consumer to producer goods branches.[51] There seems to be conflicting evidence to what extent the rise of employment in heavy industry resulted from a substitution of labor for capital

Table 19

MANPOWER IN CZECHOSLOVAKIA, 1948-65
(Annual averages in thousands of persons)

	1948	1950	1955	1960	1963	1965
Total working population	5,545	5,577	5,956	6,063	6,311	6,477
in industry	1,640	1,674	1,942	2,263	2,411	2,480
construction	253	352	404	501	506	521
agriculture	2,239	2,058	1,933	1,468	1,316	1,262
Total employed in Slovakia	1,526	1,531	1,640	1,571	1,630	1,730
Total labor participation rate of women	37.8	38.4	42.7	42.8	44.0	44.8
Labor participation rate of women in Slovakia	40.1	41.0	42.6	39.5	40.1	40.7

Source: SR 1966, pp. 22, 24, and 47.

Table 20

PERCENTAGE SHARE OF EMPLOYMENT IN THE NATIONAL ECONOMY, 1948-63

Sectors	1948	1955	1963
Total	100.0	100.0	100.0
Industry	29.6	32.8	38.2
Construction	4.5	6.7	8.0
Agriculture	40.4	34.0	20.9
Transportation	5.0	5.7	6.4
Science and research	0.4	-	2.1
Health and welfare	1.6	2.5	3.1
Education and culture	2.5	3.8	5.4
Administration	2.5	3.5	3.1

Sources: Alexej Balek, Statistika, No. 4, 1965, p. 150; and SA 1965, p. 32.

or from an expansion of productive capacities.[52] The growth of the labor force in principal branches of industry is shown in Tables 21 and 22. The largest increases in employment occurred in the metallurgy, machine-building, chemistry, power, and rubber industries. The textile, printing, footwear, leather, garment, and food-processing industries experienced a decline or a minimal increase in comparison to 1948.

The steady climb in the labor participation rate of women was a particularly important factor in the sharp over-all rise of employment. The expansion of the female labor force was a device which helped to save on investments in housing which would have had to be made if the increase of manpower had been secured by an exit from agriculture. But the gains in industrial employment were predominantly achieved by drawing on the agricultural labor force.[53] The poor performance of agriculture, its lagging mechanization, its discouragement resulting from the adverse terms of trade for agriculture, and the shortage and relatively high age composition of the agricultural labor force--all these are among the factors which make it mandatory for the government to constrain further exodus of labor from agriculture to industry.[54]

The share of manpower in the "nonproductive" sectors has increased (19.4 per cent in 1964 as against 13.4 per cent in 1950), primarily due to sharp increases of employment in education, health, science, and research.[55]

The high employment in the postwar years was accompanied by considerable labor mobility. During the first years of the 1950's in "some enterprises the entire labor force was changed in the course of the year." A number of branches (particularly mining and steel and iron mills) suffered from acute labor shortages. In agriculture, maintenance, and local administration, labor shortages were due mainly to inadequate wage incentives, poor working conditions, etc. The large general increase in

Table 21

DISTRIBUTION PATTERN OF INDUSTRIAL EMPLOYMENT, 1948-57
(In thousands of persons)

Branches	1948	1949	1950	1951	1952	1953	1954	1955	1956	1957
Total industry	1,264	1,272	1,311	1,369	1,413	1,415	1,441	1,472	1,508	1,554
Producer goods	630	656	700	758	809	828	841	849	872	895
Consumer goods	634	616	611	611	604	587	600	623	636	659
Electric power	15	16	17	17	17	18	19	20	20	20
Mining of fuels	97	96	97	97	101	103	111	111	116	123
Fuel-processing	16	15	14	13	13	13	14	15	15	15
Mining	11	10	11	12	14	14	14	14	14	14
Metal-processing	70	74	79	88	94	98	99	98	99	101
Machine-building	234	251	274	319	354	389	394	402	420	438
Chemicals	26	28	30	31	33	34	35	36	38	41
Rubber	8	8	8	9	9	10	10	10	11	12
Building materials	39	41	43	44	47	50	50	52	54	56
Glass	33	34	36	35	33	31	32	33	34	36
China and ceramics	10	10	10	9	9	9	8	8	9	9
Woodworking	49	54	60	68	72	67	68	69	69	69
Paper	23	24	24	25	26	26	27	28	28	28
Printing	16	15	16	17	15	14	14	15	15	15
Textiles	173	182	170	166	154	150	153	158	160	168
Clothing	38	45	53	51	50	47	45	48	46	47
Leather and footwear	44	44	45	42	37	33	33	35	35	41
Food-processing	105	113	124	126	120	118	118	116	116	117

Source: Ekonomicheskoye razvitie Chekhoslovakii, p. 69.

Table 22

GROWTH OF EMPLOYMENT IN INDUSTRIAL BRANCHES, 1950-64

Branches of Industry	Index (1950 = 100)				Industrial structure in percentages	
	1950	1955	1960	1964	1950	1964
Electric power	100.0	121.1	131.6	142.1	1.4	1.5
Fuels	100.0	112.2	127.6	139.8	9.3	9.3
Ferrous metallurgy	100.0	130.0	156.3	172.5	6.0	7.5
Nonferrous metallurgy	100.0	92.3	123.1	130.8	1.0	0.9
Machine-building and metal-working	100.0	139.6	173.9	186.5	25.1	33.7
Chemicals, rubber, and asbestos	100.0	119.1	155.3	178.7	3.5	4.5
Building materials	100.0	115.0	136.7	123.3	4.5	4.0
Woodworking	100.0	110.3	118.4	120.7	6.6	5.7
Paper	100.0	113.0	130.4	134.8	1.7	1.7
Glass, china, and ceramics	100.0	87.5	112.5	122.9	3.6	3.2
Textiles	100.0	93.2	106.2	102.8	13.4	9.8
Clothing	100.0	95.2	104.8	106.0	6.3	4.8
Leather and footwear	100.0	83.9	114.5	121.0	4.7	4.1
Printing	100.0	88.9	100.0	100.0	1.4	1.0
Food-processing	100.0	93.9	98.6	98.6	11.2	7.9
Other branches	100.0	125.0	150.0	175.0	0.3	0.4

Source: Miroslava Janderova and Jaroslav Volf, _Statistika_, No. 3, 1966, p. 127.

employment contributed to deterioration of performance by attracting unqualified and inferior labor. "Over-employment" contributed to the laxity of discipline. Also frequent reassignment of personnel created an atmosphere of instability and adversely affected performance.[56]

From the mid-1950's to the mid-1960's employment grew about three times as fast as average wages. There was, in fact, a marked tendency to curb the growth of wages. Apparently, among the European countries, Czechoslovakia experienced the lowest growth rates of individual wages, accompanied by an unabated wage equalization.[57] Wage-leveling was also blamed for discouraging efficiency and technical progress, and for its over-all negative effects on productivity, "labor morale," discipline, and responsibility.[58]

The sources of additional manpower are, reportedly, almost exhausted. At the end of 1964, 86.6 per cent of the economically active population was employed. About 93 and 80 per cent of the economically active masculine and feminine population, respectively, was employed. Whereas in Bohemia and Moravia almost 83 per cent of the economically active feminine population was employed, in Slovakia the rate was 66 per cent.[59] Slovak economists emphasized that a great reservoir of manpower still existed in Slovakia. They attributed the over-all national labor shortages to the unwise concentration of the processing industries in the Czech lands, disregarding the territorial distribution of manpower. Apparently from 1953 to 1963 factories were built in the Czech lands with little regard for manpower needs and territorial proportions.[60]

Critics of the apparent general shortage of labor point out that it is due mainly to ineffective utilization. According to rough estimates of the State Planning Commission (SPC), there seems to be a realistic possibility of achieving, with the present labor force, a 20 per cent annual increase in national product. Structural changes in the economy could be achieved by reallocating manpower.

It is advocated that the share of industry in total employment should considerably diminish to enable faster growth of the tertiary sector and to prevent an outflow from agriculture. Moreover, the "liquidation of ineffective plants and shops and the transfer of their workers to progressive branches is being pursued at the speed of a turtle."[61]

The rapid rural-urban migration that has taken place could probably be sustained only by tolerating and relying on imports of agricultural products, with all the consequent hardships on the balance of payments.

To ascertain the ratio of foreign trade to national income is a Herculean task, particularly in view of the existing Chinese Wall separating domestic and foreign market prices. It was claimed that the volume of foreign trade now accounts for about one third of national income, pointing to its particular role in the Czechoslovak economy. Czechoslovakia exports more than 17 per cent of its industrial output and imports the bulk of raw materials and fuels required and about one third of the food consumed.[62]

In 1937 foreign trade represented about 26 per cent and in 1948 about 35 per cent of national income. Zauberman arrived at an 18 per cent export-GNP ratio for 1956. The corresponding Czechoslovak estimate is 11 per cent, but it was probably computed on the gross output basis.[63] Jan Michal's rough estimates show the export-national income ratio for 1957 at 12 to 14 per cent and that of import-national income at 7 to 8 per cent.[64] In the Alton-Ernst estimates the index of growth of imports (1955=100) in constant prices showed 1937 at 58, 1950 as 64, 1960 as 189, and 1964 as 258. Imports as percentage of GNP in constant 1963 dollars were 6 per cent in 1937, 6 per cent in 1950, 8 per cent in 1955, 12 per cent in 1960, and 15 per cent in 1964. Imports as percentage of the industrial production index (1955=100) were 84 in 1937, 80 in 1950, 122 in 1960, and 155 in 1964.[65] It may be noted that Czechoslovak foreign trade per capita (in comparable 1956 dollar

Table 23

SHARE OF EXPORTS IN GROSS OUTPUT OF PRINCIPAL BRANCHES OF INDUSTRY, 1955-65

Branches	1955	1960	1962	1963	1964	1965
Total industry	10.2	13.4	14.0	15.6	15.6	17.3
Fuels	13.2	9.8	9.8	10.3	11.9	10.7
Metallurgy	11.3	10.0	11.0	14.2	17.5	20.3
Machinery	21.1	18.4	22.8	25.4	24.2	26.9
Chemistry	7.0	10.6	10.4	13.8	13.6	16.3
Building materials	9.2	4.6	5.4	6.6	9.1	9.0
Glass & china	39.6	34.9	40.5	41.5	42.8	42.8
Woodworking	9.9	13.7	15.1	17.5	19.5	23.4
Paper	10.1	15.2	10.4	10.5	10.7	11.0
Printing	8.7	10.7	8.9	10.5	12.9	13.6
Textiles	7.3	13.8	14.7	16.0	18.5	16.5
Clothing	3.0	12.8	7.5	14.5	14.8	25.3
Leather	5.1	14.9	21.5	22.2	20.9	26.1

Source: SR 1966, p. 429.

prices) was $248 in 1928, $99 in 1938, $137 in 1950, and $237 in 1961. In comparison to foreign trade per capita in Central and Western Europe--granted the pitfalls of such a comparison--"it seems safe to say that, in spite of the spurt achieved in the later years of the past decade, foreign commerce is still undersized."[66]

There were many consequences of the autarkic policies pursued and the one-sided orientation of trade toward the Council for Mutual Economic Assistance (CMEA).[67] For example, apart from the inefficient exploitation of domestic natural resources, over 70 per cent of the world's assortment of machinery was manufactured in Czechoslovakia, frequently at below-par quality, inhibiting automation, mechanization, and technical progress. Czechoslovakia was not only handicapped by the inferior quality of its products on the more competitive markets, but, as we shall see later, in time, the previously secure CMEA customers became more choosy and demanding.[68]

Czechoslovakia's pace and pattern of industrialization (particularly the development of the machine-building industry) were, at least during the 1949-53 period, tuned to serve the requirements of the less industrialized countries that came under the Soviet aegis and to strengthen the defense potential of the Soviet Bloc.[69] Czechoslovakia experienced then a secure sellers' market for machinery and equipment. In the Soviet Bloc, then largely isolated from world markets, the quality and technical standards of Czechoslovak machines were superior to those produced domestically by the other trading partners. In exchange Czechoslovakia received some of its raw materials and foodstuff requirements.

An increasing quantum of resources had to be allocated to the production of steel which became a key problem in Czechoslovakia. The increasing requirements for coal and iron ore were supported by costly investments in domestic foundries and mines, shifting resources away from light industry. The perennial problem of raw materials for light industries became more acute than ever as imported raw materials were predominantly destined for processing in heavy industry.

The extent to which the Czechoslovak economy became dependent on Soviet deliveries is indicated by the shares of the U.S.S.R. in the total Czechoslovak imports of raw materials and foodstuffs and exports of machinery and consumer goods, as illustrated by Tables 24, 25, 26, and 27. In 1951-55 Czechoslovakia imported from the U.S.S.R. mining equipment; drilling rigs; dressing installations; tractors; combines; bulldozers; construction machinery; and such consumer durables as watches, television sets, cameras, and automobiles. Soviet deliveries accounted for 82 per cent of the imported copper, 99.5 per cent of aluminum, 77.4 per cent of iron ore, 82.9 per cent of crude oil, and 61 per cent of wool.[70]

Admittedly the quality of some Soviet raw

Table 24

SOME CZECHOSLOVAK IMPORTS FROM AND EXPORTS TO THE U.S.S.R., 1945-70

Products	Unit of measure	1945 to 1950	1951 to 1955	1956 to 1960	1961 to 1965	1966 to 1970 Plan
Imports:						
Grain	a	1.9	4.9	6.7	6.0	6.0
Butter	b	31.3	54.5	45.7	61.4	65.0
Meat	b	33.1	45.8	70.9	82.9	75.0
Iron ore	a	4.1	12.0	19.9	33.7	45.9
Copper	b	-	33.2	98.8	99.8	159.0
Oil	a	0.165	1.3	7.3	21.5	39.6
Coniferous timber	c	-	-	739.0	853.7	750.0
Cotton	b	101.8	193.6	234.3	271.5	300.0
Caterpillar tractors	d	-	5.8	6.2	10.9	7.0
Exports:						
Footwear	e	17.2	8.0	48.4	74.3	117.3
Sugar	b	306.0	541.0	517.0	332.0	-
Tubes & pipes	b	231.0	577.0	412.0	675.0	583.0
Machine tools	d	1.8	2.5	8.2	11.6	3.8
Locomotives	f	470.0[g]	-	455.0[h]	1390.0[h]	1837.0

a - million tons, b - thousand tons, c - thousand cubic meters, d - thousands, e - million pairs, f - pieces, g - steam, h - electric and diesel-electric.

Source: Jozef Sebesta, NM, No. 16, 1967, p. 14.

Table 25

COMMODITY COMPOSITION OF IMPORTS FROM AND EXPORTS TO THE U.S.S.R., 1948-65
(In percentages)

	1948	1950	1953	1955	1958	1960	1963	1965
Total imports from U.S.S.R.	100.0	100.0	100.0	100.0	100.0	100.0	100.0	100.0
Machines & equipment	0.4	5.9	17.1	21.5	17.9	22.1	25.1	28.2
Raw materials & semifabricates	43.7	48.4	47.8	48.9	53.9	48.8	52.9	58.2
Foodstuffs	55.5	44.6	34.1	28.0	25.2	26.8	20.1	12.6
Consumer goods	0.4	1.1	1.0	1.6	3.0	2.3	1.9	1.0
Total exports to U.S.S.R.	100.0	100.0	100.0	100.0	100.0	100.0	100.0	100.0
Machines & equipment	23.1	32.1	35.3	53.3	48.4	49.2	58.3	62.7
Raw materials & semifabricates	26.7	37.9	50.8	42.3	27.2	20.0	17.0	18.6
Foodstuffs	8.7	9.5	7.0	2.9	4.2	3.9	3.1	1.8
Consumer goods	41.5	20.5	6.9	1.5	20.2	26.9	21.6	16.9

Source: Jozef Sebesta, NM, No. 16, 1967, p. 14.

Table 26

PRINCIPAL IMPORTS FROM AND EXPORTS TO THE U.S.S.R., 1961-65
(In percentages of total imports or exports)

	1961-65
Imports of materials from U.S.S.R.	39.8
including:	
Crude oil	93.7
Coniferous timber	90.6
Ferroalloys	75.9
Iron ore	75.0
Pig iron	64.3
Coal	64.3
Aluminum	62.0
Synthetic rubber	52.7
Cotton	52.6
Copper	49.7
Imports of foodstuffs from U.S.S.R.	33.4
including:	
Butter	81.1
Grain	67.3
Vegetable edible oils	46.8
Fish and fish products	40.5
Exports	
Machinery and equipment	45.7
Consumer goods	41.2

Source: Miroslav Stribrsky, PH, No. 12, 1967, p. 2.

materials is substandard posing a number of problems in processing. In the face of Soviet indifference to improving the quality of exported raw materials, the Czechoslovaks propose joint efforts to alleviate the difficulties, e.g., to pelletize the iron ore, to desalinate the oil, etc.[71]

About 50 per cent of Czechoslovak exports of machinery go to the U.S.S.R. Practically all large plants in the machine-building industry export their goods primarily to the U.S.S.R. A number of new products (e.g., mobile power plants,

Table 27

TRADE TURNOVER WITH U.S.S.R., SOCIALIST, AND CAPITALIST COUNTRIES, 1945-66
(In percentages)

Years	U.S.S.R.	Other socialist countries	Capitalist countries
1945	26.0	17.0	57.0
1948	16.2	23.5	60.3
1950	27.5	28.0	44.5
1953	35.5	42.9	21.6
1955	34.5	35.6	29.9
1958	32.5	36.8	30.7
1960	34.4	37.1	28.5
1963	38.9	35.7	25.4
1965	36.3	35.8	27.9
1966	32.3	35.7	32.0

Source: Jozef Sebesta, NM, No. 16, 1967, p. 14.

large refrigeration installations, dredges, river passenger boats, large dressing installations) were developed specifically to meet Soviet requirements. Many new products are manufactured according to Soviet instruction and with the aid of Soviet specialists.[72]

Dependence on a single market is not without serious drawbacks, for it strongly subjects the Czechoslovak economy to the influence of the winds of change in the U.S.S.R. The claimed stability is often illusory. For example, the frequent changes in Soviet requirements, due to shifting priorities, adversely affected a number of Czechoslovak machine-building producers (including those producing equipment for steam plants, chemical factories, textile mills, dairy production, and sugar mills, and those producing turbocompressors, electric locomotives, trolley buses, and motorcycles), resulting in frequent changes of production cycles, etc. Sometimes the product mix manufactured by Soviet suppliers changes without the Czechoslovak customers being prepared for the alteration. Conversely, for many years the same, unaltered, and unadaptable assortment is being delivered by U.S.S.R. producers. Consequently Czechoslovak production processes and investment activity are often deranged; capacity and manpower are underutilized; material inputs are used ineffectively; the range of assortments produced is narrowed down; and the product quality suffers.[73]

The present share of raw materials in total Czechoslovak imports from the U.S.S.R. "already represents the upper limit, even for future deliveries. It can rather be assumed that a certain reduction of this share will take place." The main raw materials base of the U.S.S.R. is shifting into remote Asiatic areas, with an inordinate rise of the cost of extraction and of primary processing. Indeed, the Soviets have extracted a high price for future deliveries in terms of investment credits advanced by Czechoslovakia.[74]

In order to assure for itself greater imports of Soviet raw materials, Czechoslovakia has extended to the U.S.S.R. investment credits on two occasions, thereby participating in accelerating the industrial exploitation of Soviet raw materials. On January 20, 1960, a bilateral agreement was concluded on cooperation in ferrous and nonferrous metallurgy. The U.S.S.R. committed itself to increase the deliveries of iron ore and of a number of nonferrous metals (aluminum, copper, lead, and zinc) over and above the quantities heretofore delivered. To share in the considerable investment costs, Czechoslovakia had to supply machinery, installations, and materials on long-term credit. Industrial equipment valued at 290 million rubles was shipped. The deliveries of the bulk of equipment for this grandiose project were supposed to end in 1967. The U.S.S.R. was said to have begun to repay the credit with increased deliveries of metallurgical raw materials.[75] In 1966 a second agreement was concluded whereby Czechoslovakia extended a 500 million ruble credit for the development of new oil fields in the U.S.S.R. Equipment accounts for 70 per cent of this credit, various materials for about 16 per cent, and consumer goods for 14 per cent. The U.S.S.R. will repay the advanced credit in the form of deliveries of crude oil. These repayments are to increase from 9.5 million tons of crude oil in 1970 to 14.5 million tons in 1975. The deliveries are ensured until 1990, thus beyond the repayment period (1984).[76]

It was suggested that the credits were designed to compensate the U.S.S.R. for the inequity in the structure of trade between the two countries. The U.S.S.R. bears the burden of developing the raw materials with which it supplies Czechoslovakia which, in return, only pays for the development of processing branches whose products are destined for the U.S.S.R. The Soviet investment expenditures include new settlements, highways, railroad lines, thousands of kilometers of gas and oil pipelines, and increased costs of exploitation and of basic processing. Czechoslovakia is in a more advantageous position for it foots the bill of less costly investments of a shorter gestation period.[77]

It is argued that for Czechoslovakia the credits are "most advantageous and a most reliable way of ensuring the long-term flow of raw materials for the growing requirements of the economy." To obtain raw materials from developing countries Czechoslovakia "would likewise have to grant credits, but on less favorable terms than to the U.S.S.R."[78]

But to many Czechoslovaks it seemed that their country was forced into a position where it had to foot the bill for Soviet expansion.[79] In order to develop additional sources of raw materials, the U.S.S.R. demands that the socialist states bear the burden of a share of her expenditures. Admittedly, the U.S.S.R. is in a difficult situation, particularly in view of the burden of its defense budget. It is interested in letting the other socialist countries share in this burden. But it should be remembered that investment costs for the extraction of oil in Tyumen (Western Siberia) are higher "than in other areas." This fact brings up a fundamental question: Is the loan to be granted for the specific production costs in the Tyumen area or is it to reflect the opportunity costs on the world market? "As far as I know Czechoslovakia is of the latter opinion."[80]

Complaints were raised that the credits granted to the U.S.S.R. were not proving to be overly advantageous for Czechoslovakia. For example, even though Czechoslovakia helped finance a project for refining Soviet iron ore near the source of extraction, it is getting only an insignificant share of its iron ore imports from the U.S.S.R. in the form of concentrate, while the U.S.S.R. is selling to Great Britain iron ore concentrate only.[81] An official of the SPC suggested that preliminary calculations indicated that such credits are only a stop-gap measure, and an ineffective one at that.[82]

It should be noted, parenthetically, that similar long-term credit agreements have been entered into with other socialist countries. Thus, Czechoslovakia has invested in the development of sulphur, hard coal, and copper mines in Poland; in the exploitation of the Medet copper deposits in Bulgaria; in the development of the potash industry in East Germany; in the construction of cellulose and steam power plants and the building of power transmission lines in Rumania; in the mining of bauxite in Hungary; in the deposits of iron-nickel ore in Albania; and in the development of ferrous and nonferrous metals in Yugoslavia.[83]

The U.S.S.R. evinces an increasing interest in procuring consumer goods. It is argued that this interest does not result from a temporary shift in policy. The Soviets could be enduring clients for such goods as footwear, textile products, and furniture. This shift in the structure of trade adds another dimension to the question of priority of heavy industry.[84]

Since the sellers' market for a large number of industrial consumer goods is particularly strong in the U.S.S.R., goods of inferior quality (both below "world market" and "acceptable Czechoslovak" standards) could be disposed of there. So far the

Soviets have concentrated mainly on imports of Czechoslovak mass-produced consumer goods (shoes, textiles). These exports are particularly import-intensive. The crux of the problem is that since imports of those inputs from the U.S.S.R. stagnate, they increasingly have to be imported from hard currency areas. The rise of the Soviet consumer opens very extensive opportunities and secures a long-range market. It is argued that even though the volume of exports of industrial consumer goods should not be predetermined by Soviet deliveries of the required material inputs, it is unrealistic, particularly in view of Czechoslovak balance-of-payments difficulties, "to count on a quick and orderly increase of imports of raw materials" from the hard currency areas. Moreover, the domestic consumer goods industries, particularly the textile plants, operate with obsolete equipment. A general expansion and modernization is one of the most urgent problems.

The basic solution advocated is to "broaden substantially the raw materials base"--meaning, first of all, to accelerate investments for the development of the chemical industry or its branches producing man-made fibers and materials. It is suggested that variants utilizing Soviet crude oil and its further processing (the petrochemical industry) may prove to be more advantageous in order to broaden the manufacturing of consumer goods. But the development of these branches as well as some branches of consumer goods should be supported by a one-shot, relatively short-term, loan from the U.S.S.R., either in the form of deliveries of equipment or as purchased licenses for production of required equipment and for modern technology and for industrial processes. Credits could be repaid by larger deliveries of consumer goods to the U.S.S.R. and also by deliveries of modern machinery for the Soviet consumer goods industry. The advantages claimed for such a solution include 1) a more effective specialization of Czechoslovak industry and 2) a better quality and wider assortment of consumer goods for domestic and Soviet markets.[85] But would such an arrangement subject the consumer goods industry to a real competitive test?

Will not efficiency be impaired in the long run? These are moot questions. The Czechoslovaks may be paying a high "price of protection" on the Soviet market.

For a number of years a buyers' market prevailed in the exchange of machinery of average and below-average standards among CMEA partners. However, a sellers' market was apparent in the exchange of high-quality machines and raw materials. Prices of raw materials remained firm, in the face of declining prices on the world market. There were powerful pressures to reduce prices of machinery regardless of the general upward movement on the world market. However, prices of machinery also generally remained stable. The importers of raw materials and the exporters of machinery of average standards found themselves in difficulty. Since Czechoslovakia qualifies on both counts, it was probably one of the hardest hit. Czechoslovakia found itself in gradually deteriorating price and credit conditions for acquiring raw materials and in gradually less profitable price and payment conditions for machinery sales.[86]

It should be noted that the exchange between Czechoslovakia and the U.S.S.R. takes place usually at higher prices than those at which either country can sell its respective wares to other parties. But such prices are considered to be still mutually advantageous, for they are lower than those at which either country could purchase those wares from other sources. For example, on shipments of Soviet oil Czechoslovakia paid higher prices than Italy, and more than double the prices at which it could have procured the oil from the Near or Middle East. But such price differentials are somewhat toned down when additional transportation charges are taken into account. Reports differ on the extent to which the Czechoslovaks are overpaying for their purchases by concentrating them on the U.S.S.R. rather than on alternative sources of supply. The available evidence seems, however, to point to a significant narrowing down of the price differentials.[87]

Research on the comparative efficiency of Czechoslovak foreign trade confirmed the conclusion that "economic efficiency declined substantially during the last decade."[88] In particular the main findings of the investigation bore out that the retrogression of the relative efficiency of Czechoslovak foreign trade is not primarily determined by alterations in product mix or by general deterioration of effective demand on foreign markets, but predominantly by a relative deterioration of efficiency (technological parameters, quality, etc.) of the goods supplied.

An investigation of factors responsible for the retrogression included comparisons of prices that Czechoslovak exporters secured and importers paid on the European Economic Community (EEC) and on the European Free Trade Association (EFTA) markets relative to the other traders. For example, the data in Table 28 indicate the average prices that the Czechoslovaks secured in 1964 as a percentage of the EFTA prices and the prices paid in relation to procurement prices of EFTA countries.

Table 28

EXPORT AND IMPORT PRICES AS PERCENTAGE OF EFTA PRICES, 1964

Products	Export price secured as % of EFTA	Import price as % of price paid by EFTA
Sewing machines	44.4	193.6
Sorting equipment	32.2	159.8
Excavating equipment	40.4	259.3
Generators and motors	38.2	182.6
Bearings	59.2	96.5
Automobiles	49.0	84.8
Metal-working equipment	43.7	118.4

Source: Jan Placek and Jan Pleva, PE, No. 7-8, 1967, pp. 615-16.

In trading with the EEC members, the Czechoslovaks, on the average, secured prices that ranged from 20 to 40 per cent of the prices received by advanced industrial capitalist countries (non-EEC members) for sewing machines, sorting and crushing equipment, extraction and excavating equipment, fuel pumps, electric motors, and generators. For tractors, metal-working equipment, bearings, and automobiles, the Czechoslovaks were able to command 40 to 60 per cent of the prices secured by Western producers. In this case the argument could hardly be advanced that discriminatory tariffs were one of the main reasons for disadvantageous prices obtained by Czechoslovakia. With the exception of automobiles, the tariff rates vary from 0 to 10 per cent and the non-EEC member capitalist countries are subjected to them.[89]

Prices of products diverge from the average due to differences in quality (technical parameters, services, delivery terms, etc.). But the premium for above-average quality and the mark-down for below-average standards do not proportionately reflect the quality differentials. For example, particularly in the market for industrial machinery, a manufacturer who supplies equipment above the average world standards (say by 10 per cent) secures a much higher price (say by 30 to 50 per cent). Conversely, equipment judged to be 10 per cent below the world standards generally can be sold only at a price 15 to 20 per cent lower than that of average quality.

Czechoslovak exports of machinery to capitalist countries fetch about 50 per cent of the average price per kilogram brought in by West European sales. The West European producers, in turn, can command less than half the price that American producers can obtain. As a rule, West European buyers are willing to pay the high premium for American equipment due to its high standards and progressive designs and East European machinery producers are having a hard time to sell their wares even at a substantial mark-down.[90]

The deteriorating terms of trade for Czechoslovak exports are brought into sharper focus with the degree of processing of the export article; the more fabricated is the product sold, the lower is generally the relative sales price it can fetch in comparison to a similar product sold by a West European firm. For example, for the less-processed rolled steel sold to EEC members, Czechoslovakia could command 60 to 100 per cent of the price secured by EFTA members, but for the more-processed steel Czechoslovakia could only obtain 30 per cent of the price paid to EFTA members. Similarly, Czechoslovakia could get 70 to 100 per cent of the price obtained by EFTA members for raw materials and semifabricates, with the exception of timber.[91]

As a result there was a relative decline in export prices earned, with a rapid increase of import prices paid. The investigation of the developments from 1955 to 1966 pointed out that the "price scissors" between export and import prices, already open at the beginning of the period, progressively widened, aggravated, inter alia, by Czechoslovak production of goods of inferior technology and imports of technically advanced products.

As long as the market was relatively secure and production facilities were overburdened with current production assignments, there were insufficient stimuli for technical advancement. As long as raw materials for processing and foodstuffs were forthcoming from CMEA trading partners, drastic measures to cope with the raw materials problems and a complete overhaul of agriculture were obviated.

The advancement of industrialization and changes in trade policies pursued by the other CMEA members altered their trading arrangements with Czechoslovakia, as illustrated in Table 29. Czechoslovakia's CMEA trading partners can now produce many products they previously had to import. Simultaneously, they absorb domestically a larger share of raw materials which they

Table 29

COMMODITY COMPOSITION OF CZECHOSLOVAK TRADE WITH CMEA MEMBERS, 1953-60

	Imports			Exports		
	Percentage in total		Index 1953=	Percentage in total		Index 1953=
	1953	1960	100	1953	1960	100
Machinery						
U.S.S.R.	17.1	22.1	237	35.3	49.2	286
East Germany	30.2	50.2	541	8.8	37.9	1375
Poland	7.4	35.8	533	77.4	56.6	92
Hungary	19.9	36.5	236	30.4	38.8	202
Rumania	11.3	19.3	289	87.9	46.6	31
Bulgaria	-	22.4	-	65.8	52.6	128
Albania [a]	-	-	-	53.9	49.7	110
Raw materials, semifabricates, and fuels						
U.S.S.R.	47.8	48.8	187	50.8	20.0	81
East Germany	64.1	36.5	188	56.9	33.6	188
Poland	78.9	57.5	80	16.7	32.7	263
Hungary	30.0	26.7	114	62.6	49.6	126
Rumania	50.6	36.9	130	10.2	44.3	251
Bulgaria	28.0	36.9	370	25.7	38.6	241
Albania	86.0	94.0	269	36.2	36.3	119
Livestock and foodstuffs						
U.S.S.R.	34.2	26.8	144	7.0	3.9	114
East Germany	0.7	1.8	871	14.2	5.8	130
Poland	13.4	4.2	35	0.9	0.3	49
Hungary	45.9	31.8	88	2.8	0.8	46
Rumania	36.5	41.8	205	0.3	1.5	290
Bulgaria	71.0	39.4	156	1.9	0.2	14
Albania	14.0	6.0	104	3.9	1.0	31
Industrial consumer goods						
U.S.S.R.	0.9	2.3	440	6.9	26.9	803
East Germany	5.0	11.1	731	20.1	22.7	361
Poland	0.3	2.5	922	6.2	15.0	212
Hungary	4.2	5.0	153	4.2	10.8	402
Rumania	1.0	2.0	371	1.6	7.5	276
Bulgaria	1.0	1.4	388	6.6	8.5	209
Albania	0.0	0.0	-	6.0	13.0	258

a - Albania withdrew from CMEA membership in 1962.

Source: Dusana Machova, CSSR v socialisticke mezinarodni delbe prace (Prague: 1962), p. 210.

previously exported. Also the migration from country to town, the increasing commitments to improving living standards, and the deteriorating agricultural performance have curbed these countries' ability to export foodstuffs. Their trading outside of the "Communist Common Market" has increased. Conditions of export from Czechoslovakia to "socialist countries are not as easy as they used to be." The trend is toward a buyers' market, while the technical standards of Czechoslovak products are "not competitive."[92] For example, Czechoslovakia delivered about twenty-five sugar refineries to the U.S.S.R., but the Czechoslovak producers relied on the customers to dictate technological improvements. As a result the U.S.S.R. "has finally been forced to buy technically advanced refineries from capitalist firms in France, England, and West Germany."[93]

As the other Soviet Bloc countries advanced on the path of industrialization, they attempted to achieve, like Rumania, "the diversification of industrial exports, the policy of exporting products in as highly processed a form as possible, and the displacement of imports of manufactures by domestic production." During the period of accelerated industrialization, exports of foodstuffs were increased while some raw materials, which otherwise would have been exported, were retained to propel the industrialization drive. Exports were also sensitive to alterations in the flow and structure of domestic output. Those CMEA members, like Czechoslovakia, that suffered from acute shortages of raw materials and foodstuffs "were forced to trade closely" with those CMEA partners "that were still willing" to exchange raw materials and foodstuffs for machinery and manufactured consumer goods.[94] In this situation the U.S.S.R. played a crucial role as a key supplier of raw materials and foodstuffs and a major, and not-too-discriminating, customer for equipment.[95]

The possibility of a regular exchange of Czechoslovak finished products for raw materials and foodstuffs has actually been limited almost entirely to the Soviet Union.[96] However, notwithstanding the stability of the Soviet market, serious problems increasingly emerge, as we have previously outlined. The inability or unwillingness of the U.S.S.R. to supply the increasing requirements of raw materials, coupled with severe agricultural crises in the U.S.S.R. in the early 1960's, forced Czechoslovakia to step up sizable imports from the West, greatly straining the balance of payments. To pay for those imports, the cream of machinery had to be exported, hindering technical advancement and retarding domestic capacity that otherwise could have been expanded. Substandard products could be sold only at a great sacrifice. The inferior quality of Czechoslovak machinery also forced abstention from the use of some domestic raw materials in order to export them for hard currency. However, the impact of the increasing trade outside of CMEA might, in the long run, be salutary for Czechoslovakia in forcing its industry to upgrade the technical standards of its output and to improve efficiency, apart from other economic and noneconomic effects.

Also in the early 1960's the loss of China as an export market for Czechoslovak machinery and as a source of raw materials considerably affected the economy.[97] The decline of trade with China left the Czechoslovaks with a stock of highly specialized equipment which could not be sold elsewhere, or, in some cases, could not even be used domestically, resulting in considerable losses from scrapping.[98] The growing aid to underdeveloped countries further burdened the already strained balance of payments.[99] Czechoslovak foreign trade with "socialist, capitalist, and developing countries" is illustrated in Table 30.

As alluded to earlier, Czechoslovakia faced choices of pattern and speed of industrialization and of the composition and geographical distribution of foreign trade. Having taken advantage of supplying the vast, and then famished, East European market with the capital goods for industrialization, it found itself in a position where by actively promoting the growth of its customers' industrial potential, it was also diminishing their reliance on the very source of supply. The real point seems to be, however, that while demand for the traditional equipment dwindled, Czechoslovakia, by and large, was not prepared to meet the growing demand of its CMEA partners for sophisticated equipment which they then sought on the Western markets. Although due to divergent conditions, comparisons are dangerous, the case of Belgium vis-à-vis its West European trading partners somewhat evokes that of Czechoslovakia vis-à-vis Eastern Europe. The industries of both countries suffered relatively little war damages, nor did they have to pay war reparations. Whereas the Belgian industry profited by the immediate postwar demand for its products in Western Europe, it was faced with a painful process of adjustment and adaptation when the demand for its products tapered off. Other ramifications aside, the point in question is that the process of adaptation to change was quicker and smoother in Belgium than the one through which Czechoslovakia is painfully going after losing touch with the demanding world market.

As mentioned, during the last decade, the participation of Czechoslovakia in the international division of labor left much to be desired. The rate of growth of imports was higher than the rate of growth of exports during the 1960's. On the average, the annual rate of growth of exports reached 8 per cent, whereas that of imports reached 10 per cent. The basic export item is machinery whose volume of export increased about 2.5 times, whereas total exports rose about 2.2 times during 1955-65. The share of machinery in total exports increased only slightly over that decade, as illustrated in Table 31.

In the 1960's there were growing tensions caused by a much more rapid growth of imports of

Table 30

REGIONAL DISTRIBUTION OF FOREIGN TRADE, 1955-65
(In million kcs.)

	1955	1960	1962	1963	1964	1965
Total turnover	16,046	26,964	30,697	33,277	36,034	38,599
Including:						
Socialist countries	11,264	19,357	22,775	24,820	26,385	28,272
CMEA members	10,226	17,198	21,467	23,120	24,657	26,271
U.S.S.R.	5,531	9,281	11,590	12,953	13,495	14,238
Capitalist countries	2,633	4,793	5,029	5,381	6,432	6,919
Developing countries	2,149	2,814	2,893	3,076	3,217	3,408
Total imports	7,579	13,072	14,904	15,554	17,489	19,242
Including:						
Socialist countries	5,433	9,316	11,034	11,438	12,694	14,121
CMEA	4,928	8,362	10,330	10,706	12,035	13,115
U.S.S.R.	2,631	4,539	5,626	6,067	6,572	6,874
Capitalist countries	1,218	2,477	2,619	2,668	3,374	3,614
Developing countries	928	1,279	1,251	1,448	1,421	1,507

Total exports	8,468	13,892	15,793	17,723	18,545	19,357
Including:						
Socialist countries	5,831	10,041	11,741	13,382	13,691	14,151
CMEA	5,298	8,836	11,137	12,414	12,622	13,156
U.S.S.R.	2,900	4,742	5,964	6,886	6,924	7,364
Capitalist countries	1,415	2,316	2,410	2,713	3,058	3,305
Developing countries	1,221	1,535	1,642	1,628	1,796	1,901
Balance of payments	888	820	889	2,169	1,056	115
Including:						
Socialist countries	398	725	707	1,944	997	30
CMEA	370	474	807	1,708	587	41
U.S.S.R.	269	203	338	819	352	490
Capitalist countries	197	-161	-209	45	-316	-309
Developing countries	293	256	391	180	375	394

Source: SR 1966, p.426.

Table 31

EXPORTS AND IMPORTS BY TYPES OF GOODS, 1955-65

		Machinery & equipment	Raw materials, fuels & semi-fabricates	Foodstuffs[c]	Industrial consumer goods[d]	Total
Exports						
1955	a	3,680	3,325	522	940	8,467
	b	43.5	39.3	6.1	11.1	100
1960	a	6,266	4,063	733	2,830	13,982
	b	45.1	29.2	5.3	20.4	100
1962	a	7,517	4,457	772	3,047	15,793
	b	47.6	28.2	4.9	19.3	100
1963	a	8,474	4,829	1,176	3,244	17,723
	b	47.8	27.2	6.7	18.3	100
1964	a	8,716	5,631	998	3,200	18,545
	b	47.0	30.4	5.4	17.2	100
1965	a	9,385	6,890	888	3,194	19,357
	b	48.5	30.4	4.6	16.5	100
Imports						
1955	a	1,005	4,064	2,198	312	7,579
	b	13.3	53.6	29.0	4.1	100
1960	a	2,831	6,935	2,869	437	13,072
	b	21.7	53.0	22.0	3.3	100
1962	a	3,903	7,589	2,766	646	14,904
	b	26.2	50.9	18.6	4.3	100
1963	a	3,978	7,759	3,228	589	15,554
	b	25.6	49.9	20.7	3.8	100
1964	a	4,918	8,476	3,432	663	17,489
	b	28.1	48.5	19.6	3.8	100
1965	a	5,758	9,395	3,083	1,006	19,242
	b	29.9	48.8	16.1	5.2	100

a - in million kcs., b - in percentages, c - including livestock for breeding purposes, d - excluding foodstuffs.

Source: SR 1966, pp. 428-29. Slightly different figures were reported for the years 1955-60 by Zdenek Sedivy, PE, No. 7, 1963, pp. 535-45.

raw materials than of national income. During 1961-65 for each per cent of recorded increase of national income, there was a 6.7 per cent increase in the import of raw materials and semifabricates.[100] In comparison to 1955, the 1965 import of raw materials was about 2.5 times as high, as shown in Table 31.

Almost 50 per cent of Czechoslovakia's imports consist of raw materials and fuels. This group of imports is expanding rapidly, while over-all exports have recently indicated a stagnating trend. Hence the deficit in this group is growing. In 1955 it was -739 million kcs., in 1960 it was -2,872 million kcs., and in 1965 it was -3,505 million kcs. In 1965 the -3,505 million kcs. balance was only just covered by a surplus of 3,627 million kcs. in the export of machinery. But the rate of growth of exports of machinery has been slowing down considerably. Even though Czechoslovakia is an exporter of industrial consumer goods, the surplus in this group (2,188 million kcs. in 1965) did not even cover the deficit in the import of agricultural and food products (-2,195 million kcs. in 1965). The deficits in so-called hard goods (raw materials, fuel, semifabricates, and foodstuffs) amounted to 5,700 million kcs. (about U.S. $792 million at the official exchange rate). Due to surplus of net exports of machinery (and net export of manufactured consumer goods), the over-all trade balance recorded a surplus of 115 million kcs. (about $16 million) in 1965. But it is noteworthy that the total surplus with the socialist countries (CMEA trading partners plus Yugoslavia, Albania, China, North Korea, North Vietnam, and Cuba) amounted to 30 million kcs. (about $4 million). Of this the surplus with CMEA was 41 million kcs. (about $6 million), of which 490 million kcs. (about $68 million) was a surplus with the U.S.S.R., pointing to a deficit with the remaining CMEA partners amounting to 447 million kcs. (about $62 million). The total surplus of 85 million kcs. (about $12 million) with capitalist countries included a deficit with so-called advanced capitalist countries of 309 million kcs. (about $43 million) and a surplus with developing countries of 349 million kcs.

(about $55 million).[101]

In evaluating the growth strategy adopted, the precedence accorded to heavy industry at the detriment of light industry, agriculture, and services, should not be identified as the only factor depressing living standards. If the same pattern of industrialization had been followed, but if consumer goods had been indirectly secured through larger imports, then standards of living and productivity might not have suffered as they did. Of course, the country's involvement in, and structure of, foreign trade depend on its comparative advantages and on its foreign policies and relations which bear on its opportunities to trade. Obviously, we are here in the realm of <u>ifs</u> and <u>buts</u> which are difficult to quantify.

As we have mentioned, the economy's development was characterized by a severe, persisting, and increasing lag of agriculture behind industry. Whereas heavy industry, and machine-building in particular, was accorded utmost priority and claim on investment and other resources, agriculture stagnated, with a widening disproportion between those two sectors. Domestic needs for agricultural products could then only be increasingly satisfied by indirect production; chiefly paid for by exporting machinery and equipment. The rising imports of agricultural products were met by increasing the export of machinery which in turn taxed the iron and steel resources. But, in view of the raw materials gap and the delays in putting steel mills into operation, the balance of payments was further strained; remedied again by increasing exports of machinery and, in the 1960's, by expanding exports of consumer goods, which again were in varying degrees contingent on imports of raw materials. The latter move impoverished the domestic market of goods orginally allocated for domestic consumption. The payment for agricultural products by exports of machinery necessitated expansion of the iron and steel industry, with massive, protracted, and capital-intensive investments,[102] as well as of the complementary industries, particularly fuel and power. Since the extraction of iron ore and coal became increasingly uneconomical, further intensification of imports was called for. This again taxed transportation facilities which became a major bottleneck. Because of taut investment plans--uncoordinated with construction, metallurgy, and machine-building capacities; accentuated by delays in putting capacities into operation, by underutilization of capacity, by the substandard quality of steel, etc.--production programs remained unfulfilled and ill-synchronized and idle capacity existed, especially in the machine-building industry. In the process, additional purchasing power was generated, without a concomitant flow of consumer goods. This was due, _inter alia_, to the dependence of consumer goods production in various degrees on imports of raw materials and to the channeling of capital goods to priority producer goods industries, leaving the consumer goods industries with largely obsolete and worn-out equipment. The lag in agriculture resulted in "excessive dependence" on foreign markets. To overcome this lag by exports of heavy industry, presumably the best of machinery, substantially limited the technical improvement of domestic production, delayed the putting of capacities into operation, and constrained the development of the chemical industry. The development of the chemical industry is a precondition for developing agriculture (fertilizers and synthetic proteins) and the consumer goods industry (synthetic fibers), for reducing the dependence on imports (synthetic rubber), and for enhancing technical development of industry in general (plastics). In other words, agriculture could not be developed without sufficient chemicals, which could not be produced because investments were poured into heavy industry.[103]

The development of the structure of the economy was propelled by a rapid increase in the share of productive investment in national income and by the "disadvantageous allocation of total investments," restricting resources for nonproductive investments and consumption. The increase of productive investments largely resulted from excessive investments in some raw materials branches and from the unfavorable structure of investments.[104] It may be argued that there was a built-in conservative bias maintaining the structure and distribution of investments,[105] accompanied by a built-in inflexibility of production to adjust to domestic and foreign demand and to meet the requirements and high standards of the competitive world market, together with a built-in inability to generate innovation and disseminate technical advancement.

ASSESSMENT OF GROWTH PERFORMANCE

Attempts to compare growth rates encounter innumerable problems of statistical measurement. Keeping in mind that the intrinsic problems of statistical concepts and practice of comparative valuations make international comparisons of growth rates particularly circumspect,[106] we could provide a general indication in Tables 32 and 33 based on official statistics and, particularly, in the Alton-Ernst recalculations in Table 34. We need only

Table 32

ANNUAL GROWTH RATES OF NATIONAL INCOME AND FIXED INVESTMENT IN EASTERN EUROPE, 1950-65
(In constant prices)

Countries	National income			Fixed investment		
	1950-1955	1955-1960	1960-1965	1950-1955	1955-1960	1960-1965
Bulgaria	12.2	9.7	6.5	13.3	18.1	9.7
Czechoslovakia	8.0	7.1	1.8	9.4	13.6	2.1
East Germany	11.4	7.0	3.5	19.6	14.3	4.7
Hungary	6.3	6.5	4.7	2.4	17.3	3.5
Poland	8.6	6.6	5.9	11.2	8.7	6.9
Rumania	13.9	7.0	8.7	18.8	12.6	12.9
U.S.S.R.	11.3	9.2	6.3	12.5	13.0	5.5

Source: EBE, Vol. 18, No. 1, 1966, p. 39.

Table 33

GROWTH OF NATIONAL INCOME IN SELECTED COUNTRIES, 1950-65

Countries	Index 1955=100							Percentages		
	1950	1960	1961	1962	1963	1964	1965	1951-1965	1951-1960	1961-1965
Bulgaria	56	159	163	173	187	205	217	9.4	10.9	6.5
Czechoslovakia	68	141	150	152	149	150	153	5.6	7.5	1.7
East Germany	54	147	153	157	155	161	169	8.4	10.5	2.9
Poland	66	137	149	152	162	173	183	7.1	7.6	6.0
Rumania	52	140	154	160	176	196	215	9.9	10.4	9.5
Hungary	74	138	146	153	161	168	171	5.8	6.4	4.4
U.S.S.R.	58	155	166	175	182	196	208	8.9	10.3	6.1
Yugoslavia	78	150	159	165	195	209	-	7.3	6.7	8.7
Belgium	85	111	116	122	126	139	143	3.4	2.7	5.2
France	81	126	132	141	147	155	159	4.6	4.5	4.8
Netherlands	77	123	127	131	135	147	154	4.7	4.8	4.6
Japan	66	161	186	195	219	243	-	9.8	9.3	10.8
Canada	80	118	121	129	135	144	153	4.4	4.0	5.3
West Germany	64	144	152	158	163	175	184	7.3	8.4	5.0
U.S.A.	81	112	114	121	125	131	138	3.8	3.3	4.2
Sweden	85	117	124	128	133	145	151	3.9	3.2	5.2
United Kingdom	86	114	118	118	122	131	135	3.1	2.8	3.4
Italy	75	132	143	152	159	165	170	5.6	5.8	5.2

Source: Wlodzimierz Brus (ed.), Ekonomia polityczna socjalizmu (Warsaw: 1967), pp. 342-43.

Table 34

GROWTH OF GNP IN SELECTED EAST AND WEST EUROPEAN COUNTRIES, PREWAR TO 1964

Countries	Index 1955=100				Annual percentage increases			
	Prewar	1950	1960	1964	1951-65	1956-60	1961-64	1951-64
Bulgaria	68	75	142	168	5.9	7.3	4.3	5.9
Czechoslovakia	79	84	137	145	3.6	6.6	1.3	4.0
East Germany	84	71	127	141	7.2	4.9	2.7	5.1
Hungary	80	76	123	147	5.5	4.2	4.6	4.8
Poland	72	79	127	155	4.8	5.0	5.0	4.9
Rumania	66	66	119	144	8.6	3.5	4.9	5.7
Total Eastern Europe	76	76	128	148	5.7	5.2	3.6	4.9
Unweighted average					5.9	5.2	3.8	5.1
Austria	62	74	129	151	6.1	5.2	4.2	5.2
Belgium	67	84	112	133	3.6	2.3	4.3	3.3
Denmark	68	91	127	157	2.0	4.9	5.5	4.0
France	66	80	126	155	4.4	4.8	5.3	4.8
West Germany	51	65	135	163	9.1	6.2	4.8	6.8
Greece	93	71	131	183	7.0	5.6	8.7	7.0
Italy	71	75	133	165	6.0	5.9	5.5	5.8
Netherlands	58	76	122	146	5.6	4.1	4.5	4.7
Norway	62	84	117	143	3.6	3.2	5.1	3.9
Total Western Europe	62	75	129	157	5.9	5.2	5.1	5.4
Unweighted average					5.3	4.7	5.2	5.0

Source: Maurice Ernst, in U.S. Congress, Joint Economic Committee, New Directions for the Soviet Economy (Washington: GPO, 1966), p. 880.

allude here to the dramatic growth of the various European economies, both East and West, and to the significant variations between countries and between postwar periods to provide a rough frame of reference.

Looking at the West European economies as an aggregate, we find that their (measured) growth during the 1950's was slightly better than that of the East European economies viewed as a whole. Although there were wide variations between countries, it should also be pointed out that on the whole the West European economies enjoyed a more sustained growth than that of the East European ones.[107] The West European rates of growth were particularly enhanced by the "economic miracle" of West Germany.

> In continental Europe the decade of the 1950's was brilliant, with growth of output and consumption, productivity, investment and employment surpassing any recorded historical experience, and the rhythm of development virtually uninterrupted by recession.[108]

Comparisons of average growth rates, according each country an equal weight, show growth rates of East European economies to be of about the same order of magnitude as those of the West European economies. East Germany excepted, the growth performance of East European countries varied inversely with per capita GNP.[109] On the whole, the East European economies were expanding rapidly in the 1950's. Rumania and Bulgaria recorded the highest rates of growth, as shown in Table 32. The lowest, but still respectable, growth rates were reported for Hungary, Czechoslovakia, and Poland. Not unlike West European economies, the East European ones displayed during the 1950's "a tendency for the rates of growth to decline somewhat from the first to the second quinquennium." The downward trend was particularly marked in Rumania, principally due to the adverse performance of agriculture, "but it was significant also in all the other countries except Czechoslovakia."[110] Improved growth performance in Czechoslovakia (following a sharp decline in the growth rates in 1953-54) and Bulgaria's upsurge in growth rates during the second half of the 1950's more than compensated for the deceleration of growth rates of East Germany where the belated recovery had come to a halt.

In Czechoslovakia, performance in the second half of the 1950's was impressive both in comparison to that of other East European countries and to that of Western Europe. Similarly to 1950-51, 1958 was considered as one of the most impressive and successful years since the 1948 Communist takeover. The pace of growth at the end of the 1950's and in 1960 was remarkable, with a slight deceleration in 1961 and a marked slowdown in 1962. By 1963 Czechoslovakia achieved the dubious distinction of a negative rate of growth of about 3 per cent.[111] It was one of the severest economic recessions in any country since the end of World War II--a case of the "inverse economic miracle" that profoundly shook the entire superstructure.

The percentage increase of GNP from prewar to 1964 was 84 per cent, with a 3 per cent decrease in population and a 90 per cent increase in per capita GNP. The percentage increase of GNP from 1950 to 1964 was 73 per cent, the population increased by 13 per cent, and per capita GNP rose by 53 per cent. During 1951-55, 31 per cent of the increase of GNP was channeled to personal consumption; during 1956-60, 55 per cent; during 1961-64, 136 per cent; and for the entire period of 1961-64, 55 per cent.[112] The increased share of consumption in the 1956-60 period may be partially explained by the political climate prevalent at the time in the Soviet Bloc, but particularly, as we shall see later, as a consequence of the economic overstrain of the preceding period. The relatively increased share of consumption in 1960-64 should be viewed against the backdrop of the noted deceleration during that period. The share of the increase of GNP from prewar to 1964 devoted to personal consumption was estimated at 43 per cent. The growth of personal consumption per capita from prewar to 1964 was estimated at 35 per cent, from 1950 to 1964 at 20 per cent, and from 1960 to 1964 at 5 per cent. Whereas prewar personal consumption per capita approached that of Germany, in 1964 it was only 57 per cent of that of West Germany.[113] Apart from the precariousness of such comparisons, it should be pointed out that the personal consumption does not take into consideration education, health,[114] and other social services which, in Soviet-type economies, are provided free, or at a minimal charge, by the state to a larger extent than in the West.

With the spread of economic revisionism throughout the Soviet Bloc, generally, the rationalization for the adoption of the Soviet growth strategy and of a command economy has stressed that the traditional model[115] was in principle fully applicable to, and generally adequate for, extensive development and accelerated industrialization under conditions then prevailing in the U.S.S.R.[116] Apparently somewhat similar conditions (such as unabsorbed or potential manpower resources, underutilized capacity, and "acute international tensions") prevailed in Eastern Europe in 1950-52 when the Soviet model was unimaginatively copied, admittedly without adapting it to the particular conditions in each country. Moreover, it was argued that a centralized model was then conducive to securing a swift concentration of the bulk of investment on leading links and to promoting rapid growth.[117] By concentrating the bulk of decisions at the center and by using an elaborate, comprehensive, specific, and mandatory network of targets and limits, the planner could mobilize resources for accelerated restructuring of the economy and could react promptly to some of the bottlenecks--probably creating other bottlenecks in the process.

The impressive over-all dynamics of economic activity (industrial production) have been more critically scrutinized in Czechoslovakia since the early 1960's. It was pointed out that past achievements were at the cost of extensive utilization of the labor force and ever-increasing investments and material inputs, with little concern for efficiency (presumably both technical and economic). Moreover, the path of development pursued resulted in deleterious unbalanced growth, with considerable fluctuations in the growth rates of production. The exhaustion of almost all sources of extensive growth made it mandatory to focus attention on intensive utilization of resources. As the reservoir of manpower neared exhaustion, the ambitious dynamics of industrial growth could not be achieved by further drawing on the agricultural labor force and by increasing the already high participation rate of women in the labor force. Reallocation of manpower from nonpriority to priority sectors had to be undertaken by both compulsion and incentives. The labor shortages, coupled with the behavior pattern developed under the traditional model, gave rise to the proclivity to overstate labor requirements, to "store" labor as a precautionary measure, and to inefficiently employ labor. The restrictions on labor mobility contributed to a relaxation of work discipline, with adverse effects on productivity. Hence the disappointing performance even when measured by the dubious index of growth of labor productivity.[118]

The doctrine that the propeller of economic growth is a high and rising volume of investment and that any decline in the tempo of growth could be remedied by pouring in more investment, is still another aspect of the extensive type of growth strategy pursued. Attempts were made to eradicate grave inefficiencies by pouring in more investments, so that eventually the incremental capital-output ratio rose steeply. According to the Alton-Ernst recomputations, the incremental capital-output ratio registered 6.5 for the economy at large in 1951-55, 4.1 for 1956-60, and 25.2 for 1961-64. The respective indexes for industry were computed as 5.1, 2.6, and 12.2. For the period 1951-64 the ratio for the entire economy was computed as 6.7, for industry as 4.4, for agriculture as 40.0, and for services as 7.8.[119] It was one of the highest ratios in Europe.[120] According to the U.N. report, the incremental capital-output ratio in Czechoslovakia for 1949-58 was 3.5, for 1949-53 it was 3.0, and for 1953-58 it was 4.0. For the same periods it was 2.1, 2.2, and 2.0 in industry; 118.5, 10.2, and -44.0 in agriculture; 0.4, 0.3, and 0.5 in construction; 8.3, 9.1, and 7.8 in transport; and 0.6, 0.3, and 0.9 in trade.[121] In the 1960's there was a marked upward trend in the capital-output ratios. According to one Czechoslovak source,[122] the incremental capital-output ratio was 2.04 in 1960, 10.09 in 1962, 24.19 in 1964, and 4.03 in 1965.[123]

Admittedly, the inordinate expansion of investments, beyond what the economy could sustain without excessive strains,[124] was largely responsible for the dramatic decline of efficiency.[125] The arbitrariness in determining the size of investment and its allocation further contributed to tensions and inefficiencies. Moreover, the traditional planning system was also conducive to waste of investment, not only because it was void of criteria for evaluating investment efficiency but because micro-units squandered capital offered to them virtually cost free; because these units were not under economic compulsion to use capital effectively; and because of an incentive system which induced waste by capital goods producers, construction firms, and design bureaus.

The major factor increasing the cost of economic growth and encroaching on consumption was the comparatively low productivity of investments. In other words, a much larger share of GNP was channeled to investment than in the market economies of Western Europe to produce roughly the same increase in output.[126]

The relatively low efficiency of investments in Eastern Europe in general could be mainly attributed to the economic policies and institutional arrangements of Soviet-type economies,[127] aggravated by the general technological inferiority of Eastern Europe--a condition which had particularly adverse effects on Czechoslovakia, because of its relatively advanced stage of industrialization. The adopted strategy of maximizing investments overtaxed the construction and machine-building industries, prolonging the period involved in commissioning new capacities. The propensity to channel the lion's share of industrial investments to building new factories, while minimizing expenditures on renovation and maintenance of the established ones, resulted in the delapidation of capital. In nonpriority industries pressures were exerted to produce more from existing capacities, with little support from investment.

Tentative as it may be, a statistical analysis by Mojmir Hajek and Miroslav Toms, applying Solow's modification of the Cobb-Douglas production function to the economic growth of Czechoslovakia during 1951-64, showed that economic growth for the period in question was predominantly achieved by contribution of extensive factors and that intensive factors were, on the average, responsible for merely 18 per cent of the growth of national income. As shown in Table 35, investment was the chief growth propeller. The over-all positive effect of the

Table 35

FACTORS PROPELLING AND CONSTRAINING ECONOMIC GROWTH, 1951-64

	Rate	Share
Over-all growth of national income decomposed into sources of growth:	5.90	100.00
1) Growth attributed to extensive factors	4.79	81.19
a) capital	4.71	79.83
b) labor	0.08	1.36
2) Growth attributed to intensive factors	1.11	18.81
a) technical progress	0.33	5.59
b) improvement of skills	1.82	30.84
c) planning system	-1.04	-17.62

Source: Mojmir Hajek and Miroslav Toms, in Ekonomicky Ustav Ceskoslovenske Akademie Ved, Studie z teorie ekonomickeho rustu (Prague: 1966), p. 112.

improvement in the quality of labor was rather high and the over-all contribution of technical progress was meager. On the whole, the most retrogressive factor was the planning system, impeding technical progress and reducing the over-all contribution of intensive factors. The estimates in Table 36

Table 36

ESTIMATES OF GROWTH OF AGGREGATE PRODUCTIVITY PER COMPOSITE OF LABOR AND CAPITAL, 1951-64

Years	Index	Years	Index
1951	100.0	1958	121.9
1952	106.9	1959	122.9
1953	109.7	1960	123.2
1954	108.8	1961	124.4
1955	114.7	1962	116.6
1956	116.3	1963	111.2
1957	119.1	1964	106.9

Source: Mojmir Hajek and Miroslav Toms, in Ekonomicky Ustav Ceskoslovenske Akademie Ved, Studie z teorie ekonomickeho rustu (Prague: 1966), p. 114.

indicated that the improvements of productivity were generally moderate and slackening; showing little improvement since the late 1950's and demonstrating a critical deceleration in the early 1960's. As shown in Table 37, the findings, following from simplified and not-too-tenable assumptions, indicated what the "potential" rates of growth might have been during that period without any of the adverse effect attributed to the planning system.[128] Thus, it is often claimed that the major factors tending to reduce the economy's growth potential are largely system-created.

It is noteworthy that Simon Kuznets, summarizing the experience of modern economic growth concluded that:

Table 37

POTENTIAL AND RECORDED GROWTH RATES, 1951-64

Years	Growth rates of national income	
	Potential	Recorded
1951	8.21	9.53
1952	7.93	10.65
1953	9.58	6.44
1954	9.45	3.54
1955	9.09	10.28
1956	8.89	5.35
1957	9.35	7.25
1958	9.59	8.23
1959	10.38	6.34
1960	10.29	8.08
1961	9.98	6.77
1962	10.04	1.40
1963	9.80	-2.17
1964	9.28	0.89

Source: Mojmir Hajek and Miroslav Toms, PE, No. 1, 1967, p. 24.

> While the results would clearly vary among individual countries, the inescapable conclusion is that the direct contribution of man-hours and capital accumulation would hardly account for more than a tenth of the rate of growth in per capita product--and probably less. The large remainder must be assigned to an increase in efficiency in the productive resources--a rise in output per unit of input, due either to the improved quality of the resources, or to the effects of changing arrangements, or to the impact of technological change, or to all three.[129]

Kuznets further remarked:

> The conclusion that increased output of man-hours and capital, as such, plays a minor role in the rise in product per capita

Chart 1

POTENTIAL AND RECORDED GROWTH RATES OF NATIONAL INCOME, 1951-65
(Based on data in Table 37)

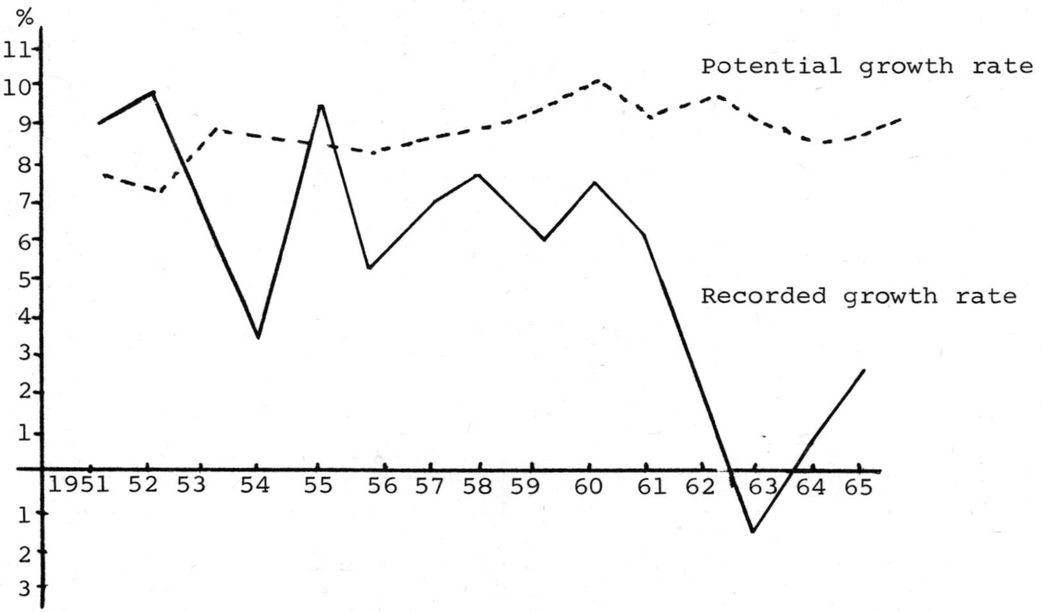

> reflects some key features of modern economic growth.

Such growth was not achieved by larger labor inputs.

> It was associated with capital accumulation, but the ratio of capital to output was kept down by capital-saving innovations, investment in human training, and other arrangements that permitted greater output with a diminished relative supply of natural resources and even of reproducible capital; and these enormous economies in the use of capital also limited the return that had to be paid for it and hence the rate of its direct contribution to current production.[130]

Interesting results were produced by Josef Goldmann, Karel Kouba, and Josef Flek,[131] in the experimental application of Michal Kalecki's model to Czechoslovak economic data.[132] The intent was to quantify the actual effect of the traditional planning system on the growth process in Czechoslovakia during the period 1950-65. Both observed and theoretical rates of growth of national income were computed.[133] They adopted Kalecki's basic growth equation as their point of departure, as follows:

$$r = \frac{1}{m} \cdot \frac{I}{D} + (u - a)$$

where r = the observed growth rate of gross national income
m = the incremental (constant) fixed capital-output ratio
I = the volume of gross productive fixed investment commissioned during a year
D = gross (material) national income
u = the coefficient of improvement, independent of investment outlays (parameter of independent improvement)
a = the rate of retirement of plant (parameter of amortization)

Goldmann modified it as follows:

$$r = \frac{1}{m} \cdot \frac{I}{D} + (u_1 + u_2 - a) \div (u_3 + u_4)$$

where u_1 = u factor <u>sensu stricto</u> in the Kalecki equation (effect on growth in gross national income of factors other than investment)

u_2 = the effect on the rate of growth of national income of the operation of the (traditional) planning system

u_3 = the effect on the growth rate of excessive accumulation (decumulation) of inventories and unfinished capital construction

u_4 = changes in growth rates due to "quasi-cyclical" and random fluctuations

The theoretical rate of growth was calculated as

$$r' = \frac{1}{m} \cdot \frac{I}{D} + (u_1 + u_2 - a)\ t + c$$

where r' = theoretical measure of the growth rate computed from the application of the Kalecki-Goldmann growth model

t = time

c = constant

$r - r' = (u_3 - u_4)$

Multiple correlation analysis supplied the regression equation,

$$r' = 0.48 \frac{I}{D} - 0.81\ t + 5.04$$

The data in Table 38 indicated the positive effects of the traditional planning model on the growth rate in the first stage of development (early 1950's) and its negative effects at the later stages.[134] Whereas in the early stages of accelerated industrialization, investment seemed to play an insignificant role and the primary factors propelling growth were noninvestment ones, in the mid-1950's investment became the decisive

Table 38

GOLDMANN'S CALCULATION OF THE GROWTH RATES OF GROSS NATIONAL INCOME, 1950-65

Years	r	I/D	t	1/m.I/D = = 0.48(I/D)	$(u_1+u_2-a)t$ = = -0.81t	c = 5.04	r' = (5) + + (6) + (7)
(1)	(2)	(3)	(4)	(5)	(6)	(7)	(8)
1950	9.7	12.0	0	5.76	0.00	5.04	10.80
1951	9.2	11.8	1	5.66	-0.81	5.04	9.89
1952	10.3	11.0	2	5.28	-1.62	5.04	8.70
1953	6.3	10.9	3	5.23	-2.43	5.04	7.84
1954	3.7	12.8	4	6.14	-3.24	5.04	7.94
1955	10.0	12.3	5	5.90	-4.05	5.04	6.89
1956	5.3	11.7	6	5.62	-4.86	5.04	5.80
1957	7.2	13.9	7	6.67	-5.67	5.04	6.04
1958	8.3	13.9	8	6.67	-6.48	5.04	5.23
1959	6.4	18.0	9	8.64	-7.29	5.04	6.39
1960	8.2	16.7	10	8.02	-8.10	5.04	4.96
1961	7.0	16.5	11	7.92	-8.91	5.04	4.05
1962	1.8	16.1	12	7.73	-9.72	5.04	3.05
1963	-1.6	16.3	13	7.82	-10.53	5.04	2.33
1964	1.2	19.1	14	9.17	-11.34	5.04	2.87
1965	2.8	20.7	15	9.94	-12.15	5.04	2.83

Source: Josef Goldmann and Karel Kouba, Hospodarsky rust v CSSR (Prague: 1967), p. 103.

factor. New capacities commissioned in 1957-61 were considered to have been the main source of growth during that period. Since the late 1950's the noninvestment factors became increasingly factors decelerating growth, consequently sharply reducing the "potential" growth rate that could have been achieved as a result of growth-promoting investments. For example, had wasteful investments and the retarding effects of the obsolete planning system not occurred in the years 1962-65, the "potential" growth might have been about 36 per cent

(Column 5, Table 38). The recorded growth for the period was only about 4 per cent (Column 2, Table 38). A revamped planning system would provide additional substantial sources of growth.[135] The estimate of retrogressive effects of the traditional planning system should be accepted with great circumspection, however. Quite apart from the simplifying assumptions and the refractory nature of the statistical data, the value of u_2 "having been estimated as a residual is, of course, subject to a particularly large margin of error."[136] No more than a very broad and rough approximation should be read into it.

In terms of Kalecki's model, the increasing "incompatibility" between the retrogressive planning system and the development of the productive forces resulted in significant changes in the strategic parameters of the growth model. Whereas the coefficient u was declining, the capital coefficient was rising, slowing down the rate of growth.[137]

Goldmann pointed to the tendency for the raw materials base to trail behind the development of the manufacturing industry in a relatively small industrially advanced economy of the traditional Soviet-type model whenever the selected growth rate exceeds the "maximum rate" that can be sustained under prevailing conditions.[138] This results from a tendency to create so-called raw materials barriers and organizational ceilings by underfulfilling the output and investment plans in the basic materials and extracting industries and by overfulfilling the production quotas at the higher stages of manufacturing. A precipitous rise in investment (overinvestment) encounters, in addition to physical constraints, organizational ceilings. As the construction activity is sharply intensified, the number of projects is extended. There is a dearth of technical and organizational personnel to cope with the mounting problems (such as discontinuous flow of supply, cooperation, etc.) further prolonging the gestation period. As import requirements are magnified, strong pressures are exerted on the balance of payments, necessarily forcing exports of the cream of machinery, enlarging unprofitable sales, and generating more investments to produce import substitutes or exportables, with the resulting aggravation of imbalances. Similarly the unsatisfactory performance of agriculture is a contributing factor.

> To sum up: the obstacle to a very high rate of growth... is the high capital outlay required both directly and as a result of the difficulties in equilibrating the balance of foreign trade and possibly also of the shortage of labour; in fact the difficulties in foreign trade may make it virtually impossible to exceed a certain level of the rate of growth.[139]

These disproportions and hypertensions can only be remedied by decelerating the tempo of expansion, with a corresponding decline in import requirements of raw materials. The pressures on the balance of payments recede and the foreign trade and materials barriers are lowered. This breathing spell continues until industry is provided with the necessary materials emanating from the facilities which were under construction in the preceding period, thus filling the materials gap. The argument continues that if the traditional Soviet-type planning system remains unchanged a quasi-cycle would resume.[140]

The crucial role of inventory accumulation is pointed to as a cycle-accelerating (reducing) factor. The rate of growth of inventories is considered to be a potent force which accelerates the tempo at which the turning point is reached in both the expansion and the contraction phases of the cycle. The inventory cycle is synchronized with, and further prolongs, the commissioning of new capacities. The dynamics of inventory cycles are said to be determined by "speculative" hoarding of materials at the peak of the cycle and by a relative or absolute drop of inventory hoarding at the trough of the cycle. This is mainly so for two reasons: 1) Growth is accelerated by increases in output originating from new capacities whose construction started near the peak of the preceding investment wave. The flow of supply increases, while simultaneously, as a result of a relatively moderate rate of growth and of reduced investment, demand declines mainly in the basic branches of industry. 2) The peak of investment activity magnifies pressures in the economy, aggravates the imbalances, causes greater hoarding of inventories, and necessitates a slowdown in the rate of growth in the immediately following period.

Thus it is held that oscillations in the accumulation of inventories and in the volume of unfinished construction are mainly responsible for alternating the increase or reduction of tensions and the ups and downs in the growth rates.[141] The accumulation of inventories reaches its peak when the growth rate has already begun to decline; the accumulation of stocks acts as a catalyst in the deceleration of growth rates. Deceleration sets in when the effects of foreign trade, materials, and capacity barriers make themselves strongly felt.

Preliminary analysis of the dependence of changes in imports of materials on alterations in the rate of growth of industrial output disclosed that the swings in the fluctuations of imports are considerably greater than those in the fluctuations of the growth rates of industrial output, since, as we have noted, a 1 per cent increase of output requires, on the average, about 6 per cent increase in imports. Since rapid expansion of exports is unlikely, the gap between import requirements and exports widens.[142] The combined effect of a synchronization of the material and foreign trade barriers demonstrates that a material barrier arises between the acceleration phase of the cycle and its peak phase. Strong pressures are then exerted on the increase of imports. As a cycle develops, the barriers become insurmountable. At first, uncontrolled deceleration sets in, followed by a throttling down of the growth rate by the authorities. As the rate of industrial output falls, import requirements decrease at a faster rate, the pressures on the balance of payments are eased, and the foreign trade and material barriers are lowered. The reduction of inventories and unfinished construction creates supplementary sources of rising consumption standards, and/or of increasing industrial capacity by investing in new projects or completing those started, and/or of investing in the infrastructure.

Summarizing the results of his research on fluctuations and secular rates of growth of Czechoslovakia, Poland, Hungary, and East Germany, Goldmann pointed to the relatively regular fluctuations of the growth rates of industrial production. Those fluctuations were sharper in producer goods production. The fluctuations in investments were more pronounced than those in the dynamics of industrial output.[143]

After an overambitious acceleration of the growth rate in the early 1950's in Czechoslovakia, the only way to mitigate the disproportions, according to Goldmann, was to decelerate the growth rates and to reduce capital formation in the 1953-54 period. Hence the slowdown of that period and the shifts in resource allocation in favor of consumption were attributed to the economic development of the preceding period, rather than to a change in the political climate--and perhaps too exclusively so. From 1954, a gradual upswing took place and accelerated development regained momentum. The new wave of industrialization and capital formation culminated about 1959-60 and, for reasons considered to be inherent in the traditional planning system, resulted by 1961-63 in a similar, but much sharper, decline in the growth of industrial output than in the period 1953-54.

Growth of industrial output was synchronized with the fluctuations in commissioning new industrial capacities. The peaks in commissioning new capacities, occurring during 1959-60 and 1964-66, corresponded to two peaks in the waves of investments in 1951-52 and in 1959-60, respectively. Generally, an interval of six to eight years was required for constructing and commissioning new projects. The shorter duration of the second cycle (1960-66 as contrasted with 1952-60) was apparently due to cutting down by two to three years on the average time required for activating new industrial capacities.

Statistical data apparently also support the contention that in the years when the increments of new industrial capacities were largest, the supply situation was vastly improved. Enterprises apparently adapted themselves to the improvements in the supply situation by sizably speeding up their inventories' turnover, with a process of relative or absolute stock decumulation. When the growth rate was again increased, sooner or later pressures developed and the supply situation deteriorated. Enterprises again resorted to hoarding, worsening the supply situation, and aggravating the imbalance in the economy. This chain reaction resulted in reduced growth rates. Such a development only terminates when the combined effect of the declining growth rate and of a new peak in commissioning new capacities reduces disproportions and pressures and eases the supply situation.

As we have seen, there was a moderately falling trend in the rate of growth of industrial output in the period 1950-64, with a tendency for the rate of growth of industrial output to fall by 0.7 per cent annually. The deceleration could not be mainly explained by such factors as the gradual exhaustion of manpower, capacity, labor productivity reserves; the achievement of a higher stage of development; and the lessening of the distorting impact of the gross value index on the statistical measurement of industry's performance. The attempt to quantify the contribution of the above factors to deceleration disclosed that actually they played no significant role.

The predominant causal factor responsible for the deceleration of the growth rate is attributed to the traditional planning system. The three key escape channels (leakages) deemed to be of sufficient quantitative importance and identified as the immediate causes of deceleration, are: 1) superfluous rise of inventories, 2) superfluous increase of unfinished construction, and 3) gradual deterioration of input-output ratios (particularly excessive use of materials). The escape channels produced by excessive inventories and unfinished construction can be fully accounted for by the traditional planning system, whereas the relative rise in material inputs is supposed to result largely from traditional planning, but also partly from structural factors.

Table 39

INCREASE IN STOCKS, UNFINISHED CONSTRUCTION, AND ACCUMULATION, 1956-64
(At current prices, billion kcs.)

Years	Increase in		
	Inventories	Unfinished construction	Total accumulation
1956	3	3	16
1957	1	4	21
1958	4	7	26
1959	1	4	27
1960	5	1	28
1961	9	10	35
1962	9	9	32
1963	6	-1	17
1964	-	-4	15

Note: There seems to be a transposition of entries in Goldmann's original article in PH, No. 11, 1964. The book version reports revised data since 1961.

Source: Josef Goldmann, PH, No. 11, 1964, p. 16; and Josef Goldmann and Karel Kouba, Hospodarsky rust v CSSR (Prague: 1967), p. 68.

The data in Table 39 indicate that a sizable share of accumulation (almost one third for the period in question) was tied up in unfinished construction and inventories which, for example, in 1961 amounted to over one fifth of national income and was about equal in size to the annual volume of investment for that year. The unfinished construction and increase in inventories absorbed often the bulk of the increase in national income, substantially infringing on the part that could be diverted to increasing consumption and for commissioning capacities. The investment in inventories remained considerably larger in relation to national income in Eastern Europe than in Western Europe.[144]

Among other growth-retarding factors, was the rather complete lack of interest in promoting technical progress due to strong disincentives built into the traditional system. A very rough estimate once again indicated that the recorded increase in labor productivity was primarily accompanied by rising investments, rather than by technical progress, as illustrated in Table 40.

Table 40

INDEX OF CHANGES IN LABOR PRODUCTIVITY AND FIXED ASSETS IN INDUSTRY, 1950-62
(First year of each period = 100)

	1950-1953	1953-1956	1956-1959	1959-1962
Labor productivity	153	118	118	114
Fixed assets	109	113	116	118
"Effectiveness of technical progress"	140	104	102	97

Source: Josef Goldmann, PH, No. 11, 1964, p. 24.

The economic structure--in many ways interwoven with the planning system--is considered to be a secondary factor responsible for the deceleration of growth rates. But massive investments would not eliminate the inefficiencies resulting from traditional planning. If, first, the basic causes for escape channels and waste rooted in the traditional model were eliminated, the resources thus released could be redirected to gradual structural transformation. Therefore, the desired structural changes do not necessarily have to be financed at the expense of living standards, since productivity would be enhanced. But this goal could not be achieved within the framework of the traditional system. Although Goldmann stressed mainly replacement of the traditional planning system--and as a policy move he advocated it as the very first step--he recognized that the way of the impasse must involve increasing, rather than reducing, the share of national income devoted to consumption and modifying, rather than intensifying, priorities of capital goods. "The elimination of relapses into notorious overinvestment" combined with a complete overhaul of the planning system "could prevent new disproportions from arising and the economic disequilibrium from being aggravated."[145]

The "inverted economic miracle" has probably had some salutary effects. Among them was the shift of the growth tempo into a lower gear forced upon the planners, together with a reduction of the commitment of resources to investment. However, the stalwarts of the traditional system overtly demonstrated their disquietude with the relative reduction of investment which they saw as a threat to growth potential. They were alarmed by what they considered to be a "catastrophic" shift in resource allocation in favor of consumption.

Some economists, particularly those associated with the SPC, attributed the stagnation of the Czechoslovak economy to the fact that in the 1960's (except for 1961) the rate of increase of personal consumption grew at a faster tempo that that of national income. They were distressed that the volume of investment was increasing at a substantially slower rate than during the Second Five-Year Plan (FYP). By reference to the structure of economically advanced countries, it was pointed out that application of modern science and technology requires the growth of such branches as chemistry, artificial fibers, power plants, and mechanical and electrical engineering at rates far above the growth of national income. Such restructuring could only be accomplished by massive investments.[146] The accelerated development of science and technology apparently makes it necessary to place more and more previously created resources into the productive sectors. The gradual increase of the share of accumulation in national income has "the nature of an objectively acting economic rule which must be observed by every conception of economic development..." To bring the structure of the economy up to the development of science and technology, precedence must be accorded to producer goods, and personal consumption must increase at a slower rate than national income. The major share of the increase of national income must be channeled to augment production.[147] The law of preferential growth was again invoked to support redistribution of national income in favor of capital formation.

In retort it was pointed out that, under Czechoslovak conditions, the tightening of the belt is not the only way, and not even a feasible way, of getting out of the impasse.[148] In the ensuing debate--which came to be known as the "are we living beyond our means?" controversy--the supporters of the latter position pointed out that a respectable growth rate could be resumed not by reducing the share of consumption, but by eliminating the escape channels. A deceleration of the growth of consumption would necessarily hinder production by its adverse effects on productivity. The rate of growth of national income does not depend only on the size of accumulation, but primarily on investment efficiency. There are sizable reserves in both capital and labor which could be tapped for increasing production. Technical progress may be capital-saving and, consequently, the "dogmatic" assertion that investment requirements must constantly grow does not hold under all circumstances.[149] Existing capacities should be reoriented in response to requirements. The advocates of fundamental structural transformation were denounced for wanting "to initiate a new cycle of investment whose consequences would make the events of 1953-54 and 1961-63 appear negligible."[150]

The cardinal problem was not in restructuring the economy, but in changing the planning system. A structural transformation, as advocated by Karel Soska and others, would strengthen central decision-making, preserve overcommitment of resources to this or that sector (branch), increase tensions, and presumably maintain administrative measures to cope with the tensions. Essentially the "prisoners of outdated views" were accused of paying only lip service to the reform of the planning system, for they advocated transformation first and reform later. They were basically opposed to reforms. They realized that with the traditional planning system they could not expect a drastic rise in efficiency that would boost output. Therefore, they resorted to methods "which seem to offer an easier solution," i.e., to raise the share of capital formation in national income.[151] They argued that the planning system cannot be significantly altered unless and until the structural changes are implemented, for the market mechanism cannot function effectively under acute shortages and dislocations. Furthermore, the restructuring was expected to last for about a decade. The unenthusiastic reformers were hoping that economic performance would improve in the meantime and that the urgency for planning reforms would abate.

The lessons of postwar economic development point to the fallacy of identifying the highest rate of growth as the touchstone of economic advancement. To aim at "excessively" high rates by overinvesting is to invite flagrant disproportions, to court ample fluctuations in the rate of economic activity, etc. The crucial questions are: To what extent does the adopted growth rate result in sustained growth and to what extent does it meet the objective function. The aim is not "any rate of growth, but one which is well-balanced." The prescription is correct, even if difficult to ascertain and to implement: "A prudent choice of growth rate, and particularly the accelerated introduction and effective application of the new system, is the only solution."[152]

CHAPTER 2 THE FUNCTIONING OF THE ECONOMY

ADOPTION OF THE TRADITIONAL SYSTEM

The planning system had undergone two major alterations of its working arrangements prior to the latest attempt.[1] The 1953 and 1958-59 reforms aimed chiefly at better-coordinated and -integrated plans; at reducing the continuous interventions from superiors; and at improving the enterprise's performance. Whereas the first was unabashedly proclaimed as a further infusion of Soviet experience, making the system more centralized,[2] the second's theme was a degree of decentralization. With different methods, both aspired at invigorating the plan as an operational document for guiding economic activity at all levels.

As we have seen, following the 1948 coup the Communists strengthened their hold over the economy by intensifying nationalization and by creating an administrative superstructure for its management, parallel to the Soviet prototype. A State Planning Office (SOP), responsible to the Council of Ministers (CM), was created, incorporating the State Statistical Office, Supreme Price Office, Center for Scientific Research, and Central Arbitration Commission. The initially few industrial ministries soon proliferated. Chief administrations, responsible for given branches of industry, functioned as intermediaries between the ministries and enterprises. Although there was a direct vertical line of subordination (enterprises--chief administrations--ministries), the SOP was formally not entitled to issue operative orders. A separate Planning Office was set up in Slovakia, as part of Slovakia's Board of Commissioners. For all intents and purposes, the Slovak office had very little autonomy and reported to the SOP on all important matters.[3]

A number of control figures--embracing a network of targets and limits of resources--was drafted by the SOP for ministries as a first step in the planning procedure. The ministries disaggregated the control figures among their chief administrations which proceeded similarly with the enterprises. After the enterprises had submitted their plans to their superiors, they passed through a process of aggregation and dovetailing until they finally reached the SOP. The latter attempted to coordinate the various inputs and outputs and submitted the draft national economic plan in summary form to the CM. After approval, the plan was disaggregated down the chain of command. The central rationing of supplies was conducted by supply centers and was later taken over by ministries under the supervision of the SOP.

By 1952 the planning system was discredited. The planners complained about the unreliability of input coefficients which were not centrally controlled and about an overwhelming lack of knowledge of the real situation at the lower echelons. The ministries' draft plans were uncoordinated. The entire burden of balancing rested with the SOP, which was essentially preoccupied with mitigating only the most transparent disproportions. There was a manifest chaos in the supply situation.[4] The enterprises often circumvented delivery orders and worked with one another directly. Due to acute shortages such relations apparently aggravated disproportions. The continuous revisions of plans, allotment of supplies exceeding the allocated amounts, and so forth, that took place at every echelon, without mutually informing each other of changes, further disrupted the process. There were also serious complaints about the low caliber of the "worker-managers" who had been appointed to top executive positions in the central agencies and enterprises.[5]

According to 1952 regulations, the bulk of investments was to be financed by the enterprise's own funds. The aim was to induce better husbandry of resources. However, central organs redistributed funds and provided enterprises with the necessary means to pay for their investments. This system soon turned into a pure formality and was abandoned. Investment financing by state grants was reverted to in principle as well as in fact.[6]

The significant changes in plan elaboration, introduced in 1953, centered on the planning procedure. Henceforth the ministries were to draft plans, guided by a less detailed set of control figures, excluding limits on inputs, emitted by the SOP. However, the ministries were expected to submit coordinated production and supply plans, to be prepared in close contact between the supplier and user ministries. While the ministries were drafting their plans, the SOP was elaborating the national economic plan, proceeding from its initial control figures. After the ministries' plans were received, they were compared with the balances prepared by the SOP, amendments were made, and the whole was submitted for approval to the CM. After ratification by the government, the plan was disaggregated along the hierarchical structure until it reached the producing unit.

Whereas before 1953 enterprises participated in the plan construction process by submitting counterplans, they were now assigned the sole task of plan executants. The shift was probably due to the disarray contributed by the former method, as the plans usually involved higher inputs which disrupted the drafting of material balances. It follows both from the logic of the method of balances and from the lack of "realism" in some counterplans, that they contributed to serious disproportions. Therefore, counterplans were frequently discarded when they reached the superiors. The essence of the 1953 reform lay in the shift of emphasis to the enterprise's meeting and exceeding plan targets which were centrally set and coordinated. But it was not grasped that, apart from the "teleological" conception of the plan and undue strains, the disparities in the degree of overfulfillment and underfulfillment of the plans contributed to unbalancing the material balances.

Basically, long-term planning remained on the fringe of the reform. In fact, from 1948 the Czechoslovak economy did not develop according to a workable FYP; after their first year or two the FYP's were shelved. The targets of the First FYP were drastically escalated by 1951. In its last year (1953) the plan proved to be entirely out of touch with reality.[7] The disillusionment with long-term planning was obvious from the announcement that for the next two years (1954 and 1955) the economy would function without a long-term plan. Stress was laid on drawing up "pragmatic" annual plans.[8] On December 2, 1955, the Second FYP (1956-60) draft directives were set and submitted to the mid-June, 1956, Party Conference. However, it was not enacted into law. Toward the end of 1957, it was revised by raising the targets, by reshuffling investments, and by reducing the growth of real wages.[9] The plan was finally enacted into law on October 16, 1958, after undergoing further surgery by mid-1958. The several revisions were explained in the light of the 1956-57 upheavals in neighboring countries and of the necessity to renegotiate trade agreements.[10] Due to successful economic performance in 1959, the draft directives of the Third FYP (1961-65) were significantly boosted by the time they came up for approval in July, 1960, at the Third National Party Conference,[11] and, as we shall see, its fate was even gloomier than that of its predecessors.

The budget was drawn up on the basis of directives issued by the Ministry of Finance (MF) to the ministries and national committees. After the latter had submitted their requirements, they were supposed to be coordinated with the economic plan. Further restrictions on financial autonomy were imposed in 1953 by enforcing the quarterly limits for the drawing of funds from the budget. As long as the annual limit was observed, the quarterly ones had heretofore been treated as mere formalities.[12]

The reform shifted more responsibility to ministries. Coefficients were increasingly used for calculating and verifying requirements. There was less circumvention of the centralized supply system, but the planning procedure did not fare well. The ministerial plans remained uncoordinated. The attempt to foster consultation among ministries failed. The SPO once again carried the full burden of interbranch coordination. Inertia set in, as the buck was being passed from enterprise to chief administration, to ministry, and finally to the SPO or to other central organs. The allocation of supplies consumed the bulk of energy exerted in planning. The lists of funded goods (distributed by the SPO and approved by the CM) and centrally allotted goods (distributed by ministries) were virtually all-embracing.

By 1954 it was decided to revert to the "gestion" system for centrally allotted goods--a system that had functioned for a short time before. Briefly, it consisted of appointing a ministry as gestor for a given good produced primarily by its enterprises. But the ministry was to prepare the balances and assign the production and distribution orders for this product also to enterprises subordinated to other ministries. Concurrently, the distribution of some goods was decentralized and given over to chief administrations. By 1955 the supply system was somewhat streamlined by instituting marketing organizations to handle the requests of small-quantity users. Moreover, since 1953 there was a gradual aggregation of the groups of funded goods and centrally set targets. As a result, the number of centrally determined targets and funded goods had not lessened considerably, but the planners' tasks were eased, for they now handled a smaller number of categories.

Since 1949 idle resources in enterprises were siphoned off and redistributed. Since 1953, when enterprise's finances were tied in directly to the budget in the form of allocations and taxes, there appeared in some enterprises above-plan funds. There were also attempts to induce enterprises to generate such above-plan funds, mainly by directing a portion of above-plan funds to a collective consumption fund--of a meager incentive role. Those above-plan funds constituted merely a temporary (within a single accounting period) benefit. At the end of the year, the unspent "surplus" was confiscated. On the other hand, shortages would be replenished, affording no real incentive for economizing on decentralized funds. Another corollary was that enterprises attempted to convert funds as quickly as they could into real assets. Enterprises that did not receive sufficient allocations, or did not generate themselves sufficient funds to meet their planned expenditures, were either granted bank loans or failed to pay suppliers, and finally forced their superiors to grant them adequate subsidies. There were vast claims on the state budget, and the state increasingly reverted to siphoning off what it considered to be excessive funds at enterprises. Such action had a particularly discouraging effect on those enterprises that were financially better off.[13]

Until 1953 credits were virtually automatically granted. The reform envisaged that credits should be extended only when the bank had reasonable assurance of repayment on time and when it had decided on the purposefulness of the credit. The bank's control over enterprises was further reinforced in 1955 by copying the Soviet system of differentiating between well- and poorly operating enterprises for purposes of credit extension.[14]

Concurrently with the 1953 revisions in planning, a so-called New Course was initiated, paralleling the movement in other East European economies and in the U.S.S.R. During the years 1953-55, the general level of investment was reduced (investments were reduced by 16 per cent in 1953 and in 1954 and 1955 remained at the 1953 level), with increasing investment in consumer goods industries, reduced investment in producer goods industries, and increased investment in agriculture. Heavy industry was slated to provide more consumer durables. More building materials were to be allocated to housing construction.[15] The intent was to raise consumption standards not only in response to the generally more relaxed political situation and to ward off the possibility of riots, such as had occurred in Pilsen in 1953 prompted by the discontent aroused by the monetary reform, but also in order to improve productivity. According to the 1954 and 1955 plans, the share of personal consumption in national income was supposed to rise from 57 per cent in 1953 to 62 per cent in 1954 and to 67 per cent in 1955.[16] At the same time, a breathing spell was required to relax the tensions which had accumulated during the interval of accelerated industrialization. But by 1956 there were already signs of a reversal of policy, reverting once again to the stress on heavy industry.[17] As can be seen from Table 7, the 1950-53 trend of faster growth of producer goods was reversed in 1954 and 1955, when consumer goods output grew more rapidly. However, by 1956 growth of producer goods again outpaced that of consumer goods, indicating a resumption of the industrialization momentum along the lines of the traditional growth strategy.

At the time the New Course was initiated, complaints of inefficiency and mismanagement were rife. The serious bottlenecks created by the coal industry gave rise to denunciations of over-centralization and bureaucratization, of the inadequate supply situation, of drastic shortages of basic supplies, and of the general waste.[18] The poor quality of output was deprecated. Consumer goods were shoddy and many were defective.[19] At the Tenth Congress of the Communist Party of Czechoslovakia (CPC), Premier Viliam Siroky upbraided industry for increasing production costs, for low productivity, for poor quality of output, for squandering resources, etc. This was echoed by the delegates from the provinces. Siroky also complained about the high labor turnover, slack discipline, lack of initiative, pronounced negligence, and widespread apathy among industrial workers and managers.[20]

THE ANATOMY OF THE PLANNING SYSTEM

Economic planning was predominantly designed as an instrument for the central authorities--or the system's directors, to borrow Abram Bergson's felicitous term--to intervene directly in determining the course, pace and pattern, choice of techniques and methods, and means for mobilizing, mustering, and channeling resources for forced industrialization. Such radical and speedy restructuring of the economy necessitated a massive and rapid transfer of resources which could be accomplished more firmly and expediently through central direct control, rather than by primarily relying on market-type measures. Planning was mainly shaped by empiricism. It was void of theoretical foundation, of rules, and of meaningful and operational criteria for resource allocation. But as the planning system was developed to serve the Soviet regime's leaders' objective of superrapid industrialization, there is much to be said for the view that the planning problem was essentially one of keeping "the circular production-flow moving smoothly without interruption" and that, under such conditions, the principles of Pareto's optimum were hardly relevant.[21]

Centralization of economic decision-making was particularly well-suited for ensuring concentration of resources on chosen key targets, for preventing their dissipation in other uses, and for imposing the central planner's will on producers and consumers. Due to the speed, extent, and efficacy of the economy's restructuring, tensions built up on resources, aggravated by a lack of reserves in planning, thus rendering the system hypersensitive to bottlenecks. No economic mechanism of adjustment for eradicating bottlenecks was provided. The goals and method for constructing the central plan, as well as the selection of strategies and of the means for implementing it, were chosen by the regime's leaders. Current production decisions were highly centralized. Planning functions were often indistinguishable from those of operational management. Administrative measures, regulations, fiat, and rationing of resources were characteristic of the system, although their intensity and enforcement varied from period to period.

A set of exogenously predetermined key targets for intermediate and final products was the starting point in plan construction. But to start economic planning by target-setting is tantamount to wandering in the fog--as Ragnar Frisch has demonstrated.[22] It seems that the plan was essentially drafted by fixing the growth rates of various branches of industry and sectors of the economy and by working from the individual industrial branches upward toward the national economic plan.[23]

Given the politically determined priorities, the state of constraints, and no market for producer goods, the central planning agencies had to construct an internally consistent and feasible plan. For this purpose, the planners elaborated a network of, generally in natura, balances of products and their uses, with the aim of equating total output (and imports) of a product with the quantities that all users (and exports) required to fulfill their quotas. This method, being a primitive version of input-output, suffered from similar shortcomings. The method of balances was also handicapped by its use of noncumulative input coefficients and by the unsophisticated methods for eliminating shortages. Basically, there was no economic verification of production.

Plan construction thus set out from given targets, such as production of coal, steel, electric power, cement, etc. These were the fixed points de repaire from which, by the method of balances and with coefficients of interdependence, a whole spectrum of quantitative relations was developed. For example, the output of steel and rolled metals conditioned the output of machines and equipment. The output of cement served to determine the resources for investments. Although the process involved already at its early stages a much wider range of indexes, nevertheless the relationships of coal-coke-electric power-iron-steel-rolled metals-machines-construction-investment was largely the pivot of the entire plan. In fact, this gave rise to a so-called planning spiral which meant that if the original target for steel was increased, it was possible by successive balancing to reach a higher volume of planned investment, which signified that investment in foundries would increase, raising steel output, and enabling a further upward movement along the spiral. Inversely, if it was found that the raw materials would not materialize as expected, a downward spiral had to be initiated.

Thus, it was possible for extended periods to continue concentrating on the production of means of production. The relatively large share of investment resources was planned as a result of the high targets set for the output of raw materials, but these investments were again enlisted for achieving the expected growth of raw materials. In spite of the high level of investment, demands for it invariably exceeded the resources due to priority allocation to the branches on which the entire process depended.[24]

Value categories were subordinated to physical planning and were vested essentially with only a recording and control function. Direct assignments of mandatory tasks to enterprises were regarded as the basic instrument for ensuring plan fulfillment. However, the implementation of such a system was constrained by the impossibility of determining the activity of the enterprise to the minutest task. A degree of aggregation was mandatory. No system of detailed indexes was capable of entirely eliminating independent action and direct inter-enterprise negotiations. It is particularly within this sphere that decisions were colored by the interests of enterprises. It may be noted in this connection that the intermediary units between the central authorities and the enterprises were not simple transmission belts, for they aggregated the reported data flowing upward and disaggregated the orders issued at the top, distorting both in the process.

Plan indexes performed a dual function: They served to assign tasks to enterprises and as such became standards for evaluating the enterprises' performance. The system was built on the assumption that the central planner would be capable of ascertaining and of evaluating the heterogeneous conditions in individual enterprises and of taking them into account when setting the entire spectrum of plan indexes. Since accounting for the varied conditions was a mammoth task, the planners were guided by the latest performance reports of particular units. For instance, in case of cost-reduction and profit-increase targets, two essential operations were performed: 1) to project the level during the planning year (essentially amounting to an estimate at the beginning of the fourth quarter of what the total results for the entire year would be) and 2) to project the data obtained above on to the planned year by applying a coefficient of reduction for costs or a coefficient of increase for profit.

Apart from the information gap, due, inter alia, to the remoteness of the central authorities from the executants, there was the serious inability of the differentiated approach to give cognizance to various conditions under which enterprises labored. Unless they were capable of resisting the pressures, enterprises with relatively better equipment and superior management were assigned higher targets and those with more backward equipment and poorer management were assigned lower targets. If the former underfulfilled their taut plans by 1 per cent, they were condemned and punished, whereas if the latter overfulfilled their slack plans by 1 per cent, they were praised and rewarded. By sanctioning varied conditions, the authorities obscured the reasons for these discrepancies, and steps were usually not taken to eradicate them. Hence, backwardness and inefficiency were just as viable as progress and efficiency.[25]

The whole system was oriented toward the enterprise's fulfillment of plan assignments. Production was essentially undertaken to fulfill the plan and not to satisfy the user's (industrial or consumer) needs.[26] When shortages prevailed, the user was at the mercy of the producer and was eager to grab whatever he could get, even if the goods did not meet his present needs. These goods could be used at times as substitutes--even if ineffectively; they could be reprocessed; they could be stored for future use; or they could be swapped for other goods. As a rule, it was not prudent to aggravate the supplier by exacting fines for the low quality of goods, for late deliveries, etc. The supplier could anyway defend himself by shifting the blame on his own suppliers. Once the plan specified the product, quantities, and contractual parties, the supplier was under legal obligation to produce the goods and the consignee to accept them, regardless of the ability of the first to produce and of the need of the second to use these goods.[27]

Because of the frequent changes of plan assignments and because input requirements had to be ordered several months in advance, the supplies received were often unsuitable for the altered production and those required were unavailable. The vertical lines of subordination frequently made for poor cooperation among enterprises subjected to different ministries.

Since enterprises were evaluated on the basis of plan fulfillment and since their employees' earnings depended on this evaluation, the enterprises were interested in obtaining low plan assignments, to ensure their fulfillment in the easiest possible manner. Since management depended on the decisions made at the center, the information it supplied was colored so as to obtain a most favorable decision. The common strategy, then, was to conceal reserves and request more resources than required. Since the rule of the game was for the producer to offer less output while asking for more inputs, the relationship between availabilities and requirements was increasingly strained. The central planner retaliated by arbitrarily increasing output quotas and by reducing input allocations, thus intensifying the pressures in the economy. The units which were less able to resist pressures got higher assignments with less inputs. The pressures built up from above and below tended to distort the data flowing up so that they would not properly reflect actual potential and requirements, and so that commands would be based less and less on data received. Consequently, the degree of plan fulfillment varied unevenly, contributing to breakdowns in interenterprise flows and upsetting the attempted internal consistency of the plan. A balance was often sought by reducing reserves and by allocating output from anticipated plan overfulfillment or from capacities slated for start-up. Since such expectations were often overoptimistic, some buyers did not receive their allocated supplies. Reserves were rapidly dwindling and pressures mounted in view of the recurrent shortages.

Knowing that superiors would cut back on their requirements, the enterprises provided sufficient padding to take care of such action and to leave them with a comfortable safety margin. The propensity of enterprises to create their own reserves was dictated by the chronic failures of the supply system to provide allocated materials in the required quantities and varieties and according to delivery schedules. Since the central planner had dispensed with market relations, the interenterprise direct exchange took on one of the most primitive forms, barter, to mitigate supply failures. Although barter was illegal, daily operations relied heavily on it. A wider variety of hoarded inventories allowed greater barter possibilities.[28] In view of the ineffective and ill-functioning supply system, the producers aimed at self-sufficiency by controlling sources of supply within a particular organizational unit or by manufacturing supplies themselves, often at exorbitant costs.

The enterprise was governed by an amalgam of often contradictory indexes.[29] Thus, there was a tendency for a single index to gain ascendency over the others, because its fulfillment was most prized by the authorities, and because it carried the bulk of rewards. Since the system was oriented toward augmenting industrial production, the volume of gross output (or that of some crucial products) emerged as the key index. Planning by material balances and the relative ease with which gross output could be controlled reinforced its importance. When evaluating performance, the first stress was on meeting the output quotas; failure to fulfill other indexes was tolerated. By the same token, the same criterion was used for evaluating performance for socialist competition, awards of red flags, press publicity, and other distinctions and praises. Above all, fulfillment of the gross output target was the criterion for awarding premiums.[30] The "cult" of gross output was reinforced by usually linking the size of the wage fund to the value of gross output or to labor productivity--computed as gross output divided by the number of productive employees.[31]

Although the central planner expanded the output composition assignments, the enterprises concentrated their efforts on fulfilling the output quota in so-called plan-satisfying assortments. The touchstone of a product's plan-satisfying ability was how material- (versus labor-) intensive it was. The most plan-satisfying product was that which maximized the yardstick by which it was measured (value, weight, length, etc.), with the least processing at the given enterprise.[32] Consequently, the assortment produced was impoverished; well-established, rather than new, product lines were produced, because the new production had to be mastered, and it might be less plan-satisfying.[33] This did not deter the producers from seeking to slightly differentiate their goods from those listed in the price lists, in order to boost their prices by manipulating costs. Since prices of goods not listed in the price lists were calculated at individual costs, the authorities _nolens volens_ circumscribed their own control over the enterprises' activity.

Growth of production was often achieved at the expense of squandering of materials, of overtime, of waste of transport facilities, of neglect of maintenance and safety, etc. With the stress on quantity, quality suffered most. There were common attempts at fraudulent reporting of achievements by redundant subcontracting, by manipulations of the stage of construction projects, by direct falsification of documents, etc. The control organs failed to detect many manipulations, for they were mainly concerned with verifying the degree of plan fulfillment, without looking into the matter of how it was achieved.[34]

Annual national economic plans were of major operational significance, but since they were often changed during the year, they suffered from a lack of coordination. In fact, ad hoc, and largely uncoordinated, interventions undermined the annual plans. Enterprises were guided and evaluated chiefly by annual (and quarterly) plans and the system of incentives was linked to their fulfillment. As a result of the proverbial limited "planning horizons," managers were preoccupied with current activity and paid little heed to technical advance. Disturbances of the status quo hampered current production activity, endangering fulfillment of key plan targets. At the most, enterprises were willing to introduce only minor technological changes. The bulk of investment was directed to expansion of capacity, while existing enterprises labored under steadily deteriorating technical conditions. With the exception of some success with a few, apparently chosen at random, directive tasks of technical development, the appeals of authorities to introduce technical progress "became only general and rather ineffectual proclamations."[35]

Technical progress also suffered at the hands of the capital goods producers. Admittedly, if enterprise A produced with large labor savings obsolete equipment for enterprises B, C, and D, enterprise A attained magnificent indexes and high premiums, but enterprises B, C, and D suffered; their plan fulfillment "limped on both legs." The main cause was attributed to the planning and incentive system, which, for a majority of enterprises, made it disadvantageous to develop and to manufacture new products.[36] Deficiencies and inconsistencies of commands, of performance criteria, of value parameters, and of methods of calculation, enabled managers to map their course of action and to exercise discretion and initiative to a much larger extent than it appears at first glance.

It is claimed that the manipulation of plan directives did not necessarily lead either to improved performance or to better satisfaction of consumers' needs. Ota Sik even went as far as to argue that, due to the nature of price formation and to the built-in rigidity of price changes, in all cases "prices tended to push enterprises in the direction of production that differed increasingly from market demand."[37] This is probably not too much of an exaggeration of what happened, but, even so, it is not quite defensible as a general rule. However, perhaps due to the extent of the illegal or "semilegal" transactions, which seem to have been widespread, the impact of some violations might not have been as adverse as it is usually professed to have been in Eastern Europe. But, of course, more evidence would be required for a meaningful generalization. A particular handicap was the absence of an economic mechanism to ensure that changes in consumers' demand would invariably elicit changes in the flow of output in the required quantity and composition, given the centrally predetermined allocations to consumption.

In the traditional system prices essentially did not perform an active role in plan construction. Prices of producer goods, set on average costs (<u>sebestoimost</u>) plus a slight profit markup, were primarily used for summarizing and aggregating heterogeneous output. Similarly, they played--at least by design--a subordinate role in plan execution. They were primarily used for expressing in summary form the enterprises' mandatory assignments and their fulfillment and to keep records of transactions. To perform those functions, the planner strove for the greatest possible price stability, irrespective of changes that were taking place in production and requirements.[38] Such a price system was unsuitable as a tool for guiding enterprises' activity. Although prices were not constructed with the former purpose in mind, their use for measuring output rendered management responsive to them. Producers' prices did not essentially perform an allocative function. Attempts were made to eradicate shortages by increasing the flow of output, but not by changing prices. Those attempts often failed.[39]

Producers' prices were readjusted en masse in five-year intervals. Consumers' prices were revised in about one-year intervals (with the tendency to lower prices, rather than to raise wages, often aggravating disequilibria), but for a number of goods they remained unchanged for longer periods. From 1953 to 1960 attempts to reflect demand and supply relations were only made for consumer goods which could not be sold. The separation of consumers' from producers' prices was considered as a fundamental principle of the price system. This principle enabled the central planner to influence either consumers or producers separately. This separation resulted in a dual price system, with different principles of price formation for producer and consumer goods and with greatly varied profitability rates on individual products.[40] Barring some cases, the differentiation was not intentional. It is doubtful whether the price relations that actually prevailed resulted from a conscious design.[41] Turnover tax was the barrier separating consumers' from producers' prices. By altering the rate or fixed amount of the tax, the changes in one type of price were not transmitted to the other. Therefore, production was insensitive to market impulses.[42]

Central price setting for the bulk of goods required the freezing of those prices for an extended period of time. The larger the number of prices to be determined centrally, the greater was the possibility that individual enterprises which supplied cost data would influence price setting, for the verification of those price proposals became exceedingly cumbersome. Prices also became outdated because each price revision took several years to prepare during which important shifts took place in the conditions and production program, so that at the outset the new price was obsolete.[43]

Producers were entirely isolated from price movements on the world market and were generally ignorant of or insensitive to the relationships of domestic to world prices and to the profitability of their particular exportables. They were reimbursed for exported output at domestic wholesale prices, set independently of foreign prices. Hence, some goods might have been produced inefficiently, yet the producer would still make a profit on them. The corollary was that the producer might turn out a better article for which the foreign trade organization would get a higher price (with a higher net effect for the economy), but if a deficit domestic price prevailed, or if the relative ratio of prices was unfavorable, the producer would be discouraged from such production. Not even foreign trade organizations were interested in the effectiveness of foreign trade, for the profit or loss on transactions was absorbed by the state budget.[44] Not only was the domestic pattern and cost of production not sensitive to the pressures of the world market, but, apparently, "foreign trade acted as a barrier, preserving the backwardness of many domestic producers and the rigidity of the domestic structure of production."[45]

Finance was reduced to the mere recording of operations in value terms and to the mechanical financing of these processes.[46] In fact, the financial plan was a mere recalculation of the production plan in value terms. The enterprise functioned on khozraschet as a self-supporting unit.[47] In principle, its current expenditures were to be covered by its receipts, with the excess kept at a minimum level in order to compel the enterprise to exercise parsimony and to prevent it from engaging in uncharted activity. The central planner not only decided what portion of the profit would be siphoned off by the budget and what portion would be retained by the enterprise, but also ruled on the apportionment of the enterprise's share among its various funds, thus cramping financial maneuverability even further. Nonetheless, irrespective of the stringent controls, the enterprise's field of maneuverability was not inconsequential and the planner was not particularly successful in completely restricting it.

One of the greatest problems encountered was that of idle financial resources, accumulated by enterprises and the population, exerting pressures on resources. Whereas control over idle resources of the population was generally particularly difficult, control over idle resources in enterprises was exercised by confiscating or blocking funds.[48]

As a rule, investments were directly assigned and distributed by the state plan and essentially financed out of state funds. It was rather a technical question of financing to determine the ratio of profit, depreciation, and the state budget's grant to which the investor was entitled. Actually, the share of the investment outlay to be financed by the profit of the enterprise and depreciation simply reduced the amount of the regular contribution of the enterprise to the budget. Since investments were virtually cost-free, the investor was unconcerned about the profitability of the investment, provided it was advantageous to him.[49] Although the cost of investment affected the producer's costs through depreciation charges, these did not constitute a potent constraint,[50] not only because the charges were insignificant, but also because by augmenting costs they inflated prices and the profit component calculated on costs.

Although, as we have seen, the manager was reluctant to jeopardize current plan fulfillment by installations of new machines and other improvements, he was eager to secure the "free" capital goods. These were often kept in storage and awaited installation for extended periods. Costs of investments were frequently understated by enterprises and their superiors in order to get the investments into the central plan. This was one of the many reasons for the protracted construction periods and the large volume of unfinished investments. Another cause was the performance criterion for the construction industry which drove builders to start as many projects as they could, since the earlier stages of construction were more material-intensive.

The logic of the system led to intensified centralization, with the proliferation of plan indexes and a trend to replace the value indexes by physical ones. But such a tendency was limited by the processing capacity of the central apparatus. It is true that with the advent of the computer the physical burden of this task was eased. However, it is argued, with the traditional planning system, a wider use of computers could not solve the problem effectively, for the major flaw lies in the planning and information process. One of the key problems would still be the vital interest of the enterprises and of other information transmitters in submitting data distorted to fit their own interest and the impossibility of enforcing execution of orders that are directly in conflict with the enterprises' interests. Increasing centralization calls for an increasing network of more detailed norms to regulate the activity of enterprises. Since the norms depend on information supplied by enterprises and since the possibility of verifying enterprises' data becomes more cumbersome as their number increases, the norms become slacker.[51] With the growing complexity of the economy, methods adopted for rapid restructuring of the economy proved inadequate for coordinating the specialized branches of industry and for coping with the increasing bottlenecks in complementary branches of industry. With the advancement of Soviet-style industrialization, the built-in inefficiencies of the economy became more acute and less tolerable.

By 1956-57 the mounting disenchantement with the planning system was publicly vented. Although, during that period, Czechoslovakia did not experience a cultural thaw of the scope of Poland's or Hungary's, the Party did not oppose the call for greater decentralization to improve the system. In fact, at its mid-June, 1956, conference, bureaucratization of the economy was denounced and there was more than a hit at economic decentralization.[52]

> Experience has shown that problems directly affecting the operation of... particular enterprises can best be solved by the plant managers... Therefore, we intend to boost the authority and responsibility of factory managers concerning planning, organization, wages, marketing, procurement, and finance and credit... Henceforth the factory manager will be authorized to approve the enterprise's plan, to alter it, if need be, to change the organization structure of the enterprise...[53]

It was decided to curtail the number of binding plan targets by 20 per cent, to reduce the number of centrally distributed goods, to establish reserves in planning, and to widen the scope of decision-making at the lower levels. A call was also made for reforming other areas of economic life, to arrive at a set of mutually consistent measures for ameliorating the functioning of the economy.[54] Although not entirely shelved, these resolutions suffered some setback in the turmoil of the internal economic situation and the unrest of neighboring Poland and Hungary.[55]

Whereas the years 1954 and 1955 were generally marked by a certain relaxation of the investment drive, as previously mentioned, the plan for 1956 specified a very drastic upsurge of investment (21 per cent). But the divergence between planned targets and performance was wide, including failures to activate key projects scheduled for 1956 completion and failures to meet planned targets for some crucial equipment (steam boilers, transformers, cranes, pumps, machine tools) and for heavy machine-building deliveries to foreign customers. The cost reduction and labor productivity indexes were not met. Wage payments exceeded the plan and signs of economic strain were evident. Production was greatly handicapped by acute shortages of fuels, power, and raw materials.[56] The events of the Polish October and the Hungarian uprising left, of course, an indelible mark. Economic policy had to be generally reoriented. Among some grave repercussions was altered trade with those same countries, e.g., the sharp curtailment of coal deliveries from Poland.

In this climate both the Second FYP, which was yet inoperative in 1956, and the plan for 1957 were revised to reflect the changes and to meet the emergencies. Investments for 1957 had to be curtailed.

> Industrial output is to be increased by better utilization of productive capacities... To meet the national economy's requirements, despite the reduced volume of investment,... there must be a maximum of economy and a full utilization of investment sources.[57]

Against this background, reforms were approved and introduced about mid-1958. It was hoped that through improved production efficiency and through raised productivity a new impetus would be given to the growth momentum.

THE 1958-59 REFORM AND ITS AFTERMATH

Early in 1957 the reform proposals were discussed at a Central Committee (CC) meeting, approved at another meeting on February 25, 1958, and publicized as the "Principles for Raising Economic Effectiveness in the Management of Industry and Construction." One of the reform's objectives was to eliminate the inertia that had set in as a result of overcentralization. But the proposed devolution of decision-making was not supposed to weaken, but rather to strengthen, the plan as a central blueprint of the economy's course. The central planner was to cease his preoccupation with minute details, with countless resolutions of conflicts, and with _ad hoc_ operational interventions, in order to devote more attention to long-term planning, which was being stressed. At the same time, the applicability of the market mechanism to the functioning of the socialist economy (advocated in neighboring Poland) was denounced, stressing the adverse effects of the market's spontaneity and the incompatibility of the plan and the market.[58]

The backbone of the reform was a broadening of decision-making at the lower echelons of the hierarchical ladder, but it stopped just short of the enterprise. A new organization was created to replace the central agencies which had functioned as a buffer between the enterprise and the ministry. These "economic production units" (EPU's) consisted of a single leading enterprise, sometimes embracing an entire branch of industry, or a group of smaller enterprises (association) producing a given assortment of goods or services. The EPU's worked on _khozraschet_ and were directly subordinated to ministries and vested with the bulk of operative management functions, such as the elaboration of production plans, deciding on technical advancement and expansion, marketing, procurement, and formation of decentralized financial resources. The ministries were supposed to refrain from interfering in daily activity and to be concerned mainly with perspective planning and with the analysis of processes. In particular, the ministries were to organize the drafting of annual plans, to prepare the norms for EPU's, to evaluate the long-term sharing in profits and depreciation, to set prices, to determine long-term development, to concentrate on redistributing financial resources, to control wage policy, and to guide over-all economic activity.[59]

Through consolidation the number of enterprises was considerably reduced. The previous 1,417 enterprises were replaced by 383 EPU's, of which 67 were associations; altogether there were 929 enterprises producing about 93 per cent of industrial output.[60] In some cases, because of regional or product mix problems, a single EPU could not be set up; enterprises were then nominated as gestors and entrusted with planning and balancing of some products, marketing, importing, and distributing some goods, etc.

The reorganization of industry released a number of employees in the central agencies. Toward the end of 1956 an attempt had been made to reduce the administrative apparatus. For example, it was reported that administrative personnel would be reduced by 22.6 per cent in the chemical industry, by 15 per cent in mining and metallurgy, and by 8.6 per cent in railroad transportation and by 16 per cent in the Ministry of Transportation.[61] However, powerful obstacles were encountered in implementing the reductions. It was found that personnel released from the higher echelons inflated the administrative ranks at the lower levels. In the timber industry the regulations were circumvented by relisting office employees as manual workers, while keeping them in their old positions. Altogether, cutting back on the sprawling bureaucratic apparatus was not an easy task. In preparation for the reform, a very harsh campaign was launched at the end of 1957 against the flowering of the bureaucratic apparatus, denouncing those who might oppose the new measures.[62] The 1958 measures were apparently successful, for it was reported that the number of employees at the Ministry of Metallurgy and Mining decreased from 1,042 to 490, in the Ministry of Heavy Machine-Building from 1,560 to 656, and in the Ministry of Construction from over 1,000 to 421.[63] Obviously, these data should be viewed with some circumspection, for, as before, the released employees might have swollen the ranks of those employed at the EPU and enterprise levels.

An advisory "technical-economic council," under the chairmanship of the EPU's director and comprising plant managerial representatives, officials of Party cells and trade unions, and representatives from research institutes and ministries, would be set up at each EPU to act in an advisory capacity on such problems as long-range development, investment planning, norm-setting, etc.[64]

By mid-1958, in anticipation of expanded managerial prerogatives at the lower levels, the authority of the Party cell at the enterprise was strengthened. Henceforth, in addition to the Party cell's right to control the activities of management, it was authorized to veto any decision it considered unjust or "socially harmful."[65] However, since the managers of the enterprises or of the EPU's were usually members of the Party cell, since the other members of the cell depended on management for their salary classification, promotion, and allotment of premiums, and since the "socially harmful" decisions might be (and usually would be) "locally beneficial," little could be expected from the local Party cell by way of a countervailing force to the increased managerial powers.

The changes in planning were to embrace the drafting of a ten- to fifteen-year "perspective" plan, of which the FYP's for various branches of industry would be the appropriate excerpts. Great stress was laid on plan stability. The drafting of annual plans, to comply with the directives of the central plan, would be entrusted to enterprises. Enterprises would share in profits and depreciation to be used for investments and working capital and greater stress would be laid on the incentive function of premiums. The underlying assumption of the reform was the preservation of the traditional function of the plan, with economic levers playing a rather subordinate role and derived from the centrally constructed and imposed plan.[66]

By 1959 innovations were being introduced in the planning system. Two novelties were the "personal incentive normatives" (p.i.n.) and "enterprise incentive normatives" (e.i.n.).

The construction of p.i.n. for raising average wages promoted the increase of targets by the EPU or the enterprise. If the latter raised their labor productivity targets, they were entitled to p.i.n. in excess of the average set for them. The starting point for setting p.i.n. for 1959-60 was the actual performance in 1958. The p.i.n. for calculating the premium fund was to be, in most cases, a stable percentage of profit or its increment. In some cases the p.i.n. was related to cost reduction or to the wage fund. However, the source of the premium fund was not profit, but wages, upon profit plan fulfillment. Moreover, its importance should not be overestimated, for premiums gravitated to around 10 per cent of basic wages.[67]

The e.i.n. was constructed so that the ministry could increase or decrease the share of an enterprise in the profits realized or in the increment of profits if the enterprise augmented its targets, or refused to accept them on the grounds that they were too taut. Some side conditions, such as the rates of cost reduction and of growth of output, were imposed. To further counteract conservative planning, from 1961 the enterprise was no longer bound to remit the budget's share in planned profits in case of profit plan underfulfillment. The shares were then scaled down proportionately to the profit achieved. The enterprise also shared in depreciation allowances which, in 1959-60, made up the bulk of decentralized resources, even though it was expected that in the future both profit and depreciation would share evenly in these resources. The share in profit was about equally divided between increase of working capital and financing investments, whereas most of the share in depreciation allowances was intended for financing investment. In total, about 75 per cent of decentralized resources had to be allocated to investments.[68] It should be noted that legally these funds did not have to be spent within the year and could be expended at any time in the FYP, without being subject to confiscation.

The following general rules were established for setting the e.i.n.: 1) the normatives were to be differentiated according to conditions in various branches and enterprises; 2) maximum stability of normatives was to be sought; 3) the share of profit was at least to amount to 20 per cent of the increment of profits; 4) the normatives were to be specified in detail for all the years of the FYP; 5) the normatives were to determine the volume of decentralized investments; and 6) the share in profits for financing investments was to increase; only in exceptional cases would all investments of an enterprise be covered by the share in depreciation.[69]

Centralized investments were restricted to the major projects so that in the early 1960's decentralized investments were about 60 per cent of all state investments. In 1958 enterprises were entrusted with large financial resources for decentralized investments, amounting to about 60 billion kcs.[70] Enterprises received directives specifying the centralized investments. On the basis of normatives prescribing the shares in profits and depreciation, they planned the decentralized investments. Before the final plan was approved, the investors were to enter into contracts with suppliers for both centralized and decentralized investments.

The FYP's investment program was to serve for elaborating the annual one which did not have to be approved by central authorities. Each enterprise notified its ministry of the annual total of those investments. Although enterprises were allowed a wide latitude in contacting suppliers and builders for their decentralized projects, of course, with the exception of funded goods, centralized projects were supposed to have precedence in cases of shortages. The authorities were able to influence the volume of decentralized investments through the centrally determined enterprise participation in depreciation allowances. The share in profit was not as easily ascertainable, but its contribution in financing decentralized investments was minimal.

In conjunction with the reform, the work norms were tightened up slowly from 1959 to mid-1960. It was reported that where the norms had been raised, the average overfulfillment dropped from 73 to 11 per cent. Concurrently there was a tendency toward replacing piece-work wages by time wages plus premiums.[71]

The planning process again reverted to enterprises. On the basis of indicators received from the EPU, the enterprise prepared its FYP and annual plan which then underwent the correction and aggregation process through the chain of command until it was finally submitted by the SPC--the reorganized and renamed State Planning Commission--to the CM for approval.[72] The process was to benefit from closer ties between the superiors and their wards and between suppliers and industrial users.

In view of the trend to widen management's horizons by means of the long-term normatives, the FYP was to become the basic guide of economic activity. Annual plans were not supposed to change the development trend established in the FYP. The growth of output index was established in the latter.[73] Directive plan indexes for output were reduced by about 20 per cent, for construction by about 50 per cent, and for labor by about 75 per cent. Cost reduction targets were eliminated from the annual plans. No indexes were to be received for quarterly plans. The indexes for FYP's and annual plans are illustrated in Charts 2 and 3.[74]

A new general measure of output was introduced: the value of output sold according to its main end uses classified as investment, private consumption, and exports. Gross value was to remain as a supplementary indicator. Only the FYP would specify physical targets; although annual directives would still specify quantities and deliveries to principal users, their number would be reduced. The FYP would include annual limits for funded goods, principally to satisfy the producers' requirements for fulfilling physical output targets.

During the drafting of the initial FYP directives, the SPC consulted with the ministries-

Chart 2

INDEXES SPECIFIED BY THE GOVERNMENT FOR THE FYP AND THE ANNUAL PLANS, JANUARY 1, 1959 (Abridged)

	Annual Plan	FYP
Industrial production and sales		
Rate of growth of output		X
Value of marketable output	X	
Value of goods for inventory	X	X
Value of goods for export	X	X
Value of machinery and equipment for investments	X	X
Deliveries of complete plant equipment for centralized construction & export	X	X
Deliveries of cooperative producers	X	X
Technical-economic coefficients		X
Production targets for specific goods in physical units		X
Material-technical supply		
Limits on key material inputs		X
Balance and distribution of limits to suppliers	X	X
Funds of key materials	X	
Labor and wages		
Limit of the number of employees in the last year of the FYP		X
Growth of labor productivity to wages		X
P.i.n.		X
Directives on manpower distribution		X
Growth of labor productivity in industry, construction, and transportation	X	X
Total annual wage fund	X	
Number of employees (for transition period only)	X	
Interregional distribution of manpower	X	
Construction		
Volume of completed construction work		X
Construction work carried out according to contractors' contracts	X	

Chart 2, (continued)

	Annual Plan	FYP
of which: total construction work carried out for centralized investments, according to ministries	X	
Central investment capacities commissioned in particular years	X	X
Construction started (completion dates, costs per unit of output, or other indicator of effectiveness)	X	X
Purchase of equipment not included in the construction budget		X
Volume and structure of construction	X	
Volume of decentralized investments in central organs where material interest norms do not apply		X
Housing construction	X	X
<u>Technical development</u>		
Tasks of development, introduction of new products, and adoption of new technology		X
<u>Financial plan</u>		
E.i.n.		X
Cost reduction		X
Transfer of profits to the budget	X	
Specific forms of transfer of profit to the budget	X	
Indicator of total profits (of the central organs where the p.i.n. and e.i.n. will not apply)		X

Source: Miroslav Rosicky, <u>CEP</u>, No. 2, 1962, pp. 69-70.

Chart 3

INDEXES PROVIDED BY THE MINISTRY FOR EPU's
IN THE FYP AND IN THE ANNUAL PLANS, JANUARY 1, 1959
(According to data of the Ministry of
General Engineering)

	Annual Plan	FYP
Output and sales		
Rate of growth of output in the last year of the FYP as compared with the previous FYP		X
Value of output of finished goods	X	
Output in physical units (broken down annually)	X	X
Value of gross output	X	
Value of marketable output	X	
Value of consumer goods	X	X
Value of goods for export	X	X
Value of goods for construction	X	X
Centralized capital construction		
Commissioned capacities	X	X
Machinery and equipment not included in the construction budget		X
Volume and structure of centralized investments	X	
Annual total value of completed projects	X	
Completion dates of specific projects	X	
Total construction work started annually	X	
Volume of centralized investments, of which: construction projects started specifically during the FYP		X
Labor and wages		
Limit of number of employees in 1965		X
Total number of employees	X	
Growth of labor productivity to average wages		X
P.i.n.		X
Total wage fund	X	

Chart 3, (continued)

	Annual Plan	FYP
Plan of material-technical supply		
Annual limits of funded material inputs	X	X
Limits of imports	X	X
Financial plan		
Share of depreciation		X
Share of the increment of profit		X
Transfer of profits	X	
Turnover tax	X	
Percentage cost reduction in the last year of the FYP compared to the preceding FYP		X

Source: Miroslav Rosicky, CEP, No. 2, 1962, p. 71.

gestors on the balances of funded goods. Thereafter, the ministries-users transacted with the ministries-gestors so as to arrive at a more concrete elaboration of the supply plan. The ministries-users then issued the "informative limits" to the EPU's which were expected to draft their supply plans by consulting their suppliers. Those plans traveled back to the ministries-users and more concrete agreements were made with ministries-gestors. When the FYP was approved by the government, definite annual limits of funded goods were transmitted to the ministries-users. In the annual plans, these limits could either correspond to the ones named in the FYP for the particular year, or they could be amended to fit a changing situation or new desiderata. In any case, the ministry did not have to distribute its entire limits among its EPU's, but could withhold reserves to meet unexpected perturbations during plan fulfillment. The procedure was similar for the allocation of centralized goods, although in that case the negotiating process was to be restricted to users and gestors without directly involving the SPC. It was reported that, at the beginning, decentralization of the supply system was rather far-reaching. For example, the Ministry of Heavy Machine-Building was planning the sale of only 6.3 per cent of its output.[75] The reduction in the number of centrally set output quotas and in the number of funded goods is indicated in Table 41. It should be noted that the

Table 41

CENTRALLY PLANNED OUTPUT, 1953-59

Years	Centrally set output quotas	Funded goods
1953	2,251	974
1957	858	380
1958	765	312
1959	228	228

Source: Miroslav Rosicky, CEP, No. 2, 1962, p. 58

drastic reduction in targets during 1953-59 was not solely due to decentralization, but was accompanied by a process of aggregation throughout the period.

EPU's and enterprises were appointed gestors for the goods that could be procured in a decentralized manner. The annual deliveries of these goods were based on long-range contracts entered into when drafting the FYP.

In preparation for the reform, wholesale prices were revised as of January 1, 1958. As heretofore, they were based on the principles of "stability and uniformity." The starting point for price formation was the planned average production cost (based on 1955-56 costs), plus a minimal profit markup. Prices of raw materials and semifabricates were raised and brought closer to costs. Subsidies were thus reduced, but not eradicated. It was advocated that prices would be lowered periodically to counteract excessive liquidity and to reinforce the budget constraint. There was recognition that prices should be used to influence the buyer and the producer. More emphasis was placed on price relations of substitutes. For example, an attempt was made to promote the use of aluminum and to restrict that of other nonferrous metals. Turnover tax was levied on those prices whose profit rate exceeded the required minimum, primarily because of the desirable price relations for substitutes or because of variations of prices for improved quality. In such a way the "excessive" profitability of nonferrous metals and high-grade steel was siphoned off. Due to great divergencies in the cost of coal extraction and, of course, to fallacious costing, settlement prices had to be set for coal.[76] The setting of prices for new products was to depart from the principle of adding a 3 per cent markup on costs. Such prices were to be set with an eye to the prices of existing similar products, to the future cost of production, and to making the price attractive for the buyer.[77] But, in practice, when prices were set for new products, the existing product chosen for comparability was not selected on the basis of its technological or other similarities, but because it was plan-satisfying.[78]

Concurrently, as of January, 1959, bank interest rates were revised. The interest rates on enterprises' current accounts were raised from 1.5 to 1.8 per cent and a somewhat higher interest rate (2.7 per cent) was offered on investment accounts to interest enterprises in accumulating funds on these accounts.[79] But, one may well wonder how effective such an interest rate might be in view of the prevailing apprehension that unspent investment funds might be confiscated, notwithstanding the previously mentioned regulation that they could be spent at any time within the FYP. Interest rates for investment credits were differentiated between 3.6 to 7.2 per cent. Lower interest rates were established for investments with "higher effectiveness" and those requiring a larger share of machinery and equipment. Instead of a 3.6 per cent interest rate on working capital credits, the new rates varied from 1.8 to 5.4 per cent. Lower rates were to enable enterprises to overfulfill their plans and the higher ones to curtail use of credit for "incorrect" activity.[80] Obviously, the differentiation in interest rates was to strengthen the influence of the bank over the enterprise's activity as an additional controlling organ.

The principal advantages of the reformed system, as it functioned from 1959 to 1961, were reported to have been its indictment of administrative methods; contraction of the purely quantitative character of the plan; restriction of the use of the gross output index; insistence on incentives for guiding activity; greater emphasis on commodity-money relationships; a widening of the autonomy of the lower echelons; an awakening of the enterprise's interest in profitability; and a stress on long-term planning. But its main shortcoming was that it consisted of a set of half-measures. Detailed central directives were, de facto, not eliminated. Insufficient weight was attached to the possible frictions between qualitative and quantitative plan indexes and commercial direct ties between producers and users. The lack of decentralized flexible price formation hampered market relations. In addition, profit was not accepted as the sole performance criterion, making it impossible to evaluate activity objectively.[81]

During the first two years of the reformed system the recorded performance improved significantly. It should be recalled that at that time a number of investments, started in the 1950's in order to widen the raw materials base, had come to fruition. The supply situation improved and tensions were somewhat relaxed. At the same time, a new wave of investments was initiated. Much credit for the improved economic situation was given in 1961 to the reformed system.[82]

The reformed system suffered much from what was left undiscarded. The relatively broad decentralization measures were still bound up in a maze of existing directives. Not only did enterprises often receive a much more detailed set of directives, but superiors frequently chose to regard all sorts of informational indexes as binding directives whose fulfillment conditioned premium distribution and expenditures from decentralized funds.

During the first two years of its functioning the new system was reported to have stimulated a certain amount of response in managers and provoked them to increase their targets. However, the enterprises were interested only in increasing production volume, without economizing on inputs and, in practice, higher output goals were achieved at the cost of additional investments, materials, labor, etc.[83] For example, in the Ministry of Metallurgy and Mining, 87 per cent of EPU's proposed higher output targets than those originally assigned for the Third FYP, but only 13 per cent raised their labor productivity targets. In the same Ministry, 60.8 per cent of EPU's raised their output quotas and 21.7 per cent boosted the productivity targets for 1961. In the consumer goods industry, 54.4 per cent of the EPU's raised their output quotas and 12 per cent increased their productivity targets. As a rule, the annual productivity targets did not evince any increases over those specified in the FYP.[84]

On the whole, the system did not induce managers to reveal their capacity because the penalty for doing so was greater than the expected benefits.[85] It was safer to aim at overfulfillment of a slack plan, since the benefits for overfulfillment were not much lower than those for increasing the plan, and the risk of plan underfulfillment, followed by nonreceipt of premiums, was minimized. The ministry often attempted to foist much higher targets on the enterprises that came up with increased plans. The long-term stable normatives were supposed to widen the managers' time horizon and to prompt them to undertake long-range projects of protracted gestation periods. However, this incentive miscarried because the long-term normatives were being annually trimmed in relation to the preceding year's performance. Such action was defended on the grounds that the long-term plan was obsolete and that to earn higher premiums enterprises were especially prone to manipulate their product mix at the expense of consumers.[86]

To augment profit, enterprises also deteriorated quality, violated price-setting rules, neglected fixed capital, etc. Attempts were made by the state machinery to unearth these practices, to extract the "unearned" profit, and to punish the responsible managers.[87] The profit incentive was said to obstruct progressive production because enterprises tended to turn out well-established goods, whose prices were high and costs relatively low, at the expense of new goods. An investigation revealed that 53 per cent of all new products introduced in 1962 was produced at a loss, and was more labor-intensive than the well-established goods.[88] The profit incentive also failed to function because of the well-entrenched sellers' market.

The gross output target was not uprooted. Superiors overlooked many shortcomings when it was fulfilled. Actually, the stress on gross output remained practically in full force, even after gross output was abolished as a directive index in 1958. It was so, because the binding wage fund was computed on the basis of gross output, while gross output also remained fundamental to the calculation of labor productivity and its dynamics, which, as we have seen, was closely tied into the p.i.n. The reformed system was to stress efficiency, but in reality it floundered in doing so. Whereas the incentive system stressed growth of qualitative indexes, in fact, it accentuated the pressures on increase of gross output. Actually, the p.i.n. for raising wages could be easily manipulated through the gross output index.[89]

At the end of each quarter there was still the same rush to meet targets. Premiums were still being paid on the basis of quarterly performance. Also, in trying to widen managers' horizons, no attempt was made to abrogate the practice of shifting top management from enterprise to enterprise.[90] Enterprises still used the entire gamut of manipulations to acquire a slack plan. Requests for materials were inflated because deliveries were uncertain. Hoarding prevailed. Departmentalism was not eliminated.

The gestion system was at loggerheads with the decentralization trend, because, inter alia, it permitted legally autonomous economic units to interfere in each other's affairs. The gestors often found persuasion ineffectual in getting the producers to turn out the required goods and all sorts of pressures had to be resorted to. The index of realized output according to end uses was not complex enough; the end uses were not specific enough and the data were not collected at close enough intervals. It was found that a larger number of computers than was available was required for this purpose. Decentralized distribution did not run smoothly. There were frequent appeals to the center from dissatisfied customers, giving an impetus to recentralization in the distribution of some goods. Differences were not easily resolved among enterprises. They were usually appealed to ministries, but appeal extended the time necessary for solution; or they remained in the "blissful" state of irresolution. Even the annual plan became less and less operative because of continuous changes and interventions.

The investment plan was strained and lacked reserves. Early in 1959 the size of enterprises' funds that were available for investment expenditures was apparently incorrectly gauged. The e.i.n.'s were so determined as to fully account for capital goods suppliers' output without leaving reserves for credit-financed acquisitions of capital goods and without any real possibility of checking demand by credit policy. Already in 1959 the profit plans were greatly overfulfilled, with consequent pressures on investments. Apparently, the e.i.n. and the share of enterprises in depreciation were not properly set, resulting in excessive liquidity in the hands of enterprises.[91]

During 1959-60 enterprises aimed at accumulating the largest possible investment funds. Enterprises requested credits for above-normative working capital and diverted their own resources to investments. In July, 1959, the Czechoslovak State Bank (CSB) was empowered to approve transfer of funds from investment to current activity and to correct the enterprises' one-sided orientation toward capital formation. In practice, many enterprises that were unable to obtain credits because of their shortcomings or those that pursued accumulation of inventories transferred unused investment funds to current activity. In order to get the situation under control, attempts were made to impose harsher bank control. The CSB was not successful in forcing enterprises to channel their own resources to supplement working capital instead of unduly augmenting investment funds. An examination by the bank of 775 enterprises in metallurgy, fuels, power, chemical industry, heavy and general machine-building, and construction revealed that the enterprises that overfulfilled their planned profit targets continued to supplement their planned working capital from their own funds, but also to channel the remainder to investments.[92]

The pressure for more investments allowed the capital goods industry to choose easily fulfillable projects, and to start many projects at the same time, thus attaining a higher index of productivity. Many enterprises acquired often unsuitable capital goods in the fear that idle investment funds would be confiscated by superiors. "Enterprises spent money on anything that the supplier was ready to offer them. Thus, the decentralized investment policy only increased tensions..."[93] The enterprises did not display interest in more effective utilization of the investment funds, since the degree of investment efficiency had a negligible effect on the employees' incomes.[94]

On the whole, decentralized investments fared much better in fulfillment than did the centralized. Whereas in 1960 the centralized investment plan was fulfilled by 91.9 per cent for construction and

91.4 for machinery and equipment, the decentralized investment plan was fulfilled by 102.8 and 127.1 per cent, respectively.[95] The over-all centralized state investment plan was fulfilled by 94 per cent, whereas the decentralized plan was fulfilled by 109 per cent. The planned decrease of the share of decentralized investment from 61.2 per cent in 1959 to 58 per cent in 1960 was not accomplished.[96]

It was found that the backward enterprises which should have been modernized, lacked the necessary decentralized funds, whereas the central planner considered that those that accumulated the funds did not need to invest so much. Hence, methods at variance with the system, to subsidize some and to take away from others, soon made their appearance.[97] Since the accumulation of funds did not coincide with planners' priorities--contrary to the "spirit" of the reform--the undesirable investment funds were blocked, disillusioning management with its new prerogatives.

Already by 1961 it was decided to cut back on decentralized projects, in order to ensure the execution of the centralized investment program. But the centralized state investment plan for 1961 was fulfilled by 92 per cent and that for decentralized investments was fulfilled by 106 per cent.[98] The 1962 plan was a substantially tampered version of the FYP figures for that year, entailing considerable revisions in the long-term normatives and other financial indicators and seriously undermining confidence in plan stability.

Strong recentralization currents made themselves felt by 1962. A number of goods distributed by enterprises were recentralized. Key material usage norms were once more calculated and enforced centrally. Mandatory cost reduction targets reappeared. The SPC returned to fixing quarterly plan assignments. Long-term normatives were abolished and enterprises were allowed only a 15 per cent share in above-plan profits. The formation of the premium fund was made dependent on fulfilling the indexes of realized output and cost reduction. Superiors reverted once again to binding targets for working capital and enterprise investments.[99]

By August, 1962, no decentralized investment exceeding 1 million kcs. was to be started, except for housing, mining, and other specific projects approved by the government.[100] The construction of less important projects and of those in earlier construction stages was to be stopped, in order to reallocate resources to priority projects.[101] The number of unfinished construction projects was supposed to have been sharply reduced by 1962. In reality, not only was this not accomplished, but new construction proliferated. In 1963 the number of unfinished construction projects and the time required for their completion were about double that which the technical and economic resources of Czechoslovakia could sustain. In the first half of 1963, 42 priority projects were supposed to be finished, whereas only 29 were actually completed.[102] A State Commission for Investments was set up to control the allocation of investment resources and to enforce their concentration on priority projects. Notwithstanding those stringent controls, there was in 1962 and 1963 a tendency to start so-called black market construction,[103] jeopardizing the completion of priority investments and freezing more investment funds in unfinished projects. Almost 800 such violations were detected. The most frequent violators were the national committees, but 60 of them were found in the Ministry of General Machine-Building, 30 in the Ministries of Heavy Machine-Building and Agriculture, and 20 in the Ministries of Metallurgy and Ore Mines and Consumer Goods.[104]

In 1963 hardly any reserves were provided for granting investment credits. Long-term credits were mostly granted in the same way as subsidies and financed an insignificant share of investments. Only in a few cases did the bank grant investment credits to the extent that other enterprises pledged themselves not to use their "excess" reserves.[105]

The relatively improved turnover of inventories

in the 1956-60 period started to deteriorate in 1961. By 1962, due to changes in plans and difficulties in allocations, hoarding of inventories grew sharply, especially in metallurgy and machine-building.[106]

In principle, the enterprise's permanent requirement for working capital was to be covered in its entirety by its own financial resources (strictly speaking, the resources with which the enterprise was endowed at its creation and which were being replenished from profit and subsidies). Any attempt to introduce a partial credit financing of a given share of the permanent requirement was regarded as an infringement on the enterprise's autonomy.[107] The volume of the permanent requirement was fixed by norms--the so-called working capital normatives which were supposed to determine the quantity of working capital permanently required to ensure an uninterrupted flow of activity. Normatives were established for different types of inventories and were supposed to express the average of the permanently required quantity. Bank credits were to be granted for financing seasonal and special requirements, above-normative inventories, etc. In insisting that the enterprise finance from its own funds the normative of working capital, the planners were hoping to induce the enterprise to speed up working capital turnover and to keep inventories at a minimum level.[108]

The working capital normatives were to be determined by the enterprises, with the stipulation that they could not assume a slowdown in turnover. The rule that the normative be financed from the enterprise's own funds and the above-normative working capital be financed by credits was not implemented in practice. Experience has shown that the attempts to determine what the normative should be have failed, as in other Soviet-type economies.[109]

Until 1963 the enterprises were allowed to decide on their own how to apportion the part of profit at their disposal between augmentation of working capital and of decentralized investments.

Apparently, the tendency was to set low normatives for working capital in order to be able to allot more funds to investments. The remaining requirements for working capital were financed by credit as above-normative working capital requirements.[110] The bank controlled whether the normative was correctly set and whether the enterprise did channel sufficient funds to supplement its own working capital. The point in question was to arrest "excessive" transfers of profit to investments. Bank approval and a credit agreement were required for the superiors to approve the enterprise's plan. In other words, the bank's refusal was followed by the superior's rejection of the plan. Ironically enough, legally, the plan was not subject to the superior's approval.[111]

It was argued that, when working capital was partly financed by the enterprise's own resources and partly financed by credits, the control system was unusually complex and bureaucratic. The problem was that constant verifications of the movement and composition of working capital were required. The financial resources and credit requirements of the enterprises also had to be constantly checked. The complex system of control and coordination was ineffective; it was purely administrative and was conducive to waste, rather than to efficiency.[11]

The enterprise's prerogatives to apportion the part of retained profit were curtailed in 1963 when the division of investments into centralized and decentralized types was abandoned. All investments were incorporated into the national economic plan, thus, reverting to the 1954-55 system.[113] Simultaneously, directives were to determine the apportionment of profit between working capital and investments. Also in 1963, to counteract "excessive" hoarding, the following measures were taken: 1) a comprehensive classification of stocks was required in order to uncover superfluous stocks which could be transferred to other enterprises, and 2) current controls over the suitability of materials for given processes were instigated.[114]

In 1964 new stress was laid on controlling and financing investments. In controlling the flow of funds, the bank was supposed to ensure concentration of resources on priority investments, in order to reduce the number of unfinished projects. The CSB was not supposed to release funds for new projects if, during 1964, the work on existing projects by the same investor was not proceeding as planned.

Enterprises were partly allowed to finance limited investments from sources such as surplus of wage funds. The ceiling imposed on so-called minor investments, those whose planned costs did not exceed 100,000 kcs., was relaxed if the enterprise could find additional financial means. To promote technical progress and better use of fixed capital, 200 million kcs. was appropriated for financing such measures. The bank was allowed to approve credits up to 500,000 kcs. to promote such measures. But such investments were not to jeopardize the investment plan by unduly claiming real resources.

Another type of credit introduced in 1964 was that for machinery and equipment, for which 150 million kcs. was set aside. The bank was charged with granting such credits over and above the investment plan limits, as long as the acquisition of assets did not infringe on the suppliers' output assigned for limited investments and did not put a claim on new production. The purpose of these credits was to induce the sale of idle assets, such as surplus assets at enterprises, of those tied up in unfinished construction projects, of those that were delivered before the project was completed and were later found unsuitable, of those produced for export or domestic use but not sold, etc. Credits for such purposes were not to be granted if these acquisitions would create needs for complementary machinery.

The government also authorized the CSB to exceed the limit on investments for renovations and machinery which were not stipulated in the project's estimates, but on which an agreement for execution had been reached with the supplier. After scrutinizing the advisability and availability of such investment, the bank could exceed the limit if the purpose was modernization, provided that it would not jeopardize planned deliveries.[115]

In 1964, experiments were conducted in granting long-term, interest-free, investment credits to replace outright state grants. However, if during the execution of the project the deadline for commissioning capacity was not met, a penalty interest rate was charged in the range of 3.6 to 7.2 per cent, depending on the extent of the investor's fault. In other experiments, the bank proposed a charge of a 9 per cent quarterly penalty rate for "undesirable" and unduly delayed projects. But when it was found that the penalty would amount to 1.8 million kcs. for the Kralove Dvur Iron Works and to 242,000 kcs. for the Lenin Mines, the Ministry of Metallurgy and Ore Mines protested vehemently and killed the experiment which was then shifted to a nonpriority sector of the consumer goods industry.[116]

In 1963-64, due to the fact that higher normatives were in the interest of the enterprise, since they would be partly financed by budget grants and partly by credits to supplement their own working capital, enterprises demanded that their own working capital be excessively increased. In a number of cases the bank had to resort to sizable cuts of working capital requirements.[117] It is also likely that enterprises were now demanding more working capital because of the restrictions imposed on decentralized investments and because of the more strained supply situation.

Once again, in 1964, the CSB was called upon to combat hoarding of supplies, with the aim of reducing working capital by over 2 billion kcs. On the one hand, the bank was to promote this aim by more stringent credit controls and even refusal of credit, if necessary, and, on the other, by more favorable credit terms.[118] However, the bank's action was of little consequence, for fulfillment of the output plan was by far the most important aim, and the enterprise would resort to other, less legitimate, sources of financing; as, for example, delayed payments to suppliers.[119]

The financing of supplies by credits exerted a negligible influence on management, inter alia, because interest charges were only an insignificant share of costs. Apparently most directors were even unaware of the amount of interest or penalties paid. Therefore, the CSB resorted to primarily administrative controls and measures to mitigate hoarding, since neither credit policy, interest, nor material incentives were sufficiently effective.[120]

Revised wholesale prices were introduced in 1964. The revision was apparently the most extensive of all price adjustments that had taken place heretofore. The principles of this revision did not depart from tradition. One of the aims of the revision was to cut back on the liquidity of enterprises. Planned average production costs for 1964, plus a profit markup (from 1 to 9 per cent) were the basis for price formation. Actual costs for 1961 were projected into 1964 by taking the planned cost reduction stipulated in the Third FYP into consideration, with an expected 4 to 6 per cent reduction in prices. However, these postulates had to be changed in the course of preparing the revision. The expected cost reduction did not materialize in 1962 and 1963. Prices were actually lowered by only 1 per cent in industry. Instead of an average 3.6 per cent profit in industry, a 1.5 per cent was set, with variations of -1.2 to +5.6 per cent among the branches. In the fuels industry prices rose by 38 per cent. Prices of pig iron were increased by 47 per cent; those of high-grade and low-grade steel went up by 10 and 47 per cent, respectively. Prices of manufactured consumer goods fell by about 5.5 per cent, whereas those of machine-building products dropped by about 23 per cent. Greater attention was apparently paid to price relations of substitutes and price differentiation for quality.[121]

The fundamental shortcomings of the planning system were not eradicated with the 1958-59 reform. The attempts to increase the scope of economic levers floundered badly because the measures were half-hearted. The directive assignments of plan indexes were retained as the basic planning tool; their fulfillment remained the fundamental performance criterion. The lower echelons were, indeed, entrusted with wider decision-making, but since price formation was not altered, prices could not be used as choice coefficients. In fact, due to these half-measures, production was apparently further divorced from "social needs." The reform failed to grapple with the problem of the market mechanism in a socialist economy and with the question of employees' incentives. The prevailing attitude was that market relations and a system of potent incentives would contradict planning in a socialist economy; that they were remnants of the capitalist system; and that they were a source of uncontrollable elements. Therefore, the measures taken had the purpose of confining these "necessary evils" as much as possible within the boundaries of the central plan.[122] The experience of the 1958-59 reform indicated that half-way, inconsistent measures have more adverse effects than retaining the traditional planning system.

There exist two diametrically opposed schools of thought in Czechoslovakia on the failures of the 1958-59 reform: One claims that the reform has gone too far on the road to decentralization; that too much hope was placed on management by incentives; and that the self-regulatory aspects of the market were overestimated. The other school propounds that these reforms were only half-measures; that they stopped short of decentralization; and that they attempted to graft the reform on the deceased body of the old system. From these opposing views derive also the attitudes of protagonists in the discussion to be presented in the next chapter: The first school would improve the system by intensifying centralization, or, at best, by tinkering with the status quo; whereas the second would push further on the road to decentralization through utilization of the market mechanism.[123]

CHAPTER 3 IN SEARCH OF MARKET SOCIALISM

PLAN AND MARKET: EROSION OF OLD MYTHS

As we attempted to outline in Chapter 1, the retardation of growth performance in the 1960's, and, in particular, the calamitous results of 1963, prompted Czechoslovak economists to take a hard look at economic realities. It is true that criticisms had been voiced in the late 1950's, and that partial reform measures were taken, as we have seen in Chapter 2. But it should be stressed that these early criticisms lacked the fervor of their Polish and Hungarian counterparts. Little was done to investigate alternative variants of the functioning of a socialist economy. The very question smacked of heresy; a positive approach to Yugoslav experiences was branded as revisionist.[1]

Perhaps three major factors contributed to that more placid state. First, there was relative prosperity. Living standards in Czechoslovakia were considerably higher than those in other East European countries.[2] There was little turmoil and dissatisfaction at the grass roots. Second, the de-Stalinization phase was half-hearted in the 1950's. There was an obvious reluctance on the part of the leadership to grapple with these delicate problems. The behavior of the political decision-makers was marked by caution and suspicion. They tried to avoid any major policy or leadership changes. De-Stalinization really only gained momentum in the early 1960's. Third, the fraternity of economists in Czechoslovakia was weaker than that of its neighbors. Even before World War II, economic science was underdeveloped and economists with international reputations were not produced.[3]

During the postwar years, with transplantation of the Soviet model, the sterile and "dogmatic" Stalinist approach to economics was also imported. Economists at research institutes and at universities were confined to reciting well-learned litanies and to finding apologia for the system. It was a highly "politicalized" economy, where political decisions were uppermost in the shaping of economic development. Yet, there was a tendency to camouflage the political nature of decisions by referring to "economic laws." It was particularly here that theoretical economists were called upon to evolve and formulate these "laws" so that they could "scientifically" justify current economic policy. Only those economists were considered as progressives who proved "that the market is capitalism and that the plan is socialism and that with the plan we must exorcise the market in the same way as the church had exorcised the devil with holy water."[4]

Perhaps the Czechoslovak reform movement of the 1960's had more _élan vital_ than that of other East European countries because the thaw came relatively late--at a time when economic performance was at its lowest ebb--so that the two factors--intellectual renaissance and disastrous economic performance--joined forces to push through radical proposals.

Also, by 1963, a new generation of economists had come of age. Although they were raised on "Stalinist dogma" and lacked training in modern economics and in mathematical techniques, they slowly became aware of the ferment in economic thought taking place around them. Their own restlessness prepared them to welcome the new winds and to evolve their own ideas. This development was described as a "revolution" in economic thought. "It was a process of basic re-examination in which theoretical fetiches were pulled down one after another, and little was left of the old stock of categories and theories."[5]

It may be noted that the first articles on mathematical economics appeared during the period 1958-59, but until 1963 the flowering science of planometrics had not made noticeable inroads.[6] Czechoslovak economists were criticized for being sceptical of the application of mathematical methods. A "completely negative" attitude was apparently demonstrated during the discussions organized by the Prague Higher School of Economics. Benedikt Korda blamed the situation on a fear of ideological deviationism.[7] This was probably true of the more "conservative" economists, but not altogether accurate of others, who often committed similar "heresies." These economists realized that planometrics could not offer immediate solutions to pressing problems and that their further refinement would delay changes by another decade or so. Perhaps it was also due to a lack of mathematical sophistication. In general, Czechoslovak economists were not attracted to "push-button" economics, but found far more appeal in the possibilities of resuscitating the market mechanism.[8]

Let us now briefly digress to a more detailed examination of the recession that beset the economy in the 1960's. The reported plan fulfillment for 1961 indicated a slight underfulfillment of the gross industrial output target, but it was still a 8.9 per cent increase over 1960. There were substantial disparities in plan fulfillment. The chemical industry registered the highest fulfillment (113 per cent). Production targets of key industrial products were not met (including hard coal, electric power, pig iron, steel, rolled metals, machines, and bricks). Although excess capacity existed in the steel industry, the acute shortages of iron ore, coke, and fuel hampered fulfillment of quotas for steel and rolled metals which, in turn, reduced output in machine-building. Delivery plans for export were curtailed. Labor shortages were particularly pronounced in mining and metallurgy. Difficulties in recruitment and poor caliber and performance of miners adversely affected production. There were persisting complaints of low labor productivity, excessive employment, violations of "wage discipline," poor quality of output, etc. Poor results were again recorded in agriculture. But, on the whole, reported plan fulfillment in manufactured consumer goods fared well. In his New Year's Day address Antonin Novotny criticized the shortage of housing, unavailability of consumer goods, and poor services. He called for a strengthening of control over the economy from the center and from below through the Party cells and the trade unions.[9]

Early in 1962 there were signs that the strains of 1961 were not being overcome. Plans were being underfulfilled in construction, freight transportation, central procurement of slaughtered livestock, milk, and eggs. The metallurgical industry, machine-building, and coal mining were lagging behind. Heavy machine-building did not meet deliveries for centralized investments and for exports. The results for the first six months were disappointing. Frequent breakdowns in supply again resulted in underutilization of capacity.[10] There were considerable shortages of numerous consumer goods. The situation was so bad that meat was virtually unobtainable and, at times, various other foodstuffs (particularly eggs, vegetables, and fats) were in short supply. On May Day students of Prague demonstrated against the prevailing situation with such cries as: "We have Gagarin and Titov, but we have no meat." Due to severe shortages prices of some consumer goods were raised. On August 14, 1962, it was announced that after two years, the Third FYP was being abandoned, to be replaced by a one-year plan in 1963 and by a Seven-Year Plan for 1964-70.[11]

Again in 1962 industrial output targets were underfulfilled by 1.1 per cent. Originally the rate of growth of industrial output was set at 9.9 per cent for 1962. It was later lowered to about 7.5 per cent. The reported performance was 6.2 per cent. Output targets were underfulfilled in electric power by 3.6 per cent, in metallurgy and mining by 2.9 per cent, in heavy machine-building by 2.7 per cent, and in building materials by 1.6 per cent. They were barely overfulfilled in fuels by 0.3 per cent, in chemicals by 0.4 per cent, and in consumer goods by 1.5 per cent. Gross agricultural production dropped to about 94 per cent of the 1961 level.[12]

As compared to 1961, investments in 1962 decreased by about 1 per cent (fixed investments by about 5 per cent), against a planned increase of about 6 per cent, later scaled down to about 1 per cent. There was about 25 per cent reduction of investments in collective farms and a 12 per cent decrease in the completion of private housing.[13] Again too many projects were begun, immobilizing, dispersing, and absorbing resources. Construction was reported to lag behind particularly in ore mining, metallurgy, heavy machine-building, transportation, the chemical industry, and the projects undertaken by national committees. The pattern was repeated: The delays provoked by the builders were accentuated by failures of machine-builders to supply machinery which were, in turn, aggravated by failures in metallurgy and ore mining. Deliveries were often incomplete and substandard materials were supplied. For instance, in metallurgy the plan for production of rolled steel had to be drastically reduced in view of bottlenecks in the supply of ores, of the imposed restrictions in the supply of gas and power to cope with the fuels crisis, of breakdowns in the operations of metallurgical plants, etc. Hampered by supply shortages, idle capacity amounted to about 25 per cent in machine-building.[14] The builders and design bureaus were, in turn, blamed for poor preparatory work and documentation, for crude cost estimates, for unwarranted changes during construction, for inordinate delays in completion, for breakdowns in operations, and for the resulting delays in activating new capacities whose output had already been allocated to users.[15]

The 1962 plan targets were generally met (or approached) by increasing employment (and/or overtime) at a rate higher than planned. Whereas the original productivity target, subsequently lowered, stipulated an increase of 7.2 per cent over 1961 (9 per cent in construction), the index registered an increase of 3.2 per cent (in construction only 2.3 per cent). Employment rose by 3 per cent over

1961, compared to a target of 2.5 per cent. The largest increases were recorded in fuels, metallurgy, chemical, and machine-building industries. There were acute shortages of manual labor in construction. Railway transporation was a major bottleneck. The cost reduction plan was not met and the norms of planned material and power consumption were exceeded. Manipulations of assortments and poor quality of output were deplored.[16]

Although the foreign trade surplus increased, it reflected largely credits extended to developing countries and the inability to procure imports from the West because of a shortage of convertible foreign exchange. A number of orders for Western machine tools was cancelled to make room for additional food imports.[17]

By 1962 the dislocations in the economy were of such proportions that drastic measures were called for to reduce the mounting tensions. Further restrictions were to be imposed on investments in 1963; greater stress was to be placed on quality, with a reorientation of production toward this goal and toward cost reduction, specialization, and better coordination with domestic demand and export requirements. Investments were to be concentrated on fewer industries than in 1962. Special priorities were to be accorded to re-equipping and developing electric power, machine-building, and the factories producing for export. Concurrently, the level of consumption was to be raised. But, by all accounts, the control figures for the 1963 plan were clumsily balanced, partly due to conflicting views within the ruling circles on the degree of reorientation required.

The 1963 plan targets were trimmed to a 1 per cent increase of industrial output over 1962, a 6 per cent decrease of investments, a 9.5 per cent increase of agriculture, a 0.7 per cent increase of productivity, and a 0.24 per cent decrease of unit costs.[18] The plan was approved late in 1962, with the understanding that its targets would be raised early in 1963. But the severe 1963 winter played havoc with the plan and unforeseen difficulties forced a further reduction of some output targets by May, 1963. At the same time, in an effort to alleviate the difficulties, the CC called for increased "action" plans to be drawn up in all branches, stipulating raised output targets. However, the "action" campaign did not fare well. In fact, the government was forced on two occasions to scale down the 1963 plan targets while the implementation of the plan was in progress (including reduction of the targets for the growth of national income, curtailment of investments, and restriction on imports from the West). Reportedly, the interventions by the government to remove some bottlenecks created others. An atmosphere of uncertainty as to plan targets prevailed. Because of the revisions, inter-enterprise and interbranch flows (poorly integrated at the outset) were further "unbalanced," aggravating the interruptions in the flow of production; the hoarding of inventories; the inefficiency of production; the production of shoddy and unwanted goods; the manipulations of product mix; and the deterioration of product quality.[19]

The results for the first half of 1963 afforded little to cheer about. Nonfulfillment of even the scaled-down investment targets and delays in commissioning new capacities were among the major weak spots. Investment expenditures recorded a 17 per cent decline in the first six months of 1963 compared to the same period in 1962. In the first six months only 39.2 per cent of investments planned for 1963 were completed. The ratio of completed investments to those envisaged in the plan was the lowest in basic industries. About two thirds of the backlog was attributed to failures to achieve the planned labor productivity targets and one third to the failure to recruit the planned man-power for construction and to arrest the sizable labor drain in construction. Delays in the deliveries of equipment and in installation significantly contributed to the difficulties. Failures to observe the plan for placing new power-generating capacities into operation aggravated the already strained fuel and power situation.

The fuels and power crisis was greatly aggravated by a transportation crisis--attributed primarily to ineffective utilization of available equipment both by the railroad and by the shippers. The failures in transportation disrupted seriously the deliveries of ore, dolomitic sand, and limestone for metallurgy; gravel for construction; and coal for the railroad itself. Labor shortages particularly hampered railways, construction, mining, and agriculture. At the same time, superfluous labor was reported in many enterprises. Although virtually in every branch the labor productivity index was set considerably lower than originally envisaged, the results were reported to have been very disappointing.[20] The campaign to curtail "wrong" output met apparently with some success, but little was achieved to advance the production of the "right" one. However, production to augment the stocks of unwanted goods continued and warehouses piled high with unsalable goods constituted a serious problem.

The reduced industrial output target was barely fulfilled (by 100.7 per cent) in 1963, but it was 0.6 per cent below its 1962 level. About 20 per cent of industrial enterprises failed to meet their output targets. Gross agricultural production increased by about 7 per cent, but remained below its 1961 figure. Throughout 1963 rejects rose by 12 per cent, materials were hoarded, and investment and production costs rose steeply. There were continuing manpower shortages and a precariously strained balance of payments. Personal consumption increased by 1.6 per cent over 1962, as against a planned 1.3 per cent rise. Employment grew by 0.4 per cent, compared to a 0.3 per cent planned rise. Labor productivity recorded a 1.0 per cent drop, compared to a planned increase of 0.7 per cent. Investment registered about 12 per cent decline, whereas the reduced plan targets had called for only a 6 per cent drop. In spite of the decline in aggregate output and the campaign to reduce stocks, they rose by about 7 billion kcs.--about twice as much as the amount by which the investment plan was underfulfilled (about 4 billion kcs.).[21]

Table 42

VARIATIONS IN OUTPUT OF SELECTED BRANCHES AND PRODUCTS IN 1963 COMPARED TO 1962

Industries	Increase of output percentage	Decrease of output percentage	Industries	Increase of output percentage	Decrease of output percentage	Industries	Increase of output percentage	Decrease of output percentage
Branches			Electric power	3.9		Electric engines		18.4
Fuels	3.7		Pig iron	1.5		Diesel engines		59.3
Power	0.7		Steel		0.5	T.V. sets		23.6
Metallurgy		2.9	Rolled steel	0.8		Tractors		9.7
Heavy machines		2.1	Steel tubing		4.2	Refrigerators	21.5	
General "		1.9	Cement		9.3	Cotton textiles		2.2
Building materials		9.8	Bricks		19.9	Wool textiles		2.6
Chemical	3.4		Synthetic fibers	1.4		Linen textiles		7.3
Consumer goods		2.6	Plastics		1.8	Leather shoes		5.3
Food	4.1		Fertilizers		0.1	Rubber shoes		16.2
			Sulfuric acid	12.8		Paper	0.6	
Products			Machine tools		14.3	Meat		1.3
Hard coal	3.9		Agricultural			Milk	1.8	
Soft coal	5.0		machines		19.7	Vegetable fats	0.6	
Lignite	8.5		Automobiles		12.2	Sugar	7.1	
			Trucks		16.0	Beer	5.6	

Source: RP, February 11, 1964.

While the Czechoslovak economists acknowledged some of the exogenous factors, such as severe draught, an exceptionally harsh winter in 1963, deteriorating relations with the Chinese, and other tensions on the international scene (apparently entailing a considerable rise in military expenditures), they realized that these were by no means the only causes for the failures of the economy.

Even though de-Stalinization had set in, the atmosphere was yet far from propitious for the first virulent attacks appearing against the system. The giant 50-foot statue of Stalin still towered over Prague in 1962. There were no tangible relaxations since the Twenty Second Congress of the CPSU. In mid-1962 the Party launched a campaign against "rotten" liberalism:

> Demagogues and enemies know how to cunningly make use of our economic problems... They have attacked the principles of democratic centralism and have preached rotten liberalism, absolute freedom of demagoguery and slander under the cover of unlimited freedom of criticism. In some cases we hear completely reactionary views violating proletarian internationalism.[22]

Two important factors brought to a head the dissatisfaction that had been brewing for some time at the very apex of the Party's leadership. One was in February, 1962, the purging of Novotny's protege, Rudolf Barak, who had been accused of embezzlement, but who had apparently fallen because of rivalry. The other was the Twenty Second Congress of the CPSU, with its further thrusts at Stalinism, which left many a Czechoslovak Communist desirous of whitewashing. At the Twelfth Congress of the CCP the CC was charged with investigating the legality of the 1949-54 political trials. This placed Antonin Novotny--the First Party Secretary and President of the Republic--in a rather precarious position, for he had been Klement Gottwald's assistant in the latter's power struggle with Rudolf Slansky and bore a large share of responsibility for the Slansky-Clementis executions and for the trial of many others. In 1953 Novotny was already First Party Secretary and was personally fully accountable for the later trials. The Czechoslovak purge was the most extensive in the satellites. Besides drawing heavily on the army and the bureaucracy, the purge removed fifty of the ninety-seven-member CC and six of the seven-member secretariat. Even though the CC's conclusions were never publicized, they were debated at an April, 1963, plenary session and caused a major rift in the Party's unity against the oncoming wave of criticism.[23] The pressures for rehabilitating the victims of the purges might have also been partly an instrument wielded by a Party faction to voice its discontent with Novotny's policies and to attempt to overthrow him.

In preparation for the Twelfth Congress of the CCP, the slack adherence to "democratic centralism" and the ensuing "one-sided decentralization" were criticized. At the Congress Novotny took up the difficulties faced by the economy and struck three notes: 1) the lack of balance in the economy; 2) the neglect of agriculture; and 3) the violations of "democratic centralism."[24] The latter euphemism has sometimes been interpreted as a call for either centralization or decentralization, depending on which word was accented.

Just two months later, Radoslav Selucky indicted the "cult of the plan" to which he attributed the brunt of economic ills. He denounced the arbitrariness and irrationality of plans whose fulfillment was surrounded by glory and nonfulfillment by opprobrium.

> What is the benefit if the railroads fulfill all the indicators, when the transport of many goods is itself useless? What is the benefit if the productivity is higher in the case of washing machines than in the case of iceboxes, when stores are overstocked with the former, while queues extend

for the latter?[25]

Mordant reproval came from Novotny, who, referring to Selucky by name, vituperated against those people "who do not recognize the principles of socialist society and who, under cover of freedom of their person and their opinion, actually abuse the freedom of socialist society." Defending the right to criticize, Novotny went on: "But nobody must touch our Communist Party, its program, and our socialist system." Referring to the scope of the Party's control, he underlined that the "Communist Party has the right to direct the cultural life of the country, just as it guides its economic life." As to the shortcomings of the planning system, he had this to say: "Of course, we are against subjectivism in planning. But we must do our utmost for the plan to carry great authority and for the state and work discipline to be strictly enforced."[26]

The undercurrent in 1963 was Novotny's unwillingness to give free reins to criticism, even to that of the "personality cult."[27] Another clash between the Party and the intellectuals came at a meeting of Slovak writers who, attempting to push de-Stalinization further, were clamoring for more sincere rehabilitations. It was, after all, the Slovaks who had suffered most in the purges. One of the harshest condemnations of the "witch hunts" and a resounding call for recantations came from Miro Hysko at the Congress of Slovak Journalists. The Party retorted by inculpating in the past wrongdoings those who were now clamoring for rehabilitations. Novotny personally criticized Hysko's speech and blamed the Bratislava Pravda (the organ of the Slovak CC) for being a platform whence "hysterical attacks" are hurled at the Party. But, in order to conciliate the Slovaks, Karol Bacilek, who was thoroughly disliked in Slovakia as a stooge of Prague, was demoted from his post of First Secretary of the Slovak Party and was replaced by Alexander Dubcek. In the latter part of June, Premier Siroky, who had been put on the dock by Hysko for having been involved in rigging the trials of Slovak Communists, spoke defiantly in Bratislava. Concurrently, Dubcek was sent on a mission to pacify the Slovaks and reiterated the need to slow down the pace of criticism and to recognize past accomplishments. Speaking in Prague, Jiri Hendrych defended the de-Stalinization pace set by the Party and denounced the Party's critics as heretics whose calls for freedom are a "manifestation of petty bourgeois radicalism."[28]

On August 8, 1963, it was announced that Slansky had been rehabilitated, but in a most ambiguous way and without removing the stigma attached to his name. The precariousness of Novotny's position was implied in Pravda which stressed that those most responsible for implementing Stalinist methods in the past were not the best suited for eradicating them.[29]

In the fall of 1963 it seemed as if the Party was losing ground to the rising call for liberalization. Many of the diehard Stalinists were removed from office. For example, Alois Indra was demoted from the post of Chairman of the SPC and replaced by Oldrych Cernik. There was a noticeable move to placate the Slovaks with the appointment of Josef Lenart as Premier and of other Slovaks to important posts. As he took office, Lenart censured "low standards" in planning and acknowledged existing economic difficulties.[30]

In the meantime, Selucky again took up the call for reforming the planning system. He stressed that the traditional model was not the "categorical imperative" for a socialist economy. He leaned toward the decentralized solution advocated by the Polish economist Wlodzimierz Brus and toward the "borrowing" of such "capitalist" ("heretic Yugoslav") notions as the profit motive, the market mechanism, etc.[31]

Ota Sik, the director of the Institute of Economics of the Czechoslovak Academy of Sciences and member of the CC, who previously had dealt with the problem of divergence of interests between the individual and the state and had emphasized the need for harmonizing these interests in a rationally operating economy, was able to soften the radicalism of Selucky's outcry, yet emerging with proposals very much akin to Selucky's "borrowing from the West," but couched in more palatable Marxist terminology.[32] At the December, 1963, meeting of the CC, Sik argued that Czechoslovakia had already depleted its manpower resources and did not enjoy the U.S.S.R.'s relative self-sufficiency. It could no longer afford to model itself on the U.S.S.R. and must solve its problems boldly and differently--by blending the plan and the market.[33]

Until about the end of 1963 the criticisms and proosals of economists were of an intermittent nature and lacked organization. Dogmatism in economic thought had been vigorously assailed by Sik and Eugene Loebl. The latter had been a victim of purges, and was recently freed and rehabilitated. In November, 1963, a round-table discussion was held to evaluate the state of economic science. It sharply deplored "dogmatism" and assailed the underlying logic of "economic laws."[34] It was argued by Milan Plachky that the preferential growth of producer goods was a "mere fiction and only a regard for authority and political expediency prevents us from tackling the question." Zdenek Haba argued that planning, nationalization, and collectivization should not be regarded as ends in themselves, but should be viewed pragmatically as means to achieve a given end. He supported Selucky's contention that there are different roads to socialism. The point was not to criticize the anomalies of the existing system, but to subject the system itself to searching scrutiny and to explore alternative institutional arrangements. Whereas the official doctrine proclaimed a unity of individual and social interests, what was needed was an examination of the contradictions and conflicts in the socialist economy. Some of the factors contributing to the dismal state in economics were spelled out; namely, the very scant knowledge of developments in economics in the West; an absence of translations of significant contributions to modern economics; the impossibility of gaining access to relevant statistical material, etc. Karel Kouba pointed out that although Keynes's magnum opus had been translated before, it had not yet appeared in print by 1963. Korda called attention to the unavailability of Soviet writings of the "golden age" of Soviet economics (1920's). Even the contributions of such unorthodox socialist economists as V. S. Nemchinov, Oskar Lange, Brus, etc., were little known and studied.

The conference seems to have given sufficient impetus and cohesion to the pressures for reforms. Its general tenor, at least among the most outspoken, favored something akin to a market-type solution. It afforded a platform for economists to get rid of obsolete ideas, thus preparing the ground where new and consistent ideas could germinate. Of course, many contributors only tackled particular facets of the system. The contention of these conservative reformers was that the shortcomings of the system could be eliminated by changing this or that of its aspects. On the other hand, there were those who claimed that only a thoroughgoing reform would be able to cope with the problems.

At the December, 1963, CC plenum both "dogmatists" and "revisionists" were berated.[35] Hints at reforms came early in 1964 when CC secretary, Drahomir Kolder, called for less "administrative" and more "economic" management. The proposed changes were only palliatives. He reiterated the need for stronger incentives and for the so-called deleveling of wages (expansion of the wage structure) as stimulants for better plan implementation. Greater stress was to be placed on technical competence and less on "political maturity" in managerial appointments. Salaries of managerial and technical personnel were to be more closely related to "economic results." The piece-rate system was to be used more extensively. The wages of foremen, construction workers, and tractor drivers were to be raised. Salaries would be higher in factories that produce better goods. New schemes to reward efficiency were to be developed and first tested on an experimental basis in pilot enterprises; if successful they would be extended to the whole economy. But no wholesale changes in the planning system were yet envisaged. The 1964 plan, Kolder said, would aim at mitigating the drastic disproportions of 1963, even though it still indicated imbalances between requirements and availabilities.[36]

Meanwhile, the January, 1964, CC meeting appointed a special committee to study and report on the ways and means of improving the system and to evaluate the proposals submitted to the CC. The report submitted to the Party's Presidium was criticized for "economic revisionism" and did not meet with approval.[37]

The breakthrough finally came when, at a conference of Party officials in mid-1964, Novotny announced that "a new system of management" was being elaborated. It looked as if he was referring to a thoroughgoing reform. He called for closing down "ineffective," obsolete, and worn-out plants. He reprimanded the bureaucracy for failure to shut down such plants in 1963. Lenart stressed the need to tie in the workers' rewards with the sales of the enterprise and its performance; he also insisted on rendering exports more competitive, and on improving long-term planning.[38]

It is noteworthy that with the first signs of the Party's acceptance of economic reform, there was a clamp-down on liberalization in other domains. On January 18, 1964, Literarni noviny published an interview with the controversial Hungarian Marxist philosopher, Gyorgy Lucacs, who had been prominent in Imre Nagy's government. Lucacs called for breaking away from Stalinist tradition, for extending freedom of expression to intellectuals, and for allowing greater information about Western developments to seep through. The Party's ideological commission issued a statement criticizing the journal's editors for not disassociating themselves from the revisionist views they printed. The intellectuals were rebuked for their independent interpretations of the Party line and for recommending closer cultural ties with the West. Two days later Novotny was reported to have said that "the comrades in the cultural journals" who deviate from the Party line were advised to leave the Party before it parts with them.[39]

Later that summer the contemplated reform was still nebulous, even though it was expected to be implemented in connection with the Fourth FYP (1966-70).[40] The objections with which the reformers had to contend came from those critics who considered reform from the angle of its fitting into the existing framework of a socialist economy--that framework being regarded as the categorical imperative. As Selucky noted, this group still rallied behind moral suasion for aligning the goals of the enterprise with "social interest." Their main contention was that the existing system could be improved by palliatives, that the number of plan indexes could be expanded, that some indexes could be replaced by others, that control could be intensified, and that more noneconomic measures could be used to influence economic activity.[41]

On October 17, 1964, Rude pravo published the "Draft Principles of a System for Improving the Economy's Planned Management," whose outstanding architect was Ota Sik. The fate of the draft principles was somewhat uncertain for a while. Instead of approving the document at its December meeting, as expected, the CC passed it to its Economic Commission for continued study.[42] The Commission approved the document in principle, but referred to the need for further elaboration of some of its concepts.[43] Evidently opposing factions within the Party had not yet been reconciled. In his New Year's Day address, Novotny indicated that he sided with the conservatives. Once again he reverted to the prominent role to be played by central planning in the reformed system, and he blamed decentralization for the abortive 1958-59 reform.[44] But he must have had a change of heart, for at the end of January, 1965, the CC finally approved the reform proposals. The impact of the reform, howerever, was softened by refusing to allow that the proposals envisaged a completely new path for the economy, and by emphasizing that they only aimed at correcting past errors. There was an appeal to the Party membership at large to oppose the erroneous view that the acceptance of these reforms constituted an incursion of liberalism into the Communist economy.[45] The final acceptance of the reform proposals by Novotny was viewed as a partial compromise with the forces of change. The point was not to allow greater liberalization in other domains.

THE DRAFT PRINCIPLES OF THE NEW SYSTEM

Understandably the draft principles hardly provided a blueprint of the reformed system.[46] A large part of the document was devoted to some of the familar criticism of the past, albeit it shunned from explicitly attributing to the traditional system the role of the main retrogressive factor. No clear-cut picture of the reform emerged. The document was particularly vague on the key changes in working arrangements.

With the view of regenerating the system, the draft principles proclaimed value parameters as the core of economic calculations. Fulfillment of quantitative targets was now to be subjected to the cost and benefit test.

To encourage enterprises to enlarge the variety and to enhance the quality of their output and to compel them to produce efficiently, they would be vested with more decision-making authority. In the attempt to harmonize and to identify the interest of the enterprise with that of the state (society), the former would always be so manipulated as to accord with and support the latter. Employees' earnings would be closely linked with the enterprise's performance. Value parameters would convey to producers information on changing conditions of demand and would force them to adapt to these conditions.

The long-term plan "must originate within the process of systematic constructive cooperation" between central planning bodies and economic units. The plan must become "the fundamental instrument for management of the socialist economy--an obligatory directive for economic policy at all levels." The shift to intensive development would require that all investments should be documented with efficiency calculations (mainly the dubious recoupment period), so that resources should not be tied up for prolonged period. Crucial investments that essentially affect the given branch and sector and that increase labor productivity, the technical level, and the quality of output--would be decided at the center. The central planning authority would be required to evaluate the proposed projects in the light of similar foreign projects. The center would judge only the key projects, whereas local authorities would evaluate those of more restricted importance. But to maintain uniformity in evaluation, the center would set the norms and standards by which the projects would be judged.

Three types of investments were envisaged: 1) centrally planned and financed investments for development; 2) branch and enterprise investments for modernization, financed by the enterprise or bank credits; and 3) overhaul and replacement of assets, financed from the enterprise's share in depreciation allowances. To curb the enterprise's propensity to press for "free" investments, a capital charge would be levied by the state budget.

Since world prices express progressive tendencies, they ought to condition domestic production. The revenue of enterprises producing for export would reflect the sales value of their products on the world market. Similarly, the enterprise that uses imported inputs should be aware of their real costs. Moreover, the export producer should be drawn organizationally closer to the foreign markets. In many cases the foreign trade enterprises would be directly tied to the producing units. The organizational forms of foreign trade monopolies would have to be amended.

The enterprises would be primarily driven to maximize their gross income (GY), but they will not be evaluated on the degree of fulfillment of planned GY.[47] GY would remain after the deduction of the costs of materials, power depreciation, and transport from sales revenue. GY would be used for paying off capital charges, bank interest charges, investments, and budget levies; the remainder would then serve for paying basic wages (together with social security surcharges, etc.) and for awarding premiums. Enterprises would still have to comply with the centrally determined wage scales and with other restrictions imposed on wage payments. The quality of management in the enterprise would be reflected in the variable part of personal income (premiums).

Since GY and its residual for remuneration would depend primarily on the realization of output, the enterprise would be under economic pressure to turn out only those products that it could sell, to adjust its assortment to demand, to analyze the market, etc. Moreover, GY would grow proportionately to savings on materials, fuels, electricity, etc. GY would also increase when prices of material inputs dropped and when prices of outputs rose (assuming elastic demand in this range). Hence the user would press the producer to decrease prices and, simultaneously, the producer would improve his product mix so as to get a higher price. The specter of speculative price increases was raised. Economic and administrative measures would have to be used to check these attempts; the most important of which would be central management of price policies. Foreign trade should also inject a spark of competition into domestic trade.

The system should provide a stimulus for reducing employment. If by reducing its staff the enterprise did not deteriorate its performance, it would be left with a larger share of GY for premiums to be distributed to fewer employees.

The draft principles emphasized that rates of budget levy on GY (akin to a tax on value added) would be uniform for enterprises of the same branch of industry. However, rebates would be used temporarily, for differences between enterprises could not be overcome at once. Enterprises that could not effectively be extricated from backwardness would eventually be shut down.

To instill greater flexibility, a three-tier price system would be created: 1) fixed prices, centrally determined for raw materials, materials, fuels, and power, and for some consumer "necessities"; 2) limited prices for standard products, with centrally determined ceilings and possibly with floors, free to fluctuate between these boundaries; and 3) free prices, set in agreement between seller and buyer, to fluctuate with changes in demand and supply. The new types of prices were to be introduced gradually, with a view to the market situation.

The draft principles called on central organs and on producers to improve their working standards, to assimilate managerial techniques, and to improve the skills of executives. Also a reorganization and redefinition of relations among enterprises, between enterprises and their superiors, and between intermediaries and the central organs would be required. The organizational level immediately above the enterprise would be changed over to operate on khozraschet to render it economically responsible and sensitive to its ward's performance. Two types of EPU's would prevail: 1) a branch enterprise with a number of subordinate plants and 2) a trust of several enterprises of the same branch. The branch directorate would head up both organizational units. The EPU's would incorporate research and design bureaus, testing laboratories, marketing organizations, foreign trade groups, etc. The branch directorate would be wholly responsible for its wards' economic performance and the salaries and premiums of its employees would depend on the enterprises' GY. The specific division of managerial duties among the branch directorate and the enterprise would be decided by the former, with the understanding that a wide scope for initiative would be left to the enterprise. Concurrently, the directorate would perform many of the functions previously solely the responsibility of ministries.

Finally, the draft principles placed the burden of success of the new system on the shoulders of enterprise managers. If the system was to function smoothly and to bring forth the expected results, managers would have to be willing to take risks, to exercise initiative, and to approach problems with know-how. The selection of qualified personnel for top positions was emphasized as an urgent matter, but it was followed up by a continuing stress on political and ideological acceptability of the "leading economic workers."

Although they were a more concrete step in the direction of reforms, the draft principles left yet many loopholes and were characterized by a lack of precision, prone to various interpretations. The various agencies and institutes were charged with elaborating certain aspects. Experience was to be gained through experimentation--as we shall see in Chapter 4. During the preparation and approval of these principles, a lively pragmatic discussion continued on the plan and the market; on the use of GY versus profit as performance criteria and sources of premiums; on price formation; on investment decision-making; etc.

PLAN AND MARKET: DEBATE ON REFORM IMPLEMENTATION

The discussion featured a radical departure from the stigma of dogmatism and exercises in sterility; revisionism in the approach to economic problems; acceptance of the apparatus of the modern theory of value and of the market and market-type instruments; and concentration on finding a more effective system for the functioning of the collectivist economy. Much of what was said leaned on Polish economic literature, with a strong flavor of Yugoslav "revisionism."[48] In many cases there was a diametrical shift in favor of a genuine market, often with an exaggerated view of what the market could and could not do. In fact, in most cases the market was viewed in its institutional sense only. The Western economist, who--to borrow Joan Robinson's expression--was brought up to inquire into the meaning of meaning--would be disappointed and probably appalled at the ambiguity and lack of sophistication of some concepts. For example, everybody was for "optimum planning" and almost everybody was for an "optimal combination of the plan and the market." The discussants were understandably more preoccupied with voicing their disenchantment with the status quo than with drawing up a comprehensive blueprint of alternative working arrangements.

The principal architect of the reform saw its basic premises in rendering enterprises more responsive to market pressures, in strengthening the "buyer-seller relationships," and in systematically uprooting the old administrative methods of planning. The postulated wider utilization of the market necessarily entailed not only the reintroduction of market devices, but also a reexamination of the methods of plan construction and implementation, in order to adapt them to the blending of the plan and the market.[49]

The central economic plan should be limited to "questions of macro-economic growth based on realistic analyses of demand trends, technological-economic analyses and computing optimal solutions." "Socialist market relations" mean that enterprises "do not work completely separately and independently of each other, according to their own interest and decisions, for a more or less unknown market." Contrariwise, their path is mapped out and coordinated by the macroeconomic plan and the "basic structure of their output programmes is regulated by over-all planning." Distribution of national income; regulation of movements of key prices; over-all price relations; the general price level; technological development, investment, and manpower policies--all these are laid down by the plan. Key investment projects are incorporated in the long-range plan in order to regulate the "main proportions." The implementation of macro-plans would be induced primarily by the use of economic and financial levers.

> The socialist market helps, within the scope of the macro-economic plan and through the direct contact of interests between producers and consumers, to encourage enterprises to undertake production of commodities that are in demand, steadily to improve their assortments while lowering production costs.[50]

Stress was laid on long-term planning to assure sustained growth and to map out the basic development of individual sectors and branches of industry. As a rule, the center's prerogative to determine the basic development pattern was not questioned. The long-range plan would primarily encompass the basic construction projects in accordance with the restructuring of the economy; the main technical progress trends, the production of critical goods, particularly those in short supply; the foreign trade trends, especially in view of fulfilling long-term contracts with CMEA partners; the forecast of the size and composition of the labor force; and the main trends in the distribution of national income. But the paramount question: What criteria would be used to ascertain what the correct proportions are?--was not elucidated. The drafting of such plans would from the start enlist the active participation of enterprises in calculating and evolving the alternative variants. Obviously, the enterprises and EPU's would have a much larger role in drafting the short-term plans.[51] In this connection the central organs would have to ensure that the more or less independently constructed branch plans correspond to the general direction of the economy.

An issue of major importance was the relationship between the managers' initiative and the extent to which plan assignments would be binding. With a few exceptions, quantitative targets could not be considered as absolute magnitudes whose overfulfillment is always beneficial and whose underfulfillment is always detrimental. Together with a few binding plan assignments, a number of guideline indexes would be issued to orient the producers about the envisaged development of their production, the shifts in the labor force, domestic and foreign sources of raw materials, etc.[52]

The mutual relations of the EPU's and the state would be outlined, specifying the resources that the state would allow them for expansion and the funds that they would remit to the state. The FYP would list the key new projects and the aggregate of investment available for each EPU for modernization and expansion. The EPU would finance replacement or overhaul of assets from a share in depreciation allowances. The EPU would also be issued guidelines on the labor force and basic raw materials that it could expect during the FYP. The branch and EPU's FYP's should not only tabulate the allocated investments, but should also stipulate the expected results in terms of labor productivity, costs, quality, technical standards, and growth of output. Hence, the FYP would estimate the volume of output, GY, and profit. The EPU could be bound to remit a given share of GY to the state. Supported by an effective incentive scheme, the system could function without binding EPU's to output, assortment, or quality indexes. However, a sharp deviation from those indexes (in any direction) during the course of the FYP, if all reserves had been exhausted, would call for a modification of the plan. The use of value parameters and incentives would regulate the enterprise's activity and induce it to fulfill its FYP. On the basis of actual conditions, these economic instruments would detail the plan further and correct its shortcomings.[53]

The techniques of plan construction were also challenged, but here generalities were particularly pronounced. There was little clarification of such thorny subjects as the objective function, choice criteria in the macroplan, economic verification of production processes, etc. Among others, Otakar Turek suggested that plan construction should start from the "conditions of the growth of production," rather than from set targets for the volume of production or consumption. He argued that, to begin with, two sets of data would be required: 1) a summarized orientation survey and 2) technical-economic studies of the development of individual branches.[54]

The survey would indicate the general guidelines for the economy's development; particularly whether investments would be primarily channeled to modernization or expansion and to heavy or light industry; what would be the general directions in manpower, fuels, electric power, etc. But at this stage no definite proportions would be predetermined. The purpose of the survey would be limited to determining the over-all concept of development. The preparation of such a survey would begin by analyzing the current economic situation and by finding alternative ways of overcoming the constraints. An analysis of the world trends in technology would serve to supplement the trends extrapolated from the analysis of the current domestic scene. The conclusions drawn from these analyses would constitute a basis for concretizing the "goals of the plan." Concurrently, it would be necessary to foresee what possible bottlenecks might arise and to attempt to eliminate them at the planning stage by anticipatory measures, structural changes, and reserves. In the final stages of preparing the survey, summary balances of foreign trade, of investment construction, of manpower, and of key raw materials and semifabricates would have to be worked out.

At the same time, studies of the development of individual branches would be prepared. They would be worked out on the basis of the announced preliminary guidelines of the survey, but without being binding, so that the variants of branch studies could serve to correct the assumptions of the survey. Turek expected that the branch studies would claim more investments than could be sustained by the economy. But this in itself would afford the planners the possibility of comparing the effectiveness of the individual proposals and of eliminating the least effective ones from "competition."

Thus, the first phase of the work on the perspective plan would be completed. Then by the method of successive approximations, the branch studies would be integrated with the survey to arrive at a balanced plan variant. In this process the method of balances would come into focus, but its importance would not be overstressed as in the past.

When shifting from extensive to intensive development, the investment projects in progress limit the freedom of choice. But resources could not be automatically set aside for completing these projects, for to do so would create the danger of perpetuating the extensive development and of restricting the scope of the shift. The unfinished projects would have to compete for resources with the proposed new ones and, if they proved less effective, they would have to be abandoned. Some losses of this nature would have to be expected when carrying out such a shift.

The perspective plan would have to be stable in its basic design, but alterations in relations could not be avoided. However, each branch and enterprise would have to be aware of its perspective tasks and would have to subordinate current decisions to them. The perspective plan would inevitably have to be amended annually to incorporate the new realities, technical innovations, etc. A form of so-called continuous planning could be evolved by projecting the next FYP during the course of the current FYP, with an over-all perspective of ten to fifteen years. The duration of operational plans could be differentiated by branches. For example, in industries with a long production cycle, plans could span several years, whereas in industries with an especially short cycle, plans could span periods shorter than a year.[55]

It was noted that, since the basic criterion

of economic growth is growth of national income--the source of investment and consumption--the pivot of the long-term plan should be the choice of the rate of growth of national income, accompanied by measures which would bring it about or approach it in practice.[56] In order to achieve or approach balanced economic growth, the constraints (barriers to economic growth--or "ceilings," as referred to by Michal Kalecki) would have to be observed. The growth rate of national income is determined primarily, _ceteris paribus_, by the share of investment and the volume of investment needed for a given increase in national income (an investment coefficient). A larger increase in national income can, _ceteris paribus_, be propelled by an increased share devoted to investment. But there are limits to the extent to which investment can be expanded, as discussed in Chapter 1. The end of the economic process is increase of consumption and investment is merely a means to achieve this end. An over-all substantiation of the volume, composition, and trend of development of consumption would be required in order to solve the whole complex of problems involved in approximating the selected growth rate of national income. Only after this phase of planning is completed would it be possible, according to Karel Kouba, to tackle the problems of the "desired and possible branch structure of production and national income, and of foreign trade," to evaluate the effectiveness of variants of technical development, and to solve the problems of demand for investments and of the envisaged supply of and demand for labor.[57]

Whereas the traditional system features "planning by directives," the basic characteristic of the central plan in the new system would be its "organic integration" with the market as one of the principal instruments for propelling economic growth.

> Integration of the plan with the market mechanism makes it possible to extend the gamut of stimulants to economic growth. In the directive system, the central plan

> strictly laid down the allocation of investment funds, raw materials, and labor force. [In the new system] the central plan will not be the unique source of stimulus to growth.[58]

It was argued--albeit with much ambiguity--that in the proposed system,

> the plan anticipates market trends and establishes their direction according to a number of aims and guiding lines for social development. The plan at the same time has an active influence on the future market since it independently affects future trends by its choice of optimum lines of development and by calculated application of social preferences.[59]

Admittedly, the quality of the plan would largely depend on the quality of market research. "The central criterion in the choice of macro-proportions is the principle of economic rationality." The focus was on the selection of the best plan variant. On the basis of previous references to Oskar Lange, it seems that Kouba understood the principle of economic rationality to be:

> a general principle of procedure when the end and means of activity are quantified. This principle assets that the maximum degree of realization of the end is achieved by proceeding in such a way that either for a given outlay of means the maximum degree of realization of the end is achieved, or that for a given degree of realization of the end the outlay of the means is minimal.[60]

Admittedly, but with little operational meaning,

> Some aims and guiding lines for development will at the same time be influenced by social preferences. These exceptions to the principle of economic rationality make it possible to give priority to

social, health, defence, or other non-economic considerations where appropriate.[61]

It was argued that in the proposed system favorable conditions would be created "for genuine participation of enterprises in the drawing-up of the national economic plan." The draft proposals would be subjected to preliminary verification on the basis of active interaction and dialogue between the center and the micro-units.[62]

Emphasizing the cybernetic approach to the plan, Oldrich Kyn stressed that it does not hold "that any activity other than that prescribed by the plan is generally worse from the standpoint of over-all interests of society than the activity that results in the fulfillment of the plan." Under the traditional system, it was questionable to what extent the plan really reflected actual needs. The essential difference between the traditional and the proposed systems is that in the latter there apparently is harmony of the goals of society and micro-units and "that it is not necessary to resolve conflicts through an interest in fulfilling the plan." The new system envisages extensive operation of the market mechanism "because only in this way can the manufacturer become dependent directly on the satisfaction of consumer demands." The plan could override consumers' preferences "only where the freely developing relations between producer and consumer are in conflict with the goals of socialist society." The plan's important role is that of a forecast of feasible economic development. But the plan drafted on the basis of a forecast must be probabilistic and not deterministic. Hence, during the course of economic development the plan must constantly be corrected by a mechanism of flexible adjustments to unforeseen changes at all levels.[63]

The supreme test is: What action would the planner take (or refrain from taking) if the economy should develop at variance with the plan? Would he accept the "unplanned correctives" as a valid verification of the plan? Or, would he stand by the plan and consider any significant departure from it as unfavorable to the economy? Would departures from the plan immediately be judged as contrary to the interest of society?

Some economists saw the main function of the central planner as steering enterprises "along lines leading to satisfaction of social needs" reflected in the political-economic goals of the long-term plan which could not be replaced by "anything else." Stress on market relations and incentives would not at all mean that the central planner would be deprived of all powers of direct intervention in the economy's development of the use of commands, although the latter would be the exception rather than the rule. Essentially, it was not envisaged to assign volume and composition of output targets and to impose limits on inputs.[64]

Central planning, it was argued, could no longer be identified with pinpointing all microeconomic processes, if only because of the information gap. The market could perform these functions much better than the "poor quality" plan assignments. The acceptance of a product by the user is the final test. In order to induce the producer to care about satisfying the users' needs, his material interest should be linked with the sale of goods.[65] The enterprises' employees would be guided by the maximization of their earnings and should be rewarded according to their performance (productivity). Bohumil Komenda insisted that the crux of the proposed system was that the plan would cease to be regarded as an instrument limiting and replacing the functions of the market, directly regulating the relations between enterprises, but would become a system of measures ensuring the development of the market and promoting the operations of all enterprises to function as buyers and sellers on the market.[66]

All economic units would act as independently operating subjects, paying for all their expenditures from their revenue, which would depend on their ability to sell their products. Guided by profit, those economic units would be entitled to make autonomous decisions on how, what, when, and for whom to produce. As long as the volume and composition of enterprises' output was essentially decided upon by the central plan which predetermined also what was delivered to whom, and users were told what they would receive from whom and when, one could not speak of utilizing market relations. In order for the market to function, the producer would have to be allowed to procure his inputs and to sell his products freely on the market. This actually would mean that the market could not be limited only to a certain sector of the economy.[67] In other words, producer goods were also to be treated as commodities traded between socialist enterprises, with the exception of "minor quantities" of goods in short supply to be rationed in "exceptional cases." The point was not only to foresee market trends and to adjust the output program accordingly, but also for the planned output to be altered in accordance with actual demand. The point in question was to get a fit between supply and demand not only in determining the structure of consumer goods industries, but eventually in determining the structure of the whole economy.[68]

Such proposals were branded by some as underrating the role of planning and overrating that of the market and as being much too radical for they would be at loggerheads with the planned character of the socialist economy and were nothing more than a brand of modern capitalist state intervention. Although Oldrych Truhlar admitted that he might be accused of dogmatism, he contended that planning must proceed by assigning directives, rather than by relying on competition. He pointed to, what appeared to him to be, a confusion in the reformers' concept of the plan and the market. If enterprises are to be guided by the plan, their assignments are to reach them by means of prices which would reflect the planned goals. But then, he contended, the system would not materially differ from the existing one in that the price would be an instrument of the plan and of the planned allocation of resources, rather than a reflection of the interests of enterprises and of the power they can wield in the national economy.[69]

Two economists of the SPC stressed that those discussing the merits of the new system often misunderstood the role of the market in a planned economy, assigning to the market virtually the role of a servo-mechanism and shifting state intervention in restructuring the economy to a secondary plane. But the long-term plan would have to be an imperative framework of development, and only within this framework could the market be a guide. On the basis of information emanating from the market, the plan would be improved and concretized. But the scope of decisions of individual enterprises would be restricted to current decision-making; for otherwise the enterprise would impede progress toward fulfilling development targets. Within this framework, they saw a limited discretion for enterprises in price-setting.[70]

Even though there were some voices in the wilderness doubting the validity of the concept of the "enterprises' material interest" and voicing qualms about having introduced it and having encouraged enterprises to act on their own, rather than in the social, interest,[71] by and large there was unanimity of opinion in favor of steering this interest in the "desired path." It was generally conceded that enterprises acted in their own interests when making production decisions, rather than in the interests of their customers. These decisions could not possibly be eliminated altogether by some sort of all-seeing and all-pervasive direction of activity from the center. Hence the problem remained to be solved by ensuring that the interests of the producers would not spur them to action detrimental to their customers.[72]

One of the more stimulating controversies developed on the subject of GY versus profit incentives. The gist of the controversy can be stated as follows: On the one hand, proponents of the GY scheme argued that wages paid from GY would have to be earned by production and sale of goods required by users. Thus "the full value of the wages paid, even if the amount is not planned by directives, will always be covered by the corresponding value of goods that are really needed." On the other hand, those who favored a profit-incentive scheme were for central planning of wage funds in order not to impair the balancing of the population's income with the availabilities of consumer goods.[73]

In the past, by using a piece-rate system, output norms, premiums for savings of inputs, etc., attempts were made mainly to cope with the technical aspects of production. If the worker complied with all technological rules and if he did not waste any time or material inputs, it did not necessarily mean that the output produced met the users' requirements or was produced in an economical way. According to the proponents of the GY scheme, in order to steer the incentive system on the right path, the employees' income must be geared to the revenue from output sold. To make the system effective, the composition of planned output must be decided by manufacturers in direct contact with users. Employees' earnings and the decentralized funds of enterprises should, in principle, depend on value newly created by the enterprise (value added).

Assuming that the enterprise has no control over price-setting, the size of GY would increase to the extent that materials and power per unit of output decreased, volume of output increased, and a larger proportion of output produced was sold. Conversely, assuming given material costs, the size of GY would alter as the prices of output changed. If the price movement should reflect alterations in supply and demand, change in GY could be used as a signal for enterprises to adapt production to demand. To promote a faster turnover of inventories, production costs should include (among costs of goods sold) also the increase in stocks of work in process and of finished goods. It was argued that an increase in the share of output sold in relation to that produced induces a change in the volume of work in process which would be reflected as an alteration in the costs of goods sold. The more products are sold in relation to total output, the relatively lower will be the cost of goods sold at a given price and the higher will, therefore, be the GY. By relating the employees' income to the size of GY, employees would be induced to save costs and to produce goods of such quality that would be most advantageous in view of demand on the market. Though the enterprise could not determine prices, it could influence them by the quantity and quality of output it produced.

There might be a number of different ways of distributing GY. As a rule, it was assumed that enterprises would finance from their own resources replacement and maintenance of fixed capital (simple reproduction); short-term credits would finance working capital; and long-term credits would be used for expansion (expanded reproduction). If the enterprise earned an annual GY per employee as planned, it would transfer a predetermined share of this income to the state budget. The remainder would then constitute the enterprise's disposable GY. The first claim on this income would satisfy liabilities to the bank (interest on credits and installments due on long-term credits). The remainder would then become the source from which employees' earnings would be paid. The total wages paid would not exceed 90 per cent of this fund, with the remainder to be distributed as premiums at the end of the year. The premiums would essentially be related to the size of the basic wages.

If the enterprise failed to attain the planned GY per employee, there would generally be no reduction in the predetermined contribution to the state budget. Each decrease in attained GY, in relation to planned, would be reflected in the diminution of disposable GY and in a decline of the workers' fund. If the decline in disposable GY were so sizable that, after meeting its liabilities to the bank, the workers' fund would be smaller than the basic wages paid, the contribution to the state budget could be reduced as an exceptional measure; such a debt would not be written off, but would constitute an interest-bearing liability. This default would become a signal for the central authorities to take a closer look at the enterprise's management and to intervene with the aim of eradicating the shortcomings. If the enterprise attained a higher GY than that planned as a result of an upward price movement, it would be advisable to increase the budget's share proportionally to the excess. For the system to be especially potent, it would have to grapple with the problem of long-term incentives. The turnover of key managerial personnel of the enterprise would have to be reduced. If such employees were transferred, they would bear the full responsibility for their activity in their previous employment.[74]

From a short-run standpoint, it was argued, resistance to technical progress would be encountered when the GY scheme was used. It would be manifest in cases where new technology might occasion temporary difficulties that would interfere with production, increasing material costs and/or decreasing sales volume, thereby reducing GY.[75] The improvement of the incentive system alone could not resolve the problem of technical progress, nor could it prevent price increases. GY would be a meaningful performance criterion only with equilibrium prices. Consequently, relations between enterprises could not be regulated by means other than prices.[76]

It was especially the problem of differentiated versus uniform rates of budget levies on GY that gave rise to the profit versus GY controversy. The proponents of the uniform rates claimed that the defects of the traditional system would be very inconsistently eliminated by using a GY scheme with differentiated rates of budget levies. The reform proposals implied that detailed targets could not be assigned to enterprises because the center could not ascertain the detailed conditions in individual enterprises. Nevertheless, establishment of differentiated levies on GY would require the center to evaluate the divergent conditions. To set such levies, it would be necessary to estimate

GY at the beginning of the period, the projected increase of GY as a result of increased sales and decreased costs, etc. The center would set levies for a maximum of three years, and it would be difficult to foresee all the changes. Such a solution would hardly evoke the enterprise's interest in its development, because within a short time the levy would be changed, and when technical improvements began bearing fruit, the levy would be reset so as to reflect the higher technical level of the given enterprise, skimming off for the state the benefits of progress.

If this solution were adopted, it would not eliminate the multitude of conflicts about the size of the levy. Since the enterprises have more accurate information than the central bodies, they could always muster more convincing arguments. The superiors would defend their estimates by the right of the strongest. There would be no great departure from the traditional haggling.

Turek's criticism of this scheme did not take the central agencies to task for their lack of knowledge of specific conditions in different enterprises, but he questioned the desirability of obliterating the degree of technical and economic efficiency at enterprises by attempting to provide them with an "equal start."[77] This approach was defended by Jaroslav Libus who claimed that, in view of the different "objective conditions," differentiated rates of budget payments would be necessary to provide a common ground for evaluating performance. However, he suggested that branch directorates assign a uniform rate of budget payments to all their wards. This rate should be set with the vanguard enterprises in view. Conditions would be equalized by allowing rebates to individual enterprises. The aim would be to pinpoint the divergencies in efficiency and to undertake measures to eliminate them.[78]

Uniform rates set for the entire branch should eliminate the subjectivity inherent in the differentiated approach. The rates would reflect the standards of the average enterprise within a branch. The strife to improve performance above average would be tantamount to gaining an advantageous position. With uniform long-term rates, the enterprise would be interested in technical progress not only because it would benefit from the increased efficiency, but also because if it failed to develop, it would bear the consequences of its action, since its rate would not be adjusted to allow for backwardness. Under this scheme, should the enterprise be persistently unprofitable, it would be forced to go out of business.[79] In this connection, a wider latitude would have to be given to investment decisions at the lower echelons. But, as we shall see later, there was much hesitance, even among the more radical reformers, in advocating decentralized investments. Turek was aware of the difficulties that such a GY scheme would encounter. During the initial period, rebates should be allowed on levies as requested by enterprises that offered reasons for their inability to meet the uniform rate. Such a solution would be tantamount to differentiated rates. But requests for rebates would have to originate at enterprises, rather than from the superiors, and would then bring into focus the factors responsible for backwardness. The exemptions would be "temporary" and steps would have to be taken to remedy the situation.[80]

Planning with adequate reserves, some free price-setting, and competition among sellers would be required to make the GY scheme workable. But, according to the scheme's critics, it was doubtful whether such conditions could be assured. In some cases they might not even be desirable, in order to take advantage of economies of scale. Therefore, it might not be advantageous to base material incentives on GY which could be distorted by increasing prices and manipulating assortments. There were words of caution against the threat of inflation, particularly affecting the employees of the nonproductive sector where prices could not increase and where wages would not outpace gains in productivity. There would also be the danger that output quality would be lowered to save on material costs in order to increase GY.

Assuming differentiated rates of levy, the number of plan indexes might not necessarily diminish, for, to derive the contribution to the budget, it would not only be necessary to know the planned sales volume, but also material costs and GY and its distribution. The possibilities of realistic determination of contributions to the budget would further suffer from the difficulties to foresee the assortments and from greater price variations. Hence the same haggling would prevail. The attempts of the enterprise to maximize wages would encroach on the funds available for capital formation. To check the increased purchasing power, consumers' prices might have to be raised. When imbalances occurred, there would probably emerge a tendency to intervene by administrative measures to control purchasing power. Even though it would be advantageous to increase the weight of the flexible part of personal income, it was feared that the GY scheme would pose the danger of too much flexibility in both directions.[81]

From a practical standpoint, objections were raised to GY on the grounds that not even the strictest control could prevent the shifting of resources in favor of the workers' fund. This was the experience in Czechoslovakia--as we indicated--when enterprises were allowed the apportionment of funds between working capital and investment. Furthermore, there is every indication that the pressures would be even stronger and the results even more dangerous, since the fund in question would serve as a source of purchasing power, and manipulations in its favor would explode the precarious balance between the aggregate purchasing power and supply of consumer goods.[82]

It was argued that even the advantages claimed for GY could be achieved better by a properly constructed incentive system based on profit. GY is not really a measure of the enterprise's efficiency, primarily because it includes wages (and social security surcharges) which in many branches constitute the main share of costs. Reference was also made to the conflict between wages and accumulation in a socialist economy. An incentive system based on profit would solve the contradiction between the employees' interest in maximizing wages and the state's interest in capital formation. The enterprise's contributions to social security, bank interest charges, charges on capital, and different payments should be treated as cost factors that decrease the size of profit.

It was considered unrealistic to abandon the differentiated approach for a long time to come, mainly because of 1) considerable leveling of wages among individual branches and groups of employees; 2) striking variations in replacing fixed assets, in remodeling plants, and in expanding them; 3) low efficiency of certain capital investments, resulting in significant cost differentials; and 4) fallacies in pricing. Those would be the basic reasons for directive determination of the wage fund. The GY scheme might endanger a uniform statewide wage policy, with resulting wide wage differentials. To corroborate his position, Miroslav Tucek claimed that the Yugoslav difficulties could be partly traced to the irrational interregional structure of wages and the unjustified sharp wage differentials.

Although with profit incentives it would not be possible to avoid differences in earnings at various enterprises, the basic wage and the employees' share in improvement of performance would not be combined. The advantage would lie in the possibility to control fairly accurately the basic income and to allow variations of only the portion corresponding to profit-sharing. Consequently, the grip over the main part of earnings (basic wages) would be stronger under this system, allowing the state a firmer control.

The ineptitude of GY was, apparently, clear in that to be effective it had to be considerably modified. If workers' earnings depended exclusively on the enterprise's performance, it would lead to absurd situations in less efficient enterprises, necessitating the introduction of guaranteed minimum income. On the other hand, should enterprises be allowed to retain the entire surplus over and above the minimum wage fund, the state would be deprived of resources for accumulation. Therefore, a progressive tax on wages, or on that part which exceeds the guaranteed minimum, was expected. At least two conditions would have to be satisfied for a purposeful implementation of GY: 1) meaningful prices and 2) all employees would have to be able to gauge the extent to which their performance would enhance the efficiency of the enterprise and, hence, their earnings. Neither condition was yet, nor about to be, satisfied.

Tucek did not maintain the necessity of assigning directive wage funds. His compromise solution was to allow the enterprise to spend on wages, provided that it met its obligations to the state budget and that it repaid credits. However, he did not specify how the wage fund was to be determined. In cases of additional plan assignments, the wage fund would be augmented from central reserves. To allow for increased sales, the enterprises would be allowed unlimited augmentation of the basic wage fund, provided that the original proportions between the fund and contributions to the budget would be maintained.[83]

A defender of GY, Zdenik Kodet, saw the crux of the controversy in the manner in which the central planner would affect the distribution of income in the enterprises. When in the past profit was used as the performance criterion, only the variable share of personal income was geared to profit. The fixed share remained dependent on various measures of productivity. Hence the friction between different indexes. Maximization of wages and maximization of profit were at loggerheads, for, _ceteris paribus_, an increase in wages, decreased profit. But the tendency to maximize basic wages was always strongest. The central attribute of the GY scheme is that directives do not separate the basic wage fund from premiums, that the decision on apportionment rests with the enterprise, and that there is no need for the very cumbersome "planning" of the basic wage fund. The advantage claimed for GY is that wages could be influenced by controlling transfers to the budget, without having to resort to directives. It is striking that those in favor of the profit scheme were censured for favoring only a modification of the traditional system, whereas those in favor of the GY scheme claimed a sweeping change of the system.

Assuming that the enterprises would not be allowed decentralized investments, Kodet argued that the pressures to shift disposable GY to the workers' fund would not be counteracted. The restraining effect could be found in resorting to differentiated rates of payment into the budget. He would, however, resolve the problem by applying uniform rates of budget payments for a group of enterprises, to remain stable for one to three years. Such rates would afford a measure of objectivity in evaluating performance. If enterprises were allowed to plow back their GY into expansion, the tendency to distribute the entire GY in wages could be checked.[84]

Assuming that the enterprise would not be told what to produce and what limits were imposed on inputs and that it would be interested in maximizing GY per worker, the price would become the most important tool for flexible steering of its activity. At the same time, the price would become an important information device; it would essentially perform a parametric function, i.e., it would be a datum for suppliers and users.[85] A general, more protracted, price stability would be practically excluded, since this scheme would require equilibrium prices.

The creation of centrally controlled, but flexible, prices would require forms of price formation different from those heretofore employed. It was argued that it would be possible to set prices centrally and keep them unchanged for a longer period only for products which were not affected by drastic alterations in production conditions and for which only slow changes were taking place in supply-demand relations. This group would include basic raw materials, fuels, electric power, key metallurgical products, some products of the chemical industry, and building materials. Fixed prices for such products would have a stabilizing effect on costs of all branches of the processing industries. But, the argument went, for products such as machines or consumer goods, the underlying supply-demand relations were constantly changing and prices cannot be centrally determined for each product. Since central price control was considered necessary, in order to prevent enterprises from raising prices and restricting output, it was argued that price formation should be guided indirectly by setting limits on prices. Such prices would set either a ceiling or a floor which market prices would not be allowed to exceed, or would provide a range within which market prices would have to remain.[86] Upper price limits could also be fixed for so-called standard products, chosen as most representative of certain groups of goods. In such a manner, the range of prices of similar products would be delimited. The authorities would have to check whether a sufficient quantity of standard goods was available on the market. If it were not, because the producer was trying to force buyers to purchase a similar product at a higher price, then, either by administrative measures or by imposing a "speculative" tax, the authorities could force the producer to produce the standard item. If, however, there were few standard products on the market because of a shift in demand toward the newer similar goods, then the authorities would consider the latter to have become the standard products.[87]

The largest number of products should fall into the limited price category. Central approval would be required for changing price limits. Limits could be set for groups of products aggregated according to some common characteristic. This type of pricing would be applied to products of crucial significance (e.g., machinery) whose specificity could not be determined a priori and which were subject to obsolescence and also to those products whose prices might be threatened by monopolistic practices. The prices of products which were not within the above categories could be set by negotiation between supplier and user.[88] But, as Sik emphasized, this group "takes in articles of minor importance from the standpoint of economic progress and the standard of living."[89]

According to another variant of the three-tier price system, fixed prices would be used where there were usually a single producer and several buyers. The formation of such prices would not differ much from the past. The relative stability and uniformity of prices would be preserved. Free prices would be used for goods produced by several suppliers for one or more buyers, and would be set by agreement between them. The proposals to introduce limited prices should emanate from the supplier or buyer, but not from the center.[90]

It was argued that the center's inability to determine effective prices did not signify that it should not control price formation. The problem was one of combining the center's prerogatives with a much wider jurisdiction for producers to determine prices on the basis of mutual agreements with buyers. Central control over prices would also be exercised through a system of taxes and subsidies and by issuing regulations on price formation, on cost calculations, etc. Also, in exceptional cases, the center might intervene by setting prices on products which did not fall into the fixed price category, thereby overruling the lower echelon's pricing prerogatives.[91] Here lay the danger that the center might find too many reasons for overruling pricing prerogatives too often.

It was contended that, even for modern capitalism, direct price controls were indispensable and that indirect controls were insufficient. "The central organs cannot be denied the right to make directive decisions to increase or decrease prices whenever and wherever the economic situation warrants it."[92]

Whereas in the traditional system the buyer was virtually uninterested in arresting price increases by the supplier--he might even have favored them, since they enhanced the reported plan fulfillment--in the envisaged scheme the buyer should vigorously resist the supplier's attempts to raise prices. This was expected to become an effective brake on the supplier's efforts to escalate prices. Another restraining factor would be the deliberate state policy to create a buyer's market. Apparently producers would enjoy considerable reserves, achieved by more balanced planning and orientation of production to the market. The distribution of GY was expected to play an important role in providing for the growth of real output to outpace that of earnings, arresting demand for consumer goods.

Objections to decentralization of price-setting by advancing the monopoly argument were considered to be exaggerated. Monopolistic practices would be restricted by the increasing importance of foreign trade. Exporting enterprises would be under the fire of competition. If enterprises are able to choose between domestic and foreign supply, there would be effective pressure on domestic producers. Secondly, an antimonopolistic policy could be applied. Enterprises' interest in enlarging sales volume could be largely strengthened by assigning greater weight to fixed components of costs, by lump sum taxes, and/or by fines for speculative price increases, for deteriorating quality, and for violating terms of delivery. Production-purchasers councils, composed of representatives from the main buyers, from superior organs, from the CSB, etc., could be set up to act as control organs. Monopolistic positions, due to concentration and specialization of production and resources, would not necessarily be detrimental. It was the traditional system that failed to use these opportunities adequately as do many advanced capitalist countries.[93] Finally, on the assumption that administratively created monopolies would be dismantled, it was argued that the problem would be rather one of oligopoly which would not necessarily hamper technical progress.[94]

Even in cases of pure monopoly, it should not follow that GY would rise as a result of price increases. Whether an increase of GY per employee would result from a price change would depend, _inter alia_, on price elasticity of demand and on cost-volume relationship.[95]

The wholesale price reform should not be confined simply to incorporating new charges, for such prices would not necessarily be equilibrium prices. After the establishment of new wholesale prices, the prices would have to be varied to approach market prices. As a result of those price changes a number of enterprises would find themselves in difficulties: some because they would have to cut prices in order to sell their output, and others because of the increased costs of material inputs. There would be a storm of protests against the allegedly "spontaneous and speculative movement of the entire price level." As a result, various administrative interventions might be called into play to control the market. Obviously, the narrower is the scope of free prices and the larger that of fixed prices, the more restricted is the sphere of operation of the market.[96]

The center of administrative interference should shift away from price formation to influencing supply or demand. If this condition should be met, all pricing could be entrusted to enterprises. The market mechanism could not function properly if the price movement, resulting from a change in supply-demand relations, was not transmitted to both the producer and consumer. The restoration of the market would require elimination of the existing independence of wholesale from retail and world prices. Turnover tax, as the difference between two independently fixed prices, should be abolished and replaced by a tax as a rate to be added to the wholesale or retail price. In the same vein, special coefficients should be used so that the relations of wholesale prices should approximate those of world prices.[97]

At a conference in March, 1964, sponsored by the State Price Office (SPO) on the role of prices in the new system, serious doubts were expressed on the actual feasibility of a flexible price system. It was argued, not without good reason, that under conditions of a sellers' market in producer goods, it would be difficult to expect a flexible price policy to have beneficial results. Moreover, it was pointed out that a flexible price policy might have a detrimental effect on management's long-term planning.[98]

Even the term "flexible" price was ambiguous. For example, Julius Branik of the research department of the MF, argued that the reason for introducing a more flexible price-setting system was to "actively attempt a stability in price relations by means of flexible changes in the price relations." He advocated the closer relation of prices to costs and price development to cost development and the retention of the dual price system, which, apparently is so suitable for "creating price relations in wholesale and retail prices independent from each other."[99]

Granted that the existing price system was not established with the same purposes in mind as those that motivate its reform, two pricing experts of the SPC asked whether it would be feasible to dismiss the functions that prices had heretofore performed. How well would flexible prices serve for planning (aggregating, accounting, controlling, and comparing) past, present, and future assignments? According to them, central planning could not do without these functions.[100]

The miscarriage of the 1958-59 reform in the investment area was probably responsible for the unwillingness on the part of reformers to invigorate the role of decentralized investment in the contemplated reform. It seems, however, that any such reform proposal, with restricted investment decision-making, would be inconsistent and would incorporate within itself the germs of recentralization, for it would be, inter alia, a potential brake on the long-range outlook of the enterprise.

In connection with the GY scheme, Jiri Tesar recognized the need for decentralized investment, but to encompass mainly modernization and to be financed by interest-bearing, reimbursable bank credits. The bulk of investment should be decided centrally and financed directly by the budget. The enterprises should pay a capital charge computed at a uniform rate on the basis of the depreciated value of fixed assets. To counteract the protracted construction periods, charges should be levied from the planned date of completion. The capital charge should be deducted from GY. Reimbursement of credits for decentralized investments and payment of interest on those credits should be made from the enterprise's share of GY. Such a method would arrest unplanned increase of investment.[101] It was also suggested, that credit be used for financing centralized investments and that the interest be charged to the investor, rendering him sensitive to construction costs. Higher interest rates should prevail when planned completion was delayed.[102]

In his scheme of things Turek visualized the perspective central investment plan as one that would allot specific investment funds for the modernization or development of given branches of industry, based on bids submitted by the branches, indicating the effectiveness of the proposed undertaking. A given share of investment would remain to be distributed annually in the form of credits that enterprises could secure for investments on the basis of the criterion of the recoupment period. One of the means to stop abuse of centrally allotted investment would be the levy on capital.[103]

As for working capital, it would be advisable to finance it entirely by bank credits, with differentiated interest rates for various purposes.

Normatives would be no longer binding, but would be used as data for establishing a credit plan with the bank.[104] The bank would be allowed discretionary powers in differentiating the interest rate and would control the state of inventories. The planning of working capital would be confined to negotiations between the enterprise and the bank.[105]

The profitability test should be the touchstone for deciding whether credit will or will not be extended. The state budget would subsidize activity if criteria other than profitability should be the basis on which decisions are made.[106]

In order to impart greater efficiency to foreign trade, a rapprochement between the producers and foreign trade organizations and the reflection of world market prices on the performance of industrial and foreign trade enterprises were suggested. The key bone of contention seems to have been the extent of organizational integration. The reformers generally favored a larger degree of integration, whereas the officials, and especially those responsible for foreign trade, were for a greater independence and autonomy of foreign trade. Several organizational solutions were envisaged: 1) The foreign trade enterprise that functions as a middleman under direct supervision of the Ministry of Foreign Trade. Such an enterprise should be endowed with considerable autonomy and should be fully responsible for the effectiveness of its operations. This form would be particularly suitable for import trade. 2) The foreign trade enterprise that functions on <u>khozraschet</u> and is directly subordinated to an EPU and also to the Ministry of Foreign Trade. Such a variant would provide for a close contact between production and foreign trade, but would pose the problem of dual subordination. This form would be particularly suitable in the export trade. 3) Joint boards of cooperation between producers and foreign trade. Such boards would consist of specialists from both areas with sufficient authority to act on long-term and annual plans for developing foreign trade, on questions of incentives for both areas, etc.

4) Finally, a joint technical and commercial division. This organization would be set up to act as a coordinating link between foreign trade and producing enterprises, in order to eliminate work duplication.[107] The Minister of Foreign Trade elucidated the draft principles by affirming that foreign trade would continue to be centrally conducted by foreign trade enterprises under the direct aegis of his Ministry. He seemed to reject any integration of foreign trade enterprises into EPU's and his solution for closer cooperation ran along the lines of variant 4. In his opinion, such technical and commercial service divisions, staffed with foreign trade and production specialists, would provide industry with participation in foreign trade to the extent to which it is entitled.[108]

It was suggested that the directive plan indexes be restricted to over-all volume so as to permit more flexible adaptation to foreign trade requirements. In the case of obligations to CMEA trading partners, the assortment could be itemized in physical and value terms, if required--probably to ensure the meeting of quotas specified in the material balances of CMEA importers. The affidavits, stating that the domestic producer could not supply a given product before the product could be imported, would have to be foregone if imports were to promote a competitive spirit among domestic producers. Both producers and foreign trade enterprises should share in the benefit derived from obtaining a higher price in export. The production and foreign trade plans would be calculated in foreign prices and price relations, expressed in kcs. by means of conversion coefficients.[109] The producer should be allowed a share of foreign currency for exceeding his export targets, to be used for importing equipment, etc. He should also share in the savings of foreign currency derived from importing a cheaper new material and should be rewarded for introducing new products into foreign markets.[110]

Among the various shades of opinion expressed on the workability and viability of the proposed system, a particularly noteworthy criticism from the more conservative circles came from Miroslav Sokol of the SPC. While admitting the "basic correctness" of the ideas, he argued, often not without good reasons, that the application of the proposed scheme would be fraught with inconsistencies and difficulties.

The basic idea of the GY scheme would be to use market relations to determine the short-run volume and composition of output and to tie in employees' incentives to the enterprise's GY by determining their share in the fluctuations of GY's size. In the long run the economy's basic proportions would be largely determined by the plan and executed by the volume and structure of centralized investments. The proposed system should be, to a degree, a self-regulating mechanism automatically assuring balanced development. One of the major problems would be that of feedbacks. Should the price of a bottleneck product increase, the manufacturer should take measures to expand production of the product in short supply. But the response mechanism could be operative only if certain conditions were fulfilled: such as sufficient elasticity of production. In order for the enterprise to be able to increase the flow of production, obviously, it must either have the available productive capacity or the right and means to expand capacity. Among other conditions, the enterprise must have the opportunity of procuring the necessary inputs. The enterprise may still respond to the market by reorganizing its product mix--provided it is a varied one--within the constraint of fixed capacity, if it can obtain the required inputs.

Sokol argued that it is questionable whether, under Czechoslovak conditions, sufficient supply elasticity can be attained, particularly since the proposed system would limit the scope of the market in many respects. Most investments would be centrally decided. Prices of raw materials would largely be centrally set and stable, and there would still be central wage-setting policy and controls of the labor market. The contention that supply will outpace demand could not be maintained. For instance, employment is exceptionally high. The labor reservoir in agriculture is exhausted. Shortages are not uniformly spread. But an over-all increase of employment does not seem feasible. The experience of many capitalist countries indicates that problems of labor supply are acute even at a much lower employment rate than the one attained in Czechoslovakia. When the new system was introduced in Yugoslavia the situation was different in that Yugoslavia had a large army of unemployed; over half the population was employed in agriculture, and women in the labor force amounted to only 24 per cent.

Czechoslovakia probably could not increase foodstuff production in a relatively short period without substantial price increases, with adverse effects on living standards. Sokol argued that market equilibrium should be established <u>before</u> the new system was introduced. He questioned whether this could be achieved with administrative methods. He warned against inflationary pressures, citing Yugoslav statistics in support of the contention that an inflationary movement manifested itself primarily in the sphere of retail prices and personal income, and to a smaller degree in that of wholesale prices. This was probably due to the maximization of current income of employees and to attempts to channel GY primarily to increased wages.

The proposed scheme would attempt to remedy the encroachment of enterprises on investments and the inflationary pressures, essentially by two methods: 1) by imposing restrictions on disposable GY and 2) by imposing differentiated tax levies on GY.

As others had done, Sokol also warned against monopolistic malpractices. Such monopolistic trends would be particularly accentuated in branches where sizable investments were required. It would be unrealistic to hope to counteract monopolistic tendencies by sizable foreign exchange reserves or by creating conditions of competition. In the case of consumer-oriented products, flexibility of wholesale prices could be combined with flexible retail prices, but even in this sphere there would be serious problems in view of different turnover tax rates. However, substantial difficulties would be encountered in the case of capital goods, because the predominant share of investment would be centralized and assigned as binding directives to the investors. Under these circumstances, it would be unrealistic to expect market pressures to be applied to the suppliers of these investment projects. As long as budgetary grants were received for financing investments, it would be wishful thinking to rely on the investor to exert sufficient pressure to lower investment costs.

It was anticipated that centralized investments and deliveries for export would essentially claim the entire capacity of the key enterprises of heavy machine-building. How could prices substantially influence producers under these circumstances? Sokol referred to the system as a "double-faced" one, for it would create the superficial impression that management has a wide scope of discretion and that it is not subjected to directives; whereas the producer would be actually assigned what and for whom to produce, and the user would be told what has been allotted to him. It seemed likely that the prices of investment and other key producer goods would be kept fixed at the level approved in the investment plan. But without flexible prices the new system would be paralyzed. The solutions for consumer-oriented industries and for those producing producer goods were inconsistent. Sokol, correctly, pointed out that if prices of, say, fibers for textiles were fixed, it would be necessary to ration these fibers as long as excess demand prevailed. This direct distribution would condition the output volume of the processing industry which would not be able to adapt to the pattern of demand for its products.

Inflationary pressures might result from attempts to translate the largest possible share of GY into wages. The size of wage payments would be determined basically by differentiated levies on GY to the state budget. While in Yugoslavia a relatively large portion of GY is left with the enterprise which is empowered to decide its allocation among wages, investments, and various other funds, in the Czechoslovak proposals this scope of decision-making was considerably restricted. The differentiated tax payments would supposedly determine relatively accurately the desired wage fund. Sokol questioned the feasibility of making such differentiations and pointed out that the differentiated rate could be effective for only two or three years, with all the ensuing disadvantages of the short-run viewpoint. As other critics had pointed out, he criticized the consistent and detailed differentiation of levies on GY according to the objective conditions of the enterprise as suffering from all the errors and subjectivity of the traditional planning system.

How would the introduction of the new system affect the saving of labor? On the face, it would seem that enterprises would aim at reducing their labor force as much as they could. But this would not be necessarily so. The enterprises would be interested in cutting down on employment if additional employment would tend to decrease wages below the level already attained. However, if, as a result of additional employment, it were possible to increase the personal income per employee previously attained, the enterprises would naturally tend in this direction.[111]

As a footnote to this discussion it would perhaps not be an altogether sterile endeavor to note the position of those who stood for a modification of the traditional system, rather than its overhaul.

Due to the reformers' acceptance of pricing and wage restrictions on the enterprises, Truhlar claimed that their contention, that in the reformed system the enterprise would be an "independent commodity producer," was merely an unsubstantiated assertion. The interest of the enterprise would in such a system manifest itself only to the extent that it could offer premiums to its employees. And this is not at all the same thing as the interest of the "commodity producer," which is to survive, to renew, and to develop as an independent and self-supporting producer. Since the proposed reform is not a thoroughgoing revision of the entire system, but merely an amendment of the existing one, to render it more flexible and adaptable, it would not be objectionable on ideological grounds. However, Truhlar doubted whether the long-term plan goals would really reach the enterprise, whether the regimentation of GY would really be effective in eliminating the negative effects of the market mechanism, and whether the market would really be helpful in determining development.

Truhlar suggested that the improvement of the management system should aim not only at streamlining and promoting development of the economy, but also at removing some of the serious economic dislocation that had accumulated. But these cannot all be tackled at once, but progressively by choosing one or two problems and solving them consistently, so as to eliminate them in the shortest possible time. This would mean selecting the basic link and devoting resources to it, in order to rapidly achieve a high standard in this area, and then to move to another. This, of course, could only be done at the center, and would be best implemented by central allocation of resources. The backbone of such a system would be the national economic plan, with a given number of assignments _in natura_ and a network of balances. But some of the planning and balancing functions could be delegated to the lower echelons, including enterprises. Maximum work discipline and "full material responsibility" should be expected from enterprises. This discipline would be perforce tied into assignment of tasks and control of their execution. To improve quality control, control could be exercised by the buyer in cases of large shipments and important materials, as has been successfully practiced in cases of military shipments. The authority of enterprise directors should be broadened in the final elaboration of the output program, in organizational changes, in forms of remuneration of various employees, etc. In connection with the material interest of employees, Truhlar would favor a substantial increase in the basic pay of managerial personnel, to replace the existing system of making up for the low salaries with various more or less certain higher premiums which often drive the employees' interest into "undesirable" directions. The entire premium system would have to be streamlined so that the retained premiums would not be offered for fulfilling obligations, but for efforts over and above the call to duty.[112]

Jaroslav Vejvoda argued for central control over investment and for competition among firms so as to produce the "right" product mix and to reduce costs. Premiums should be geared to cost reduction. The firm's independence could only be confined to current activity. The total accumulation should be extracted and concentrated at the center from where it would be channeled in conformity with the central plan, with the center deciding on the direction, the recipient, and the type of investment. The enterprise should not have control over accumulation in order not to contravene the center's investment priorities. Modernization of fixed assets should not be entrusted to enterprises, but should remain within the center's purview. The enterprise's autonomy in investments should be confined to maintenance of fixed assets in working order and to some general improvements. In order to impose strict controls over the investment system, the price that constitutes the producer's revenue should not include the surcharge for capital formation.

Although the state would be supreme decision-maker, it would allow the beneficiary of the investment to contact builders and suppliers independently and to engage them to execute the project. The aim would be to have the executants compete for the projects determined at the center, so that they should fully utilize their capacity, improve the quality, and execute the project according to users' needs. The beneficiaries of investments should exert pressure on contractors to execute the project as cheaply as possible, for investment costs would influence production costs through depreciation charges.

The output of the enterprise would no longer be centrally assigned to it, but would have to conform to market demand. The forces of competition should compel the producer to abide by consumers' needs as expressed in the orders received. Vejvoda sanctioned market relations between producers and users of producer and consumer goods, as long as the state would have firm grip over investment activity and investments would be undertaken in accordance with central priorities and not in response to market forces.[113] Even so he was criticized by Kocman for underrating the role of planning and for overrating that of the market.[114] And a strange market it would be, for Vejvoda favored centralized price-setting, with prices including only the c + v components, so that the producer would be deprived of the surplus product and could not manipulate it to boost wages. The only avenue open to him to increase wages would be to reduce costs.[115]

In mid-1967, when the reform was being implemented--albeit hesitantly, as we shall see--voices were still being heard in the fraternity of economists that the new system transplants capitalist production relations into socialism. Vejvoda and Felix Oliva evinced a strong preference for rigid, all-embracing central planning. Vejvoda again stressed that the entire surplus product should be extracted from the enterprise, as otherwise it would be channeled to wage increases, for pressures to maximize current income could not be resisted, and investment activity would suffer. He was still calling for centrally determined prices to cover the planned average production costs of individual products. But the impracticality of the proposal rested, <u>inter alia</u>, in disregarding the limited information at the center and the enterprise's interest in inflating cost data--as the 1967 price revision had shown. Vejvoda was in favor of eliminating all market influence on prices, but, as Sik retorted, Vejvoda offered no substitute for market signals, and provided for no process of adjustment. Reminiscent of Mises in reverse, Oliva contended that competition can only exist where there is private ownership of the means of production; where there is collectivist ownership there can be no competition.[116]

Parallel to the discussions that were taking place, the first hesitating steps were being taken early in 1965 to give life to the draft principles and to initiate--what has since come to be called--the transitional period.

CHAPTER 4 BLUEPRINT FOR THE NEW PATTERNS

THE IMPLEMENTATION SCHEDULE

After approval of the draft principles by the CC at its plenary session in January, 1965, the government passed in March Resolution No.83 on the time table for introducing the reform measures. The main problems to be resolved in 1965 were outlined as: 1) creating conditions for implementing by January 1, 1966, the basic principles of the new system; 2) preparing the drafts of the 1966-70 FYP and of the 1966 national economic plan on the basis of the new system; 3) smoothly reorganizing the administrative apparatus; 4) determining the relationships, responsibilities, and prerogatives of the reformed central agencies; 5) elaborating the principles and methodology for revising wholesale prices; 6) initiating experiments to test particular features of the proposed reform; and 7) drafting proposals for incorporating the new system in other sectors of the economy (especially, agriculture and transportation) at a later date. A reorganized State Commission for Organization and Management (SCOM) and the SPC were charged with participating actively, coordinating, and cooperating in this work. The SPC's Committee for Improved Planned Management was enlarged by a number of additional experts. Various work groups were assigned to solve specific problems, with central agencies responsible for over-all coordination.

Obviously, successful reform implementation was contingent on observance of the schedule for introducing new measures. Whereas the assignment of control figures for the Fourth FYP and for the plan for 1966 was to follow the old administrative channels, using old prices, the draft plans would be submitted along the reorganized administrative lines and would be expressed in revised prices. The conversion of the plan would be an absorbing task. Hence, reorganization would have to proceed at a swift pace and such a method and scope of price changes would have to be selected as not to disturb the "over-all value relationships of the plan and the factors conditioning the use of economic management instruments."

It was envisaged that the following would be accomplished before the end of March, 1965: 1) control figures for the Fourth FYP and the 1966 plan would be drafted, and, as soon as they would be approved, they would be transmitted to the ministries and branches; 2) the proposal for the government regulations on the new system would be drafted, together with a proposal for planning instructions to be issued by the SPC; 3) instructions would be issued for preliminary branch calculations of budget levies; and 4) the administrative apparatus would be reorganized.

The preparation of control figures was considered to be an especially complicated undertaking. The new rules could not yet be directly applied. But the SPC was supposed "to have taken them into consideration," not only in preparing the control figures, but also in assigning them. The control figures were supposed to reflect "actual conditions and potentialities," without creating "excessive" tensions by diverting "excessive" amounts to investment and by demanding an "excessively" rapid growth rate. The binding indexes would be reduced in number. A more flexible execution of directives was anticipated for the latter part of the FYP.

The determination of contributions to the budget was, at the first stage, beset with many difficulties. The branches were expected to provide the necessary information by mid-1965. Also, it was expected that by mid-1965 the second preparatory stage should be reached, consisting of: 1) transmittal of Fourth FYP and 1966 plan control figures to the reorganized apparatus; 2) definite determination of all payments to the budget, except for the so-called basic payments which should be determined on the basis of the anticipated fulfillment of the 1965 plan recalculated in January 1, 1966, prices so as not to affect the minimum wage level; 3) completion of preparations for price revision and subsidies in order for branches to reach the required profitability; 4) specification of the methods of future price revisions; 5) completion of the reorganization and the assignment of new functions to central agencies; and 6) completion of methodological instructions on the implementation of the new system.

It was expected that the third stage of preparatory work should be concerned with finalizing the plan and with the transition to the new system so that it could be implemented by January, 1, 1966. An important part of this phase should have been improvement of internal management and organization of enterprises, drawing those at the lower managerial ranks into the preparation of reforms. In this phase the reports on experiments should have provided the necessary guidance.[1]

ADMINISTRATIVE REORGANIZATION

Reorganization, along the lines specified by the draft principles, took place by mid-1965. It was by no means a drastic reorganization, requiring the setting up of new agencies and the drawing up of new lines of subordination; as, for example, that of the U.S.S.R. at the beginning of 1966, where, although the form was not new, reorganization altered the administrative pattern. In Czechoslovakia, on the other hand, the administrative pattern was retained and only some links were streamlined. Thus, the administration of the economy by industrial ministries, as extensions of the state, was retained. Simultaneously, the existing grouping of enterprises into EPU's, functioning as intermediaries between the ministries and their enterprises, was also preserved. The most significant change seems to have been a process of consolidation which has reduced the number of EPU's by more than 50 per cent, i.e., from 236 to 102 EPU's.[2]

Both vertical and horizontal integration were resorted to. Vertical integration took place mainly in metallurgy, machine-building, and the chemical industry. By the end of 1965, the merging of three ministries, the Ministry of Metallurgy and Ore Mining, the Ministry of Heavy Machine-Building, and the Ministry of General Machine-Building, into the Ministry of Heavy Industry was considered necessary in order to avoid serious overlapping of supervision by various ministries over the same EPU which created great confusion and contributed to weakened central control. In construction, fuels, power, consumer, and food industries the planners mainly had recourse to horizontal integration. Of course, the process of integration was less intense in the less-developed branches of industry. However, its force and scope may be gauged from the following example. The former Ministries of Metallurgy and Ore Mining, Heavy Machine-Building, and General Machine-Building, respectively, supervised 28, 21, and 37 EPU's. After the initial changes, their EPU's were, respectively, reduced to 4, 7, and 12. After their amalgamation into the Ministry of Heavy Industry the total number of EPU's supervised by this Ministry became 22.[3]

The process of integration reinforced the specter of monopolies. It is quite possible that, guided by their interests, the branch directorates might curb competition between their wards. Therefore, it was suggested that it would be necessary to increase the independence of enterprises vis-à-vis the branch directorates.[4] But then it would be difficult to make the branch directorates accountable for the enterprises.

Faithful to the centralistic tradition, 41 out of 102 EPU's were located in Prague. This action was justified on the grounds that the subordinated enterprises were scattered throughout the country and that the Prague location would afford proximity to buyer and supplier EPU's, to foreign trade agencies, and to the central organs. Some attempts were made to locate the branch directorate in the largest enterprise of the group and in the area where most enterprises were concentrated. The average EPU grouped enterprises whose total employment amounted to 30,000 and whose gross output was about 2.1 billion kcs. Table 43 gives the distribution of EPU's by number of employees and by branches of industry and Table 44 the breakdown by gross production volume.

Table 43

DISTRIBUTION OF EPU's BY NUMBER OF EMPLOYEES AND BY BRANCHES OF INDUSTRY

Number of EPU's	Number of employees	Industries
12	1 - 5,000	Food and consumer goods
29	5,000 - 20,000	Consumer goods, food, construction, small machine-building
38	20,000 - 50,000	Machine-building, chemistry, metallurgy, fuels
8	50,000 - 100,000	Machine-building, metallurgy, fuels
3	100,000 and up	Iron metallurgy, automobiles

Source: HN, No. 20, 1965.

The general characteristics of the EPU's are: 1) subordination to the ministries, but as legal entities, responsible for their own financial results (the consolidated profit and loss statement of all their enterprises); 2) sole accountability to the state for fulfilling the binding indexes set for the branch; and 3) responsibility for effective management of the enterprises entrusted to their care. An EPU is managed by a branch directorate, whose director is responsible for the EPU's operations (one-man responsibility). Research and develop-

Table 44

DISTRIBUTION OF EPU's BY ANNUAL INDUSTRIAL GROSS OUTPUT

Number of EPU's	Annual gross output (million kcs.)
19	up to 500
12	500 - 1,000
53	1,000 - 5,000
6	5,000 and up

Source: HN, No. 20, 1965.

ment activity at the EPU's was strengthened. Out of the 30 organizations formerly attached to ministries and then transferred to EPU's, 22 were research institutes. Concurrently, the EPU's include specialized service, supply, marketing, and other services. Generally, the EPU's function as trusts in which one enterprise is of primary importance and the others are related to it by the production cycle. However, there are also EPU's functioning as combines (mainly in some branches of the consumer and food industries). In some cases, rather few in number, the combines do include enterprises which are endowed with considerable economic and legal independence.

As a rule, the degree of autonomy of subordinate enterprises differs in various EPU's. For example, the process will be more centralized if the end product of the enterprises is more complex. In some cases it is the EPU that decides on the volume, type, quality, and delivery terms of its enterprises. However, in most cases, the enterprises remain fully responsible for the organization of production, for their technology, and for costs. On the other hand, in cases of horizontal integration, where the production program and the customer-buyer relations are relatively stable, the role of the EPU is mainly limited to developmental policy.[5]

A consultative body, composed of representatives

from enterprises, Party cells, trade unions, the CSB, and the major customers, is attached to the branch directorate. This body deliberates on the key aspects of financial and production plans, on the allocation of investments, and on the distribution of the workers' funds. It also evaluates the performance of enterprises.

As far as the relationship between the ministry and the branch directorate is concerned, it was admitted that the ministry had not transferred all its operative activities to the branch directorates. It has retained some of them because "all prerequisites for utilizing economic management instruments have not been fully created." It was expected that these activities would be only carried out by the ministry through the transitional period and would be gradually relinquished to the EPU and the enterprise.[6]

The discernible tendency is to vest the larger scope of decision-making with the EPU. There are undoubtedly good economic reasons, such as the advantages ensuing from concentration and specialization. Moreover, the development parallels some of the organizational patterns of the West and its background could be traced to the prewar tendency for concentration in industry. However, the prevalent motive for the administrative creation of monopolies is probably the expediency of exercising control over a small number of relatively autonomous large units. The very fact of allowing EPU's to decide individually on the degree of autonomy they are going to allow their enterprises, is likely to produce overcentralization at the EPU level, mainly because the management of the EPU's is conscious of its responsibility vis-à-vis the center, because of inexperience with the new system, and because of a fear of manipulations at the enterprise level.

Among the cardinal problems in organizing the division of labor among central agencies, especially among the SPC, the State Commission for Technology (SCT), and the State Commission for Finance, Prices, and Wages (SCFPW), was that of coordination to avoid overlapping. In drafting the long-term plan, the SPC is expected to proceed from the submissions of government agencies, ministries, the Slovak Planning Commission, and the national committees. Proposals are submitted to the SPC by the specialized agencies; e.g., price and wage policies are submitted by the SCFPW. In turn, during plan implementation, these agencies are responsible for the carrying out of policies within their spheres, e.g., the SCFPW, in conjunction with the MF and the CSB (the head of the SCFPW is also head of the MF), is accountable for the implementation of the financial, credit, and incomes policies.

In order to provide for stricter control and inspection over the new system, the statistical service was divorced from the former Central Commission of People's Inspection and Statistics. The new State Statistical Office has been charged with providing more accurate data on the economy to all administrative bodies, with increasing the supply of data for planning purposes, and with improving financial, price, and wage statistics. The Central Commission of People's Inspection is an agency of the National Assembly (NA) and of the government. It prepares reports on observance of laws, regulations, and resolutions issued by the government, its agencies, and the Party. It supervises a network of control bodies charged with inspection and control at the lower echelons. In the sphere of control the MF is responsible for verifying payment of contributions to the state budget. The ministries regularly control the work of branch directorates which proceed similarly toward their enterprises. It is interesting to note that in 1967 the services of non-government auditing organizations were being tested on an experimental basis. Control over price observance is performed by the organizations empowered to set the different prices. This control will be guided by the SCFPW. Quality control is also expected to be improved owing to the services of the state testing system, subordinated to the SCT.[7]

EXPERIMENTS

The idea of using experiments in connection with implementing the new system underwent modification. Originally, it was contemplated that the very principles of the system would be extensively tested and then, after about two years, the final decision on implementation would be made, based on results of the tests.[8] But the pressing need to solve the problems faced, speeded up the implementation process. At the inception of widespread experimentation, early in 1965, the concept of experiments shifted. Tests were then viewed as preliminary work to the changeover on a national scale. The experiments were no longer expected to provide answers to questions, such as: Would profit or GY constitute the core of the incentive system? They were expected to smooth the way for the changeover by pointing to the difficulties encountered in the practical application under the diverse conditions of different branches. Having only a year's headstart on full-scale implementation, it was not expected that the results of experiments could offer concrete guidance for this implementation, but rather that some of the data gleaned quarterly from the experimenting enterprises might help to forestall initial problems. It was expected that, even when the actual changeover took place, there would be much room for experimentation; for the system would not be a rigid and ossified structure, but one open to trials and errors.[9]

Obviously, unlike an experiment in the natural sciences, an economic experiment cannot be conducted under laboratory conditions; hence, it cannot produce conclusive evidence on the correctness of a given thesis. Basically, there were two extreme views on the experiments: those belonging to the believers in the all-healing effects of the new system and those belonging to the skeptics. The latter jokingly pointed to the proposed experiment to alleviate heavy traffic in Prague in which fifty cars would be chosen to drive on the left while the others continued to drive on the right side of the road.[10]

Qui vivra verra!

The experiments were largely affected by the attitudes of management. Some managers feared that a successful experiment (where resources were revealed) would be followed by more exigent payments into the budget for the next year. Furthermore, those intrinsically opposed to the new system could conduct tests in such a manner as to prove their uselessness.[11] The many unsolved problems at the higher echelons also created an atmosphere of uncertainty at the level of enterprises. Distrust of experiments was manifested in doubt that the principles of the new system would be given life, in suspicion that the uncovered reserves would be projected into tauter norms, in suppositions that improved performance would only benefit the managers, in expectations of continuing reorganizations, etc.[12]

In the course of experiments the immediate superiors of the enterprises were blamed for their lack of foresight. Instead of hiring experts who were capable of analyzing the situation, they encumbered themselves with larger staffs and held on to the operative management of production. It was repeatedly emphasized that the ministries should be at the helm of the experimenting enterprises, propelling them in the right direction and creating favorable conditions for their activity. Several ministries were singled out as deserving praise for their leadership, but, in most cases, the ministries continued in their rigid approach to the new system. They were particularly inflexible in their approach to unconventional proposals, subjecting them to "bureaucratic scrutiny." They always had so many doubts and qualms that more often than not the initiative of the enterprises was thwarted. The Party cells were urged to cease being "economic guilds" and to devote more time "to deal with social and political problems."[13]

Since the experimenting enterprises were, so to speak, islands within the sea of enterprises working under the old system, their results may largely have been invalidated. Difficulties were encountered in the ties between the experimenting enterprises and those working in the traditional way. The SPC demanded that prior to initiating experiments, the pilot enterprises must come to an agreement with their suppliers and buyers. Furthermore, free prices had to be mutually agreed upon between supplier and buyer and disputes had to be mediated by a third party. Offsetting the difficulties arising from the isolation of experimenting enterprises, there was a trend to widen the field of experimentation to include enterprises doing business with each other.[14]

Failures in the supply system were a serious stumbling block in the path of experimenting enterprises. For example, the production plan at the Tatra Furniture Plant was threatened with breakdowns because of shortages of supplies. Other enterprises reported similar conditions. Some of the supplies which they could not get were good quality yarn, silk thread, buttons, elastic, leather, glue, cardboard, zippers, buckles, etc. Hence, these were not centrally distributed producer goods. The director of the Drukov enterprise accused the supply system of obstructing the tests: "And when we apply penalties we can expect that finally we will get nothing at all." Premiums to induce faster delivery from suppliers were not a solution because there was no way for the producer to pass this payment for better service on to the consumer in the form of higher prices.[15]

The 1965 experiments were conducted in 440 organizations, including 142 industrial enterprises, 39 construction and building materials enterprises, 7 transportation enterprises, 80 domestic trade units, 69 enterprises of local industry, and 103 cooperatives. Of these enterprises, 384 tested GY and 56 profit incentives. The experiments were started either on January 1, or on April 1, 1965. The experimenting enterprises produced about one fifth of Czechoslovak industrial output. It was claimed that the sample was sufficiently large to permit drawing pertinent conclusions.

Table 45

EXTENT OF 1965 EXPERIMENTS

Branches	Share in total: Production volume	Share in total: Manpower
Metallurgy and ore mines	44.8	39.5
Fuels: pit coal	80.2	49.8
bituminous coal	23.0	-
Chemical industry	28.6	25.8
Heavy machine-building	23.7	20.5
General machine-building	16.3	17.9
Construction organizations	12.0	19.8
Building materials	26.8	23.3
Consumer goods	24.2	24.5
Food-processing	7.6	6.4
Domestic trade (retail sales)	23.0	20.0
Health	24.0	20.0
Local (including services)	19.0	19.6
Producer cooperatives	30.5	33.0
Consumer cooperatives	6.6	5.3

Source: Bohumil Krejcar, Karel Prochazka, and Jiri Tesar, PH, No. 1, 1966, p. 31.

In many cases the testing enterprises' share of manpower was lower than their share in total output, indicating that either the more mechanized enterprises were chosen for the experiments--a conclusion which is supported by the contention of many reporters that only the better-operating and better-managed enterprises were selected--and/or indicating the greater waste of manpower in the non-experimenting enterprises.

In most cases the system was not tested in all its facets and the measures tested were different from those which would later come to form the new system, simply because the latter had not yet been elaborated. Most of the enterprises were still bound by directive targets which they had to fulfill;

hence, they were not interested in changing delivery dates, assortments, prices, etc. Although this largely distorted the experiments, it has been argued that it was helpful in providing information on how well the new system could operate if it were bound up by a number of directives.[16]

Incentives in the form of wages and premiums were incorporated in all experiments. The criteria used were usually GY or profit and the output or sales plan. The emphasis was on GY, particularly in enterprises which could improve their function as suppliers by improving quality rather than by increasing quantity.[17] The reason for this was probably that the authorities were understandably suspicious of the functioning of a GY scheme in a sellers' market. Similarly almost all experiments included the three-tier pricing system. Most of the principles of the new system were to be tested, but the extent of experimenting with pricing, capital levies, and the effectiveness of foreign trade was particularly limited. In some cases the enterprises were not charged for the total working capital credit, in others no charges were levied on fixed capital; there were serious divergencies in the manner of paying interest and fines or in the manner of distributing the sums among the enterprise's funds, etc. The officials in charge were instructed not to create a "hothouse" atmosphere; on the contrary, they were instructed to apply tauter norms, which could later be relaxed if needed. One of the shortcomings noted in the preparatory stages of many experimenting enterprises was the lack of dissemination of information about the experiment among the staff of the enterprise. Some central agencies modified certain facets of the system "allegedly because of special conditions," but, reportedly, they did so to suit their own purposes and to improve their own advantage.[18]

The experiments tackled the so-called intra-enterprise management, i.e., the introduction of the <u>khozraschet</u> system into cost centers. A relatively elaborate intra-enterprise management system was achieved only at the Klement Gottwald

New Metallurgical Plants, the Trinec Iron Works, and the Vitkovice Iron Works. These enterprises specified output and financial indicators for individual cost centers and interested workers in their results by tieing in about 20 per cent of the workers' earnings to the center's results. The individual centers were given latitude to develop production and to improve performance. In dealing with each other the centers used prices based on the level of wholesale prices in case of planned assignments, and in above-plan transactions they used free prices.[19]

The inclusion of intra-enterprise management in some experiments brought out a host of problems, including the setting up of cost centers, intra-enterprise prices, operational planning, incentives, accounting, and external influences. The fundamental step was the setting up of cost centers that would parallel existing organizational units and that would be subdivided so as to form a closed circle of activity. Usually it was possible to create either large centers (following existing plants) or smaller ones (following existing shops). Although the large center could use the existing administrative staff, the responsibility of employees could not be sufficiently identified with the center's performance. But the smaller center, where such responsibility could be more closely identified with performance, usually increased paperwork and its creation signified an expansion of administrative staff. The experiments mainly concentrated on the larger center.

Perhaps the most vital aspect of intra-enterprise management was the formation of meaningful intra-enterprise prices. The following alternatives were evolved: 1) at the level of production costs (without a profit markup); 2) at the level of planned costs plus an intra-enterprise profit markup; and 3) at the wholesale price level. Mostly the first alternative was used because it was far less complicated than the other two, even though it was also far less effective. In the experiments in ferrous metallurgy, interdepartmental transfers were invoiced at prices approximating wholesale prices. The system has apparently proven advantageous in raising output quality. It also afforded a measure of commensurability in departments that received semifabricates both from the outside and from other departments. When the second or third alternative was chosen, a department recorded a share of profit not yet realized and which might not be realized if the enterprise failed to sell its final product. Enormous difficulties were being encountered in setting the intra-enterprise prices because of a shortage of reliable data and of a lack of accurate standards in costing on which valuations could be based. At some enterprises the problems were resolved by forgoing intra-enterprise prices, replacing them by calculations in natura.

To be effective, the intra-enterprise system would have to be so constructed as to reflect departmental performance in the employee's earnings. Basically, two methods were evolved for the distribution of premiums: 1) premiums were paid in proportion to basic wages, thus assuming that the participation of each employee in improving over-all performance was commensurate with his basic salary, and 2) premiums were paid out according to the complexity and responsibility involved in a given post, thus assuming that basic wages failed to do so. The problem here was to find so-called objective criteria for differentiating premiums. There was also the danger that employees, especially manual workers, might resent these differentiations.[20]

As a rule, the wage-premium systems adopted featured the following: 1) a portion of above-plan funds (or the total) was set aside for reserves of wages and premiums; 2) to prevent undue fluctuations, managerial premiums for a given period were delayed to take into account performance in the following periods; 3) premium criteria combined individual with over-all enterprise performance; and 4) managers were allowed to reward their subordinates from a special premium fund. The potentials of the premiums system were handicapped by the tendency to pay out premiums in relation to basic wages.[21]

The profit-sharing fund was related to and drawn from GY plan overfulfillment, rather than fulfillment. Budget levies and price subsidies were computed so as to relate GY and basic wages to comply with directives of the SCOM that "means are not created for the workers' sharing in economic results; the enterprises will have to create these means thereafter." The obvious incentive was to encourage plan overfulfillment, thus assuming that premiums would be forthcoming only when an extra effort was made, as, for example, at the Kablo enterprise where in the first half of 1965 GY was overfulfilled by 17 per cent and the workers' fund increased by 10 per cent. The quite obvious pitfall into which such a scheme stumbled was that of the familiar understatement of the plan at the drafting stage. If such overfulfillment was due to an increase in sales (output) by means of an enlarged labor force, the entire increase of the workers' fund could not be used for profit-sharing premiums, for it had also to be allotted to wages of the additional workers. Such was the case at Kablo where employment rose by 1.3 per cent and 4 per cent of above-plan GY had to be used for additional wages.

Table 46

COMPOSITION OF ABOVE-PLAN GY AT KABLO, JANUARY 1, TO JUNE 30, 1965

Sources of above-plan GY	Share in above-plan GY
Sales of goods and services	33.20
Price surcharges	24.80
Sale of packaging supplies	35.90
Adjustment of inventories	3.40
State grants	1.05
Others	1.65

Source: Ladislav Klinko, HN, No. 40, 1965.

At Kablo premiums were distributed on the basis of differentiation coefficients established for and within various groups of employees. The coefficients ranged from 0.25 to 0.5 for workers and up to 4 for managerial and technical personnel. The thirty-five- to forty-fold difference was considered necessary to counteract the equalization of salaries that had intensified in the early 1960's.[22] The trade unions rejected the proposal on the grounds that such differences were "incommensurately high." It was claimed that the premium system alone could not undertake to solve the problem of differentiating earnings which should be solved in the area of basic wages and salaries, i.e., centrally by differentiating the wage rates.[23]

The experimenting enterprises of the chemical industry worked under a GY scheme which specified that if the plan were underfulfilled, the budget levy on GY would be proportional to the actual achievement. In case of overfulfillment, 60 per cent of the above-plan GY was to be paid to the budget and 40 per cent could be retained by the enterprise. A reserve fund had to be created to amount to 0.4 per cent of the annual wages paid, and to be mainly used for paying additional wages.[24] For example, at the Fatra enterprise contributions to the budget from GY were in a fixed rate of about 23 per cent. The retained above-plan GY was allocated as follows: 10 per cent for enterprise investments, 1 per cent for the reserve fund, 29 per cent for the workers' fund for premiums. It was claimed that the low share of the enterprise in above-plan GY had a disincentive effect on increasing output of "desirable" products.[25]

In the chemical industry all wage payments were to be drawn from the workers' fund which was to be initially determined on the basis of the planned wage and premium funds for 1965.[26] But in the future its size was expected to depend wholly on GY. The basic wage was to include those components which were previously also part of the wage scheme plus premiums for work in hazardous environments and night work, foremen premiums, premiums for reducing labor time, and piece-rate premiums. All other premiums previously paid were to be amalgamated and paid out of profit-sharing.

The reserve fund was to serve for wage payments if the enterprise should fail to meet its targets during a given period and would not have enough funds to pay wages. In addition, special payments could be made for financing extraordinary projects involving the entire enterprise (e.g., taking preventive measures against accidents, etc.) At the end of the year a part of the reserve fund would be apportioned among the various departments; managers would be paid premiums from this fund and a balance would be carried over as a base for next year's reserve fund.

The planned profit-sharing fund was still considered as simply an addition to wages. Such premiums, distributed in relation to wages, perpetuated the wage-leveling tendencies and deficiencies of the qualification tariffs. The foreman's fund was an entirely new instrument, allowing more decentralized premium distribution. This fund usually consisted of savings of planned wages. In 1965 this fund was extremely low. The maximum per worker was between 40 to 80 kcs. per month. In most cases it was much lower and in others the fund was not even created. But in 1966 an effort was made to increase its weight.[27]

In 1966, criteria for determining premium coefficients were improved, but the tendency for leveling wages picked up momentum. Where widespread discrepancies among coefficients prevailed in 1965, they were being reduced in 1966. Apparently, this tendency was reinforced by the enlarged prerogatives of the lower-level enterprise management in deciding on premium distribution. The leveling tendencies continued to be the main reasons for procrastinations in preparing new individual merit criteria, for refusing to distribute premiums on the basis of new coefficients, and for turning the growing foreman's fund into an addition to wages. Because of these tendencies the foremen, as a rule, followed only the criteria of extreme merit or exceptional violations for differentiating premiums.[28]

Within the incentive system the rules for remunerating managerial personnel were of utmost importance due to these employees' larger responsibility and wider scope for exercising initiative. The premium part of earnings carried greater weight among them. But just how wide is this field for initiative? To what extent is this field limited by superiors? What is the meaning of "socialist entrepreneurship"? What would be an adequate reward for entrepreneurship? These questions still remained unanswered.

Profit incentives were tested on a much smaller scale in some enterprises of metallurgy, general machine-building, transport, health services, producer cooperatives, and local enterprises. The profit scheme was particularly designed for enterprises which would be directed by a relatively larger number of binding indexes and where the volume and assortment of output would be administratively controlled.

The budget levies on profit were specified for enterprises of the Ministry of Metallurgy and Ore Mines as 1) 10 to 25 per cent of wages and 2) 45 to 65 per cent of the remainder of profit. Relating the budget levy to wages was supposed to induce economy on wages.[29] For example, at the Klement Gottwald Ironworks in Vitkovice the main premium criterion became fulfillment of the profit plan, with supplementary indexes to emphasize this or that task. During the first quarter of 1965, the premium of plant managers and assistant managers averaged 30 per cent of salaries. The premium regulations were so set up that a maximum of 40 per cent of salaries could be paid.[30]

Most experimenting enterprises were reported to have overfulfilled their GY (profit) plans. On the average, during the first half of 1965, the overfulfillment was about 9 per cent. On the average, cost reduction accounted for 54 per cent of the above-plan GY and increased sales for 46 per cent. Cost reduction was responsible for 71 per cent of above-plan profits. The highest beneficiaries from above-plan achievements were the workers' and premium funds. During January to July, 1965, the workers' funds were exceeded by almost 7 per cent and premium funds by more than 40 per cent. But the unspent balances in these funds corresponded generally to these surpluses. It was claimed that, although their achievements did not justify it, many enterprises would dispose at the end of 1965 of a so-called thirteenth salary premium per employee and in some cases of even more. At the beginning of 1966, it was reported that in the best-operating experimenting enterprises the premium fund averaged about 1,000 kcs. per employee. But the enterprises had some misgivings that these funds would be withdrawn from them by the state.[31]

The objections raised against the initial experience of the guinea pigs were that the initial measures taken to improve performance were short-run and that they were not followed by increased investment activity, rationalization, and major repairs. There were immense pressures to increase the workers' funds and premium funds at the expense of leaving the investment, technical development, and welfare funds at their minimum limits. For example, whereas 69 million kcs. were allotted to premium funds, only 2 million kcs. were allotted to the technical development funds, and, in enterprises testing GY, the workers' funds amounted to 220 million kcs. and the technical development funds to 4 million kcs. It was claimed that the reluctance to allot funds for investments stemmed from unavailability of real assets, and a suspicion that superiors would siphon off the funds if the assets proved unobtainable.[32]

In the drive to increase GY (profit), many enterprises resorted to reduction of outlays on repairs and maintenance, to "undesirable" alterations of the product mix, to "excessive" reduction in the volume of work in process, etc. It was reported that the experimenting enterprises increased their

Table 47

ALLOTMENTS TO AND EXPENDITURES FROM THE WORKERS' AND PREMIUM FUNDS IN EXPERIMENTING ENTERPRISES, JANUARY 1, TO JUNE 30, 1965

Ministries	Type of Incentive System	Fulfill-ment of GY (P) in %	Actual formation of workers' (premium) funds in %	Balance of workers' (premium) fund		
				Total in million kcs.[1]	Kcs. per worker	In % of average wages
Electric power	GY	111.0	98.0	1	808	4.1
Metallurgy	P	106.0	133.0	83	934	4.1
Chemistry	GY	120.0	107.0	34	794	4.2
Heavy machinery	GY	108.0	110.0	55	1,080	5.7
General machinery	GY	105.0	-	8	438	2.6
General machinery	P	130.0	104.0	30	-	-
Consumer goods	GY	104.0	150.0	46	356	2.2
Food-processing	P	121.0	109.0	3	240	1.5
Construction	GY	111.0	-	60	1,169	5.8
Total (including other testing enterprises)	GY	109.4	105.8	247	-	-
	P	113.4	141.7	118	689	-

P - profit.

1 - for profit-sharing premiums and for technical managerial premiums.

Source: Vladislav Jebavy and Josef Kepecky, HN, No. 38, 1965.

workers' average earnings and that the possibility of increased earnings usually lessened the drive for more workers.[33]

There was a tendency to enhance the share of premiums in earnings. Whereas this share accounted for 25 to 28 per cent in 1964, in 1965 it was expected to reach 30 per cent and to be further significantly increased by the annual distribution from the unspent balances.[34] Apart from the very real and recognized pressures to increase current earnings, there is a possibility that the experiments were constructed with the view to palpably increasing earnings at experimenting enterprises as a propaganda tool. It is not unlikely that in order to break down (or at least to relieve) the employees' resistance to the new system--a resistance which may stem, inter alia, from a distrust of the goodwill of reformers and an unwillingness to change well-entrenched ways of doing things--the shifting of a bulk of funds to remuneration was encouraged to show that the new system really would be as good as its promises.

The tinkering with price-formation was most inconclusive. As a rule, limited prices hovered around the limit either because production costs were high, a better-quality product was offered, the producer exploited his monopolistic position, or the price increase was used to cover up inefficiency in production and/or organization.[35] Regimentation of price-setting was reduced by shifting some pricing prerogatives to lower organs. But price flexibility was greatly stifled in cases where the supplier--presumably because of allocations--could not refuse to deliver if the buyer was not willing to pay a higher price than the recommended one. There were attempts to boost prices by inflating costs, by spuriously changing the attributes of the product, etc. In many cases quality surcharges substantially exceeded the claimed improvement. Hence many buyers demanded standard quality at standard prices, but due to either shortages or a monopolistic position, they had to buy the "quality" product at a surcharge.

Table 48

SHARE OF INDIVIDUAL PRICE CATEGORIES IN MARKETABLE OUTPUT OF EXPERIMENTING ENTERPRISES

Price types	Heavy machinery		General machinery	
	Expected 1/1/65	Actual 7/1/65	Expected 1/1/65	Actual 7/1/65
Fixed	8	8	62	42
Limited	78	79	22	42
Free	14	13	16	16

Source: Vladimir Kadera and Karel Prochazka, HN, No. 39, 1965.

The relations with nonexperimenting enterprises greatly hampered the utilization of both free and limited prices. Free prices were actually restricted to apply only to products for the internal use of enterprises or branches. The fact that most contracts for 1965 were concluded in 1964 was also an impediment in testing the new prices. No attempt was made to reflect the price structure on the foreign markets in domestic prices. Hardly any adjustments were made in retail prices, except for raising retail prices on fashion articles, on goods of "exceptionally high quality," and on technical novelties. The profit rates exceeded those originally planned. For example, at the Lenin Cotton Mills only one free price was tested--the price of a fabric called Texas. It reached a profit margin of 21.6 per cent, with an average of 8.2 per cent for the entire EPU. The free prices on three types of fabrics at the Hedva EPU indicated a 29 per cent profit, with an average 0.6 per cent deficit for the entire EPU. These results were achieved without changing retail prices, but by using an averaged turnover tax rate for an entire product group.[36]

Many enterprises experimented with credits for the current account. The enterprises dealt with the bank on the basis of a credit contract. This system apparently introduced greater flexibility and the bank was able to influence enterprises through such means as discriminatory interest rates. Efforts to lower inventories were reported, as illustrated in Table 49.

Table 49

INVENTORIES IN EXPERIMENTING ENTERPRISES IN SLOVAKIA, FIRST QUARTER, 1965

Industries	Actual inventories compared to plan	Work in process and supplies
Chemical	97.3	96.5
Machine-building	92.8	91.3
Consumer goods	97.1	96.6
Building materials	91.9	93.3
Total	96.7	94.7

Source: Frantisek Hatar and Jan Jamrich, PH, No. 6, 1965, p. 50.

The bank's extension of credit was evaluated as having both positive and negative facets: 1) The relations between the bank and the enterprise were much simplified. 2) Since the enterprise could use any operative funds for financing working capital, there was less pressure on credits. 3) More potent interest rates, a large enough share of credit in operation, and the influence of the interest charged against disposable GY combined forces to speed up turnover of inventories. 4) All the enterprise's needs, whether judged "desirable" or "undesirable" by the bank, were covered by credits, as long as the limit on credits in the credit agreement was not exceeded. 5) When establishing the contract, there were countless disputes between the enterprises and the bank; the former demanding a higher limit to have a safety margin and the latter insisting on a lower limit in order not to tie up its funds. The bank officials were even of the opinion that the enterprise should be made to pay an interest charge for the unused credit funds it has tied up in a contract. Of course, the rate should be considerably lower than that for credits used.[37]

One of the more comprehensive foreign trade experiments was conducted by the Jablonex Corporation--a producer of costume jewelery--under the auspices of the Ministry of Consumer Goods Industry. The aim was to establish closer ties between foreign trade and production. The tested tenets were 1) the link between the amount of foreign exchange obtained from the sale of Jablonex's products and its employees' material incentives; 2) the influence of price fluctuations on the foreign market on Jablonex's "economic results"; and 3) the efficacy of the new organizational ties which merged some foreign trade activities with production.[38] The testing of relations between producers and foreign trade organizations did not take off smoothly and was generally inconclusive. The producers were usually unaware of the world prices of their products and obtained such information with difficulty.[39]

A grave inadequacy in analyzing the results of experiments was that the old "quantitative" criteria were applied in measuring achievements of the "qualitatively" oriented system. This was reinforced by the manner of compiling statistical data in ministries. Masses of data were redigested on plan fulfillment, on the growth of production, and on cost reduction, but little was made of the new system's effect on management and of its influence on economic processes in enterprises and branches. Relative to the last few years the reported performance of most enterprises and branches improved in 1965, thus largely obfuscating to what extent good results were due to the tested system and to what extent they were due to the general improvement. Evaluation of the results of experiments was hampered by 1) the short life of the experiments; 2) the selection of above-average enterprises for experimentation; 3) the impetus given by the initial rationalization measures, etc.

Usually enterprises found it beneficial to reduce their inventories of hoarded materials as a substantial one-step attempt at improving results. The disposal of old supplies had a relatively speedy effect on the increase of revenue. Such action "created an exaggerated impression, suggesting that the whole experiment was successful." It was expected that after the initial high performance was achieved by experimenting enterprises--mostly through exploitation of the backlog of reserves--much more effort would be required to maintain this level without which results might deteriorate, causing a general disillusionment with the system.[40]

The following example was offered to illustrate how improved results were often achieved. The Ton Factory fulfilled its GY plan by 111.3 per cent and its workers' fund plan by 110.6 per cent in the first quarter of 1965. Savings amounted to 2.3 million kcs. and their achievement is illustrated in Table 50.

Table 50

SAVINGS AT TON FACTORY, FIRST QUARTER, 1965

Itemized savings	Thousands kcs.	Share in total savings
1. Revaluation of work in process	165	7.1
2. Correction of accounting errors	740	31.7
3. Savings on material inputs for prisms	420	18.0
4. Savings of electricity	151	6.5
5. Spread of overhead over larger output volume	322	13.8
6. Savings on depreciation	242	10.4
7. Effect of prices	638	27.4
8. Total effect of factors intensifying GY	2,678	114.9
9. Reduced GY because of failure to improve technology	- 347	- 14.9
10. Total net increase of GY	2,331	100.0

Source: Ladislav Hula, PM, No. 11, 1965, p. 505.

The reporter warned that on Items 1, 2, and 7 there might be possibilities of manipulations which would have to be verified.[41] The measures taken in Item 9 seem rather spurious. Obviously, they were taken to punish the enterprise for not carrying out some technical progress measures. However, if the system was to be effective, the punishment should have been automatic and reflected in the enterprise's future performance--not an arbitrary ruling from above. Of course, the testing of the system was not visualized as a long-run process to indicate how present actions would affect future performance. Nevertheless, arbitrary tampering with the mechanism was unhealthy--to say the least.

The results of the first quarter of 1965 indicated that the degree of plan overfulfillment was higher in the experimenting enterprises than in the others, as indicated in Table 51.

Table 51

PLAN FULFILLMENT IN THE CHEMICAL INDUSTRY, FIRST QUARTER, 1965

Indexes	Percentage fulfillment	
	All enterprises	Experimenting
Gross output	101.4	102.5
Marketable output	101.6	102.7
Sales revenue	102.3	103.7
Financial result	201.7	270.9

Source: Bohumil Krejcar and Jiri Tesar, HN, No.23, 1965.

Apparently the best results were to be found in enterprises that had adopted intra-enterprise management and where internal prices had been set on semifabricates transferred among departments. It was also reported that a large number of enterprises achieved higher average selling prices even where free or limited prices were not in effect. In most cases enterprises reduced the number of workers in "unproductive posts," especially in metallurgy and in the chemical industry. In other branches, enterprises were fulfilling and overfulfilling their plans with a below-plan labor force. It was confirmed that the wage-premium system helped in silencing demands for more manpower. It was claimed that one of the foremost contributions of experimenting enterprises was a moderate reduction of manpower tensions.[42]

It was found that some of the various methods used for distributing the GY were unsatisfactory in that the rates of budget levies were too low, resulting in a faster growth of the workers' funds. It was deplored that the improvement benefited the state budget only slightly.[43]

For the period January to September, 1965, the planned GY (profit) was, on the average, exceeded by over 10 per cent. The enterprises were still not induced to reveal their potential at the planning stage. About 45 per cent of above-plan GY (profit somewhat less) was due to increased revenue, dispelling the apprehensions in some quarters that the new system would not stimulate growth of output. More than 50 per cent of above-plan GY and almost 80 per cent of above-plan profit were achieved by reducing operating costs. The results of experimenting enterprises of some industries were as shown in Table 52.

Reports indicated that reduced interest charges, capital levies, fines, etc. considerably increased disposable enterprise funds, altering, to a large extent, the key for allocating funds between the enterprise and the state. It was recommended that this factor be watched when the system was introduced on a large scale--a sign of the persisting belief in the advisability of allowing the enterprise only a limited financial maneuverability.

The contributions to the budget and allocations to the workers' and premium funds were the highest beneficiaries of above-plan funds, as illustrated in Table 53.

Table 52

RESULTS OF EXPERIMENTING ENTERPRISES IN FUELS, CHEMICAL, MACHINE-BUILDING, AND CONSUMER GOODS INDUSTRIES, FIRST THREE QUARTERS, 1965

Sources	Millions kcs.					
	GY as incentive			Profit as incentive		
	Planned	Actual	Fulfill-ment in %	Planned	Actual	Fulfill-ment %
Total revenues	15,534.4	16,403.5	105.6	5,651.8	5,887.9	104.2
Receipts from sales	15,020.4	15,806.3	105.2	4,884.5	5,076.6	104.4
Adjustments & corrections	+ 249.1	+ 225.4	90.5	+0.1	-39.8	-
Total operating expenses	11,271.0	11,709.3	103.9	5,256.1	5,282.9	100.5
Material costs	9,931.0	10,398.5	104.7	2,631.5	2,720.1	103.4
Depreciation	828.3	824.8	99.6	435.6	431.4	99.0
Labor costs	-	-	-	1,701.7	1,685.2	99.0
GY (profit)	4,512.5	4,919.6	109.0	395.8	585.2	142.8

Source: Bohumil Krejcar, Karel Prochazka, and Jiri Tesar, <u>PH</u>, No. 1, 1966, p. 33.

Table 53

DISTRIBUTION OF GY(PROFIT) BY EXPERIMENTING ENTERPRISES OF THE FUELS, CHEMICAL, MACHINE-BUILDING, AND CONSUMER GOODS INDUSTRIES, FIRST THREE QUARTERS, 1965

Distribution		GY as incentive			Profit as incentive		
		Planned	Actual	Fulfill-ment %	Planned	Actual	Fulfill-ment %
GY (profit)	a	4,512.5	4,919.6	109.0	395.8	565.2	142.8
	b	117.8	118.6	-	422.9	328.6	-
Budget levies	a	371.5	517.2	139.2	187.6	281.9	150.3
	b	9.7	12.6	-	200.4	163.9	-
Fixed capital levies	a	122.5	118.8	97.0	110.5	110.0	99.5
	b	3.2	2.9	-	118.0	64.0	-
Interest on working	a	174.9	159.8	91.4	0.6	0.5	83.3
capital credits	b	4.6	3.9	-	0.6	0.3	-
Allocations to enterprise	a	3,836.2	4,113.0	107.2	93.6	172.0	183.8
funds	b	100	100	-	100	100	-
Investments	a	15.2	22.6	148.7	39.5	48.9	123.8
	b	0.4	0.5	-	42.2	28.4	-
Technical progress	a	89.9	92.7	103.1	-	0.1	-
	b	2.3	2.3	-	-	0.1	-
Welfare fund	a	20.0	26.2	131.0	1.0	3.2	320.0
	b	0.5	0.6	-	1.1	1.9	-
Reserve fund	a	12.1	72.2	596.7	-3.2	8.2	-
	b	0.3	1.8	-	-3.4	4.8	-
Workers'(premium) fund	a	3,699.0	3,899.3	105.4	56.3	111.6	198.2
	b	95.4	94.8	-	60.1	64.9	-

a - absolute figure in millions kcs., b - ratio of allocations to enterprise funds.

Source: Bohumil Krejcar, Karel Prochazka, and Jiri Tesar, PH, No. 1, 1966, p. 37.

It appears that the design of the profit scheme was such that enterprises stood to benefit much more from plan overfulfillment, i.e., nondisclosure of reserves at the planning stage. The results indicated strong pressures in the experimenting enterprises to allocate the largest possible sums to the workers' or premium funds. It was naively suggested that managers ought to be appealed to "to act as responsible managers and to reckon with their enterprises' long-term interests."[44] The experiments indicated the usefulness of the reserve fund not only as a source for mitigating fluctuations in activity, but also as a receptacle for "excess" funds which could not be distributed to employees, but which could not be legally extracted by the budget.

Due to the sellers' market, the experimenting producers did not, as a rule, attempt to improve quality, variety, or services. Compared to a similar period in 1964, during the first three quarters of 1965 the number of complaints from buyers did not drop significantly. There was a tendency to turn out only highly profitable or otherwise advantageous (from the producers' standpoint) goods. Enterprises also tended to exploit monopolistic positions by often raising the surcharges to even 100 per cent of the original prices. The buyers were usually too weak to resist these pressures. It was admitted that this was a serious danger, for such a situation is prone to recentralization, to the setting up of more directive indexes, and to the enacting of various measures by central agencies. Such measures would collide with the very principles of the new system. For example, a restriction on assortments in one industry would have an infinite chain reaction on the assortments in other industries.[45]

The exponents of radical reforms were generally not in favor of widespread experimentation. Admittedly, such experimentation cannot be conclusive when the conditions under which the majority of enterprises are working have not been altered. The experiments were a tinkering with this or that aspect, whereas the radical reformers believed that only a dramatic overhaul of the system could eradicate past deficiencies--and such an overhaul did not lend itself to experimentation. But, although these and similar arguments were voiced, all with good reason, what probably was uppermost in the minds of the radical reformers was that the time was ripe for a dramatic overhaul of the system, and that it would be a serious tactical error to allow the withering away of the reform momentum. As it usually happens, the advocates of the status quo preferred to postpone action, arguing that practical experience had to be gained and a more thorough study of reform measures had to be undertaken before over-all changes could be introduced. They hoped that time was on their side, which was exactly what the reformers feared. After the slump in 1963 it was anticipated that economic activity would improve and such an improvement would be a good practical reason for delaying action.

CHAPTER 5 THE INCIPIENT PHASE

PLAN AND PERFORMANCE

The main factors responsible for the improvement of performance in 1964-65 could be catalogued as follows: 1) As a result of the second industrialization wave set into motion in the late 1950's, additional production capacity was brought into operation, primarily in the basic branches of industry. 2) The pace of growth of manufacturing industries (including machine-building) was relatively decelerated and the tensions between requirements and resources slackened. 3) From 1961, the share of consumption in national income increased somewhat and that of accumulation declined. The share of accumulation in 1964-65 was considerably lower than in the 1958-62 period, whereas it approached the average of the period of consolidation (1954-58). There was no major increase in investment activity, thus somewhat lowering the raw materials barrier and alleviating the balance of payments.[1] The share of accumulation in national income dropped by 34 per cent from 1961 to 1964, but the increment of fixed capital declined by only 18 per cent, indicating a reduction in the growth of inventories. During the 1962-65 period the retarding effect of the obsolete planning system was particularly in evidence; the negative effect of decelerating factors was considered to be stronger than the positive effect of new capacities. Moreover, difficulties were encountered in staffing the added capacities, resulting in their underutilization and in the underfulfillment of the plans.[2]

A review of the economy's performance in 1964 indicates a slight recovery. With a planned increase of national income of 1.4 per cent over the disastrous results of 1963, the actual performance recorded a 0.6 per cent increase. Personal consumption was supposed to increase by 2.3 per cent, whereas the reported rise was 3.0 per cent. Accumulation decreased by 5 per cent. The planned growth rate of gross industrial output was 3.6 per cent. The output plan was reported to have been exceeded by 1.9 per cent, registering a 4.1 increase over the depressed 1963 results. Employment in industry was slated to rise by 0.8 per cent and was reported to have risen by 0.6 per cent. The respective figures for labor productivity were 2.8 and 3.5 per cent. There was a relative slackening of tensions in the supply of metallurgy--where output rose by 8.5 per cent--and of power--where output rose by 7.4 per cent. The rate of increase of output in various industries were rather erratic. Although the output of producer goods appeared to have grown faster than that of consumer goods, there were some exceptions to the rule. Whereas the output of heavy machine-building, building materials, and chemicals grew by 6.1, 6.7, and 7.5 per cent, respectively, that of general machine-building and fuels increase by only 1.6 and 2 per cent, respectively, and that of manufactured consumer goods and of food-processing grew by 1.8 and 1.9 per cent, respectively. In the over-all results, the momentum picked up by industry was considerably dampened by the poor showing of agriculture. Agricultural output had been planned to grow by 6.5 per cent; the reported increase was only 0.6 per cent. Although the investment plan was slightly underfulfilled (investment rose by 12.2 per cent, instead of 13.6 per cent), investment activity reached about the 1962 level, with a slightly lower level in construction and with a higher one in the acquisition of machinery. The construction industry was once again taken to task for the perennial failures to activate new capacities, for protracted construction periods, for poor performance of newly installed capacities, etc. Idle capacity, ineffective utilization of resources, inefficient production, and other failures of the planning system were once more criticized.[3]

Even though there was little cause for jubilation, there was an appreciable improvement of performance in 1965, albeit without a tangible abatement of the extensive-type development. National income increased by 2.5 per cent (subsequently revised to 3.7) over 1964, as against a planned 4.1 per cent. Damages caused by floods and bad weather reduced national income by 8 to 9 billion kcs. Personal consumption rose by 4 per cent (subsequently revised to 5.1), instead of the planned 3 per cent. Accumulation increased by 1 per cent. The planned and reported figures for growth of industrial output, employment, and labor productivity were 5.5 and 7.9, 1.1 and 1.8 (subsequently revised to 2), and 4.4 and 6.0 (subsequently revised to 5.8) per cent, respectively. The growth of labor productivity was apparently responsible for about 75 per cent of the growth of output. The latter was the second largest in the past quinquennium. The industrial output plan was overfulfilled by 2.8 per cent. Losses due to waste in production were apparently reduced by 30 per cent.

The consequential growth of industrial output centered on producer goods, with the main exception of fuels whose production rose by only 0.9 per cent. Thus, whereas the output of energy, metallurgy, heavy machine-building, general machine-building, building materials, and chemicals rose by 7.8, 9.9, 8.1, 14.0, 9.2, and 11.2 per cent, respectively, that of manufactured consumer goods and food-processing rose by only 7.0 and 1.9 per cent, respectively. Moreover, a considerable share of the increase in output was actually industrial inputs rather than final products. It was estimated that the excessive use of inputs was instrumental in reducing national income by 3.5 billion kcs. Although the supply situation improved somewhat, it still remained below par in many areas. Though metallurgy overfulfilled its output quotas (by 4.1 per cent), its assortment was reported to have been unsatisfactory in meeting the requirements of the machine-building industry. Similarly, notwithstanding the considerable overfulfillment in the output of machine-building (by 4 per cent) and building materials (by 7.2 per cent), the demand for them exceeded supply.

Once again agriculture's performance--registering a 3.3 per cent decrease of gross agricultural output over 1964, representing a 9.2 per cent decrease of crop output and a 2.3 per cent increase of animal output--was instrumental in attenuating the over-all 1965 results. The investment plan remained underfulfilled. Whereas it called for a 8.4 per cent increase of investment over 1964, only a 6.6 per cent rise was reported (subsequently revised to 7.8 per cent). Investment in industry increased by 5.8 per cent, in agriculture by 3.9 per cent, and in the nonproductive sector by 6.7 per cent. By far the largest rise of investment was in the construction industry which reported a 34.1 per cent increase. Substantial increases were also reported for trade and transport where investments rose by 18.5 and 14.2 per cent, respectively. There was a slight rise in the share of machinery (from 43.5 to 44.5 per cent of total investment).

Again the outstanding failures of the traditional system were noted: extensive use of resources, poor quality and inferior standards of products, wrong assortments, the perennial failures of construction, mismanagement in industry and agriculture, underutilization of industrial capacity, increase in the material input-output ratio claiming over two thirds of the increase of gross industrial output, etc.[4]

The incipient phase of reform implementation coincided with the first year of the Fourth FYP.[5] The FYP was being drafted simultaneously with the elaboration of the reform measures. Hence, it would have to bear the stamp of the reform's aspirations.

After many years of preparatory work on the plan, the CC approved in April, 1965, the directives of the Fourth FYP for the period 1966-70. The work was, however, not completed. Indeed, Novotny admitted at the Thirteenth Congress of the CPC that a "fully balanced plan" could not be presented to the Congress as a definite framework for discussion of economic matters. The directives were elaborated essentially according to "the old methods, administrative lines, and prices, without the effect of economic management instruments." Admittedly, one of the basic deficiencies was that the role of the plan and its content were not given sufficient attention. The plan was not based on a comprehensive forecast of development trends and the criteria for assessing specific variants of development were lacking. The work on long-term forecasting was only then beginning.

A major aim of the Fourth FYP was to provide definite guidelines and to relatively stabilize conditions for enterprise operations. The plan expressed greater concern for "qualitative" achievements. Among the top priority desiderata were the urgent tasks of increasing efficiency and of speeding up technical progress. Reliance on noninvestment sources of growth was particularly stressed for the first years of the FYP. The stock of fixed capital would have to be utilized more intensively, materials and power would have to be economized, and the reserves that had accumulated in the past years would have to be tapped more consistently. The problem of efficiency was also brought to the fore in stressing the need to take advantage of the international division of labor. There was increased solicitude for the population's living standards and, in particular, greater preoccupation with alterations in the pattern of demand.

The planned average annual growth rates of national income for the Fourth FYP were 4.1 to 4.4 per cent (with the aim of approaching 5 per cent in the last two years of the FYP), hence they were significantly higher than those recorded in the past quinquennium, but still well below those planned for that period. National income was supposed to grow by 22 to 24 per cent, with over 75 per cent of the increase attributable to industry.

Labor productivity was expected to rise by 22 to 23 per cent, implying that the increased productivity should account for the bulk of increased output. Productivity in construction would increase by 18 per cent, with half of the increase due to technical advance and organizational improvements.

It is not quite clear what effect, in terms of efficiency, the macro-decisions, especially those touching upon the investment pattern, will have. Past policies were bound to have an impact on the economy for some time to come and rectification of some past errors may well be detrimental in the immediate future. For example, performance might not be improved quickly by the efforts to modernize industry and to promote technical progress. The increasing reorientation toward international specialization--necessitating a protracted process of readjustment at almost all levels of the economy--might prove of little tangible benefit within a short lapse of time. Thus, it would seem that macro-decisions could not be instrumental in precipitating palpable improvements in efficiency in the short run.

The declared precepts laid down for the investment plan aimed at an investment policy that would not overstrain the economy and that would not tie up and commit future development to a predetermined pattern. The share of accumulation in national income would be maintained at the 1966 level and was not expected to increase. The aim would be to cut down on the number of unfinished projects and to shorten the construction periods. The share of investments for the nonproductive sphere would markedly increase, with a relative decline of the share of investments for production. A relatively modest target of 14.5 per cent increase of construction work was to be primarily absorbed by investments in the nonproductive sphere. The growth of investment in industry, agriculture, and transportation would be mainly channeled to machinery and equipment. In compliance with the call for modernization and re-equipment, the share of machinery deliveries in total industrial investments would rise from 55.5 to 61 per cent.

The incremental capital-output ratio was expected to be 6.70. Capital intensity was planned to increase _pari passu_ with labor productivity. Accumulation was slated to rise by 20 per cent over the quinquennium. Investments were supposed to increase by 22.5 per cent throughout the period. Whereas investments in the processing industries were expected to grow by 22 per cent, those in the basic industries were supposed to increase by only 12 per cent--hence, an appreciable shift of emphasis on the processing industries. In basic industries a significant growth of investments was foreseen for the chemical industry and for electric power, 45 and 41 per cent, respectively; a 60 per cent drop in metallurgy; and a stabilization of investments in fuels. In the processing industries investments were planned to increase by 46 and 48 per cent, respectively, for manufactured consumer goods and food-processing. Investments in machine-building were to remain at the level of the previous period. Investment in transport was expected to increase by over 50 per cent.

The problem of developing Slovakia was perhaps more acute than ever. Although Slovakia would provide over 50 per cent of the nation-wide manpower increment, its share in over-all industrial investment would only amount to 30.9 per cent--a rise of 1.9 per cent over the preceding period. Industrial investments would account for about 42 per cent of all investments in Slovakia, with about two thirds concentrated on electrical engineering, metallurgy, and chemistry. About 48 per cent of investment outlays would go to projects started before 1966. In adopting the Fourth FYP guidelines, the government recommended that the relocation of certain investment projects from Bohemia and Moravia to Slovakia should be seriously considered to make up for, what was considered by the Slovaks to be, an unequitable distribution of investments, favoring the Czech lands.

The main structural changes in the Fourth FYP derived primarily from the desired long-run transformation of the economy, and centered on electric power, chemistry, and machine-building. There would be a shift in the primary sources of power. The technical base of railroads would be modernized. A reconstruction and modernization program for the road network would be initiated. To accomplish these long-run goals, the following structural changes would have to be achieved by 1970: 1) the share of the electric power industry in gross industrial output would rise to 4.1 per cent, with the share of gaseous and liquid fuels increasing; 2) the share of chemical output would grow from 8.9 in 1965 to 10.4 per cent in 1970 (according to the earlier draft, it was reported that chemistry's share would rise to 12.6 per cent); 3) the share of output of machine-building would rise from 30 in 1965 to 32-33 per cent by 1970 (with precedence accorded to expansion of output of machine tools, machines for the textile, leather, tanning, and food industries, production of trucks, antifriction bearings, pumps, etc.); 4) the share of sheet metal in the total output of rolled metals would increase from 20 in 1965 to 34 per cent by 1970, the share of welded pipe would rise from 27.2 to 35.7 per cent, and the output of nonferrous pipes and precision tubes would by 1970 be twice as high as in 1965; and 5) in manufactured consumer goods the output of glass and porcelain would by 1970 rise by 33 per cent over 1965 and the share of synthetic fibers in gross output of textile raw materials would double.

The expansion of the electrification system would primarily rest on cheap deposits of brown coal. The pilot nuclear power plant was to start operation in the Fourth FYP and plans were being drawn up for constructing another one with a reactor of 250-300 MW performance. A total electric power-generating capacity of 50,000 million KWh was expected by 1970 (70,000 million KWh by 1975), with an annual average increase of consumption of electricity by 7.6 per cent during the quinquennium.

The share of crude oil and gas in the fuel and power balance was to grow from 15 per cent in 1965 to 20-22 per cent by 1970 (to 28-30 per cent by 1975).

Following the completion of the unfinished pressure gas works, the expansion of the use of gas should be derived from natural gas. Concurrently, the liquidation of obviously unprofitable coal mines was being contemplated in order to halt the rising costs of coal mining, to save on the investment outlays on coal mines, and to release badly needed manpower for other activities.

The speedy development of the chemical industry would heavily depend on the refinement of crude oil. The main areas of concentration were to be the output of chemical fertilizers and of sprays to protect agricultural produce from pests and diseases and the production of synthetic fibers, plastics, synthetic rubber, etc. The development of oil refining was envisaged at 10 to 11 million tons by 1970 (17 to 18 million tons by 1975). The center of attention would gradually shift to highly specialized production of synthetic materials and plastics for which propitious conditions for research and development and domestic supplies were available.

Metallurgy would be developed on the basis of existing capacity and of facilities in the process of construction, with particular stress on the continuous production processes to be established at the East Slovakia Iron Works, upon their completion. Special attention would be paid to reducing inputs of basic materials and to improving the quality and variety of goods. A modernization of the older metallurgical plants was contemplated in the period after 1970. Greater use of imported high-quality iron ore was anticipated, in order to enhance economical operation of foundries. Domestic ore production would be limited to those mines which could successfully compete with the imported ore. Those mines where costs could not be reduced to an "appropriate" level, within a given lapse of time, would be shut down.

The mining and processing of nonmetallic minerals would be developed at a substantially faster rate than in the past, in order to intensify their use in domestic production and to use them more effectively in export. The quality of magnesite mined in Slovakia would be improved to meet the standards of the work market. The mining and processing of kaolin would be expanded. There would be stress on the development of raw materials for the china, glassware, and construction industries, such as sand, clays, and slates.

Significantly, the development of the machine-building industry would rest primarily on the reconstruction and re-equipment of existing facilities. In order to increase the effectiveness of domestic machine-building and to raise the economy-wide technological level, import of high-quality equipment would grow, making it also possible to restrict the range of domestic machine-building production.

It is interesting to note the stress on consumer goods production as a potential source of exports. To this end, the reconstruction and re-equipment of porcelain, glassware, and footwear industries was anticipated, together with the modernization of the printing and textile industries. The aforementioned expansion of the production of synthetic fibers and other materials, such as synthetic leather, would serve for the development of these consumer goods branches. The output of porcelain and glassware industries was to increase by about 33 per cent and its share in total gross output of the consumer goods industry was to increase from 9 to 10.3 per cent in 1970, displacing the relative shares of the textile and woodworking industries.

There would be a slowdown in the growth rate of the food industry whose average annual growth rate would not quite reach 3 per cent. Precedence would be accorded to the expansion of meat, milk and dairy products, and fruits and vegetables, at the expense of fats and flour consumption.

Mainly traditional building materials would be used in construction, although some light pre-fabricated materials would be developed. Use of prefabricated materials would increase markedly after 1970.

Transportation would be modernized. By 1970, 90 per cent of railway activity was expected to make use of electric traction and Diesel locomotives. Measures would be taken to prevent railway transportation bottlenecks and snarls by adequate reserves in equipment and by untangling overburdened traffic centers. A speedy reconstruction and modernization of highways was planned, concentrating at first on the main routes.

In agriculture higher per-hectare yields were expected for grain by 14 per cent over the average in the preceding period, for sugar beet by 16 per cent, for potatoes by 30 per cent, and for perennial fodders by 20 per cent. Livestock was mainly to be expanded in the production of cattle for slaughter and milk. The share of investment in agriculture was slated to decline (about 30 billion kcs. was allocated for the entire period), with a shift in its structure. The share of machinery and equipment would increase from 34 per cent during 1958-60 to 50 per cent in the Fourth FYP. Concurrently, investments in branches producing for agriculture were expected to increase. Fixed assets in agriculture would rise by 17 per cent by 1970 over 1965. The increased deliveries of artificial fertilizers were expected to raise the pure nutrients per hectare of agricultural land, from about 120 kilograms in 1965 to about 186 kilograms by 1970. It was anticipated that there would be additional incentives for the agricultural labor force: increased income with the growth of marketable output (by an average of 4.5 per cent annually) and with cost reduction; wage increases for some skills to match similar employment in other sectors of the economy; and improved housing (about 70,000 new apartments), services, and other amenities.

The Fourth FYP anticipated a considerably reduced increase in industrial employment, especially in comparison with the previous period. Employment in the economy as a whole would by 1970 be 2.7 per

Table 54

PLANNED CHANGES IN INDUSTRIAL FACTOR INPUTS AND OUTPUT, 1965-70

	1965	1970
Net output	100	127.0
Employment	100	103.5
Fixed capital stock	100	128.0
Labor productivity	100	123.0
Capital productivity	100	99.0
Capital intensity	100	124.0
Capital-output ratio	100	101.0

Source: ESE 1966, Chapter 2, p.46.

cent higher than in 1965; in the productive sphere it would be 1 per cent higher and in the nonproductive sphere it would be 9.5 per cent higher. Concurrently, with the aim of stabilizing employment in agriculture, attempts would be made to increase the proportion of men, to increase the number of experts, and to increase the number of younger people engaged in agricultural work.

The planned annual growth of gross industrial output was 5.1 to 5.4 per cent, but of consumer goods only 3.4 per cent--indicating the continuing preponderance of output of producer goods, as indicated in Table 55.

The growing caution and "realism" in planning was also demonstrated in setting the quotas for agriculture. Even though the Fourth FYP set generally higher targets than the reported results of the preceding period (calling for a 2.8 per cent average annual growth rate and a 20 per cent growth of agricultural output over the period), they were substantially lower than those planned for the previous period.

Foreign trade turnover was slated to rise by 32 per cent, with an increase of exports by 36 per cent

Table 55

PLANNED CHANGES IN GROSS INDUSTRIAL OUTPUT BY MAIN BRANCHES, 1965-70

	1965	1970
Total industry	100	130-132
Fuels	100	113
Electric power	100	143
Metallurgy	100	134
Machine-building	100	143
Chemicals	100	152
Food-processing	100	117
Manufactured consumer goods	100	119
Transport of goods	100	120

Sources: ESE 1966, Chapter 2, p. 49; and Vaclav Rendl, CEP, No. 9, 1967, p. 11.

and of imports by 27 per cent. There would be a relative expansion of trade with the capitalist countries which was expected to increase by 39 per cent, compared to a 35 per cent growth of trade with the socialist countries. The leading items in the structure of imports would consist of fuels, power, and consumer goods (38 per cent); industrial raw materials and semifabricates (29 per cent); and foodstuffs and agricultural raw materials (17 per cent). It was anticipated that the share of machinery in exports would rise substantially, with a relative decline of raw materials and foodstuffs.

No drastic changes were envisaged in the improvement of living standards. An 18 to 19 per cent growth of real wages over the quinquennium was planned, with a 17 to 19 per cent rise in personal consumption. The respective annual average rates of growth were 3.4 to 3.5 and 3.2 to 3.5 per cent. It was expected, however, that these targets were conservative; they were considered rather as lower limits. The rise in living standards was supposed to be mainly effected by increasing personal, rather than collective, consumption. About 460,000 apartments were slated to be built, including 127,000 in Slovakia alone. It was anticipated that from 1970 on, 105,000 to 115,000 apartments would be built annually. The working week would be curtailed to a five-day, forty-hour week for jobs particularly injurious to health and to a forty-two hour week in other occupations. The changes in the structure of personal consumption would center primarily on the growing importance of consumers' durables (especially automobiles), on the expansion of services and recreational facilities, on a shift toward gaseous and liquid fuels in household use, and on the development of household use of electricity.

By mid-1965 the reform measures were elaborated and approved by the government. Although these instructions were not to be rigid--and it was expected that some of the measures would be altered in the course of reform implementation--they nevertheless provided a rather comprehensive set of directives to guide planners and managers at all levels.

GUIDELINES FOR REFORM

Three types of economic plans were to prevail: the perspective, long-term, and operative plans. Enterprises and EPU's were to participate actively (by submitting their own projections) in the construction of all types of plans. The obligatory nature of the plan was to be altered, with extensive use made of economic incentives and of financial, credit, and price policies to ensure fulfillment of the plan. Most plan goals were expressed in percentage increases or decreases, rather than in absolute amounts. The EPU's were expected to specify these goals concretely after analyzing market conditions. Plan quotas were established with ceilings and floors within which they could be varied to meet a specific situation. The production plan carried about 6 to 7 per cent of the obligatory indexes previously assigned to each industry. Instead of reporting the volume of gross output, the producer would henceforth report the percentage changes in sales. Evidently, the scope of directive plan guidance would vary substantially depending on the nature of the product mix and its destination. At a bird's-eye view, the basic changes lay in forgoing central assignment of gross output and sales, of production costs, of labor productivity, and, in most branches, the regulation of labor costs and of average wages.[6] There was a significant shift in emphasis away from linking employees' material incentives to plan fulfillment.

The new industrial output plan was an amalgam of the plans for industrial production, marketing, and supply. The plan incorporated the following groups of data: 1) indexes of volume of gross output (semifabricates, marketable goods, and others for particular branches); 2) indexes of volume of goods delivered on order to customers (for domestic consumption, export, or producer goods); 3) indexes by category of production and consignment as per plan and standard industrial classification; and 4) indexes of imports (volume and categories). The essential difference was that most of these indexes were to be informative (guideline), rather than directive. Output quotas for exports at parity prices were to remain binding. Minimum binding limits were to be established on some products. These could be exceeded if demand for the product warranted it. Maximum quotas were to be set for some goods produced from inputs in short supply.

For example, whereas before January 1, 1966, the EPU's of the chemical industry were given about 180 binding assignments for production and delivery, this number was sharply cut to only 3 mandatory tasks in the production and delivery of chemical fertilizers, rubber, and fuel.[7] But apparently in practice the difference between the directive and informative indicators was blurred.[8]

Producers would be obliged to sign contracts for the delivery of output specified in the binding quotas. Due to the priority of export orders and to the lack of interplay of economic forces in this domain, binding export assignments were to be set for each

Table 56

OBLIGATORY AND INFORMATIVE PLAN INDEXES, 1964-70

Type of index	Number of indexes 1964	1965	1966	1966-70
Output quotas for funded goods	435	380	-	-
National goals not centrally prorated	305	140	-	-
Output quotas set by ministries[a]	600	600	-	-
Total binding quotas	1,340	1,120[b]	66[b]	48
Informative indexes	-	-	333	351
Firm indexes	-	-	111	113
Total indexes in industrial output plan	1,340	1,120	510	512

a - rough estimate.

b - another source claimed that indexes were reduced from 1,200 in 1965 to 67 in 1966. Miroslav Sokol, ZG, No. 10, 1967; cf. Josef Lenart, NM, No. 1, 1966.

Source: M. Kulich and V. Markvart, PH, No. 7-8, 1965, p. 29.

industrial branch. Wholesale prices would be used for computing the output, but parity prices would be indicators for the producers and the customers. The output of capital goods would be computed in value terms and a balance would be kept by central purchasing organs for each branch. In case of specifically approved investments, deliveries of capital goods would be reckoned separately and would be mandatory. In consumer goods, binding assignments would be set for only a few important "necessities."[9]

Supply of labor, allotments of capital funds, and the balance of payments would remain under central aegis. The labor plan would take account of the ceiling on the number of employees which would apply only to the Ministry of Labor and to the national committees. As long as those organs would supply their planned quotas of employees, no quotas were to be set for EPU's and enterprises. In some cases the wage funds would still be centrally determined and limits on the number of employees would still be imposed. Investment limits would be set by the plan, but wider variations would be permitted if an EPU or an enterprise would have their own investment funds or could arrange for credits. The prerogatives of enterprises and EPU's in the investment field were increased by reducing the volume of centralized and increasing that of decentralized investments. Binding directives would also be issued for research and development activity and for defense requirements.

The financial plans were considerably altered by including the estimates of the formation and allocation of GY and profits. Concurrently, the importance of these plans within the entire planning system was to be greatly enhanced.

Should the enterprise suffer any financial losses because of the centrally determined assignments, it could claim indemnification from its superiors. Furthermore, the enterprise was entitled to protest some of the directives and seek remedial action from its superiors.

One of the plan's main shortcomings was the lack of criteria for optimalizing the plan, attributed mainly to deficient research in this area, to defects in pricing which seriously hindered application of efficiency criteria, and to the flagrant shortcomings in the gathering and processing of information.[10]

It was fully realized that, in many respects, especially in plan construction and criteria for plan verification, the transitional system greatly resembled the traditional one. Essentially, the practice of balancing virtually in natura--without resorting to the equilibrating mechanism--was not abandoned. Whether, when, how, and what criteria would be used to construct an optimal plan remained a moot question. The problem of deriving parameters from a plan that was "arbitrarily" constructed continued to haunt the planners. At best the plan could be implemented better--by itself no mean achievement--but economic verification would still be virtually absent. Scarcity prices--emanating either from a genuine market, conceived as shadow prices, or derived *à tâtonnements* by a central planning board--would be required for the economic verification of production. As we have seen in Chapter 3, the Czechoslovaks, contrary to their East European confreres, demonstrated a propensity to rather trust genuine market prices. They often bypassed the other alternatives, sometimes giving the impression that they were not fully aware of the opportunities offered by planometrics.

In the new system the plan could not be used effectively without having an orderly operating market. The market was regarded, *inter alia*, as beneficial in providing the entire planning process with objective criteria and freeing it from continuous disputes between enterprises and central agencies--usually arbitrarily settled. But there was no such market. Its introduction was considered as a key problem to be effectively solved only by the central agencies. One could hardly quarrel with the earthy comment that "it will, to a considerable extent, depend on the central agencies' approach to the problems involved and on the methods employed by them whether at all, how soon, and how intensively" the enterprises would be placed in a position compelling them to work efficiently. In this context the plan was regarded as a fundamental tool for managing the economy which would "supplement and inject a solid long-term element into market operations, would accelerate the progressive results achieved by the market, and would enable society to consider noneconomic aspects in economic development."[11]

Market pressures were to force inefficient enterprises to improve their operations and to concentrate on a product mix that could be profitably produced with existing equipment. The "inordinately inefficient" enterprises would have to be liquidated. However, such a policy was unsuccessfully advocated in the past and it was doubtful whether it would be more successful in the future.

The theses of the Thirteenth Congress of the CPC held in May, 1966, alluded to the partial implementation of the reform by January 1, 1966, because the work had not progressed far enough and because "economic practice had not, so far, created sufficient certainty and stability about the instruments and regulations." This situation was labeled "a temporary phenomenon accompanying the introduction of the new system, while the old way of thinking still survived." The delay was also blamed on the fact that so far the problem of creating instruments for more economical production had been attacked without sufficient attention to redistribution of national income and to the ensuing structural changes.[12]

THE 1966 VERSION OF THE NEW SYSTEM

One of the partial changes introduced at the beginning of 1966 was the use of the GY scheme in most industries, with the profit scheme used in exceptional cases (e.g., the food industry). The creation and distribution of GY (profit) is schematically illustrated in Chart 4.

At the enterprises where profit incentives were used, the distribution of profit was similar to that of GY, but wages were included in costs and, instead of the workers' fund, a premium fund was created.[13]

It was expected that the repartition of the aggregate 1966 GY (profit) was going to be: 1) remittances to budget, 26 per cent (of which 55 per cent should represent basic levies, 14 per cent levies on the increase of GY, and 31 per cent levies on capital); 2) insurance, bank interest charges, fees, etc., 13 per cent; 3)

Chart 4

CREATION AND DISTRIBUTION OF GY, 1966

I	Sales revenue and other income		
	± (i)	changes in the stock of materials, work in process, and finished goods	
	+ (ii)	price subsidies	
	- (iii)	turnover tax	
	- (iv)	material inputs	
	- (v)	depreciation on fixed assets	
II	GY created		
	- transfers to the state budget		
	(i)	levy on capital	
	(ii)	basic transfer from GY	
	(iii)	transfer from increase of GY	
	(iv)	supplementary transfers	
III	GY net of transfers to the state		
	± (i)	penalties, fines, etc.	
	- (ii)	bank interest charges	
	- (iii)	installments on bank credits	
IV	Disposable GY allotted to:		
	(i)	fund for replacement of assets	
	(ii)	welfare fund	
	(iii)	reserve fund	
	(iv)	risk fund (in some cases)	
	(v)	workers' fund	
V	Allocations of workers fund to:		
	(i)	basic wages and salaries	
	(ii)	profit-sharing premiums	

allocation to the enterprises' funds and to the bank accounts, 2 per cent; 4) allocations to workers' (premium) funds, 59 per cent. The basic levy was to be remitted pari passu with the degree of GY plan fulfillment. However, in case of overfulfillment, 50 per cent of GY would be remitted to the budget and the remainder would be left at the enterprise.[14]

Obviously, the size of the transfer to the state determined not only the budgetary revenue, but also the size of GY retained by the enterprise. By ruling on the size and methods of transferring to the budget, the state exercised considerable control over the size and distribution of GY (profit). It was emphasized that, in order for the transfers to be successful economic tools of indirect management, the rates and regulations should be "objectively" determined, should remain stable over a number of years, should aim at equalizing conditions for all enterprises, and, in particular, should not put well-managed enterprises at a disadvantage. It was decided that several levies, which could be easier manipulated to fit the different conditions, would be more propitious than one. The following explanations were offered for the functions assigned to the different levies and the manner of their determination and transfer:

1) The levy on capital was introduced to promote better utilization of fixed assets, to induce enterprises to carry out expansion and modernization economically, and to reject investments that bring in low returns. The capital levy should express the minimum profitability on investments. In principle, the rate of the levy should be uniform for all branches of the economy. The charge was 6 per cent of the depreciated cost of fixed capital in industry, transportation, construction, and trade (3 per cent on the distribution network, on structures in railway transportation, and on retail outlets and their equipment)--seemingly, a below equilibrium rate. No capital levy was imposed on fixed assets for housing,

welfare and social services, and water and air purification installations. The uniformity of the rate adopted in industry was apparently not dictated by a particular stand taken on the raging controversy of differentiated versus uniform capital charge rates in Eastern Europe. It was not necessary to allow for differentiation of rates in various branches since the differentiation of the contributions to the budget from different branches was ensured through the other levies, especially through the basic levy on GY and the levy on the increase of GY.[15] The levy on capital was to become a significant source of budgetary revenue. It was expected that eventually it would overshadow the turnover tax.[16]

2) In differentiating the size of the basic transfer to the state budget, the planners aimed at providing an equal start for all enterprises.[17] The basic transfer was calculated by recomputing what the GY was in 1965 and the need of the enterprises for decentralized resources.[18] This reference base served as a starting point in computing the amount that could be siphoned off in 1966 in the form of the basic transfer. When computing the basic transfer, allowances were made for capital levies, bank interest charges, and appropriations for the welfare fund. But no allowances were made for penalties, fines, etc. and for allotments to the reserve fund and to the profit-sharing fund. Thus, a redistribution of funds among enterprises was accomplished. In the understandable attempt to put enterprises on an equal footing, the volitional methods were reintroduced by the back door. By attempting to neutralize the effect of fallacious prices and costing, the planners were once again placing the better-operating enterprises at a disadvantage and were favoring those with better bargaining abilities. Furthermore by relating disposable GY to 1965, the planners were perpetuating the fallacies of the traditional system. The basic transfer was to be determined on the basis of the plan as a lump sum differentiated annually, but set at the outset of the FYP. However, in the case

of the 1966-70 FYP, the annual transfers were to be set only for 1966, 1967, and 1968. Basic transfers could only be altered in case of price changes and other essential changes. The basic transfers were to be centrally determined for ministries, which would disaggregate them among their EPU's, which would break them down among their enterprises.

3) The rates of transfer from the increase of GY over the preceding year were to remain constant for the entire FYP (or in this case from 1966 to 1968). These rates too were differentiated by branches, EPU's, and enterprises, if there were significant differences in their initial conditions and cost structures. The rates were centrally determined for individual EPU's which would break them down for their enterprises. This scheme aimed at inducing overfulfillment of planned GY. When determining the basic transfer, although the increase of GY would be taken into account, the above-plan GY would not, thus allowing the enterprise to retain a larger portion of the above-plan GY. Soon after its introduction this system of transfers from GY was discredited. It was particularly criticized for being too tightly interwoven with the plan. Apparently, it did not provide a reliable basis for judging performance.[19]

4) Supplementary transfers were set up as punitive measures against "unjustified" price and wage increases.[20] For example, to curb wage increases in prosperous enterprises, a pointedly progressive tax was imposed on the difference between the actual workers' fund and that derived from a multiplication of the number of employees by the 1965 average wages. The progression of the tax would ultimately impose a ceiling on the rate at which wages could increase. The issue whether to aim at a rapid wage rise, with the consequent heavy taxation, or to devote a larger share of GY to other funds, was one to be decided jointly by the enterprise's management and the trade union representatives.

To strengthen the role of interest, interest

charges were excluded from costs and were deducted from GY only after the obligations to the budget were met, so that the enterprise alone would shoulder the burden of the interest charge. Moreover, such a procedure focused attention on the deduction of interest from GY, whereas as a cost element it would be lost among the other multifarious elements. Interestingly enough, no reference was made to the usual Marxist argument that interest is a part of surplus product and not of costs.[21]

The enterprise was bound to earmark funds for the reserve fund. The minimum reserve fund was to be determined for branches as a percentage of the total wage fund. Similarly, superiors were to determine the minimum rates valid for two to three years to form the reserve funds at their subordinate units. The reserve fund was designed primarily for paying wages in case of shortages in GY and for financing other requirements, such as supplementing the fund for replacement of assets, but only if such spending should not encroach on the minimum level. The enterprises were also obliged to finance working capital from the reserve fund if and when the bank refused to extend credit. In 1966, enterprises were bound to set aside 1.5 per cent of the wage bill (1 per cent in case of enterprises working on the profit scheme) for the reserve fund. Otherwise, they were not entitled to boost average wages over the basic rates agreed upon in the collective agreement.[22] Similar, and in addition, to the reserve fund, the risk fund was created, particularly, in trade organizations. The risk fund was to be used, for instance, for compensating for losses from clearance sales.

The fund for replacement of assets was to serve for financing the enterprise's investments. It was left entirely up to the enterprise to decide whether to overhaul an asset or to replace it. The major sources of this fund were to be depreciation, allotments from GY, and proceeds from the sale of assets. In 1966, it was decided to transfer the entire depreciation to the state budget.[23] Within the next few years no significant increase in enterprise investments were expected to come from this fund.

The welfare fund was to be primarily earmarked for the collective needs of the workers; i.e., culture, health, recreation, etc. The minimum rate of contribution from GY to this fund (identical for all branches of the economy) was to be expressed as a percentage of the wage fund. This fund could also be used for extending loans to provide for employees' cooperative housing and for scholarships for employees continuing their education. The fund could supplement the workers' fund if the latter was insufficient, even when supplemented by the reserve fund, for paying the guaranteed wages. Funds could be transferred to the fund for replacement of assets.

The workers' fund was to be used primarily to pay wages and premiums for individual performance according to existing wage scales. During the year those rewards were to be paid from the workers' fund and at the end of the year, should the results warrant it, the employees were to participate in profit-sharing. The rules for profit-sharing were to be determined in advance by collective agreements between management and the trade unions. Although the premiums were to be related to the over-all performance of the enterprises, the size of profit-sharing for individual employees was to be tied into the performance of particular cost centers. Advances on profit-sharing could be made during the year. It was estimated that in 1966 the share of workers' fund devoted to premiums would amount to about 30 per cent and would rise in the future. In case of inadequate funds, the enterprise was to pay wages from the reserve fund, and if the latter were insufficient, the enterprise could dip into the welfare fund. If all these funds were insufficient, the superiors could place a share of their own reserve fund at the enterprise's disposal, or the enterprise could seek a payroll credit at the bank. But then it would be obliged to cut individual wages to the guaranteed level of 92 per cent of basic wages.

When establishing the transfers from GY for their wards, the EPU's assured for themselves a certain income by keeping a portion of what was transferred to the state. The EPU's other financial resources included a share in depreciation and a share of funds designated for promoting science and technology. The EPU's diverted these funds to a reserve fund, an investment fund, and a technical development fund (not created at the enterprise as originally envisaged). The EPU's were also to use their resources for settling the current loans of their wards which they had guaranteed and for financing their own administrative expenses.[24]

Early in 1966 a new decree on pricing was issued to become effective on March 1, 1966.[25] Selling prices were defined as prices at which products were sold on the domestic market: 1) wholesale prices were prices at which products were sold to socialist organizations to be used in production, in construction, for export, and for defense; 2) trade prices were prices at which domestic trade organizations procured goods for resale at retail prices; 3) retail prices were prices at which goods were sold to the consumer; and 4) procurement prices were prices at which authorized organizations bought agricultural products from agricultural producers. Foreign prices were defined as: 1) world prices, at which current trade agreements were concluded; 2) actual prices, at which imports were bought and exports were sold; 3) prices f.o.b. Czechoslovak border, adjusted for expenses incurred abroad to consummate the transaction. Special prices were those listed in tariffs, selling prices of buildings, price limits (i.e., ceilings on prices of new products in the research and development plan and on imports), price estimates for products not yet in production, and settlement prices.

The wholesale prices consisted of the average branch cost of production (sebestoimost) plus a profit markup. The markup was to be calculated so as to cover interest on capital, basic levies from GY, additional levies, appropriations for installment payments of investment credits, and appropriations for the enterprise's funds. Generally, costs included research and development expenditures, licenses, patents, premiums for inventions, design and assembly work, and packaging costs. In special cases, wholesale prices were raised or reduced by price subsidies or reductions to promote or restrain output. Generally, a trade price consisted of the wholesale price plus turnover tax. The retail price consisted of the trade price plus the trade margin.

Three types of prices were distinguished: fixed, limited, and free prices. Fixed prices encompassed primarily key materials and other goods which 1) were prime determining factors of the key production program and were the costs and prices in successive processing; 2) had to be centrally distributed in view of persistent shortages; 3) significantly affected the pattern of consumption and claimed a large share of consumers' budgets; and 4) for social and political reasons, had to have low, uniform, and stable prices.

Limited prices applied mainly to goods produced in a large variety and whose product mix was subject to frequent changes. The limits could be specified as 1) a ceiling or a floor on the price and 2) a directive price limit which served as a base from which individual selling prices could be raised or lowered, with the ceiling on these variations usually stipulated as a percentage of the limit or fixed amount, sometimes together with a floor or without it.

Free prices applied to goods: 1) which were produced under competitive conditions; 2) for which a buyers' market existed; 3) whose prices were essentially determined by fixed or limited prices of substitutes; 4) which were luxuries and fashion and technical novelties; 5) whose prices did not perceptibly affect either production costs or consumers' budgets; 6) which were exported and whose prices were set corresponding to world prices; 7) which were sold by the producers' own marketing outlet; and 8) for special services rendered by the research and development departments. It should be noted that consumer goods could have either free or limited prices only after the turnover tax rate was established.

If the selling prices of free- or limited-price goods indicated an "undesirable" trend, the appropriate agency would initiate a reclassification. Presumably the limited prices would then become fixed and the free would become limited. A product not explicitly included in the free- or limited-price categories was regarded as a fixed-price good.

The decree took pains to elucidate that new prices could only be set for new goods, in order to circumvent price inflation. As in the past, prices of new goods were set by referring to similar existing goods.

The prices of buildings could be determined by negotiation between builders and investors as definite selling prices on the basis of the builder's approved cost estimates. This procedure also applied to subcontracted equipment.

Article 18 was particularly noteworthy. It specified that prices of exports and imports were set like those of goods not subject to foreign trade and only when approved by appropriate central agencies could prices of such goods be set with reference to foreign prices.

Since increased stress was placed on injecting flexibility into price setting, it might be instructive to see what a proposal for price revision was to contain: 1) the reason why the existing price was to be revised: 2) a calculation of how the new price would affect the producer, the user, and the budget; 3) a statement from main customers expressing their viewpoint on the proposed price change (in case of major disagreements a statement from experts, technical agencies, institutes, etc. would have to be provided). The proposal for setting the price of a new product was to contain: 1) a detailed description of the new product's attributes, supplemented by a sample, photograph, and drawing, detailed description of technical attributes, and possible usages; 2) reason for the product's introduction; 3) itemized cost calculation; 4) price comparison data; 5) comparison between proposed and preliminary prices, with justifications for deviations; 6) sales estimates; 7) suggested inclusion in a price category, 8) the reaction of main customers to the proposed price and the main points of eventual counterproposals, and 9) description of the product according to standard classification.

In a nutshell, the price-setting procedure was prescribed as follows: The proposal for a price revision or for setting a price for a new product was to be prepared by the supplier or his superior. If the supplier's branch directorate was entitled to set the price, it could proceed only after consulting the branch directorate of the main user. If price-setting was the prerogative of the ministry, the branch directorate was to submit the proposal to all the central agencies involved. The appropriate ministry could set or revise the price only after consulting the main user's ministry. If the new price affected the state budget and if the turnover tax was not imposed at a fixed rate, the appropriate ministry had also to consult the MF. The same procedures applied to setting fixed and limited prices.

An organization which benefited from "unjustified" price increases would be instructed to transfer the full amount of improperly acquired funds to the state budget and, as a rule, another 50 per cent additional levy would be imposed if the "improperly" acquired funds were detected by a central control organ.

The SCT, in conjunction with the SCFPW, enacted pricing measures in order to promote technically advanced goods, decided upon revising fixed prices and price limits in the construction industry, and exercised jurisdiction over prices of design work and engineering services. The ministries ruled on: 1) fixed prices and price limits for new products, unless the SCFPW (or SCT in case of construction) reserved the right to do so; 2) revision of fixed prices and of price limits, with the general revision of the price level decided by the government or the SCFPW; 3) classification of goods into price categories, only if such goods were produced and used within the same branch; 4) which products were technically advanced and the period for which the novelties would be included in free prices; and 5) lowering prices on obsolete products. The ministries also submitted proposals to the SCFPW on classification of products in price categories and on changes in fixed prices and price levels.

In case of goods sold directly by the branch directorates or their wards, the former ruled on: 1) the price limits for new products in those cases where they were especially authorized to do so by the ministries and 2) price limits for products at the research and development stage. When the branch directorates concluded contracts they listed agreed-upon fee and limited selling prices. But the statute of the enterprise might specify that it would have to seek the branch directorate's approval of selling prices of products included in the free and limited price categories, prior to entering into a contract.

The price revision conducted according to the foregoing instructions was expected to be completed by the end of 1966 so that the new prices could go into effect on January 1, 1967.

It was reported that as of January 1, 1966, a partial adjustment of wholesale prices took place, affecting 10 per cent to 15 per cent of industrial products, predominantly in the consumer goods and machine-building industries. On the average, wholesale prices increased by about 4.1 per cent. It was expected that 92 per cent of foodstuffs and 59 per cent of manufactured consumer goods would carry fixed prices. About 32 per cent of manufactured consumer goods would be sold at free prices, and

Table 57

WHOLESALE PRICE INDEX, 1966
(1965 = 100)

Industries and selected products	Index	Industries and selected products	Index
Industry	103.5	Chemical industry	102.4
Mining	100.1	petrochemical products	104.3
hard coal	100.1	paints and varnishes	99.4
brown coal and lignite	100.0	Construction	99.7
Energy and power	102.4	concrete products	100.2
electricity	103.2	building ceramics	97.5
Heavy industry	102.5	Consumer goods	115.1
electric appliances	100.1	lamps	111.0
broadcasting, television, and		saw mill products	107.5
reproduction equipment	110.3	wooden furniture	111.9
time-measuring devices	104.8	porcelain	120.4
office equipment	116.3	cotton fabrics and fibers	101.8
measuring equipment	118.3	silk fabrics and fibers	116.2
mechanized hand tools	106.1	woolen fabrics and fibers	133.9
grinding tools and equipment	105.9	knitted underwear	117.2
air conditioning equipment	105.4	bed linen	114.2
trolley buses	116.0	clothing	132.8
electric locomotives	112.3	leather footwear	101.5
household electric appliances		furs	130.3
and refrigerators	101.3	Food industry	100.0

Source: SP, No. 2, 1967, pp. 47-48.

19 per cent at limited prices, in order to allow for flexibility in pricing those goods which possess fashion and technical novelty attributes. By mid-1966, only 7 per cent of goods were sold at free prices. Fixed prices encompassed two thirds of the entire sales volume. At the end of 1966, it was reported that the shares of fixed prices were 71.5 per cent, limited prices 24.4 per cent, and free prices 4.1 per cent. The dual prices system continued to prevail: "So far we have not been able to achieve an immediate relationship between the movements of retail and wholesale prices, which still isolate the decisions concerning production from actual market demand."[26] Price subsidies were not eliminated. To avoid the sharp increases in wholesale prices--required to meet the new levies and the new financing provisions--"temporary" subsidies for the old prices were introduced. Income of the enterprises became dependent on usually "subjectively determined grants," creating uncertainty and disincentives. In 1966 the budget subsidies were to amount to about 7 to 8 per cent of industrial earnings. It was admitted that such subsidies were incompatible with the new system and were bound to evoke many conflicts.[27]

Like with any other subsidy system, the main problem encountered was the danger of rewarding lagging enterprises for their inefficiency. About 13 per cent of required subsidies were replaced by reducing capital levies; 23 per cent were set as fixed amounts in order to curtail output of some goods; 17 per cent were set in kcs. per unit of specified output; 24 per cent were established as percentage of sales of given goods; 11 per cent were set as percentage of markups of foreign and domestic trade enterprises; and the rest were set as amounts per standard unit of some raw material inputs, to mitigate special increases in cases where raw material costs went up and the prices of output remained unchanged. Attempts were made to replace subsidies on sales revenue by subsidies per unit of output to influence the desired product mix.[28]

A wider use of self-financing (enterprise funds

and credits) was envisaged for investment activity, but still a substantial share of investment was to be financed from the state budget. The centrally planned investments were to be financed from the central purse. Branch investments were to be financed by specific branch funds and credits. Enterprise investments were to be primarily self-financed (with a floor of 6 per cent on the enterprise's resources and a ceiling of 9 per cent on credit). Investment credits were to be used on a wider scale than heretofore for financing branch investments, but they were not anticipated to play any role in financing central investments. Their role in financing enterprise investments was to be confined to temporary advances and the financing of modernization.[29]

The structure of investments was planned to consist of: branch investments (21 per cent), enterprise investments (14 per cent), specifically identified central investments (16 per cent), and nonidentified central investments (49 per cent). The sources for financing those investments were: 51 per cent from the enterprises' and branches' own funds; 3 per cent from credits; and 46 per cent from the state budget. The 1966 budget envisaged the over-all share of enterprises in total investment outlays at 41.7 per cent--a considerable increase from the 32.8 per cent share in 1965. The plan for 1966 called upon enterprises to share (at a rate of 15 per cent) in the investment outlays expended on them. The bank was still called upon to control investments, particularly to uncover such failings as dissipation of investment funds, undue extension of completion dates, and failure of the project to meet specifications after it was put into operation.[30]

It was argued that although profitability of investment was much higher in the Czech lands than in Slovakia, it could not be the only criterion because then the already industrialized regions would attract resources and manpower. Hence, direct intervention of the state was required to redistribute resources and to channel them to underdeveloped areas. Some specific measures were to be used, such as a larger share of subsidies for underdeveloped regions, lower interest rates on credits (reduction of the rate from 8 to 2 per cent), and reduction of the capital levy from 6 to 4 per cent.[31]

Research and development activities were to be undertaken and financed mainly by central agencies and EPU's. A curious novelty was the specification that enterprises should in the future compensate the state for any benefits they might derive from state-subsidized research activities.

In 1966 the working capital of enterprises was confiscated and replaced by credits. But enterprises were not left entirely without funds at the beginning of 1966. Permanent liabilities and other enterprise funds which were often used as temporary sources of working capital still remained at the enterprises' disposal, amounting to about 28 per cent of their working capital needs.[32] The confiscation was justified on the grounds that otherwise the enterprises that were in more favorable positions in the past would be favored because they would use less credit and would save on interest.[33]

To save on interest charges, enterprises could attempt to muster their own funds to replace credit. For example, if an enterprise earned a larger GY and did not immediately increase wages, the excess of GY would remain on the current account, reducing the need for credit, therefore, saving on interest and increasing the enterprise's disposable GY.[34] But if the share of interest in total costs was so insignificant that the minimization of interest charges would not be a prime objective for management, or if, in cases of shortages, supplies would have to be accumulated at almost all costs, it was doubtful that there would be any real drive to replace bank credits by the enterprise's own funds. Moreover, the enterprise might not entirely get rid of bank control by mustering its own funds. In addition, the insecurity of the transitional period--the length of which was inderterminate--would make management suspicious of future confiscations of working capital to replace it once again by credit. Therefore, the incentive to generate its own resources and to convert them into inventory acquisitions, etc., during a given period would be stronger than that to save on credit.

In the old system a multiplicity of special-purpose bank accounts had to be kept, with restrictions on transfers. The purpose was to control that funds earmarked for particular purposes were spent for those purposes only. Therefore, one could hardly speak of financial autonomy under the *khozraschet* system, as traditionally practiced. By establishing the current account at the bank from which all current needs were to be met, a step forward toward financial autonomy was made. Enterprises were thus allowed a larger field of maneuverability of funds.

The credit contract between the enterprise and the bank stipulated, *inter alia*, that: 1) the separation of working capital and investment funds would be retained; 2) a single current account would suffice, with no subaccounts required; 3) the enterprise pledged itself to use credit only for working capital and exclusively for efficient and profitable endeavors, usually understood to mean the speeding up of working capital turnover; 4) the enterprise would promptly exact payment from its customers; 5) the enterprise would give precedence to its own excess operational funds (e.g., reserve fund, welfare fund, workers' fund) for financing working capital, with once again the stipulation that investment funds could not be used for this purpose; 6) wages would be paid from the current account in accordance with the formation of the workers' fund; 7) the enterprise was to submit to the bank an impressive number of reports on actual and planned operations, including inventory reports; and 8) the bank would extend credit in the amount stipulated in the contract, charging a 6 per cent interest rate in 1966, and would credit the enterprise with an 1.8 per cent interest rate on the unused credit balance in the current account.[35] The amount of credit stipulated in the contract would be based on the reports submitted by the enterprise. The enterprise would, of course, be inclined to submit such data as to get a larger possible credit allowance for the duration of the contract, in order to provide a safety margin for hitches in production and supply to be drawn on without having to face the bank with explanations for additional credit. The interest offered by the bank on the unused credit balance, instead of counteracting this tendency, gave it additional impetus, although not a very potent one. Moreover, the inducement to save on credits was not very strong either.

Should an enterprise overdraw its credit limit and, after a grace period, fail to remedy the situation, a progressively higher interest rate (differentiated by branches) would be charged, depending on the duration of the overdraft. The highest penalty that the bank could impose on an enterprise for mismanagement of working capital would be to refuse further credits. It then would set a maximum limit on credits, actually freezing them at the amount already extended. Then, enterprises would have to pay off their debts to the extent of receipts, only with the exception of wages for which credits could be obtained. But enterprises might finance their needs through non-payment of debts. It would then be unlikely that the superiors would not come to the rescue and pressures might be exerted on the bank to re-extend credit.[36]

Separate credit contracts were concluded for working capital (the current account) and for investments. Contracts for the current account were concluded for a calendar year, to coincide with the annual plan. The contracts for investment credits were concluded separately for each project.

It was reported that construction enterprises were reluctant to provide for the improvement of working capital turnover. The bank insisted on an average reduction of inventories by 4.8 per cent compared to the actual stocks of 1965, but the contracts concluded specified only an average reduction of 2.3 per cent. In submitting data justifying their credit requirements, construction firms deflated their permanent liabilities and underestimated their own funds. In many cases the credit contracts were concluded only after protracted negotiations and intervention by superiors.[37]

Although generally great hopes were placed in the somewhat magic role of the interest rate, more sober voices were also heard. It was pointed out that enterprises might not be inclined to allocate a part of their GY to finance working capital in order to reduce the interest charges. The enterprise's price for saving on the interest might be too high. For example, during the first year an enterprise might have to forgo 100 kcs. from the workers' fund to save only 6 kcs. in interest charges. "The possibility of immediate distribution of premiums would unquestionably outweigh for a long time the incentive of a benefit that would materialize only in a few years."[38]

It is interesting to note that it was anticipated that if the generally applicable interest rates would not induce parsimony of working capital, the CSB would be allowed to gradually increase the interest rate until an effective rate was reached.[39] It might be that the *à tâtonnements* process, if it was to produce palpable results, might require some interest rates which might be unacceptable as a policy weapon.

On the basis of an investigation of forty-six enterprises for the first quarter of 1966, it was found that most enterprises were using relatively less credit than planned, but their average stocks markedly increased. It was obvious that this form of financing was ineffective as a tool for discouraging hoarding. Generally, punitive rates and other sanctions were not applied because the bank kept extending the grace period for enterprises that exceeded credit limits and failed to apply sanctions even when it was clear that the enterprise would not rectify the situation. There seemed to be a laxity on the part of the bank to ensure repayment of credits.[40]

Management complained that the CSB officials were not convinced themselves of the potency of the interest rate to curtail demands of enterprises for larger working capital credits, for otherwise they would not interfere in the planning of working capital requirements. Apparently the bank officials did not abandon their predilection for regulating inventories of enterprises. Contrary to other opinions, this source claimed that interest was a potent factor in restraining inventory accumulations, since it represented about 10 per cent of the workers' fund.[41]

As an anti-inflationary measure, attempts were made to induce enterprises not to spend immediately their above-plan funds by allowing the CSB to credit the enterprise's account with interest if the reserve fund exceeded the minimum and was kept for at least one year. Interest of about 8 per cent would also be credited to the accounts of enterprises that froze their own investment funds for at least three years.[42]

One of the novelties introduced in 1966 was the granting of foreign exchange credits by the CSB to enterprises for imports with a short and "guaranteed" return of the foreign currency. The bank was to extend credits for imports of machines, licenses, patents, or raw materials which were not included in the plan or which exceeded the plan and whose utilization could increase in inflow or reduce the outflow of foreign exchange. The enterprise would be obliged to repay the credit at the same exchange rate within the same year. The enterprise would also have to justify how the goods produced with the help of the imports would enhance exports, or to what extent they would curb imports.[43]

PERFORMANCE IN 1966

The moderate growth momentum picked up by the Czechoslovak economy since the fateful recession of

1963 continued in 1966. The reported increase of national income of 7 per cent over 1965 (as against a planned rise of 3.8 per cent) was the highest since 1960.[44] Personal consumption was reported to have risen by 4 per cent--slightly less than the 5.1 per cent increase in 1965. There was also a moderate drop in the growth of gross industrial output which rose by 7.4 per cent as compared to the 7.9 per cent increase in 1965. However, the plan for 1966 called for only a 5.5 per cent rise in industrial output. The increase in employment by 2.6 per cent was higher than that of 1965. The rise of industrial labor productivity by 4.7 per cent was slower than that recorded in 1965. Industrial performance was less satisfactory than in 1965. The improvement in performance relied heavily on extensive growth factors. In 1966, 64 per cent of the growth of industrial output was attributed to labor productivity, with a plan target of 77 per cent. It would appear that the efforts to modernize capacities and to improve performance did not produce significant results, at least as measured by the admittedly spurious index of labor productivity.

The increases in output of various branches of industry were more evenly distributed than in the past two years, as illustrated in Table 58. In almost all branches there was a slowdown in the rate of growth of industrial output. The deceleration was particularly acute in the chemical and metallurgical industries. The rate of growth of electric power approached that of 1965. Only the food industry showed a considerable acceleration--from 1.8 per cent increase in output in 1965 over 1964 to a 4.9 per cent increase in 1966, the highest since 1961. This was particularly due to the better than average performance in agriculture. While in most cases the rates of growth of output decelerated, they exceeded the plan targets, some even substantially as in the machine-building and chemical industries. But the planned rate of expansion of electric power was underfulfilled by 1.4 per cent.

A faster growth of inputs and inventories than

Table 58

GROWTH OF GROSS OUTPUT IN INDUSTRY IN 1966 OVER 1965

Industries	Percentage increase of 1966 over 1965	
	Planned	Reported
Electric power	8.4	7.0
Metallurgy	5.0	8.2
Machine-building and metal-working	8.1	10.6
Chemicals	7.0	9.2
Manufactured consumer goods	3.3	6.4
Food-processing	3.9	4.9

Sources: HN, No. 7, 1967; CFT, No. 4, 1967, p.8; ESE 1966, Chapter II, p.8; and Oldrych Cernik, RP, December 19, 1966.

that of output recurred. Moreover, the relative increase in industrial and trade inventories was indicative of the lack of success in the efforts to adapt the structure of production to the pattern of demand. The lack of headway achieved in "qualitative" improvements was noted; not much was accomplished to enhance the technical level and quality of output. The existing constraints, which were hardly removed by the very fragmentary reform measures introduced in 1966, were considered to be the main obstacles.

Even though some improvement of the product mix was noted in metallurgy, chemistry, and machine-building, such as increased production of high-grade metals, plastics, and spare parts--output of spare parts for passenger cars rose by 39.8 per cent, for trucks and buses by 19.6 per cent, and for agricultural machines by 49.7 per cent[45]--industrial performance continued to be plagued by underfulfillment of customers' orders, low quality of raw materials and semifabricates, and a persisting shortage of spare parts.

Table 59

PRODUCTION OF SOME INDUSTRIAL GOODS IN 1966
(1965 = 100)

Goods	Index	Goods	Index
Electric power	106.8	Nitrogen fertilizers	114.0
Hard coal	96.8	Phosphorous fertilizers	101.2
Brown coal	101.2	Synthetic fibers	104.9
Coke	99.7	Plastics	114.7
Steel	106.1	Cement	107.3
Rolled materials	107.0	Lime	102.4
Steel tubing	107.8	Masonry materials	109.7
Machine tools	87.2	Timber	100.8
Roller bearings	110.0	Paper	104.9
Agricultural machinery	102.3	Cotton textiles	103.3
Tractors	92.2	Silk textiles	104.3
Locomotives	76.5	Linen textiles	103.6
electric locomotives	80.3	Wool textiles	102.8
Trucks	109.1	Footwear	101.8
Passenger cars	119.3	Meat	97.1
Washing machines	94.7	Milk	100.0
Refrigerators	114.7	Butter	100.7
Television sets	83.1	Beer	103.1
Sulfuric acid	105.2	Flour	97.1

Source: SP, No. 2, 1967, pp. 49-51.

A number of problems arose in the supply of inputs to enterprises. Apparently, the central plan largely provided for limiting central distribution and rationing and for normalizing the commercial relations between enterprises. But this was not always borne out by the plans at the lower levels. At times, additional directives for deliveries were considered as binding. There were definite tendencies to administratively distribute products on the part of the lower echelons, fortified by an enduring sellers' market.[46] There were persistent breakdowns in supplies. For example, the construction enterprise in Ceske Bujovice was able to get confirmed deliveries for only 10 per cent of some of its requirements. It had concluded contracts promising delivery of only two thirds of its requirements of polyvinyl chloride flooring. It was compelled to place the "finished" apartments at the disposal of tenants who were to provide themselves the flooring material. It was quite common for suppliers to confirm contracts with the stipulation that they would deliver their products if they could secure inputs. For example, the North Moravia Brickworks in Hranice informed the Prague Industrial Construction enterprise that it could not assume responsibility for delivery of bricks because it experienced difficulties in getting the required railroad cars. Enterprises were unwilling to reduce inventories until they could be reasonably assured of a regular flow of supplies.[47]

With a 7.4 per cent rise in industrial production, there was only a 4.4 per cent increase in final products for investment, consumption, and export. Although the rates of growth of final products were considerably lower than in 1965, the highest increase (9.9 per cent) was registered for investment, with a 3.3 per cent rise for consumption and a 4 per cent rise for exports.

The improvement of the capital-output ratio, begun in 1965, persisted in 1966. The share of liquid and gaseous fuels in the fuels-energy balance increased, indicating progress along the lines of one of the chief restructuring aims of the Fourth FYP.

Agricultural output increased by 10 per cent--an unmatched rate of growth since 1955. The trend of the preceding two years for the rate of growth of livestock output to outpace that of crop output (which, in fact, decelerated) was diametrically reversed, with crop output registering a 20.5 per cent growth rate and livestock increasing by only 1.6 per cent. Of course, the accelerated growth of crop output was partly an optical illusion produced by the sizable decline in 1965. The weather was favorable. Yields of all key crops were higher than in 1965. Increased investment and industrial supplies for agriculture were criticized on the grounds that they were both too large and too small. In the first place, they were disproportionate in relation to the growth of productivity and significantly boosted production costs. In the second place, they were both quantitatively and qualitatively insufficient to compensate for the exodus of manpower from agriculture to industry.

The 8.9 per cent growth rate registered in investment expenditures was 1 per cent higher than the planned rate. Outlays for investment were 9.5 per cent higher than in 1965. The share of investment outlays on equipment accelerated significantly--continuing the modernization trend initiated in 1964, so that between 1964 and 1966 investment expenditures on machinery and equipment increased by almost 50 per cent--whereas the volume of construction was again underfulfilled. There was a continuing rise in the volume of unfinished construction work. The persisting failures of the construction industry were again sharply felt. Centrally issued orders for starting new construction aggravated this situation. The stock of fixed capital was about 885 billion kcs. at the end of 1966, or about 5 per cent higher than in 1965.[48]

No radical reallocation of investment resources among sectors was noted, with a preferential allocation of investments to the chemical and energy

Table 60

INVESTMENT IN 1966
(1965 = 100)

	1966
Total investment	108.9
construction	106.8
Investment for:	
state sector	109.4
cooperative sector	108.3
social institutions	81.6
private sector	104.5

Source: SP, No. 2, 1967, p. 45.

branches recorded. Among the more important additions to existing capacity were 100,000-ton sulphuric acid facilities in the chemical industry and 660 MWh and 220 MWh additions to the Vojany and Ledvice power stations, respectively.

Whereas the means for a rapid expansion of consumption (both individual and collective) were largely provided by the propitious performance of agriculture and the good showing of industry, the rates of increase of both types of consumption (4 per cent in each case) were disappointing and showed a decelerating movement in comparison to 1965, even though they were still the second largest in the 1960's. With only a 0.5 per cent natural increase of population, the increase in per capita consumption was somewhat higher. The growing allocations to accumulation seem to have been mainly absorbed by unplanned growth of inventories.

The accelerated growth of the population's total income since 1964 continued, although the 5 per cent rise in 1966 represented a downward trend in comparison to the previous years. The growth of income was mainly absorbed by the 2.6 per cent rise in employment--exceeding the planned level--primarily achieved by further drawing on the dwindling feminine labor force reservoir. Average wages rose by 2.4 per cent--a slight acceleration in comparison to 1965--whereas the budget for 1966 provided for a 3.3 per cent rise.[49]

The cost of living was reported to have risen by only 0.3 per cent, evincing more stability than in 1965 and being the lowest rise since the 1960 and 1961 decreases in living costs. But the almost stable level of retail prices until October, 1966, was later sharply offset by price increases of foodstuffs, beverages, and services, resulting in a swifter growth of the population's expenditures than of its income in the last quarter of 1966, drawing on the net balance of outstanding consumer credit and having a decelerating effect on savings. As a result of a multitude of price variations, their impact was not easy to assess. The complaints voiced against the price increases and their general tenor might be indicative of an understatement of the recorded statistical averages.

Real wages were reported to have increased by 2.1 per cent, hence faster than in 1965, but slightly slower than in 1964. The unplanned rise in employment hampered the faster growth of average wages which would have been more in line with recorded productivity achievements. It also apparently retarded the movement toward wage differentiation.

Retail sales turnover rose by 5.2 per cent (by 0.7 per cent more than planned), indicating a slight deceleration in comparison to 1965 (5.6 per cent increase), but remaining the second largest since 1960. An increase in consumer goods imports apparently widened the range of goods on the market. The consumer was also said to have benefited from the application of higher quality control standards. The plan for 1966 had called for a 3 per cent rise in food sales and a 6 per cent rise in other consumer goods sales. The plan for food sales was underfulfilled (with a rise of 2 per cent) and that for sales of the other consumer goods was overfulfilled (with a 9 per cent rise). The rise in food sales was the smallest since 1963 and that of other consumer goods sales was the largest since

1960. Shortages of light industry's products, such as bed linen, clothing from synthetic fabrics, knitwear fashions, toys, jewelery, packaging materials, beer, etc., were noted. The sharpest rise was registered in the sales of automobiles which went up by 68 per cent (44,000 cars sold in 1966 as against 26,000 sold in 1965), closely followed by sales of television sets which rose by 19 per cent. However, the size of the waiting list for automobiles was continually swelling.

The plan for housing construction was underfulfilled by 85 per cent. Whereas the plan had called for the construction of 82,000 dwellings, only 75,000 were built. It was the smallest number of dwellings built since 1959 (3.7 per cent less than in 1965). The most acute decline was in the state construction of housing which dropped by 21.4 per cent, whereas the cooperative housing construction increased by 4.1 per cent, and private building rose by 0.8 per cent. The private building of dwellings which had recovered from 1960 (18,000) to 1961 (30,900) and dropped again gradually to 19,200 by 1965, recovered only slightly by 1966 with 19,400 dwellings. The reduced number of dwellings completed by the state sector in 1966 was not counteracted by an increased number of flats constructed by housing cooperatives. There were sharp fluctuations during the year. Whereas only 9,000 dwellings were built in the first quarter, 33,000 were supposedly completed in the last quarter, with a marked deterioration of quality in the construction work. Unfinished housing projects grew by 12,000 dwellings, inflating the number of unfinished dwellings to 119,000 by the end of the year.

In order to alleviate the severe shortage of housing and to siphon off purchasing power, private individuals were permitted to pool interests to construct cooperative apartment houses, where any individual was entitled to own only one apartment. Tenants of old houses could buy the apartments which they occupied, but only if all of them decided to do so.[50]

Total foreign trade turnover increased by 2.3 per cent (imports by 2.4 and exports by 2.3 per cent).[51] Trade with the socialist countries dropped by 1.9 per cent, and the sharpest decline was registered in trade with CMEA partners as a whole (-3.6 per cent), of which the most significant decrease took place in trade with the U.S.S.R. (-7.2 per cent). Trade with the U.S.S.R. in 1966 was even lower than in 1964--registering a drop of 2.1 per cent. Whereas both imports from and exports to the socialist countries and CMEA partners as a whole declined about evenly, imports from the U.S.S.R. dropped by only 4.2 per cent and exports to the U.S.S.R. fell by 10 per cent. Trade with the socialist countries amounted to 69.1 per cent of total turnover.

There was a remarkable shift in trade toward socialist countries non-CMEA members. However, it should be noted that because of the inconsequential share of some of these countries in Czechoslovak trade, the growth of their trade with Czechoslovakia was not overly significant. For example, imports from Albania increased by 43.1 per cent; exports to Yugoslavia rose by 37.3 per cent; imports from North Korea went up by 40.4 per cent, whereas exports dropped by 38.2 per cent; exports to North Vietnam increased by 39.4 per cent, whereas imports declined by 27.1 per cent; and both imports from and exports to Cuba rose by 22.9 and 11.1 per cent, respectively. In the trade with CMEA partners, besides the noted decline with the U.S.S.R., there was an even sharper decline in trade with Poland, with exports falling by 4.9 per cent and imports diminishing by 13.9 per cent. Trade with Rumania and Hungary did not evince pronounced change. Imports from Bulgaria declined by 28.3 per cent, but exports rose by 32.1 per cent. Both imports from and exports to East Germany rose by 10.5 and 7.3 per cent, respectively.

Total trade turnover with the capitalist countries rose by 13.2 per cent, registering an increase of 13.9 per cent with the developed countries and an increase of 11.9 per cent with the developing nations. Imports from the capitalist countries rose relatively faster than exports to these countries (by 14.3 and 12.2 per cent, respectively). Whereas imports from the developing nations rose by only 10.1 per cent, exports to these countries went up by 13.1 per cent. The reverse was reported for the developed countries. Exports to these countries increased by only 11.7 per cent, whereas imports rose by 16.0 per cent, indicating again the difficulties encountered in selling Czechoslovak manufactured goods to the technically more advanced markets.

Both exports and imports registered a remarkable increase in trade with Italy (25.1 and 43.6 per cent, respectively), Greece (33.3 and 21.7 per cent, respectively), the United Kingdom (11.5 and 30.9 per cent, respectively), and the U.S.A. (36.3 and 122.5 per cent, respectively). Growth of trade with Finland and France was more one-sided, with imports increasing by 33.3 and 61.6 per cent, respectively, and exports remaining relatively stable. While imports from Japan and Canada declined significantly, especially in the latter case as a result of the improved Czechoslovak agricultural performance, exports to these countries rose by 41.0 and 50.8 per cent, respectively. Among the developing nations, trade with the U.A.R. increased considerably, with imports rising by 71.6 per cent and exports by 20.0 per cent.

Notwithstanding the relative ups and downs in trade from 1965 to 1966, the U.S.S.R. remained Czechoslovakia's chief trading partner (with a volume of trade amounting to 13,212 million kcs.) followed by East Germany (with a volume of 4,432 million kcs.). Poland, Hungary, and West Germany retained their third, fourth, and fifth places. Yugoslavia came up from eighth to sixth place and the United Kingdom from ninth to seventh place. Rumania and Bulgaria dropped from their sixth and seventh places to eighth and ninth. Italy remained in tenth place.[52]

The 1966 composition of exports and imports did

Table 61

COMPOSITION OF EXPORTS AND IMPORTS, 1965-66

Products	Exports		Imports	
	1965	1966	1965	1966
Total	100.0	100.0	100.0	100.0
Machinery	48.5	49.7	29.9	32.4
Fuel and raw materials	30.4	29.4	48.4	45.4
Fuel, mineral raw materials and metals	20.3	18.9	27.5	24.0
Chemicals, fertilizers and rubber	3.8	3.9	7.6	7.6
Building materials and components	1.5	1.6	1.2	1.2
Agricultural raw materials	4.8	5.0	12.5	12.6
Livestock	0.2	0.1	0.2	0.1
Foodstuffs	4.4	3.9	15.9	16.3
Manufactured consumer goods	16.5	16.9	5.2	5.8

Source: SA 1967, pp. 83-4.

not vary significantly from the preceding year, as illustrated in Table 61. Whereas, notwithstanding official pronouncements, there were no conspicuous shifts in the shares of trade of consumer goods and foodstuffs, some changes were effected in the machinery and raw materials areas; both the shares of exports and of imports of machinery increased perceptibly, and both the shares of exports and imports of raw materials dropped. Imports of machinery from capitalist countries increased by 46 per cent; the share of machines in total imports from these countries was 24 per cent. Imports of machines from the socialist bloc increased by 12 per cent. Czechoslovak exports of machines to capitalist countries was stagnant. The expected increase of export's effectiveness through export of more profitable assortments did not materialize.[53]

The share of exports in total industrial gross

output increased by 1.7 per cent. There was an accelerated growth in the share of exports in gross output of metallurgy (2.8 per cent), machinery (2.7 per cent), chemistry and rubber (2.7 per cent), clothing (10.5 per cent), and leather goods (5.2 per cent). The purchase of licenses was considerably expanded. Whereas 55 licenses had been purchased in the period 1960-65, 64 were bought in 1966. The continuing poor quality of exports was again responsible for sales at cut-rate prices.[54]

The small active balance of payments of 115 million kcs. in 1965 was significantly improved, with a reported balance of 814 million kcs. in 1966--almost at the 1962 level. There was a significant shift in the balance of payments with the socialist countries, registering a total of only 101 million kcs. This represented a total deficit balance of payments with CMEA countries as a whole (-24 million kcs.), of which the active balance with the U.S.S.R. was unusually low in comparison with previous years (only 42 million kcs.). The bulk of the active balance of payments came from the capitalist countries (713 million kcs.). But it was offset by a deficit balance with the developed countries, in the amount of -125 million kcs. (perceptibly lower than in the past), as contrasted with the active balance of 838 million kcs. with the developing nations. The active balance of payments did not represent freely expandable purchasing power, for the sales to developing nations were made on long-term, low interest-bearing credits.

The statistical material should be treated with utmost caution due to changes in CMEA prices as of January 1, 1966. Whether there was a reorientation of foreign trade territorial patterns or a temporary shift (or simply a statistical illusion) is yet difficult to determine.[55] Official pronouncements stressed that Czechoslovakia would continue to orient its trade toward the socialist bloc and that the predominant role of the Soviet Union would continue.

To sum up: Even though Czechoslovakia registered in 1966 the highest growth rates of national income since 1960 and had a record harvest, the growth of personal consumption declined, average wages did not increase faster than in the preceding two years, the balance of payments continued to be strained, and the tension between the raw materials' base and the requirements remained. One of the main causes for these phenomena could be found in investment construction--in the increase of investments under way, in the increase of prices, and in the fact that many projects were not commissioned on schedule. The fact that many requirements were not satisfied resulted in an increase of inflationary pressures in the entire economy. Other escape channels were the unwarranted growth of inventories and the disproportionately high use of materials. It was disclosed that one third of the growth of national income was an increase in inventories and that one fourth of this increase of national income was investment construction in progress. About one third of the increase of inventories was considered undesirable.[56] In 1966 the steep rise of inventories and of the volume of unfinished construction was higher than the increment of consumption or of fixed capital assets. It was claimed that the year 1966 was, in some respects, fatally similar to 1961--taken as the starting point of the decelerating trend culminating in the 1963 recession.[57]

Some of the tensions generated in 1966 originated in the safety factor conditioning the behavior of the enterprise. An investigation of about fifty enterprises of various branches revealed that the bahavior of the enterprises resulted from apprehension for the stability of the economic levers used.[58] And for good reason! By April, 1966, it was announced that new wholesale prices and a revised set of economic levers would be introduced by January 1, 1967. In anticipation of these changes the enterprises reacted by increasing inventories and employment, by starting new investments, etc.

According to provisional figures, GY exceeded the expected figure by 6 billion kcs. Reportedly, analyses at individual enterprises indicated that in many cases they were able to find new sources of cost reduction, or that existing reserves were much better utilized.[59]

Table 62

GY in 1966

Distribution	Million kcs.	Quarterly Index	Monthly Index
First quarter	30,330	100.0	
January	9,221		100.0
February	9,534		103.5
March	11,575		125.5
Second quarter	33,164	109.3	
April	10,678		100.0
May	10,962		102.8
June	11,524		107.9
Third quarter	32,716	107.9	
July	10,221		100.0
August	10,841		106.0
September	11,654		115.0
Fourth quarter	33,962	112.0	
October	10,969		100.0
November	11,464		104.5
December	11,529		105.1

Source: SP, No. 2, 1967, pp. 38-9.

The pattern of fluctuations of GY, as illustrated in Table 62, was much like that established for many years in the flow of gross output. Thus, there was a tendency for the amount of GY to increase every quarter, so that the amount reported in the fourth quarter was substantially higher than that reported in the first quarter. Furthermore, within each quarter there was a noticeable tendency for reported GY to rise every month, so that, in most cases, a higher GY was registered in the third than in the first and second months. At the same time, the GY reported for the first month of the following quarter was in all cases substantially lower than that registered in the last month of the preceding quarter. GY fell by 7.7 per cent from March to

April, by 10.1 per cent from June to July, and by 5.9 per cent from September to October.

The average annual amount of profit-sharing premium was 501 kcs. in industry and 408 kcs. in construction, with wide variations among branches and enterprises. Mining attained the highest level, with 933 kcs., power engineering reported an average of 665 kcs., and the chemical industry 613 kcs. The lowest levels were reported in the food industry, with 380 kcs., and in the consumer goods industry, with 304 kcs.

According to a survey of sixty-nine enterprises conducted by the CSB, on the average a manager received 173 per cent and an office employee 102 per cent of the profit-sharing premium paid to the manual worker. It was also found that the differentiation of premiums among manual workers was considerably narrower than among other employees. Whereas the premiums for managerial and office staff varied within a 100 per cent range, those for manual workers varied only within a 25 per cent range. Whereas 91.3 per cent of managerial staff and 84.5 per cent of office staff received profit-sharing premiums, only 82.4 per cent of manual workers were so rewarded.[60]

In the food and consumer goods industries profit-sharing premiums were the lowest and were distributed in relation to wages, thus perpetuating the disincentives in the existing wage scales. This was particularly surprising in view of the small improvements in performance in these industries that could produce palpable results. Moreover, improvements could be mainly expected from a better utilization of manpower because of the continuing pattern of investments favoring other industries. Finally, the quality of consumer goods output had to rise and the range of assortments had to be widened as a stimulus to employees in other industries.

In other industries profit-sharing premiums were distributed on the basis of points which were supposed to account for professional qualifications, degree of responsibility of the job, the length of employment, and individual merits as determined by the immediate supervisor. Since the contributions of individual cost centers to the profitability of the enterprise were in the main inadequately determined, there was no significant differentiation of the wage levels of various cost centers.[61]

The role of working capital credit grew significantly. Whereas 56,794 million kcs. was granted in 1965, 111,583 million kcs. was granted in 1966--an increase of over 96 per cent. However, the rather insignificant role of investment credits in 1966 and their inconsequential growth were indicated by a 13,384 million kcs. outstanding balance at the end of 1966, with 3,842 million kcs. used since the beginning of the year (while total investment outlays amounted to 46,634 million kcs.) compared to 13,155 million kcs. investment credit granted in 1965. As in the past, the investment credits went in 1966 primarily for cooperative housing construction and to the agricultural cooperatives.[62]

The supplementary levies imposed on the prosperous enterprises to siphon off "excess" funds for subsidizing those enterprises that were performing poorly had a double disincentive effect, for neither enterprise was then keen on improving its performance. Hence the center had to again resort to direct measures to improve performance.[63]

Actually enterprises did not gain substantially in the scope of decision-making, and there was virtually no abrogation of the center's authority and of its interference with current operations. The creation of EPU's and branch directorates by administrative fiat, rather than by voluntary formation of associations of producers, was deplored. Such administratively created branch directorates, with a deceptive independence, would tend to obey the center's orders, rather than to fight for the producers' interests. Apparently, the authorities continued to appoint politically reliable managers who were not particularly well-qualified professionally. Hence the center continued to watch closely over their activities and to interfere with them.[64]

Although there was every indication that trade unions would continue to serve the Party as a tool for implementing its will on the workers, there were already indications that they may play a larger role in representing some of the workers' interests. For instance, pressures were exerted to introduce what essentially amounted to unemployment insurance benefits. It was confirmed that in a number of enterprises, workers had attempted strikes to protest the government's measures to differentiate wages and to discontinue ineffective production.[65]

It was widely claimed that one of the main reasons for the fragmentary nature of the 1966 reform measures was the postponement of a thorough price reform. By January 1, 1967, new wholesale prices were introduced. To what extent did these approach scarcity-equilibrium prices, and how effectively could they perform the function of coefficients of economic choice?

CHAPTER 6 PRELUDE TO THE 1967 CHANGES

THE PRICE REVISION

The adopted procedure for revising prices was to take place in two phases: 1) the alteration of the levies and relationships of wholesale prices so as to give more cognizance to costs, especially to the cost of capital and 2) the adjustment of individual wholesale prices to reflect the relationship between supply and demand for particular products and the impact of foreign trade. Whereas Phase 1 could essentially be implemented by a single adjustment of the wholesale price level of the branches, Phase 2 requires a gradual and flexible adjustment.[1]

Phase 1 reflects only the supply conditions in wholesale prices and it disregards market conditions. The latter would be reflected only when individual prices were adjusted to retail (market) prices and world prices (Phase 2). Phase 1 is only confined to price ratios within the state sector and cannot perceptibly affect the general level of retail prices and income distribution. The turnover tax would generally absorb the wholesale price increase. Under Phase 2 prices of individual goods must deviate from their averages to reflect the state of supply and demand, to promote introduction of new products, etc. For these reasons prices of individual goods should, in most cases, be established directly by individual branches and enterprises.[2]

Phase 1 would create calculated prices which, in order to become "economic" prices, must reflect the specific conditions of production and of the market. Phase 2 would involve extensive price changes also because of the chain reaction of prices. In contrast to past experience, wholesale prices were not to be rigid, but to constitute merely a point of departure for evolving equilibrium prices. Prices were gradually to approach the equilibrium level, determined by the interplay of supply and demand, by means of decentralized price decision-making. When prices varied from their point of departure there would be a tendency toward sharp differentiation of the rates of profit. It was expected that restoration of the tendency toward profit rate uniformity would result from market pressures which would bring about lower prices, forcing the producer to reduce costs. Better utilization of capacity, added capacity, and the impact of foreign trade should restrict increases in profit rates due to shortages on the market.[3]

The first step in the price revision (Phase 1) was the changing of the wholesale price level in order to reflect "more realistically" production costs in the over-all price level and in the prices of individual branches and groups of products, with the aim of eliminating sizable budget subsidies. Such revised prices were introduced on January 1, 1967.

In preparing the 1967 wholesale price revision (and in drafting the price development plan until 1970), a simple mathematical model was used for price planning and high-speed computers were employed. Experimental calculations were performed by using several alternative price formulas (point of departure prices), in order to ascertain how the adoption of a particular price formula would change the major price relations within the economy and how it would influence demand, supply, utilization of fixed assets and of manpower, and other crucial variables.[4] These experimental calculations were conducted by the Econometric Laboratory of the Czechoslovak Academy of Sciences (CAS) and by the SPC. Empirical data for these calculations were obtained from a 96-sector statistical input-output table for 1962. In both cases the data were modified in different ways to update them. A simple Leontief-type model was used. It was admitted that:

> More sophisticated optimalization models exist today, which can give an optimal price system as their solution. But these optimalization models still present a number of unsolved problems and also the information necessary for their use is not available and so makes them impossible to use for the practical planning of prices in the near future.[5]

In order probably to avoid heresy, the price formulas used were, with some modification, the familiar concepts encountered in the Soviet and East European controversies.[6] Several variants, featuring a uniform base for apportioning the surplus product among prices (in order to abrogate the dual price system), were proposed, including: 1) the value type (Capital, I), where the surplus product is apportioned in proportion to the wage bill;[7] 2) the cost type (sebestoimost), where the surplus product is apportioned in proportion to cost; 3) the price of production (Capital, III), where the surplus product is apportioned in proportion to capital; 4) the two-channel price (a combination of 1 and 3), where a part of the surplus product is apportioned in proportion to the wage bill and a part in proportion to the stock of capital; and 5) the income price, where the entire GY (wages + profit) is allocated in proportion to the stock of capital.

At the CAS the original 96 sectors were aggregated into new 48 sectors to simplify the matrix and to allow for the unavailability of data on capital stock (particularly in machine-building) in the required disaggregation. In order to express the total output of each branch in homogeneous prices, turnover tax was deducted from the input-output data and adjustments were made for the distribution of depreciation allowances. The influence of foreign trade on prices was not taken into consideration. All the cost elements, including those of imported products, were assessed according to prices of domestic output. Formula 4 was adopted in practice; the less interesting results of computations (using Formulas 1, 2, 3, and 5) were published and indicated wide discrepancies. On the whole, sizable price increases would have been necessary in each case. After all is said and done, one wonders what the real significance of the variances is. In interpreting the size of variances not too much should be read into them, for they obviously depend on questionable frames of reference. In any case, the various prices would have generally markedly diverged from equilibrium prices.

Before selecting the final price formula, the SPC conducted further computations of different price formulas, including alternative variants of the two-channel price. As a backbone for its work the SPC also used the statistical 1962 input-output table, disaggregated into 92 sectors, adjusted for prices as of January 1, 1964, and modified for the planned structural changes for 1966. The matrix of fixed capital assets was obtained from a special statistical inquiry conducted in 1964, adjusted with the aid of branch indexes for 1966. Fixed assets were divided into two groups: 1) buildings and 2) machines and equipment, subdivided into eight subgroups. Buildings were revalued by using price coefficients of the change in the price level of buildings. Machines and equipment were revalued by using appropriate price coefficients for each subgroup. Working capital was revalued by means of price coefficients of the branches where the assets were used. Reportedly, two alternative computations were made: 1) with imports included in branches of production and 2) with imports excluded. In the first alternative the prices of imported goods changed in the same manner as those of domestic goods. In the second case imports were revalued in "reproduction costs" ("by an index of change of the price level of exports needed to obtain a currency equivalent to buy imports"). It was resolved that for purposes of wholesale price formation, when imports constitute the bulk of supply, or the only source for satisfying domestic demand, the reproduction costs will be "represented by the amount of goods in new wholesale prices to be exported in order to buy these imports." The level of wholesale prices of goods which are partly imported and partly domestically produced "will be determined in different ways, according to economic interests": 1) by using the average cost of imported and domestic goods and 2) by using reproduction costs in case of imports and production costs in case of domestic goods.[8]

The procedure followed in preparing the general wholesale price reform can be briefly summarized as follows: 1) The two-channel price was selected, but the dual price system was retained. Several alternative percentage surcharges on the wage bill and interest on capital were experimented with. It was decided to impose a 22 per cent surcharge on the wage bill and a 6 per cent interest on capital. The dual price system was apparently retained to reinforce the budget constraint. The stated rule was that the enterprise should be left virtually without any funds for self-financing after it had met its payments to the budget and the wages to employees--obviously in violation of the spirit of the new system. It would seem that the interest on capital and the surcharge on the wage bill were arbitrarily determined in the sense that the interest on capital did not approach the equilibrium market price for capital and that it is doubtful whether the surcharge on the wage bill represented the measure of the differential between wages paid and the full social costs of recruiting rural population, investment in human capital, etc. 2) Price change coefficients were calculated on the basis of the adjusted 1962 input-output table disaggregated into 92 sectors. These coefficients were directly used to revalue capital stock and depreciation. 3) Price coefficients for new price levels for 92 sectors were passed on to ministries and enterprises which, guided by general indicators, elaborated new prices for their main products. On the basis of data derived from enterprises, price change coefficients were calculated at the center for 24,000 (some sources report up to 27,000) groups of products. The data obtained from enterprises were aggregated into matrices of 420 X 420. Price change coefficients for 420 groups of products were computed and disaggregated into 24,000 groups of products. Only three iterations were carried out during the disaggregation. 4) The price change coefficients for groups of products were to be used for recalculating individual prices of specific products.

The mathematical techniques adopted allowed some measure of success in coping simultaneously with price-cost interdependencies which in previous sequential treatment from primary to processing industries could only be tackled in the crudest fashion. Also the preparation of the reform was accelerated; whereas previous wholesale price revisions took three to four years in preparation, the latest lasted about eighteen months. A general wholesale price reform involves changes in about 1.5 billion prices, taking into account all interdependencies. Obviously the much greater extent of aggregation was instrumental in rendering the entire undertaking of dubious validity, even if its initial premises be accepted. But, above all, the sources of contamination of data were not removed.

According to the regulations issued by mid-1966, the aim of the price revision was to provide the same initial provisions for profitability of all enterprises as envisaged by the 1966 plan, with the exception of the tariff rates of the transportation network (as of 1965), fuels extraction (1968), and higher profitability in the food industry (40 instead of 22 per cent to wages).[9] About three quarters of profit was distributed in proportion to capital and one quarter to labor. It was argued that in view of the fact that profit distributed in proportion to labor costs influences $\underline{c}$ and $\underline{v}$ to the same extent, fundamentally such a distribution of profit would amount to a transition to the price of production. The directives for overall price adjustments stipulated that of total costs submitted as basis for new wholesale prices, costs of "marginal" enterprises (those that have just initiated operations and those slated to be shut down) should be excluded from calculations, particularly if this brought domestic prices closer to world prices. In addition, changes would be introduced in establishing price levels and price relations of important products so that the level prices of such products would better reflect the costs of inputs.[10]

Prices with differentiated profit rates were approved for exports and imports. Limits were set on markups and discounts to induce a more favorable structure of exports and imports. It was reported that prices of goods directly involved in foreign trade were adjusted to world prices, but not those of goods in the domestic market, even though such goods could potentially be subject to foreign trade. Analogous steps were not taken to centrally differentiate profit in the new wholesale prices, partly because of: 1) diversity of views on the scope of the January 1, 1967, price revision and 2) the notion that some of the lagging branches or groups of products should be given a chance to progress since their failures might stem from the old system.[11]

The price adjustment was to create conditions for a transition to uniform budget levies from GY. Should the new budget levies and the removal of subsidies be reflected in prices, an average increase of 20 per cent of the industrial price level would have been required. Chart 5 shows that the entire profit included in the new prices would be siphoned off. Enterprises should be able to acquire additional funds for free disposal only by increasing the planned profit.[12]

According to the Deputy Chairman of the SCFPW, the imbalance of the economy in 1966 did not augur well for the development of prices. Prices would tend to increase. Price controls would not be

Chart 5

PROFIT IN THE 1967 WHOLESALE PRICES

1 - Formation of Profit	2 - Allocation of Profit
a) 12 per cent markup on wages (1966 plan)	A budget levy of 22 per cent of wages (equal to a + b) or alternatively an 18 per cent charge on GY
b) 10 per cent health insurance surcharge on wages	2 per cent minimum stabilization tax
c) 3 per cent minimum increase of profitability over the 1966 plan	1 per cent minimum on wages as a contribution to the development fund
25 per cent of wage costs (equal to a + b + c)	25 per cent on total wage cost
d) 6 per cent capital charge	6 per cent charge on fixed assets 2 per cent charge on inventories and prepaid expenses 4 per cent interest on working capital credits

Source: Supplement to HN, No. 30, 1966.

sufficient to check this tendency and to rid the economy of the imbalance.[13] Among the strong pressures for price increases, the following were noted: 1) shortages in the domestic market which could not be mitigated by imports; 2) the policy of income differentiation and the tendency for wages to rise; and 3) price increases of product with inelastic demand within a pertinent range. Hence, it was noted that if free reins were given to prices, serious inflationary pressures would develop, reinforced by the monopolistic structure of industry. Barriers had to be opposed to such pressures. The following factors were felt to contribute to price reduction: 1) incentives to reduce inputs; 2) equilibration of supply of and demand for products with a high coefficient of elasticity within a certain range; and 3) anti-inflationary measures, such as a transition to self-financing of investments, control of the investment policy of enterprises through the "magical" interest rate, the fight against monopolistic practices, creation of state reserves (especially of foreign exchange), and pressures of the world market.[14]

It was expected that during 1967 changes would be made to correct price levels of groups of products, particularly by adjusting prices of final products, by turnover tax, or by supplementary charges. Such adjustments would be made in cases where actual profitability proved to be much higher than that expected, because enterprises and branches calculated costs with a safety margin or because of calculation errors.[15]

There were indications that the plans for the years 1967-68 of the Fourth FYP were particularly taut. The increases in production were to be in the main achieved by investments and imports. The imbalances that would be created would hardly be conducive to the functioning and full impact of the market mechanism, particularly since sharp price increases were ruled out. Under such circumstances, there would be considerable central control over prices. Even though the logic of the new system called for restraining administrative interference in price formation, the scope of decentralized price formation had to remain within the confines of the plan. The central control of prices was to be primarily oriented to the development of price levels of product groups and "only in exceptional cases to prices of individual products." The prices of individual products were to be formed between the parties to the exchange. But such price formation would be centrally supervised. The basis for the central price control would be the long-term price development plan, prepared as a part of the long-term national economic plan, providing the enterprises with a sort of blueprint on what the center's price intentions were.[16]

The contention was that the price development plan, supported by credit, subsidy, and tax policies, should become one of the main regulators of revenues of enterprises. The primary functions of this plan were: 1) to forecast the movements of prices and costs and to provide measures for ensuring its fulfillment; 2) to stipulate the binding price levels and to establish price relations; 3) to correct "disproportions" in the growth of profits in various sectors and branches; 4) to give priority to the branches or to the products whose profitability was above average compared to world prices; 5) to attempt to eliminate disproportions by having each branch generate sufficient funds for accumulation; 6) to take into consideration demand-supply conditions; and 7) to curb monopolistic trends. But no operational price development plan was expected for 1967. The contributions of the enterprises to the budget were predetermined until the end of the Fourth FYP. But prices were to be determined centrally according to the price development plan which was not communicated to enterprises. Apparently, managers complained that the security provided by predetermining their liabilities was more than offset by the insecurity of their revenues.[17]

The control over price movements would be twofold: 1) direct control by central determination of binding fixed prices and price levels and 2) indirect control by setting prices or price limits for key products; by creating conditions forcing the producer to adhere to planned price movements (primarily by inviting competition from imports and by stimulating competition among producers); by promoting foreign trade; and by taxation, wage, and credit policies. If indirect control should prove ineffective, direct controls would be resorted to by reverting to central fixing of obligatory prices.[18]

Central price control distinguished between the following price categories:

1) Fixed prices which could be set for the most representative, i.e., key types, of products, within a group. Fixed retail prices would be determined primarily for "basic necessities," particularly for key expenditures in consumers' budgets. Fixed procurement prices would be set for agricultural products, particularly where those prices affect considerably the incomes of farmers. Fixed wholesale prices would be set for key raw materials, and other materials which substantially affect prices of producer goods.

2) The price level of free prices would be controlled indirectly by the turnover tax, discounts, markups in foreign trade, and fixed prices of standard products when used as inputs or as substitutes. Those prices would be in effect, as a rule, where a buyers' market already existed. Free prices would apply to a majority of exports and imports "in connection with the application of related domestic and foreign prices." Free prices were also to be used in connection with technically advanced products.

3) Limited prices would be determined and altered in principle on the basis of agreements between parties to the transaction. The level of these prices would be limited centrally in different ways, depending on the specific conditions of individual branches. Those prices would apply to all products not covered under 1 and

2. If the product were sold below the price limit, the central organs would not guarantee a subsidy to the seller to cover the difference. The crux of the matter was that central organs would not dictate the price of the individual product.[19]

Limited prices would be arrived at in the following manner: 1) A price agreement would be drawn up between the central organs and branch directorates, specifying the limits of price levels. Such a price level of individual branches or groups of products would have to be adhered to, even when prices of individual products were set by enterprises. If such an agreement were not arrived at, existing prices would be declared as maximum prices and the enterprises would be restricted in varying them. 2) Central organs would have to be informed of a proposed increase of prices which could only become effective with the center's approval and possible specification of conditions under which the price level might be altered. If the central organs judged the proposed price increases to be undesirable, measures other than prices would have to be used to remedy the situation which prompted the enterprise to suggest the price increase. 3) The purpose of the agreement was to instigate analyses of production and market conditions by branch directorates and enterprises. These analyses would be submitted to the central organs for evaluation from the over-all economic standpoint.

In some cases the agreement might stipulate that the price limit might vary with changes in world prices and that it might vary relatively with changes in prices of key raw materials. In cases when the agreement would stipulate a price limit that would allow the producers to reap "exceptionally high" profits, the agreement might contain a clause regulating the manner of distributing these profits (e.g., specifying increased production of "desirable" goods). In such a manner central direct specification of what to produce was reintroduced. This also gave off a particularly strong impression that the planner was not convinced that "desirable" goods would have such prices as to make them attractive to produce and that improving the quality of goods would be sufficiently compensated by higher prices.

It was stressed that central price control would become more rigid and particularly oriented to: 1) control of price-setting for new goods, in order to maintain the prescribed limits and ratios; 2) control of adherence to fixed prices; and 3) control of adherence to price agreements. In case of violation of agreements, the central organs might revert to instituting or increasing the turnover tax; to eliminating or deducting the subsidy; to cancelling the producers' share in foreign exchange; to altering markups or discounts for exports or imports; to extending the use of fixed prices; to using less-aggregated product groups; etc. In addition, the central organs might penalize violators by siphoning off the "unjustified" difference, plus a 50 per cent penalty.

At the end of 1966 and during 1967 prices were to be classified on the basis of proposals emanating from the lower echelons. The extent of fixed and free prices was to be altered. Gradually limited prices were to be introduced. The first agreements on limited prices were to be signed, especially where there were no significant deviations from the January 1, 1967, level. The bulk of agreements was to be signed during 1967.[20]

As alluded to, the wholesale price reform was not to affect the retail price level. The added state revenue from imposition of the capital levy and reduction of subsidies would be counterbalanced by a reduction of turnover tax, without necessitating an increase of retail prices. At the end of 1966, Novotny pointed out that retail prices for many goods and services were drastically below cost and required subsidies in the order of about 6 billion kcs. After introduction of new wholesale prices, the subsidies required would have to be increased to about 11 to 13 billion kcs., excluding subsidies of hundreds of million kcs. for agriculture. He warned that those state subsidies would be eliminated gradually by increasing retail prices.

However, such price increases would be compensated by increasing nominal wages in order to forestall a drop in living standards. Novotny attempted to negate rumors of a general price hike. He warned, however, that if waste in production were not checked, the freezing of wages, an increase of prices, and a reduction, rather than maintenance, of living standards would be necessary.[21]

The reform guidelines pronounced a gradual reduction and eventual elimination of "economically unjustified" differences in turnover tax rates and discrepancies between foreign and domestic prices. From January 1, 1967, generally the same turnover tax rates would be applied in the state and cooperative sectors.

In order to bridge the gap between producers' and consumers' prices, the adoption of proportionate turnover tax would permit changes of retail prices under market conditions to be reflected in wholesale prices. Alternatively, changes in wholesale prices, due to changes in supply conditions, would be transmitted to retail prices. The proportionate turnover tax would become effective gradually in the whole range of assortments, even in those that have fixed prices. Ultimately, it would entirely replace differentiated turnover tax. The proportionate turnover tax could not, however, be counted on in the near future because it would introduce many changes in retail prices and in the composition of consumer goods which could not, as yet, be handled. Hence, for the time being differentiation of turnover tax for large groups of commodities would be retained.

On January 1, 1967, new turnover tax rates were introduced for 2,797 groups of products. Those rates were applicable to free and limited prices only. It is important to note that with respect to fixed prices--and the reader hardly needs to be reminded how <u>exceptional</u> these were--the existing system of differentiated turnover taxes remained in effect, to be replaced only by new rates at some unspecified date. It was acknowledged that although the group turnover tax rate was preferable to the differentiated rates, it conflicted with price controls.[22]

REGULATIONS FOR 1967 CHANGES

On December 12, 1966, Czechoslovak Government Decree No. 100 was issued, legalizing the many features of the new system as they were to be introduced on January 1, 1967.[23]

At the outset the decree stressed the FYP's primordial role in the development of the economy. In principle, the position of the plan as the basic instrument of management of the economy remained unchanged. The set of national economic plans would assert and concretize the state's economic policy. These plans would be implemented by means of economic devices, binding targets, and binding limits.

The FYP performs the function of a comprehensive development plan, specifying the manner of carrying out structural changes and the distribution of income. It determines the binding indexes, it allocates key resources, and it provides the framework within which economic devices will be used. The annual national economic plans formulate more precisely the FYP's targets and limits, adjusting for changing conditions. The relative independence of enterprise plans is wider in areas where the state plan is less explicit. Together with the plan of development of the national economy--which is the cornerstone--the system of state plans embraces the state budget; the credit plan; the treasury plan; the foreign exchange plan; and, of course, the plans of national committees, of ministries, of branch directorates, and of other state organs.

Binding targets are set for a) state research and development and geological prospecting, b) state investment projects, c) growth goals of Slovakia and other individual areas, and d) deliveries for defense. Binding (upper) limits are set for a) state grants or subsidies and b) financial relations between the state and the national committee budgets. A proviso has been inserted allowing the setting of additional binding targets and limits, "if the goal envisaged by the plan cannot otherwise be attained." Additional binding targets can be set for 1) deliveries in physical unit; 2) personnel training and youth recruiting drives; 3) job assignments to high school and university graduates; and 4) allocation of manpower among regions. Additional binding limits may be set for 1) sale of "some" products to "some" customers; 2) production and delivery of wood and coniferous lumber; 3) investment projects carried out by budgetary organizations; and 4) the budgetary organizations' wage funds. Furthermore, binding targets and limits may be set with respect to a) experimenting enterprises, for levies on profit, for depreciation allowances, and for other additional levies and b) subsidized enterprises, for total investment volume for the wage fund, for levies on depreciation allowances, and for other additional levies.

Binding targets, limits, export and import quotas, and, if necessary, the ratio of exports to imports, will be set for a "limited" period in the foreign trade sector. The obligations assumed when entering into international trade agreements are binding for the responsible organs. But if the execution of a given assignment should result in losses for the executant, the agency that issued the assignment is bound to compensate the executant.

In enterprises operating under profit system, the wage fund may be set as a binding limit.

It should be noted parenthetically that twelve binding assignments for production and delivery of goods (and binding limits for purchase of goods) were prescribed by the SPC in drawing up the 1967 plan, and only six such assignments and limits were set for elaborating the 1968 plan. Binding assignments were set for buses, trucks, and white sawn timber for export, and for the import of corn and meat.

The state determines the total volume of investment which binds it in its granting of budget subsidies and circumscribes the CSB's credit policy. The state may also limit the amount of estimated costs for unfinished construction. Separate (tentative) indexes are set for the volume of construction and investment credits in Slovakia.

The binding indexes are incorporated into the FYP, the annual national economic plans, and the budget. Those indexes are then broken down by superiors for their subordinates. During the disaggregation process the binding indexes should neither be lowered nor raised. However, the binding targets for exports may be raised or the export-import ratio may be improved. Binding indexes can only be revised by the government and by the organs authorized by it to do so.

Central or regional agencies are not allowed to expand the number of binding limits. They may, however, impose additional "extraordinary" binding targets. In the process of disaggregating the binding indexes the branch directorates may increase their number only to the extent that such action is in conformity with the statutes of the EPU's. Otherwise, the additional binding indexes must be identified as "extraordinary," and only then would the branch directorate be obliged to idemnify the enterprise for losses it might have incurred while complying with the "extraordinary" binding index. But, if the imposition of additional binding indexes is within the realm of what the branch directorate can do in exercising its functions, then it bears no responsibility vis-à-vis the enterprise with regard to the assignment's effects on the enterprise's performance. The greater leeway granted branch directorates in expanding the number of binding indexes was motivated by the material responsibility they shoulder for the aggregate results of their branch.

Hence, it was left up to the directorates to determine the degree of decentralization in production decisions most propitious in their particular branch.

Generally, if an enterprise fails to abide by the binding indexes, superiors must impose an additional levy to siphon off the benefit gained. If a branch directorate fails to do so, its superior will siphon off the amount and retain it. Additional levies may also be assessed on foreign trade organizations which fail to fulfill the binding export target or fail to maintain the export-import ratio. Should a management organ fail to disaggregate binding indexes among its subordinates and should these indexes remain unfulfilled, the MF may siphon off any benefits so derived.

The organ assigning a binding index must ensure that such an index will not be detrimental to the desirable wage trend and investment activity. If an organ assigns a binding "extraordinary" index, it will be held financially responsible for any demages resulting from its fulfillment. The above responsibility also applies in cases of plan changes during its course.

Economic tools are classified as a) long-term and b) operative. The following are considered long-term economic tools, chosen before preparing the plan: levy on GY (profit), charge on fixed capital, charge on inventories, stabilization tax, and levy on depreciation allowances. The operational economic tools are: prices, surcharges and discounts, bank interest rates, subsidies, and turnover taxes; wages, additional levies and reduction, varying allocations to different funds; operating and investment credits; foreign exchange credits; incentives to improve profitability of foreign trade and to save on foreign exchange; discriminatory measures to promote industrialization of underdeveloped areas; levies to siphon off "unlawfully" obtained funds; and punitive damages, fines, etc.

In calculating the GY of an organization,

Chart 6

FORMATION AND DISTRIBUTION OF GY IN 1967

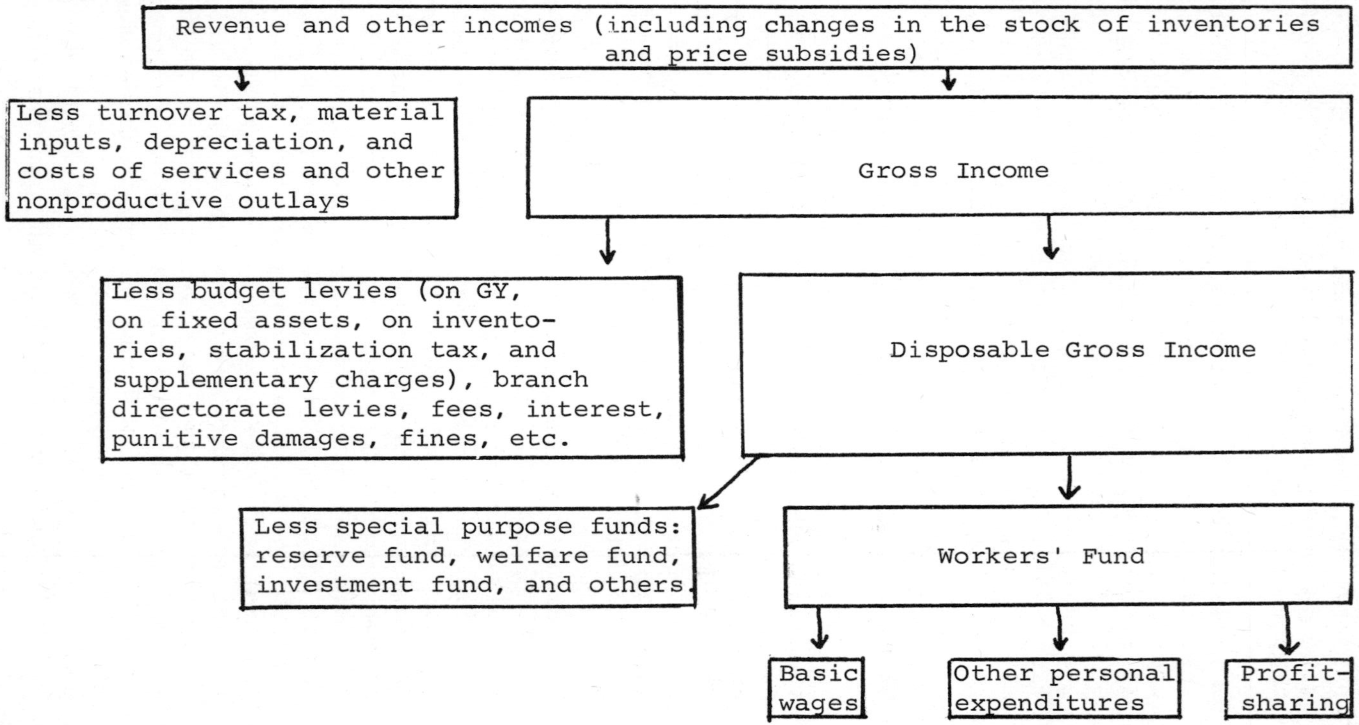
Revenue and other incomes (including changes in the stock of inventories and price subsidies)
Less turnover tax, material inputs, depreciation, and costs of services and other nonproductive outlays
Gross Income
Less budget levies (on GY, on fixed assets, on inventories, stabilization tax, and supplementary charges), branch directorate levies, fees, interest, punitive damages, fines, etc.
Disposable Gross Income
Less special purpose funds: reserve fund, welfare fund, investment fund, and others.
Workers' Fund
Basic wages
Other personal expenditures
Profit-sharing

revenue from operations, sales of fixed assets, and other income is first computed. In calculating revenue, price surcharges and discounts and subsidies increasing revenue are to be allowed. Revenue should then be reduced by the amount of material costs and depreciation on goods sold, by the turnover tax, by proceeds from the sale of fixed assets, by allocations to the risk fund (where it is set up from receipts from sales), by costs of inventories sold, and by other non-labor operating expenses. Unless the cash method is used, GY is to be increased or decreased by the changes in the stock of inventories. An organization's profit is computed by deducting labor costs from GY.

The primary claimants on an enterprise's GY (profit) are: 1) budget levies; 2) insurance premiums (other than health insurance which is considered an integral part of the levy on GY), fees, interest, punitive damages, fines, etc.; 3) repayment of credits extended for wages; and 4) levies of branch directorates. After meeting the above claims, the enterprises use GY (profit) for setting up and replenishing a) the reserve fund; b) the welfare fund; c) the investment fund; d) other special-purpose funds; and e) the workers' (premium) funds.

The budget levy on GY (set at 18 per cent in industry and construction) is computed on GY reduced by the levies on fixed assets and inventories; by interest on credits (only up to the basic interest rate), with the exception of credits for wages; by insurance premiums; by levies of the branch directorate; by contributions to the technological improvement fund; and by payments to the state budget to compensate for forgoing agricultural production on land used for industrial purposes. The levy on profit, set at 32 per cent, in enterprises working on the profit scheme, is computed on the basis of profit reduced by allocations from profit to a minimum specified premium fund; by levies on fixed assets and inventories; by interest on credits; by insurance premiums; by levies of the branch directorate; and by the compensation for forgoing the agricultural use of land.

In addition, in enterprises working on the profit scheme, there will be a 15 per cent levy on all disbursements from the basic wage fund and the premium fund. The rates of these assessments cannot be increased by more than 1 per cent during the course of the year. National committees participate in the levy on GY of state enterprises. Their share amounts to 1 per cent of the GY (2 per cent of profits). The apportionment of this share among the various local, district, and regional committees is arranged between the branch directorate and the regional national committee.

A 6 per cent levy on fixed assets is based on the depreciated cost of assets. The levy is also applied to unfinished centrally assigned projects which have not been completed on schedule. The following assets are exempt from levies: 1) those used as factory housing and for welfare and cultural purposes; 2) those used for water and air purification and for the improvement of working conditions; 3) those used for maintaining historic monuments; 4) those used for civil defense purposes; 5) those that are temporarily idle; 6) land; 7) those assets (or part thereof) that were self-financed by the experimenting enterprises since 1965 and by the others since 1966--this proviso to apply only until the end of 1970; and 8) highways and roads. The levy on capital assets will be reduced by one third for a period of five years for enterprises whose construction has been subsidized. This refers to investment projects in specified areas qualifying for a special state subsidy amounting to 15 per cent of the project's cost.

A 2 per cent levy is paid on all inventories.

A stabilization tax is paid to the state budget by enterprises subject to the GY or profit scheme. The stabilization tax is set at the rate of 30 per cent on that part of the total volume of payroll disbursements which exceeds the product of 90 per cent of the average annual wage planned by enterprises for 1966 and the number of employees in the year for which the levy is computed. The tax is increased by 1 per cent of total payroll for each per cent of annual manpower increment. For each per cent annual decrease of manpower, the stabilization tax will be decreased by 0.3 per cent of the total payroll.[24] It is stipulated that the government will list the specific instances where the increased tax will not apply. The stabilization tax (S) is computed according to the following formulas:

$$S = 0.3\left[P - 0.9(w_1 \times m)\right] + P\,\frac{(m - n)}{n}$$

$$S = 0.3\left[P - 0.9(w_1 \times m)\right] - 0.3P\,\frac{(n - m)}{n}$$

where P is the actual average wage (say 1967) times the actual number of employees (1967), w_1 is the planned 1966 average wage, m is the number of employees (1967), and n is the number of employees (1966). It should be noted that the average annual wage is controlled and approved for the enterprise by its immediate superiors in conjunction with the CSB.

Rather obvious and not fundamental conclusions seem to be evident. Should there be no change in the average wage rates and employment in 1967 over 1966, the firm would pay 30 per cent tax on 10 per cent of 1967 payroll (or 3 per cent of total 1967 payroll). Should there be no change in employment, the total tax paid would increase with an increase in average wages, and, hence, the stabilization tax is intended to discourage it. The total stabilization tax would decline, with the decrease of average wages. In case of a decrease in employment by 10 per cent, with no changes in the average wage rates, the enterprise would pay no stabilization tax. Should employment drop below 10 per cent, again without changes in the average wage rates, it seems that the state would have to credit the enterprise's account. The most severe provision, of course, pertains to the burden of the tax on the increase of manpower. The marginal cost of employing additional workers is substantially increased in the effort to discourage additional employment.

The idea is to create potent economic pressures against increase of employment. The argument is advanced that augmentation of GY through manpower increases would have to entail a saving equal to 100 per cent of the incremental payroll, plus an 18 per cent charge on GY.[25]

It should be borne in mind that this tax is bound to contribute to misallocation of labor because it largely sanctions the allocation of labor in 1966 which, by all accounts, appears to have been drastically wasteful; and because it makes reallocation of labor expensive, it does not provide potent enough incentives to reduce employment, and it artificially increases the price of labor, hindering the approach to clearing levels for labor. At the same time, it makes for inefficient substitution relations by artificially and arbitrarily raising the cost of labor in relation to that of other factors.[26]

The functions of the stabilization levy are envisaged as follows: 1) to create in the budget funds in proportion to wage increases in production, which could be used to maintain the proportions between wages in the productive and non-productive spheres and 2) to influence the combination of factors of production, in particular, to make labor more expensive to promote labor-saving substitution, and to utilize the released labor for the growth of other branches of the economy.

It is provided that in some cases there will be a need to reduce the impact of the stabilization tax. The following deviations are sanctioned: 1) in determining the annual changes in employment in special areas designated by the government neither the alterations in the number of employees nor the changes in the employment of partly disabled workers are taken into account; 2) in high-priority investment projects and in the production of building materials in short supply only 0.3 per cent of wages will be levied for each per cent of the annual increment of manpower; and 3) in areas recognized by the government as having low employment rates, only 0.5 per cent of the volume of wages will be levied for each per cent of the annual increment of workers.

The government sets individual stabilization rates for newly built large enterprises. The immediate superiors of the enterprise are allowed, with the CSB's consent, to adjust the average annual wage or changes in manpower, for purposes of computing the stabilization tax, in cases where substantial organizational changes have taken place.

It would seem that the effect of this tax will be considerably reduced not only because, under conditions of a seller's market, the burden of additional cost of labor would be somewhat lessened, but also because, under pressures, exemptions and reductions are bound to proliferate.

Subject to the SPC's approval, the regional national committees of highly industrialized areas suffering from a labor shortage can introduce a surcharge on the stabilization tax in those enterprises that are judged to have a superfluous labor force. The surcharge may not exceed 2 per cent of the current annual wage fund. The surcharge is to be divided among the national committees in the area.

Payments from depreciation on fixed assets are made to a special state account. They are computed on the basis of the average 1966 enterprise depreciation allowances, reduced by the part earmarked for capital repairs, and multiplied by a coefficient of 1.5. The size of the levy will remain constant every year until the accumulated levies equal the base which is computed on the net depreciated cost, recalculated at current prices, and the volume of unfinished construction as of December 31, 1966. The base will not include, inter alia: 1) investment outlays in 1966 (in experimenting enterprises also in 1965) which were not financed by budget grants; 2) fixed assets used for civil defense purposes; 3) assets temporarily withdrawn; 4) assets financed by the trade union organization, workers' premium funds, welfare funds, etc.; and 5) land, if its price is included in the base.

The purpose of the levy on depreciation allowances is to recoup from enterprises the value of depreciated fixed assets as of December 31, 1966. The intention is again to level out differences in endowment so that enterprises that are re-equiped or expanded after January 1, 1967--in which case they would self-finance the investment--should not be at a disadvantage vis-à-vis those that had been modernized prior to that date. Those enterprises that previously benefited from virtually free fixed capital should not be placed in a position of commanding more means for financing capital than those that were underprivileged. The general tenor of this argument was unfavorably received in Slovakia. It was claimed that this less-developed area would have to carry a relatively heavier burden of depreciation extraction--because of its more modern plants--and would be left with relatively more meager own resources for future development.[27]

The branch directorates impose the following levies on enterprises: 1) contributions to the operating costs of branch directorates; 2) contributions to the branch directorate's special funds, such as technological development, geological exploration, and compensation damages; 3) contributions to the combined EPU's funds; and 4) contributions from depreciation allowances to the combined EPU's funds in case of enterprises which will be shut down in the near future, if these enterprises are not to construct new production facilities. Uniform rates of contributions under 1, 2, and 3 are set by the branch directorate for all enterprises under its jurisdiction.

The branch directorate is entitled to impose an additional levy on the prosperous enterprises to be used for subsidizing enterprises which are in financial difficulties. In such cases the rule should be that those enterprises on which an additional levy has been imposed should still, after redistribution, have a higher GY (profit) per worker than those which benefit from the extraordinary grants. The additional levies for redistribution can be imposed at the latest at the time when the enterprise's draft plan is being discussed. These means can only be granted to enterprises that apply for them and that, at the same time, propose definite measures for improving their positions and for ending their dependence on grants. If an enterprise should not take these measures, the branch directorate can either reduce or stop the grants.

With the government's approval, central agencies can redistribute funds among EPU's in cases where there are marked divergencies between the attained profitability rates and those envisaged by a price revision. The redistribution is conducted in a way similar to that among enterprises.

In order to advance the development of its branch, the directorate may pool different funds for important investments for the entire branch. Besides bank credits, the directorate may use long-term loans from enterprises, a share of enterprise funds, budget grants, and other funds siphoned off from enterprises, as previously mentioned.

Due to costing and pricing vagaries, the enterprises endowed with different quantities and qualities of capital and other resources must be afforded a relatively equal start, since otherwise the divergencies in reported profit could not be essentially attributed to performance. However, as previously pointed out, the equalization measures would generally reintroduce by the back door the voluntarism of the old system. As it seems, the law governing the operations of the new system sanctioned the introduction of a host of measures which essentially amount to the subsidy of poorly performing enterprises by the well-operating ones, with all the ensuing disincentive effects.

In cases when agricultural land is permanently taken over, compensation is made to the budget out of the investment funds and included in capital outlays. In case the land is only temporarily taken over, payments amounting to the annual gross crop production are made to the budget from the enterprise's GY or from profit.

Besides stipulating the direct levies on GY, the state exercises a good measure of control by prescribing the apportionment of the disposable GY into special enterprise funds to be used for distinct purposes.

In order to mitigate fluctuations in the revenues at the enterprise, the setting up of a reserve fund, whose minimum size is determined by the government, is imposed. Until this minimum is reached, the fund can only be used for meeting the guaranteed wages. The excess over the minimum can be used for other purposes. If the reserve fund falls below its minimum level, no profit-sharing premiums can be paid. In 1967 the minimum level of the reserve fund was to be 2 per cent of the annual payroll (3 per cent in research and development organizations). In 1968 the minimum level of the reserve fund (in industry, mining, and construction) was to be a composite of two rates--6 per cent of the annual payroll and 25 per cent of the GY reduced by budget levies. In other areas it was to remain at 3 per cent of the annual payroll.

The investment fund must be set up from a share in depreciation allowances, from allocations from GY (profit), from proceeds from the sale of fixed assets, and from other sources. Additional funds may be obtained from allocations from superiors (or from the state budget), from contributions from other enterprises, and from transfers from other funds. Besides new acquisitions, the enterprise may use its investment fund for repaying investment credit installments and for contributing or lending to other enterprises.

The rate of allocation from GY (profit) to the welfare fund is specified by the government. The minimum allocation to that fund in 1967 and 1968 was set at 0.8 per cent of the annual payroll. It could be raised somewhat in agreement with the trade union organization. It could also be increased by transfers from the workers' fund and from the reserve fund. However, no transfers from the welfare fund to the reserve and workers' funds are allowed even though transfers to other funds are permitted, in agreement with the trade union organization. No profit-sharing premiums could be paid as long as the minimum allocation to the welfare fund has not been made.

Besides drawing on GY (profit), after meeting other commitments and setting up the aforementioned funds, the workers' (premium) fund can be augmented by rewards from socialist competition, contributions from supervisors, and transfers from the reserve fund. Transfers from other enterprise funds to the workers' fund or redistribution of workers' funds among enterprises are not allowed. All rewards and payments to employees must be confined to the workers' fund.

Working capital is financed from permanent liabilities, from temporarily idle enterprise funds, from temporarily undistributed GY (profit), and from short-term credits. The basic interest rate on working capital credits is 6 per cent (2 per cent for domestic trade and 3 per cent for agriculture). A 4 to 5 per cent interest rate is charged on loans to supplement shortages in payroll due to seasonal fluctuations. Enterprises' bank deposits earn 1.8 per cent interest. From January 1, 1968, these rates were to be revised upward as follows: basic rate 6 per cent and short-term and seasonal credits 8 to 10 per cent. Should the bank refuse credit, the enterprise will have to revert to its own funds or those loaned by superiors or other enterprises.

The regulations for industry and construction broadly apply to other sectors of the economy, with some notable modifications. In domestic trade a 3 per cent levy is set on fixed assets. Inventories are exempt from levies. In case of service enterprises, the levy from GY is 16 per cent and the levy on fixed assets is 3 per cent. The government is to designate the enterprises of wholesale distribution that will benefit from the same exemptions as domestic trade.

In enterprises engaged exclusively in research and development, the levy on GY amounts to 10 per cent of wages paid and no levies are imposed on fixed assets. These enterprises are allocated foreign exchange to procure the required machinery and equipment for fulfilling the state plan of science and technology. They can undertake also above-plan projects and they can procure the additional foreign exchange from their own funds. Independent design bureaus pay a 16 per cent levy on GY and no levies on fixed assets.

Air transport pays 16 per cent on GY and makes no contributions from depreciation allowances.

Agricultural procurement and supply enterprises pay a 3 per cent charge on fixed assets, with many exemptions. Inventories are also exempt from levies. Until the end of 1970 increases in manpower do not entail increases in the stablization tax and no levies will be made on depreciation allowances.

The state budget may specify the volume of financial reserves for central agencies and the Slovak National Council. These reserves are to be used for counteracting problems arising from plan revisions or from the imposition of additional assignments and for securing stability. The funds for these reserves will be granted from the state budget and from other sources. Generally, only the government can dispose of the central reserves embodied in the state plan, budget, and credit plan.

It is stipulated that the commercial relations between socialist enterprises will be based on a free choice of domestic supplier and buyer, with mutual agreement on deliveries, on services, and on terms of cooperation. Significantly, there is no mention of the mutual agreement on prices. Superiors are not allowed to hamper these relations by restricting competition, by granting monopoly rights in sales, etc. The prerogatives of enterprises are circumscribed by the binding targets and limits and only beyond these can they develop a production program that will accord with market demand. The needs of the national economy are to be analyzed through market research. In order to improve the supply of consumer goods in domestic trade, many regional and branch restrictions were lifted (e.g., allowing producers to sell their wares on the market and to offer the relevant services). But regulations governing the sale and procurement of agricultural products were not abrogated.

Socialist organizations are allowed to enter into agreements with one another for the purposes of combining certain operations, pooling funds for accomplishing a specific objective, etc. Superiors cannot hamper such action. On the basis of such an agreement, a new socialist organization can be set up with the consent of superiors.

If, in the course of the audit, the fiscal agency discovers that binding indexes have not been adhered to and that penalties were not paid, the organization in question will be instructed to pay a 50 per cent surcharge to the budget in addition to the existing penalties. Superiors are bound to remit to an enterprise any supplementary levies that were unlawfully exacted. If an enterprise has unlawfully increased a fund or disbursed it, it must remit to superiors the amount by which the fund was augmented or disbursed. In case it has not done so and the auditor discovers the omission, the 50 per cent penalty would apply.

The government can grant exemptions for these regulations. The MF, together with the SPC, is allowed to grant exemptions from the regulations pertaining to experimenting and subsidized enterprises. The decree is effective on January 1, 1967.

According to Decree No. 101 of December 20, 1966, on remuneration, centrally set wage scales, levies from GY, stabilization tax, price controls, and other policy measures--all are to be used to achieve the desired distribution between consumption and investment and the desired wage proportions between the individual sectors, branches, and enterprises.[28] The wage policy is to aim at shifting the labor force from the branches where there is relative overemployment to those that suffer from chronic labor shortages (e.g., services). It is also to promote the transfer of manpower from the inefficient to the prosperous enterprises. Steps were taken to facilitate termination of employment and the system of central allocation of the labor force has been discontinued. The temporarily unemployed (due, for example, to the shutting down of inefficient enterprises) will receive financial succor from the MF. The costs of retraining them will also be borne by the state.

Collective agreements are to be used for regulating wages in individual branches and enterprises. The guidelines for concluding these agreements are issued by the Central Council of Trade Unions (CCTU), but the provisions concerning wages must be approved by the SCFPW beforehand. Supervisory agencies must ensure that the provisions of the collective agreements are in conformity with the state plan targets and guidelines on wage trands. The superiors may reject such agreements if they do not satisfy these conditions.

It appears that another device for restricting excessive channeling of GY to personal earnings is to stipulate in the collective agreement how GY will be distributed. The key is provided by the SCFPW; agreements will not be approved if they significantly deviate from this key.

It is stipulated that the guaranteed wages must be paid in full, irrespective of the enterprise's financial position. The bank is obliged to extend credit to the enterprise for this purpose. Guaranteed wages are defined as 92 per cent of the product of the initial average wage and the number of employees of the enterprise, increased by the amount of premiums specified beforehand and by the premiums for inventions.

In order to spur the growth of revenues of the enterprise, wages should be substantially differentiated according to work performed and to the contributions of the individuals to fulfillment of plan targets and to achievement of good results. Wages should not only be differentiated according to skill, complexity, difficulty of work, and the working conditions, but also according to the quality of performance.

Central setting of wage scales is recognized as a direct instrument of state control. Wage scales list either firm rates or ceiling and floor rates for each occupation in a particular branch. Employees of exceptionally high abilities can receive a salary that is 50 per cent higher than the appropriate rate. However, if the wage scale lists a floor and ceiling only, such employees are then paid the highest rate.

Basic wages are supplemented by premiums and profit-sharing. A share of the workers' fund can also be set aside for foremen's or plant managers' funds, which would be disbursed at their discretion in premiums to their subordinates. The profit-sharing premiums are distributed only after the results for the past year have been assessed. Only those employees whose work influences over-all financial results can share in annual results (i.e., management). The increasing implementation of the intra-enterprise management system should make it possible to determine the individual results of cost centers and to have the workers share in these results. These shares could be disbursed for periods shorter than one year. The employees of branch directorates are rewarded on the basis of the over-all financial results achieved in the past year.

Enterprises are entitled to decide on the use of specific wage forms for specific groups of employees, on the apportionment of wage funds, and on other wage problems, unless the wage regulations have vested these prerogatives with superiors. The branch directorates issue wage directives to their enterprises within the confines provided for them by the central agencies and supervise the application of wage instruments and control. Central agencies are responsible for preparing guidelines for wage development and supervising its implementation in their sectors and branches according to the measures taken by the government and the SCFPW. To ensure the implementation of these measures the central agencies promulgate wage regulations for their subordinates.

The entire hierarchy of superiors verifies whether the wage payments of enterprises are in line with their financial results. The bank serves in controlling wage payments through its credit and interest policy. When concluding credit agreements, the bank not only evaluates, but also participates in the preparation of collective agreements. It is entitled to examine the plans for creation and apportionment of GY, for withdrawals from the workers' fund, etc. The bank is also supposed to report to central agencies on the effectiveness of the use of material incentives and to carry out period checks on wage developments.

Exemptions from the above decree may be granted by the SCFPW.

INVESTMENTS IN THE NEW SYSTEM

In the area of investment, the emphasis of the new system was on central decision-making in investment policy. This policy was to be reflected particularly in the FYP's which should provide "sufficiently comprehensive" guidelines for investment. The country-wide extent of capital construction is determined at the center. This governs the allocation of state grants and the CSB's credit policies, taking into account to what extent enterprises use their own investment funds. This limit does not reach the enterprise level, but imposes on the bank the burden of verifying and controlling the enterprises' formation and disbursement of investment funds so that the specified volume of construction should not be exceeded. Concurrently, the government sets guiding indexes on the volume of capital construction in Slovakia, in order to further its aims of industrializing that region.

The investments in the annual plan had to be balanced against the capacity potential of construction enterprises, machine-building plants, and their suppliers and had to reckon with the volume of still unfinished projects, so as not to dissipate resources.[29]

In preparing their investment draft plans for 1967, the enterprises decided, in principle, on their investment projects and had to self-finance them. In some exceptional cases, subsidies were to be granted. Before the annual plan was drafted by enterprises, the branch directorates, in conjunction with the CSB, selected those projects that could be started or completed during the planned year. It was stipulated that the investment plan could only list those projects that the CSB had agreed to finance.

The 1967 plan envisaged alterations in the nature of investment limits and in the classification of investments into categories. Wherever the new system was not implemented in 1967 (e.g., housing projects), the volume of investment was set as a definite and binding limit. In those cases where the new system was introduced, the plan targets were to be enforced, above all, by economic devices.

To ensure the selection of the most "profitable" projects, binding limits could not be imposed on the volume of investments in specific branches. Such limits would prevent the undertaking of highly profitable projects exceeding the limits, and, at the same time, the limits would allow the undertaking of less profitable projects wherever limits had not been reached. Therefore, binding limits for individual branches and investors were replaced by guideline limits. The bank was not compelled to adhere to the guideline limits for branches if the profitability criterion was not satisfied or if the credit could be used more profitably in other areas.

Such guideline limits would be specified before the selections were made. But the plan would already reflect not only the selections, but also the negotiations with the contractors. The new system did not preclude enforcement of central investment decisions where "it would be considered necessary and advisable," with the center ruling on the "necessity or advisability" of intervention. There was really no potent constraint imposed on the center, nor did it seem to be relinquishing its powers. The regulations were worded to leave loopholes for recentralization so that, when and if recentralization should become a fact, the existing regulations would not have to be entirely rescinded.

On the basis of the 1966 experience with the new system, and its limited scope in investments, it was pointed out that due to the strained relations between the supply of real resources and the needs of investment projects, investment construction would continue under central aegis for some time.

The investment credit policy aimed at combining commercial criteria with safeguarding the macroeconomic proportions of the plan. It was stressed that, whenever possible, central control should be implemented by economic levers. A reasonable compromise, combining the autonomy of the enterprise which was directly responsible for the high profitability of the investment with the protection of the state's interests required that such tools as the evaluation and approval of "certain" investment projects be used. The instructions for 1967 stipulated that to ensure structural changes, interbranch proportions, priority distribution of production potential, and a limitation of unfinished construction, central agencies would enumerate the key projects which they would have to evaluate and to approve before the annual plan was drawn up. It was argued that the central evaluation of certain projects did not imply that those projects would have to take precedence in fulfillment, but, since the state commands the real inputs, in case of shortages these projects would probably be accorded priority.

Whereas the 1966 regulations distinguished between specified (individually listed) projects, branch projects, and enterprise investments, the 1967 regulations abandoned this classification and the planners faced the solution of the problem of top priority that the specified projects had previously enjoyed. To ensure the availability of materials and manpower to carry out these projects as planned, there was an insistence on thorough elaboration of requirements to be taken into account before the plan would be drawn up. Those projects would be regarded as directly ordered by the government. As a rule, these projects also had to meet the profitability criterion and to be self-financed by enterprises or branch directorates. But the government reserved the right to relax the above requirements.

The sources for financing investments were to be: 1) investment credit; 2) accumulated depreciation on fixed assets; 3) the portion of GY earmarked for investment; 4) grants from the state budget; 5) funds from disposal of fixed assets; and 6) appropriations from funds earmarked for social and cultural purposes. It was envisaged that the economy-wide distribution of the sources for financing would be 2 + 3 = 24 per cent; 1 = 60 per cent; 4 = 15 per cent; and 5 + 6 + others = 1 per cent.

The GY funds earmarked for financing investments would have to be accumulated by the enterprise' extra effort to secure a larger GY. The investment would have to be highly profitable to meet the relatively high cost of investing.

The advantage of the predominant credit financing of investments was that it constituted a deferred payment from the enterprise's own funds, thus making the investor responsible for incurring the investment costs. The big questions were: To what extent would this responsibility be enforced? Would an enterprise that was unable to pay back be forced to shut down? And if not, what other measures were foreseen to make the responsibility really stick?

In limiting the volume and distribution of investment credits, the CSB was to be guided by the state plan and the bank's selection of investments according to profitability. Should the demand for investment credit exceed the supply of funds earmarked for this purpose, the bank would restrict credits by imposing stricter terms and, alternatively, it would relax the terms should the opposite happen. Investment credits were to be extended on the basis of the over-all volume of investments, specified in the national economic plan, the investments' estimated costs, and the preliminary distribution of investments among branches in accordance with development policy. Investment credits were supposed to become an important economic instrument employed by the center in allocating investments; it was expected that credit would possibly correct the macroeconomic control figures for different sectors and branches.

The purpose seems to be to promote justification of projects by adding the additional check of the bank on the profitability test. Hence, if relatively unprofitable projects are submitted and detected by the bank and are below the limit set, for instance, for metallurgy, credit should not be granted. The bank should then extend credit to a more profitable investment in this branch or, if none is submitted, then, but only in agreement with the SPC--the significance of which cannot be overstressed--can the bank redistribute the funds to other branches. In this connection some more fundamental unresolved issues come to mind: How will the central plan be constructed? How will the guideline limits be determined? What will be the amount of credit and how will it be distributed? Will the prices be rational and will profitability be meaningful? Exactly how will the "standard" profitability rate be determined? What weight will be assigned to other factors? Will only the anticipated profit on a particular venture be taken into account or will the over-all investor's financial situation be decisive, with financial considerations on the ability and promptness of repayment given precedence over the project's profitability? How will the investor's calculations be verified? Will the bank's personnel be able to perform meaningful and independent efficiency calculations, or will it still have to depend on data generated by the investor? What will be the reward and penalties to be borne by the bank for making the right or wrong decisions? More important, will the bank's incentives be such that it will strive to make the right decisions?

It was pointed out that the profitability principle could not yet be really implemented. The results of the wholesale price revision would only be apparent long after the completion of the selective procedure and even then it was questionable whether profitability would become a reliable criterion. In an ambiguous way it was claimed that, therefore, the 1967 plan limits should be abided by.

It is noteworthy that in evaluating the investor's application, the CSB would not give as much weight to his calculation of the anticipated profitability as to the credit repayment terms which he is able and willing to assume. Those terms were to depend on the "actual" project profitability (as computed by the bank and not as declared by the investor) and on the over-all financial position of the investor. Hence, financial considerations and the general stature of the investor would be the weighty factors in the selection process, whereas the marginal expected profitability of the project would not necessarily be important. Admittedly, the verification of profitability posed many grave problems, but we do not find here a sharp departure from tradition, for predominantly financial, as distinct from economic, criteria were resorted to. Inter alia, it seems that there would be a tendency to favor projects with shorter periods of credit repayment and many projects that require a longer gestation period would be discriminated against. Undoubtedly, some of them would find their way through the "good offices" of the central planner. But in the smaller investments, whose cumulative effect might be considerable in the over-all transformation of the economy, the CSB's conservatism might be detrimental.

The CSB was supposed to give preference to the investment projects that showed a higher profitability so that from the profit achieved on these particular investments, the investor could repay the credit in larger installments, thereby reducing the repayment period as compared to the service life of the asset. Furthermore, in cases where the profitability rates did not diverge markedly, the CSB would give preference to the projects that offered shorter credit repayment periods. To guide the CSB in the selection, the following formula was offered:

$$k = p/n - 100/m$$

where $k/100$ is the profit rate, $p/100$ is the percentage of credit required for financing the investment, n is the credit repayment period (years) and m is the service life of the investment (years), based on depreciation rates in effect, reciprocal to the depreciation rate.

The credit repayment period (or the credit pay-off) is arrived at by dividing the amount of credit required by the annual repayment installment:

$$n = I(p/100)/a$$

where I is the cost of the investment and a is the annual repayment installment and algebraically is

$$a = I/m + (k/100)I$$

Consequently, the credit repayment period is computed as:

$$n = \frac{I(p/100)}{I/m + (k/100)I}$$

Therefore, the repayment installment consists mainly of the depreciation allowance which remains entirely at the investor's disposal (in case of assets acquired after January 1, 1967) and the profit that should accrue from this investment. Two illustrations are offered to illuminate the application of the formulas. In the first example, the investor requests a credit amounting to 70 per cent of the project's costs, offers repayment within 10 years, and the project's estimated service life is 25 years. The competing project requires 100 per cent credit coverage, with repayment within 8 years and with an estimated 10 years' service life. The bank will favor the first project because $k_1 > k_2$.

$$k_1 = \frac{70}{10} - \frac{100}{25} = 3 \quad \text{and} \quad k_2 = \frac{100}{8} - \frac{100}{10} = 2.5$$

In the second example, the investor requires 100 per cent credit to be repaid within 10 years, with a service life of 20 years. The competing project also requires 100 per cent credit financing to be repaid within 4 years, with a 5-year service life of the project. Although the profit rate here is identical ($k_3 = k_4$), the bank will grant the credit to the second contender because preference is given to the investor offering a shorter repayment period.

$$k_3 = \frac{100}{10} - \frac{100}{20} = 5 \quad \text{and} \quad k_4 = \frac{100}{4} - \frac{100}{5} = 5$$

It was recognized that the formula was only to assist the bank in evaluating competing projects, but that no standard profit rate or credit pay-off period was provided. Without justifying its derivation, a 6 per cent (net) profitability rate was adopted. On the assumption that about 60 per cent of investments were to be financed from credits and that the average service life of fixed assets is 25 years, then the standard profit rate should amount to about 15 per cent of investment projects, or the annual return of the investment should be 15 per cent of its costs. The computation was derived as follows: Since a 6 per cent charge would be levied on depreciated capital assets and 6 per cent interest would be charged on bank credits for investments (from 1968 the rate on interim investment credits was to go up to 8 per cent)--once again it is not clear how these figures were derived--and since a 6 per cent (net of all capital charges) profit rate was stipulated, the source of funds for the annual credit installment should in this "standard" case amount to:

$$a = \frac{I}{m} + \frac{15}{100} I - \frac{6}{100} I - \frac{6}{100} I \cdot \frac{p}{100}$$

The planners seemed to have been preoccupied with explaining that the 15 per cent is only an approximate rate, rather than with examining the logic behind, what seem to have been, arbitrarily adopted figures in each case.[30] Since

$$n = (I.p/100)/a$$

by inserting the value for a

$$a = \frac{I}{m} + \frac{15}{100} I - \frac{6}{100} I - \frac{6}{100} I \cdot \frac{p}{100}$$

we arrive at

$$n = \frac{pm}{100 + 3m(3 - \frac{2p}{100})}$$

Hence, the credit repayment period is 6 years.

Essentially, three instruments would be used in the investment credit policy: 1) the amount of credit, its distribution, and the share of credit in financing the investment; 2) the credit repayment period; and 3) the interest rate. It should be noted that only the use of the first two was stressed and there seems to have been some hesitation about the third. The investment credit policy had to deal with the problem of divergent profitability and varied conditions in individual branches in view of the past investment pattern and of the peculiarities of the wholesale price revision. In "exceptional" cases subsidies from the state budget would be granted, to wit 1) for investment projects already begun which were deemed beneficial for the economy, but were beyond the scope of a single enterprise; 2) for civil defense projects; 3) for water and air purification projects built for already existing enterprises (up to 50 per cent of investment funds); and 4) for new construction to promote a particular region (up to 15 per cent of the investment costs).

Furthermore, subsidies would be granted for special purpose projects as proposed 1) by the Central Electric Power Administration for the construction and expansion of power-distributing systems and for the construction of new large-scale projects; 2) by the Ministry of Mining for new mines, new gallery system, and new pipelines; 3) by the Ministry of Domestic Trade for enlarging the retail outlet network; and 4) by the national committees for expanding services for the population. In each case the total subsidy per project could not exceed 50 per cent and the total subsidies for a given unit could not exceed a certain percentage of the total investment undertaken by that unit. There again it was expected that eventually the subsidies for special-purpose projects would be displaced by price increases in these branches. As a rule, no other investment subsidies would be granted; only "quite exceptionally" would the state allot subsidies for individual projects from a special reserve fund.

The rate of annual transfer of depreciation was to be computed as follows:

$$\frac{6 \times \text{enterprise depreciation rate for replacement of assets}}{4}$$

where 6 refers to an average rate of remittance for the economy; the enterprise depreciation rate for replacement of assets refers to an enterprise average rate in force in 1966, minus the 1966 average rate for capital repairs; and 4 refers to the average rate of depreciation for replacement of assets in the economy. On the basis of the average for the economy, it was expected that on the average it would take seventeen years to pay off these depreciation allowances to the state. The computations were roughly based on the following assumed relationships: On the average, the depreciated value at the end of 1966 was 17/25 of the original cost (25 years is the average service life); 6 per cent was an average remittance on depreciated cost (17/25 of I). Should the enterprise rate for replacement coincide with the average (4 per cent based on the original cost, or 0.04 of I) 150 per cent of depreciation based on original cost was about 6 per cent of depreciated value.

In cases where unfinished construction was sizable and the transfer would have to exceed the accrued depreciation, the CSB might defer payment of such excesses. Obviously, the amounts contributed to the budget could, at best, aim at an accounting equal start and not at an economic one. Apart from the other shortcomings (including subsidies) that we have pointed out, the Czechoslovak crowns do not represent replacement costs of assets.

On the average, about 27 per cent of depreciation allowances on fixed assets purchased as at the end of 1966 would be left with the enterprises for the partial replacement of these assets. This might be the share of depreciation earmarked in the past for capital repairs. The entire amount of depreciation of fixed assets purchased after January 1, 1967, was to be retained by enterprises, no matter how these investments were financed.

However, the branch directorates were empowered to request a transfer of a share of the enterprise's depreciation to the EPU to be used partially for financing strategic investments for the branch.

As of January 1, 1967, depreciation would be written off at the fixed asset's original cost and the previously included charge for capital repairs would be eliminated. Expenditures on major and current repairs would be treated as operating costs. Renovations would be defined as investments. Revaluation of fixed assets was expected by January 1, 1967, in connection with the general price reform: Machinery and equipment was to be adjusted by a general index of 123 and buildings and construction by an index of 119.

ASPECTS OF FOREIGN TRADE POLICY

Concentration on foreign trade with the socialist bloc, particularly with the U.S.S.R., was stressed.[31] It was argued that capitalistic markets were unstable, that a major shift toward them would be an adventurous undertaking, and that trade with those countries must accord with the principles of foreign policy. The capitalist countries were differentiated as those that apparently misuse foreign trade as an instrument of "imperialistic" policy (U.S.A. and West Germany) and those that are guided by more "commercial principles." State loans from the West seemed to be out of the question,[32] but a wider exploitation of the possibilities of long-term self-repaying credits was supported. Long-term foreign credits extended to enterprises would be promoted. The flexibility of Soviet policy in acquiring long-term credit for specific business projects (Fiat) was praised.[33]

Long-term foreign credits to procure up-to-date equipment and to rejuvenate industry were favored and the policy of self-sufficiency was criticized. Imports should be financed by long-term foreign credits, rather than at the cost of consumption.[34] Another advantage of increasing imports was seen by

Premier Josef Lenart as subjecting domestic producers to the competitive test and as improving the welfare of the consumer by widening the choices open to him. He pointed out that the share of imported consumer goods (about 5 to 6 per cent of marketable commodities) was too low for both purposes. As a bare minimum the share ought to be at least 20 per cent.[35]

The sale of foreign exchange for imports of machinery from capitalist countries would require proof of the ability to pay back the purchase price in the same foreign currency, with compound interest. Foreign exchange was to be allocated to investors on the basis of competitive bids. The basic criterion would be the repayment period and profit computed in foreign exchange. Those allocations were to assume a form of credits in foreign exchange, committing the enterprise to sell back the amount involved to the bank in foreign currency. All exporters were bound to sell the foreign currency they received to the bank.

In order to encourage exports that were profitable on the capitalist markets on the basis of an export-import ratio, the bank would allow enterprises "a little balance of trade" account. It was expected that enterprises would gradually enjoy greater discretion in dealing with foreign currency.[36]

CHAPTER 7 THE FALTERING WINDS OF ECONOMIC CHANGE

THE LESSONS OF 1967: EFFECTS OF PRICE REVISION

As past experience in Czechoslovakia and elsewhere in Eastern Europe has shown, under conditions of a taut plan, where the engine of economic growth is propelled mainly by investments, acute disproportions and shortages are bound to create tensions, which do not permit the restoration of the price mechanism. In 1967 tensions were bound to magnify, creating one of the main obstacles in reviving the price mechanism.[1] In view of the acute inflationary pressures, it was apparently not possible to allow prices free rein to fluctuate with the market.[2]

Ota Sik maintained that under the existing sellers' market, price movements had to be restrained and a broad range of centrally controlled prices had to be retained. Consequently a large number of fallacious prices remained. Rigid central price formation was the main brake in equilibrating demand and supply which could not be fully and flexibly achieved by varying production only. The 1967 wholesale price revision was confined merely to revising prices of broad groups of products.[3] Considerable discrepancies in the profitability of individual products were not rectified. Moreover, high profitability often resulted from the ability of some branches and enterprises to inflate their cost data. The point in question was not so much the divergent profitability, but that these variations were not indicative of scarcity relations. Before individual prices were negotiated between supplier and buyer within the limits allowed, the point of departure price for the group had to be rectified to eliminate "unjustified" price increases indulged in during the price revision. Only after a "sound system of price statistics and control" would be instituted, could the movement of individual prices be relaxed without the danger of rampant inflation.[4]

Originally it was estimated that as a result of the 1967 wholesale price revision, prices would increase by 19 per cent, whereas they were reported to have actually risen by over 29 per cent.[5] It was revealed that even after the revision, enterprises succeeded in raising wholesale prices by all kinds of surcharges, increasing the level of wholesale prices in the first quarter of 1967 by 0.7 per cent.[6]

The price revision reportedly eliminated 17.5 billion kcs. (or about 90 per cent) of the subsidies introduced in 1966. During the price revision, which increased the price level of groups of products, some adjustments of individual prices were made (in about 30 per cent of individual products.)[7]

In investment construction there was a pronounced increase of prices over the anticipated increase. For example, the prices of mechanical installations rose by 34 per cent instead of 23 per cent and the prices of construction work rose by 32 per cent instead of 19 per cent.[8] In the second quarter of 1967, the CSB inquired into the effect of revised prices on 1,100 constructions. It was found that estimated costs rose by 54 per cent, the increases varying between 35 to 100 per cent. It was reported that builders' costs increased by 47 per cent, their revenues by 36 per cent, and their GY by 13.5 per cent, indicating a decline in the effectiveness of construction. However, the manipulations involved cost inflation at the planning stage, with underestimation of GY in order to qualify for subsidies. To make up for the increased estimated costs, the investors were to use 10.3 billion (or 14.8 per cent) from their own funds, 27 billion (or 38.7 per cent) from credits, and 32.5 billion kcs. (or 46.5 per cent) from budget subsidies.

Table 63

WHOLESALE PRICE INCREASES IN MAIN BRANCHES OF INDUSTRY IN 1967
(1966 = 100)

Branch	Index
Solid fuels	149.9
Power	138.7
Machinery and metallurgy	128.9
Chemical industry	147.1
Building materials	142.3
Consumer goods	120.1
Food industry	120.5
Pharmaceuticals	112.9
Average	129.3

Source: Oldrych Novotny, Supplement to FU, No. 8, 1967.

The CSB, in conjunction with the SCT, conducted a survey of the effect of the new wholesale prices on virtually all unfinished construction projects whose estimated costs exceeded 1 million kcs., involving 5,964 constructions at an estimated cost of 159.5 billion kcs. The findings revealed that as a result of new prices, the estimated costs rose by 49.6 per cent, of which construction costs were responsible for about 48 per cent and equipment for about 52 per cent. The survey indicated that there was considerable cost inflation and the MF initiated a comprehensive audit of all projects financed by the state budget or by bank credits.[9]

In order to encourage export production, the producer was allowed a share of the positive difference between the foreign and domestic price of a product and was granted state subsidies to cover the negative difference. It seems that the latter subsidies were instrumental in the Ministry of Heavy Industry's fulfillment of the volume of exports for the first quarter of 1967.[10] Evidently in this case no significant departure from the traditional system was made, for instead of making the producer more sensitive to market impulses, it preserved the barrier between the producer and the market for his products.

Since the price revision pertained only to wholesale prices, the perennial problem of the dual price system had to be solved. Namely, what to do if the new wholesale price would exceed the existing and essentially unchanged retail price? Products and services whose wholesale prices exceeded retail prices had grown in number.[11] As usual, the problem was solved by resorting to sizable subsidies. Reportedly, the over-all level of retail prices increased only by 0.1 per cent in the first quarter of 1967. On the whole the prices of services went up by 1.5 per cent. However, various price changes were made within groups of goods, and, although the statistical evidence does not clearly bear this out, there seem to have been more significant increases of prices which affect the cost of living.[12]

According to the 1967 plan fulfillment report the share of free prices in total retail turnover dropped from 23-25 per cent in 1966 to 13 per cent in 1967. The share of free retail prices was reported to have been 10 per cent in the Ministry of Consumer Goods, 34 per cent in the Ministry of Heavy Industry, 3 per cent in the Ministry of Food, 1 per cent in the Ministry of Construction, and 55 per cent in local industry and cooperatives. The relatively more restricted use of free prices was justified on the grounds that a hike of retail prices caused by increased wholesale prices had to be prevented. The restricted use of free and limited prices was explained by the Domestic Trade Minister, Jindrich Uher, as due to a continuing sellers' market, especially for industrial consumer goods, and a monopolization of industry which was yet not counteracted by sufficient import of consumer goods.[13]

Uher complained that the proclivity to fix too high limited and free prices for newly introduced products was all too frequent. Prices of products of low profitability were often increased, whereas those of highly profitable goods were left unchanged. Hence, as long as there was a sellers' market, enterprises should be subjected "to more severe conditions" for fixing free and limited prices. Regulations were issued requiring that products be priced at calculated prices (based on costs) with not higher than an average profitability on comparable products (hence reverting to the past procedure). Admittedly, the verification of prices of about 350,000 to 400,000 products was virtually impossible, but imposition of stringent controls in the best tradition was at least to be a brake on price manipulations.[14]

To the conservative Party stalwarts and to the functionaries of the SCFPW and of the MF, inflation is an anathema with which they associate, often not without some good reasons, major ills. The population was apprehensive that restoration of equilibrium might entail a deterioration, or at best stagnation, of living standards. Although early in 1967 there were some signs that a moderate inflation might be reverted to, by mid-1967 Oldrych Cernik rejected such a solution by declaring it to be politically unacceptable. Cernik warned that monetary and fiscal policies alone could not be relied upon to avert or arrest inflationary pressures. A "radical restriction" of effective demand would, in Cernik's view, be tantamount to a crisis situation, involving idle capacity, unemployment, and a drop in the living standards. In view of the existing striking imbalances, economic instruments alone could not be counted on to alleviate dislocations.[15]

Apprehensive of losing the essential controls over price formation, terrified by inflationary price movements should curbs be relaxed, and conscious of possible popular unrest in response to retail price escalation, the SCFPW maintained the dual price system and retained firm and direct authority to determine crucial price relations and to regulate, to control, and to approve the bulk of prices or, at least, to influence their formation.

The fear of inflation leads central authorities to continue freezing prices. But imposition of price controls often further aggravates the situation; it requires widespread governmental intervention into the details of economic activity. Rigid prices do not eliminate inflationary pressures, but, at the most, suppress them. Suppression prevents the price system from working, thus hampering the economic mechanism that would elicit eradication of shortages.

Originally, at the price revision stage, profitability to wages was planned at 22 per cent, but in the 1967 annual plan of enterprises a 53.5 per cent profitability was envisaged. The reported profitability for the first quarter of 1967 was 71.5 per cent.[16] The Deputy Minister of Finance reported the profitability to have been a startling 75 per cent.[17] Still another source reported the profitability to wages to have been 76.5 per cent and 12.5 per cent to costs in the first quarter of 1967.[18] There was a wide dispersion of profitability between

Table 64

PROFITABILITY IN THE FIRST QUARTER, 1967

Branches	Profitability (percentages)	
	To wages	To costs
Mining	97.5	23.7
Power	106.8	11.8
Heavy industry	66.1	12.0
Chemical industry	120.1	14.6
Consumer goods	62.1	13.8
Food industry	94.2	5.2
Average	76.5	12.4

Source: Oldrych Novotny, Supplement to FU, No. 8, 1967.

individual enterprises. For example, the Spolana enterprise "planned" a 19.87 per cent profitability when the price revision was being conducted. Its

1967 plan envisaged a 36.85 per cent profitability. The reported profitability for the first quarter 1967 was 101.97 per cent.[19] Of course, the example used might not be a typical one.

Profitability in industry and construction in the first half of 1967 was on the average as much as 70 per cent of wages paid and by the end of the third quarter 1967 it was 85 per cent, exceeding the planned average for the whole year by more than one third.[20] There was very wide "unintended" dispersion between the profitability of various branches and various products.[21] Significant and entirely random differences in profitability occurred among groups of products.[22]

Official spokesmen condemned the process of price recalculation for having allowed flagrant manipulations and for having been open to obvious errors resulting in "illegitimate" profitability, which seriously and intolerably deviated from assumed proportions. The process actually consisted of setting prices on the basis of planned costs for 1966, which, with the benefit of hindsight, have proven to have been considerably overstated. Apart from price machinations and infractions on regulations, some additional price adjustments in machine-building and construction were responsible for boosting the price level.[23] Substantial improvements were achieved in more consistent calculations, in reckoning with interdependencies (but significantly not in removing the sources of contamination of data), and in the techniques and the speed of carrying out the price revision. Price coefficients were determined by a method which did not break with tradition, but merely modified it. The faulty prices thus obtained would not have mattered so much if the second phase of the price reform--the adjustment of prices to reflect market conditions--had been carried out. As it happened, enterprises continued to be guided by fallacious signals and choice coefficients, impeding any effective decentralization.

One of the main causes for the exceedingly high

profitability was attributed to the enterprises' submission of plans which understated GY by 10 billion kcs. in 1966 and by 17 to 20 billion kcs. in 1967. Once again, when preparing the 1967 national economic plan, the enterprise and ministerial plan drafts were "marked by excessively high demands for allocations from central resources and by concealment of their own possibilities." Bargaining with superiors continued. Enterprise plans provided for all sorts of hidden reserves. According to an estimate of the Ministry of Heavy Industry, the plans submitted to it understated GY by about 4 billion kcs. Premier Josef Lenart called upon Party cells to scrutinize and tighten up their organizations' plans,[24] but as usual the exhortation proved to be of little avail. "Audits of individual enterprises revealed great miscalculations." Amounts often reaching the 100 million kcs. mark were involved. The government requested a thorough investigation of how the enterprises had carried out the price revision. The SCFPW investigated selected EPU's and enterprises in heavy, consumer, and food industries; in construction; and some local enterprises to verify the cause for higher profitability in the first quarter of 1967. It was revealed that in preparing the data for revised prices the enterprises and EPU's did not abide by the central directives and many violations were reported. Since computation of wholesale prices was based on enterprise 1966 plans--plans which were slack and were overfulfilled both in terms of quantity of output and of unit costs--profits were inflated at the outset by about 6 billion kcs. in centrally managed industry and construction.[25]

The higher rate of profitability achieved as a result of the price revision was also attributed to shortcomings in calculating depreciation which was not accurately estimated at the center.[26] As of January 1, 1967, the MF decreed new depreciation rules. Fixed assets were classified into eight classes. Within each class three subdivisions were made. The depreciation schedule was considerably simplified. A straight-line method based on original cost was used. Provisions for repairs were excluded from the depreciation rates. Reportedly, the over-all impact of the new depreciation policy was an increase in enterprises' GY of about 24 billion kcs. As a result of new prices and increased volume of fixed assets, the depreciation base in 1967 was on the average increased by 4.5 per cent, increased by 20 per cent as a result of revaluation of fixed assets, and reduced by 19.8 per cent as a result of excluding fully depreciated assets and of excluding assets below 3,000 kcs. from depreciable assets. The largest decrease in the depreciable cost of fixed assets occurred in the consumer goods and food industries because of their obsolete capital stock. The abolition of depreciation on fully depreciated assets enhanced the taxable GY, but allowed the previously underprivileged plants an opportunity to accumulate investment funds.

While preparing the 1968 budget, the MF evaluated the possibility of increasing depreciation in some branches. However, it was rejected, for in such cases the contributions to the budget would decrease because of both a reduced GY base and a decreased stock of assets on which a budget levy is imposed. There remained still many unsettled problems of depreciation policy. Among them was the dubious proposition of making the depreciation rate contingent on the size of the enterprise's GY.[27]

At the September, 1967, Party Plenum a complaint was echoed that wholesale prices were so inordinately high as to make it impossible to distinguish between effective and ineffective enterprises.[28] As it was later observed: "Judging by the income situation of the enterprises, it is difficult to find at all any really inefficient enterprises, although there is no shortage of them."[29] Virtually every producer could make a profit. It was feared that if such a situation continued, it would elicit the introduction of more and more directive measures. The profitability of most enterprises was spurious and grossly misleading. Financial resources were ill-distributed. Generally excess funds were not available to light industry branches, but inflated the pockets of heavy industry. As Otakar Turek observed:

> The abundance of money is not necessarily concentrated in the more effective production units so that higher income can result in expansion of production either through investments or by attracting additional manpower.[30]

Moreover, for yet another reason, the price reform had no effect on ineffective producers who continued to receive substantial state subventions (subsidies, reduction of turnover tax, surcharges on exports, reduced budget levies, etc.). On the other hand, the "income of numerous effective producers was being drained off by various means."[31] On the whole, the price revision was instrumental in creating "soft," rather than "hard" economic conditions, thus largely eliminating the pressures on which the reformers had relied to force efficiency on producers.[32] The reform relaxed the budget constraint without introducing scarcity prices which would have contributed to providing the efficiency constraint.

The objective of the new system was to create conditions which would exert pressure on enterprise managers providing incentives to uncover reserves, to improve utilization of fixed and working capital, to raise productivity, to enhance quality, and to adjust output to demand. But the experience indicated that the enterprises' GY was so large that there was no pressure for significant improvement.[33]

> Enterprises are not forced to seek innovations and improvements, but have sufficient funds to pay substantially higher wages, and, in most cases, they do not have any problems in providing funds for investments... This is not a healthy climate for initiative. We need a situation on businesslike terms that would compel the enterprises to constantly seek improvements.[34]

The ample funds were primarily translated into wage increases and accumulated funds. It was claimed that because of slow "progress" in investment construction there were no potent pressures for enterprises to increase the allocation of their funds for investments or to apply for credits. Nevertheless, where warranted by ample liquidity, enterprises embarked on "wild" investment spending, without concern for economy and "regardless of whether or not they could complete these constructions within a reasonable time."[35] Credits were of little consequence in investments and even in current activity. The increased liquidity of enterprises and the ensuing inflationary pressures added fuel to recentralization forces.[36]

There were persisting strong tendencies typical of the old system. The sellers' market was vigorous. Essentially world market conditions did not affect producers. In many cases, enterprises were shielded by state subsidies. The production of unwanted goods for both the domestic and foreign markets continued, leading to superfluous accumulation of inventories. The credit policies were ineffective.

NEW POLICIES AND THEIR EFFICACY

The distribution of investments was gradually changed: Especially, investments in heavy industry were curtailed and investments in processing branches and the nonproductive sphere were increased.[37] As far as structural changes were concerned emphasis was placed on accelerating the development of the chemical industry; on increasing the share of liquid and gaseous fuels; on restricting the extraction of solid fuels; on expanding the output of glass, textiles, and building materials; on speeding up the development of the fodder industry; and on increasing the supply of agricultural chemicals.[38] The allocation of investment subsidies is illustrated in Table 65. Investments were fully subsidized in cases where "the state interest substantially outweighed that of the enterprise." To restrict investments, apparently individual investment grants were to be subjected to a very strict control. Subsidies were granted only for

Table 65

BUDGET SUBSIDIES FOR INVESTMENTS IN 1967

Branches and sectors	Million kcs.	
Mining	1,367	
Power	1,608	
Heavy, chemical, construction, consumer goods, and food	348	
Centrally managed industry		3,232
Agriculture	1,168	
Bulk buying	500	
Forestry and water	1,650	
Transportation	1,850	
Communications	620	
Centrally managed organizations		9,020
Economic organizations under national committees		1,301
Others		600
Total		10,921

Source: Leopold Lerr, FU, No. 10, 1967, p. 654.

specific investments.[39]

Out of a total of about 3 billion kcs. idle investment funds as of June 30, 1967 (2 billion kcs. accumulated as of March 31, 1967, and 1 billion kcs. in the second quarter), the largest share was accumulated by enterprises in heavy industry (especially in metallurgy), whereas the lowest share was accumulated by the chemical industry. Admittedly the surplus of available funds on the enterprises' investment accounts should have amounted to "twice the actual amount," because the enterprises were in no hurry to transfer the share of GY to the investment accounts and were keeping these funds in their current accounts.[40] Conceivably enterprises reacted this way because, inter alia: 1) real investments were difficult to come by and they were reluctant to leave idle funds on the investment account which they suspected might be frozen; 2) of the propensity to spend on wages; and 3) of the advantages of hoarding inventories.

The low share of credit in financing enterprise investments attested to the exceptionally favorable financial situation at enterprises. An investigation of credit agreements disclosed that the CSB could only influence about one third of all industrial enterprises through the conditions under which it would extend investment credit. As could be expected, the price of investment credit--the interest rate--was ineffective. An official of the MF argued that it would be desirable to raise the interest rates, but in view of the macroeconomic disequilibrium the credit policy alone would be insufficient. "It can be said that today no interest rate could be high enough."[41] Whereas enterprises had planned about 50 per cent of their investment outlays to be financed by credit and 10 per cent from GY, the enterprises' revisions of plans in the course of 1967 decreased the share of credit to below 30 per cent and increased that of GY to about 25 per cent. The shares of budget subsidies (about 17 per cent) and depreciation (about 18 per cent) remained virtually unchanged, while other enterprise resources increased by 10 per cent. The statistics of plan execution revealed that as of June 30, 1967, the share of investment credits was only 24 per cent, budget subsidies increased to 19.5 per cent, and the enterprises' own resources rose to 56.5 per cent.[42] A survey conducted by the Ministry of Heavy Industry revealed that whereas credit was supposed to finance 65 per cent of investments in that Ministry, it was determined that only 23 per cent of investments were so financed.[43] By mid-1967 it was expected that 21 per cent of productive investment would be financed by credit; 52 per cent by subsidies, depreciation, and various transfers; and 27 per cent of investment would be self-financed.[44] It was envisaged that in 1968, 26 per cent of investment of the Ministry of Heavy Industry would be financed by credit, 66 per cent in the Ministry of Chemical Industry, 51 per cent in consumer goods, 60 per cent in food-processing, and the share of credit in financing investment in glass and ceramics industries would be substantially higher.[45]

From 1965 to 1966 the number of unfinished construction projects increased from 15,032 to 16,239 and the estimated costs of unfinished construction as at end of year increased from 161 to 170.3 billion kcs. This was mainly attributed to increased liquidity at enterprises and EPU's.[46] As of June 30, 1967, it was reported that the volume of unfinished construction was excessively high in all branches, except mining.[47] Although some decline in the number of industrial projects under construction was evident in 1967,[48] unfinished construction mushroomed in the regional sector under national committees "so that for all practical purposes, nothing has changed in the over-all situation." Moreover, the average period of completion of construction was further extended.[49]

One of the reasons for the failure to reduce the volume of unfinished construction was the underfulfillment of the investment construction program, attributed to the lack of materials for finishing the work, to breakdowns in deliveries of subcontracted components (especially electrical installations, air conditioning, heating, plumbing, etc.), and to a lack of skilled labor. The construction suppliers continued to enjoy a dominant position, with their production capacity unadapted to the requirements of builders. So much so that the Chairman of the SCT was lead to say that the "structural allocation of investments is becoming less a matter that lies within the competence of central bodies and is becoming increasingly a matter that lies in the province of suppliers." Investors were competing among themselves by offering higher prices (surcharges) to suppliers. Another reason was the continued excessive starting of new constructions while those in progress were not being completed.[50] Furthermore, the volume of unfinished construction grew because of the excesses of actual over estimated costs and due to new prices.[51] The perpetual problems of considerable dispersion of investments, of insufficient preparatory work, and of failures to abide by estimated costs were not overcome.[52]

The bank performed a regular check on estimated costs of projects financed from the budget or by loans. It was found that unfinished construction projects were being expanded by including new projects; that the contractors added in many cases unsubstantiated charges; that engineering costs were inflated; etc.[53] One of the problems encountered was the difficulty in verifying the prices of machines and equipment generally made to order. This was a source of "illegal" price hikes, just as it had been in the traditional system.[54]

Failure to put new capacities into operation continued. For example, in 1966 the construction of various plants for the East Slovak Iron and Steel Works was delayed. The same was true of projects in the power, chemical, food, and consumer goods industries. Education, health services, and housing investment targets were also underfulfilled. The often-aired past complaints about investment construction were again heard. The construction industry's capacity could not meet the demand for investments. Suppliers of capital goods continued to dominate investors. Investors continued to press for inclusion of their projects into the plan and for starting work on it. It was still more advantageous for the construction industry to start more projects, rather than to complete those on hand. Investors were still being invoiced for fragmentary work done.[55]

The most serious threat of inflation came from investment activity. The May, 1967, Plenary Session of the CC called for restricting the demand for investments to remain within the FYP's indexes and for decreasing the volume of investments in the productive sphere. But there was no effective response. The principal causes were attributed to the perennial problem of large volume of unfinished investments and to the ineffectiveness of the credit policy. The enterprises' GY was so "excessively" high that it undermined the role of investment credit. Thus the old administrative methods crept back into the system in order to tackle the problem of restraining new investments.[56] It was particularly difficult to check the inflationary pressures exerted by investments whose estimated costs did not exceed 1.5 million kcs. and which enterprises could start without having to resort to the bank's selective procedure. Constructions whose estimated costs exceeded 1.5 million kcs. were subject to the selective procedure. The deadline for submitting projects to the selective procedure was May 31, 1967. The investor could not start in 1967 a project that had not been submitted prior to that date.[57] It was expected that by applying the new investment credit policy the unfinished construction in industry, construction, and domestic trade at the end of 1967 would be reduced by over 8 billion kcs. in comparison to 1966. However, the results of the selective procedure were disappointing and enterprises did not resort to credit as much as expected.[58]

The enterprises' fear of possible withdrawal of idle funds on the investment account prompted them to vehemently promote projects which did not pass the selective procedure tests. The enterprises often clamored for increases in wholesale prices in order to push a "weak" project through the tests. To prevent the recurrence of such manipulations, it was decided that world market prices would be used in calculating the efficacy of investments. But the extent to which this was done, the selection of price weights, and the validity of the selective procedure are yet other questions. Apart from the shortcomings which we discussed in the previous chapter, the selective procedure in itself was deficient, for bids were confined to narrow branches; e.g., the effectiveness of a project in heavy industry was not allowed to compete with the effectiveness of one in chemical industry. As was pointed out, "the manner of allocating investments has hardly changed."[59]

Since the curbs on unfinished construction failed, the authorities resorted to applying the selective procedure for purposes of reducing the number of projects started in 1967. Reportedly, the construction of six buildings at an estimated cost of 31 million kcs. was stopped and the work on 32 construction projects was limited by 1.7 billion kcs. The volume of new constructions subjected to selective procedure was apparently reduced by 20 per cent due to the restrictive measures. The restrictive measures applied to investment credits and budget subsidies were effective. But admittedly they "involved direct interventions, partly of an administrative nature."[60]

At the May, 1967, CC Plenum, Cernik reported that the 1967 investment plan was cut below the level envisaged in the Fourth FYP. Investment credits were to be reduced by some 2 billion kcs. and new construction was cut to 12.5 billion kcs. The revised 1967 investment plan modified the assumption of the Fourth FYP in that it called for increasing the share of investments and for accelerating completion of investments in chemical, consumer goods, and building materials industries at the expense of investments in basic industries.[61] In comparison to the original targets of the Fourth FYP, the output of coal and the generation of electric power were to be reduced, allowing a reduction of investments in fuels and power. For example, the construction of a hydroelectric power station in North Bohemia was abandoned and some approved "political" investment projects in Slovakia were shelved. Preference was to be given to investments in industries that might help to alleviate the balance of payments.

In 1967 the CSB was not permitted to extend credits for new enterprise investments, except for agriculture, domestic trade, and economic organizations under the aegis of national committees. Due to the ample liquidity of a majority of enterprises, even complete restrictions on credits could not significantly curtail the volume of unfinished investment projects.[62] In extending credit, the bank was supposed to discriminate according to the enterprise's state of liquidity, mainly on the basis of information furnished by the enterprise--by itself probably of dubious validity. Within the credit limits set at the center, the bank was to accord precedence to enterprises that could contribute to improvements of the balance of payments, that could help to alleviate market shortages, and that could promote new technology. Moreover, preferential credit would be extended for completing unfinished projects.[63]

To limit investments, an enterprise commencing an investment project was required to have set aside for that purpose at least 50 per cent of its own funds necessary for executing the project.[64] One of the major inequities involved in such a measure is that enterprises that were able to achieve and retain the highest liquidity would be in more enviable positions, whereas those enterprises whose ability to inflate prices and to retain liquidity was less effective were prevented from investing. Of course, due to the fallacy of prices, liquidity was not a measure of efficiency. Hence, it is quite conceivable that enterprises that were prevented from investing would be the ones where investments were most needed, especially since they might have been the ones that were traditionally underprivileged.[65]

Under the reformed system, bank credits were to finance working capital. Stringent controls over such credits were lifted. Indeed, it was pointed out that the credits were virtually automatically granted. The facility of financing inventories by low-cost short-term credits, in fact, prompted increases in inventories. In view of the inflationary pressures, enterprises tended to accumulate inventories.[66]

Complaints were raised that goods were "to a great extent made only for storage." From January 1, to September 1, 1967, resources frozen in stocks in industry and construction grew by about 6.5 billion kcs., with the rate of increase of inventories exceeding the rise in the flow of production. During the first half of 1967 inventories of materials rose by 4.2 per cent, of work in process by 6.2 per cent, and those of the largely unsalable finished output by 14.2 per cent. The increase of inventories of materials and work in process was attributed to deficiencies in the flow of supplies. On the other hand, increased liquidity removed the pressures on producers to manufacture goods in high demand; the stockpiling of unsalable output had little effect on them.[67]

Insufficient technical progress and low returns on investments were still compensated by enlarging the investment front, which, in turn, boosted demand for producer goods, intensified pressures on imports, and made exports more imperative. To alleviate the balance of payments, more and better machinery had to be exported at the expense of domestic industry, impeding technical progress and cost reduction.[68]

The seller remained well-entrenched in his privileged position. Together with the excessive degree of monopolization, this situation was blamed for disregarding consumers' demand, for neglecting technical advancement, and for slighting improvement of efficiency.[69] Admittedly, the enterprises showed a lack of concern for technical progress. Some changes in planning and financing technical progress were introduced, but "they have not gone to the root of the matter. The key to the problem lies not solely in the ways of creating resources for financing technological advance, but primarily in stimulating the enterprises' economic interests in such an advance."[70] Comprehensive anti-monopolistic measures were still lacking. The Central Commission for Peoples' Control reported that the producers' monopolistic practices were increasing. The sellers' market pressures continued to force buyers to overlook quality shortcomings and to agree to all kinds of surcharges. It was also corroborated that "socialist graft" was not a dying art.[71]

The persisting sellers' market made it necessary to protect buyers from suppliers, often by administrative methods typical of the traditional system. The reliance on such methods was explained as a necessity of the transitional period. The difficulties in making use of the market were attributed to the fact that the central planner was inclined and continuously prompted to protect enterprises from losses that they would incur if they were unable to adjust promptly to new conditions.[72]

The problem of production for the sake of production persisted, with an accumulation of inventories of finished goods and work in process. Apparently, "not much has changed in this respect." With the persisting sellers' market, the reduction of output assignments resulted in "a considerable deterioration of supplier-buyer relations." In order to ensure the availability of supplies, enterprises bought up large quantities of materials in short supply "whenever they could get hold of them," while EPU's consistently interfered in the relations between buyers and sellers. Taking advantage of their monopolistic positions, many suppliers made their deliveries contingent on different surcharges, shares in foreign currency, etc. Enterprises were reported to be rather fickle in their attitude toward the new system, depending on whether they assumed the role of buyers or suppliers:

> As suppliers they demand the fullest operation of the new system, utilization of the market, free price formation, etc.; while as buyers they insist on fixed prices, binding allocations of materials and technical supplies, etc.[73]

Even though, generally, demand outstripped supply, there were also significant individual instances pointing to the contrary.[74] The Institute of National Economic Planning investigated the extent of the sellers' market by sending a questionnaire to all enterprise directors of centrally managed industry, to which 80 per cent replied.[75] It was reported that 52.3 per cent of enterprises replied that orders received exceeded their "capacity to produce"; 17.4 per cent replied that demand for their products was below their "capacity to produce"; and the rest replied that orders received "balanced out" with their capacity.

Table 66

MARKET SITUATION IN 1967:
CRUDE RELATIONSHIP BETWEEN SUPPLY AND DEMAND
(Percentage of replies)

	Relationship of orders to capacity		
	In excess	Equal	Short of
Investment goods for domestic market	45.0	45.0	10.0
Material inputs for domestic market	40.0	38.0	22.0
Consumer goods for domestic market	45.0	34.0	21.0
Exports:			
to capitalist countries	20.0	32.0	48.0
to socialist countries	22.0	41.0	37.0

Source: Zdenek Vergner, RP, October 26, 1967.

The investigation's findings are illustrated in Table 66. However, in view of the techniques employed, definition of terms, reliability of replies, and the degree of aggregation, not too much should be read into the results obtained. Moreover, the problem was not only one of insufficient capacity, but also one of its ineffective use, of "wrong" product mix, and of spurious combination of inputs.

About 69 per cent of enterprises disclosed that they expected in 1968 a "rise in demand" for their products (of which 60 per cent envisaged that they would be unable to meet the requirements), 25 per cent anticipated that demand would remain virtually unchanged, and 6 per cent expected a reduction in demand (particularly in the fuels industry where 20 per cent of enterprises expected a fall in demand). About one third of the enterprises anticipating a rise in demand stated that they would be unable to meet added requirements for exports, 48 per cent indicated that they would be unable to supply the domestic consumer market, and 54 per cent disclosed that they would be unable to meet deliveries of materials for production. The shortages pertained mostly to ferrous and nonferrous foundries; partly to the machine-building industry; and to a large extent to the woodworking industry, to the manufacturing of building materials, and to the glass and fine ceramics plants.

An investigation of a committee of the NA conducted in the fall of 1967 revealed that there was a flagrant shortage of consumer goods on the market (amounting to about 3 billion kcs.). It was reported that one of the reasons for the unavailability of certain consumer goods was the amalgamation which narrowed the range of assortments produced by the individual plants.[76]

Planning in domestic trade still apparently bore many marks of the past. In those cases where trade enterprises were allowed to set prices (e.g., fashions and technical novelties) goods apparently appeared on the market and market disturbances were alleviated. But there were only sporadic cases of pressure on producers.

Branch directorates still allocated materials to their wards thus largely predetermining the enterprises' volume and composition of output. The practice of setting material input norms and sales quotas continued. In such a situation the timid attempts of trade organizations to exert some pressure to obtain what was wanted (even assuming the transmitter's knowledge), to raise quality, to improve appearance, packaging, etc., were ignored by the "monopoly" producers who were anyway in a position to do so because their sales were assured to other customers, foreign trade organizations, etc.

Producer cooperatives and local industries were generally incapable of competing with the "state monopolies." The former were still "severely restricted by the system of balancing and allocating raw material. Being technologically at a disadvantage in comparison with big industry, they too found the new economic rules a hard nut to crack."[77]

It is interesting to note also some demonstration of the weakening of the sellers' market, particularly for agricultural implements. With a dwindling agricultural work force, the need for farm mechanization was steadily emphasized, but, in fact, the sales of agricultural implements were declining.[78] Many reasons were offered for this phenomenon: Marketing difficulties stemmed from financial difficulties attributed to the manner of implementing the new management system in agriculture and to the price reform. Discriminatory prices for equipment designed for agriculture were abolished. The financial situation of the farm was strained not only by upward adjustments of machinery prices, but also by those of other products and services that the farmer buys. While the procurement prices of farm products increased by about 25 to 30 per cent and the new incentive scheme was slated to further boost farm income, agricultural income fell short by 860 million kcs. of the estimate prepared by the CC of the Agricultural Commission. Though it is difficult to quantify the shifts in effective demand due to a reduction in cooperatives' purchasing power, there are indications that at higher prices a sizable reduction in quantity demanded took place. Moreover, farmers were said to be postponing purchases in the belief that they would force a reduction of machinery prices. But a more likely result would be a reduction of farm machinery output. Some cooperative farmers pressed for funds to be distributed among the members of the collective rather than to be diverted to purchases of equipment and fertilizer. Reportedly, as a result of gradual integration of collective farms, better care was taken of farm machinery, prolonging its service life. Also, the quality of machinery supplied improved, so that it did not become as rapidly obsolescent as before. Last, but not least, fallacious marketing surveys and projections of demand for agricultural implements were blamed for erroneous production scheduling.[79]

Inferior quality and poor assortment of machines were the main complaints voiced at the January, 1968, meeting of young farmers held in Prague. In 1967, 800 million kcs. of agricultural implements remained unsold because of their unsuitability, and production of thirty-five kinds of agricultural equipment was discontinued.[80]

The 1967 ample liquidity at enterprises posed the question of credit restrictions to counteract the cogent pressures for translating ample funds into personal earnings, investments, and hoarding of inventories. Minimum contributions to the reserve fund, earmarked for financing working capital, were to be made. Enterprises were to increasingly ensure the financing of working capital from their own resources. Operational credits were to cease to be an automatic source of working capital. Interest rates on these credits were to be raised to at least 6 per cent. In the future, the interest on working capital and investment credits was not to be deducted, as heretofore, in calculating the GY to which the budget levy rate would be applied. The intent was to increase the burden of interest charges by an indirect hike of interest rates. Interest rates on working capital credits were differentiated according to the amount of credit required, with the intent of penalizing the enterprises that accumulated ample funds. The old "subjective" approach was thus largely reintroduced.[81] However, it was reported that in practice in the area of credit policy there was such overcentralization that directors of the CSB branches did not have sufficient leeway to apply differentiation as most of the problems were tackled strictly by directives from above. This observation was duly negated by CSB officials.[82]

Most enterprises had such ample funds that even after satisfying all their requirements they retained free resources for a protracted period. As an anti-inflationary measure attempts were made to induce enterprises to part with these funds by offering lucrative interest earnings on long-term deposits or on the purchase of State Bank Bonds carrying higher interest than the deposits. To facilitate directing the funds where they might immediately and effectively be used, the CSB agreed to the joint accumulation of excess funds by enterprises for the financing of common investments and, significantly, to the mutual (among enterprises) extension of medium- and long-term credits from excess funds (e.g., to finance effective investments).[83]

In spite of the greatly increased liquidity, the rates of contributions to the budget were not increased. It is noteworthy that the intended stability of the new measures was not undermined. However, it was argued in some quarters that "a direct regulation of income is necessary beyond doubt," calling for a change of the rates of contributions to the budget. Concurrently, it was asserted that such action would not deprive the reform of the trust of enterprises.[84] There is probably more than a grain of truth in this assertion, for it would be difficult to lose something that one never had in the first place. About 80 per cent of the enterprise directors replying to the questionnaire issued by the Institute of National Economic Planning doubted that the rules promulgated on January 1, 1967, would remain stable until 1970.[85] It would be surprising if it were otherwise, for there were many intimations from official quarters that the stability of the regulations could not be guaranteed.[86]

A set of financial measures was adopted to counteract "excessive" liquidity at enterprises and the ensuing inflationary pressures. These measures generally departed from the principle of uniformity adopted in the rates of budget levies. For example, the minimum size of the reserve fund was to be differentiated according to the volume of GY allocated to wages and particularly according to the size of retained profit. In order to reduce liquidity ensuing from the price hike, the enterprises where profitability was higher were to set aside a larger share of GY for the reserve fund.[87] The increased compulsory contribution to the reserve fund would compel the enterprises to finance increased working capital from this source.

In centrally managed industrial enterprises the unused balances as of June 30, 1967, in the workers' funds, welfare funds, and reserve funds, amounted to 5.8 billion kcs., an increase of 2.6 billion kcs. within six months. In the socialist sector of the economy the reserve fund reached 4.8 billion kcs.; i.e., an amount about three times as large as the minimum required for the entire year was accumulated within six months, even before the increased rates of contribution went into effect.[88]

In 1966 the average wages in the economy increased by 2.7 per cent, in industry by 2.5 per cent, and in construction by 3.5 per cent. The rate of increase of average wages for the first quarter of 1967 was for the economy (excluding agricultural cooperatives) 5.3 per cent, for industry 5.4 per cent, and for construction 6.3 per cent. The rate of increase of wages outpaced the measured increase in labor productivity. The recorded increase in labor productivity for industry as a whole was 3.6 per cent.[89] Reportedly, the high increase in enterprises' GY and acceleration of average wages have primarily resulted from price revision rather than from improved performance.[90]

The root causes for the strains, stresses, and inflationary pressures in the economy in 1967 were attributed to ineffective adjustment of production and foreign trade to changing demand. Under the impact of inflationary pressures, it was necessary to resort to stricter control of wages. But, "the serious danger of a return to the 'tested' and well-known old administrative methods is inherent in any regulation of wage development." There were a number of such signs in 1967, such as an assigned schedule regulating the relationship between average wages and labor productivity (as traditionally measured by dividing gross output by the number of employees). The intent was not to have a directive labor productivity target established for the enterprise by superiors, but to have one stipulated in the contract negotiated with the trade union. The role of the trade union in this respect was not taken too kindly by the workers.[91] Branch directorates were, however, assigned the relation between labor productivity and growth of wages as an informative index. Therefore, in many instances, this was inevitably translated into a directive index for the enterprises.[92] A warning was sounded:

> If these methods of regulating wages were to prevail, it would practically mean the end of the new management system--a fact which must be realized, although many people do not, or do not want to, understand it.[93]

Nevertheless, official circles maintained that in view of the liquidity situation even the prevailing, fairly strict, wage controls had to be tightened. But, admittedly, the solution did not lie in the imposition of greater wage controls, but in a more effective economic policy.[94] Cernik announced that notwithstanding inflationary pressures, there would be no return to wage ceilings.[95] But Otakar Turek depicted the atmosphere as one where "the enterprises were beginning to suspect that somebody above was watching wages and, therefore, it was not advisable to reveal all reserves." The psychology of the wage ceiling was again on the rise.[96] The government ruled to suspend advance payments on the profit-sharing premiums in the enterprises where developments in wages were considered to have been unsatisfactory.[97]

According to investigations conducted by the CSB there were very few instances of assigning improvement of profitability as a performance criterion for premiums in the individual departments within enterprises. Moreover, such a performance criterion for individual cost centers would have required, as mentioned in Chapter 4, the setting up of internal prices and an appropriate internal accounting system. For the most part these conditions remained unfulfilled and the reported results of the cost centers were often spurious.[98] As a result, either premium funds were allocated among the individual departments in case of shortages, or the funds reported by the department were partially frozen. In either case the system had little incentive effect.

A survey conducted in the industrial enterprises of the Kromeriz district suggested that employees, regardless of the type of work performed, still viewed wages in their distributive role (as affecting living standards), rather than as a reward for the quality of performance--as a measure of skill differentials, qualifications, and productivity. Wages were treated as a kind of equalitarian social allotment, and "so far, not much has been changed in the remuneration of workers." The wage tariff in force did not provide for sufficient wage differentials. On the whole, the wage differentiation, on which so much hope had been placed, was carried out with little success. Employees were simply reclassified into higher-paid positions in the wage tariff instead of higher wages being paid to reward better performance or to compensate for higher skills or qualifications.[99] The only solution possible--probably apart from reclassification of the employees into higher wage brackets--was a differentiation by means of the variable portion of earnings, which--profit-sharing premiums aside--gravitated around 10 per cent of wages. The variable portion of wages was, however, much higher at the Technoplast Plant as per Table 67.

As can be seen from Table 67, although the shares of premiums went up considerably from 1966 to 1967 and were slated for another increase until 1970, it is worth noting that the spread between the lowest and highest qualifications was not significantly enlarged and, if anything, it was to be slightly contracted by 1970. Moreover, the experience of the Technoplast Plant could not be safely regarded as typical; it was described to indicate what efforts were made at wage differentiation, thus implying that, on the average, wage differentiation

Table 67

AVERAGE SHARES OF PREMIUMS IN WAGES
AT THE TECHNOPLAST PLANT (CHROPYNE), 1966-70
(Percentages)

Qualifications schedule	1966 Reported	1967 Reported	1970 Planned
2	21.9	26.5	30.0
3	27.3	28.8	32.0
4	24.7	28.1	33.0
5	24.6	29.2	34.0
6	26.7	32.2	35.0
7	26.7	34.1	36.0
8	27.9	34.2	37.0

Source: Vladimir Bradik, RP, November 28, 1967.

did not even reach that niveau--a conclusion which could also be drawn from the general tenor of complaints about lack of wage differentiation.

Thus whatever wage differentiation was undertaken centered primarily on the variable portion of earnings. As indicated in Table 68 the growth of average earnings in 1967 as compared to 1966 was primarily due to the increase in the variable share of earnings, while the growth of basic wages was roughly the same as in previous years. There was, on the average, a slower increase in the rate of growth of earnings of manual workers than of management and office employees. In 1967 the rate of growth of average industrial wages was 4.3 per cent. In a number of enterprises the growth of average wages exceeded considerably the 4.3 per cent average. For example, out of 700 national enterprises investigated by the State Statistical Office (SSO) in 84 enterprises annual wage increases exceeded 7 per cent and in 11 of these enterprises average wages rose by over 10 per cent. Reportedly many enterprises were not only able to increase significantly average wages, but also to largely increase employment.[100]

Table 68

BASIC AND VARIABLE SHARES OF AVERAGE INCOME, 1966-67

	All employees	Of which: Manual	Technical and managerial	Office
Average monthly income				
1967 (kcs.)	1,683	1,609	2,288	1,452
1966 (kcs.)	1,613	1,550	2,177	1,372
Index	104.3	103.8	105.1	105.8
Basic wages				
1967 (kcs.)	1,414	1,355	1,854	1,276
1966 (kcs.)	1,390	1,338	1,812	1,236
Index	101.7	101.3	102.3	103.2
Premiums				
1967 (kcs.)	216	210	332	123
1966 (kcs.)	190	183	303	104
Index	113.7	114.8	109.6	118.3
Profit-sharing				
1967 (kcs.)	53	41	102	53
1966 (kcs.)	33	29	62	32
Index	160.6	151.7	164.5	165.6

Source: Jaroslav Kux, HN, No. 20, 1968.

Attempts at wage differentiation were made between categories of employees, rather than within categories, as illustrated in Table 69. For example, the head economist of the Technoplast Plant reported that premium differentiation within categories was an exceedingly trying task. Department heads and foremen were given a relatively wide latitude in this area. Thus, in 1966, a lathe operator in qualification schedule No.7 was entitled to premiums varying from 28 to 30 per cent of wages, whereas in 1967 the spread was enlarged from 22 to 45 per cent. But the decision-makers apparently proved unequal to the challenge. They lacked the necessary courage to put into effect the principle of individual premium as a potent reward for the

Table 69

WAGE DIFFERENTIATION, 1966-67

	Manual workers	Mana-gerial	Office staff
1966			
Average wages (kcs.)	1,549	2,176	1,373
Increase over 1965 (%)	101.4	105.3	104.1
Index	100.0	140.5	88.6
First quarter of 1967			
Average wages (kcs.)	1,598	2,300	1,441
Increase over 1965 (%)	105.1	105.2	106.2
Index	100.0	143.9	90.2

Source: Emil Moravec, PM, No. 6, 1967, p. 243.

quality of performance.[101]

It was pointed out that such an approach to wage differentiation was insufficient and lacked the necessary stimulus for employees. Moreover, it created disturbances among manual workers who were under the impression that the widening of the wage scale was directed against them.[102] The differentiation of salaries for managerial and technical personnel was also mainly conducted through the variable portion of earnings. A fund for managerial premiums was established, for example, at the Technoplast Plant amounting to 6 per cent of savings on materials and to 16 per cent of savings on wages--indicating the strong pressure on wage savings exerted by the stabilization tax. Here again significant problems were encountered in determining individual premiums.[103]

There was widespread criticism among workers of profit-sharing premiums being awarded mainly to management.[104] The tendency was to award the largest profit-sharing premiums to management, as illustrated in Table 70. The workers' dissatisfaction reverberated in demands for imposing a ceiling on the individual profit-sharing premium.[105]

Table 70

EARNINGS AND PROFIT-SHARING
DIFFERENTIALS IN INDUSTRY, 1967

	Manual workers	Managerial personnel	Office staff
Total earnings	100	142.2	90.2
Profit-sharing	100	232.0	120.0

Source: Jaroslav Pokorny, PM, No. 5, 1968, p. 211.

Reportedly, distribution of these premiums was conducted so as to offset the lack of rewards for managerial activity implicit in the existing wage tariffs. For example, the point scheme evolved at the Technoplant Plant for profit-sharing premiums of various salary groups adopted qualifications and education as criteria, as illustrated in Table 71.

Table 71

CRITERIA AND POINTS FOR PROFIT-SHARING PREMIUM
DISTRIBUTION AT TECHNOPLAST, 1967

Salary groups			Points according to qualifications-education	
			Complete	Incomplete
D2	A4	T2	0.5	0.5
D3	A5	T3	0.6	0.6
D4	A6	T4	0.7	0.7
D5	A7	T5-6	0.9	0.7
D6	A9-10	T7-8	1.1	0.9
D7	A11-12	T9	1.3	1.1
D8	A13	T10	1.5	1.3
	A14	T11	1.7	1.5
	A15	T12	1.9	1.7
		T13	2.2	1.9
		T14	2.5	2.2
		T15	2.8	2.5
		T16	3.1	2.8

Source: Vladimir Bradik, RP, November 30, 1967.

Additional points were adopted to reward managerial activity per se: foremen, 1.0; group foremen, 1.5; workshop foremen, 2.0; subdepartment heads, 2.5; department heads, 3.0; subdivision heads, 3.5; division heads, 4.0; and plant managers, 4.5. The profit-sharing premiums distributed for 1966 amounted to 4,931 kcs. for the plant manager and to 369 kcs. for the lowest schedule No. 2 worker. On the average, the workers' premium was 600 kcs., that of managerial-technical personnel 1,582 kcs., and that of office staff 1,040 kcs.[106]

Out of the 700 enterprises investigated by the SSO, 552 (or about 80 per cent) paid out profit-sharing premiums in the fourth quarter of 1967. Together with advances made in the second

Table 72

DISTRIBUTION OF PROFIT-SHARING, 1967
(In 700 national enterprises)

Average profit-sharing per employee (kcs.)	Number of enterprises
No profit-sharing	148
1- 200	131
201- 400	240
401- 600	123
601- 800	37
801-1000	11
1001 and over	10

Source: Jaroslav Kux, HN, No. 20, 1968.

and third quarters (amounting to 144 million kcs.), profit-sharing premiums amounted to 929 million kcs. in these enterprises.[107]

Apparently, profit-sharing and above all advance payments were adversely affected by Government Decree No. 228 of July, 1967, which stipulated that advances of profit-sharing could be paid exclusively where "proper relationship is maintained between labor productivity and average wages." But this relationship became a mere formality: It was computed so that funds were always available for profit-sharing. The stipulated terms were modified by numerous exemptions, revisions, etc., with mounting requests for subsidies.

During the course of 1967 the principal industrial branches made advance payments of premiums totaling 812.3 million kcs. (about 25 per cent more than in 1966). The average share paid to industrial workers in 1967 amounted to 836 kcs. or to 3.2 per cent of the average annual wage. Similarly to 1966 the largest average share per worker was achieved in mining and the lowest in the consumer goods industry. The ranking of the shares essentially preserved the existing pattern of wage differentials between branches. The proportion of profit-sharing in total earnings was largest in the extraction of ores (4.8 per cent) and lowest in machine-building (2.5 per cent). In comparison to 1966, there was a relative drop in the average share in the chemical industry and a relative increase in the consumer goods industry.[108]

The trade unions were blamed for opposing wage differentiation. Admittedly, even Party and trade union officials have not drawn workers into the management process. Even the drafting and discussions on the collective agreements took place without the staff's participation.[109]

While announcing an extensive investigation of irregularities, the government requested that enterprises should verify and rectify on their own their records, and without punitive measures should remit to the state purse before September 15, 1967, the difference in profits due to errors in calculation. However, the enterprises were not especially eager to divest themselves of their earnings and altogether only some 270 million kcs. was conceded,[110] with the remittances from construction amounting to only 6 million kcs.[111] Apparently 6 to 7 billion remained with the enterprises, suggesting that they had already spent the difference.

Lubomir Strougal argued at the September, 1967, CC Plenum that in view of the prevailing situation "it is not only the right of the central bodies, but their solemn duty to intervene and redress the situation."[112] Some 400 auditors, including many experts from the central organs, were reported to have started investigations and it was expected that their findings would "obviously be different from those submitted by enterprises." In order to relieve the authorities from the burden of producing incriminating evidence, rather drastic methods of price control were approved. The auditors were to scrutinize 10 out of every 100 cases. On the basis of these findings an assessment was to be made on the whole lot. Those enterprises that would protest these findings would have to provide thorough evidence. Enterprises were to turn over the assessed amount increased by 50 per cent as a punitive measure. On the basis of these findings "the authorities and Party organizations would decide on the measures to be taken against managers responsible for the price machinations."[113] Vladimir Janza attested to the problems involved in extracting these sums from enterprises:

> I was present at some of the audits. The comrades concerned were ready to pay, having admitted their errors. But it was difficult to make them pay the additional 50 per cent.

Apart from the question of enforcing state discipline, the siphoning off of "unearned" profits was supposed to check inflation and clamp down on investments, even to the extent of stopping those that had already been begun. If the enterprises were not to abandon the started projects, they were to be left at the mercy of the bank.

Complaints were raised that in the past controls had been ineffective in view of the shortage and lack of qualifications of the auditors. Steps were taken "to improve the situation substantially." It was claimed that the audits and removal of "unearned" profits were just necessary stop-gap measures. The audit was to be concluded at the end of 1967, but the specter of further checks would remain: "We shall come back, perhaps in three years' time. Thus enterprises will always be in danger of the 50 per cent fine, if they are discovered to have speculated."[114]

Even though by mid-1966 the enterprises were generally aware of the changes that were to take place in 1967, judging by past experience, they expected that these changes would still be altered just before their implementation. The slackness of the 1967 plan was attributed to the generally prevailing feeling of insecurity.[115] It should be noted that when preparing the 1967 budget the authorities assumed a 7.5 per cent increase of GY over 1966, whereas the enterprises planned an increase of less than 4 per cent. The difference between the plans amounted to 16 billion kcs. and was attributed to higher estimates of output and cost reduction by the authorities. By mid-1967, results indicated that the plans of the authorities were very conservative.[116] The considerable overfulfillment of the GY plan was, however, not an indication that it was accomplished through substantially increased output and reduced costs, as expected, but the brunt of evidence seems to point to the price revision as a source of increased GY.

The 1967 budget amounted to over 142 billion kcs. The revenue from enterprises amounted to almost 90 billion kcs., including turnover tax in the amount of 39 billion kcs., contributions from GY (profit) of almost 20 billion kcs., levies on fixed assets of 12.5 billion kcs., contributions from reserves of 2 billion kcs., stabilization tax of 3.5 billion kcs., and additional contributions of over 3 billion kcs., which were redistributed as subsidies. The rest consisted mainly of transfers of depreciation allowances. The revenue from income and other direct taxes amounted to 16.7 billion kcs. Expenditures consisted of 68.1 billion for the national economy (markedly less than in 1966; the comparison is, however, tenuous in view of changes in methods of financing and prices), 58.8 billion for cultural and social welfare measures, 12.3 billion for defense and 3.2 billion kcs. for administration.[117] The budget's expenditures included subsidies to national committees amounting to almost 24 billion kcs. and subsidies to centrally managed enterprises amounting to almost 32 billion kcs., of which 9 billion was for investment subsidies. The subsidies for current activity included price subsidies of over 8 billion kcs., GY subsidies of over 2 billion kcs., agricultural price differentials of over 5 billion kcs., subsidies for deficit output assignments of 1.5 billion kcs., subsidies for technically advanced output of 1.3 billion kcs., and redistribution among EPU's of 2.5 billion kcs. Subsidies for current activity were expected to be cut by 10 billion kcs. for 1968-70 and subsidies for price distortions were expected to be eliminated.[118]

There was a tendency to understate GY in order not to fall prey to redistribution of funds among enterprises by EPU's:

> The enterprise that is supposed to contribute tends to show in its plans 'how much it cannot give' rather than to seek additional reserves and ways of improving the situation. A draft plan which reflects a higher capacity to fulfill the given obligations is disadvantageous because when the plan is finally approved the original additional contribution may be further raised.[119]

At the enterprise level it was felt that central agencies were again resorting to the old stated policies, "this enterprise has more funds; therefore we will increase its payments, say, its depreciation charges; and we will increase the planned subsidies of that enterprise." As a result, funds would, as a matter of course, be transferred from enterprises that were working effectively to those that lacked funds, with an enormous disincentive effect.[120]

Admittedly, enterprises were granted a wide scope in the choice of production programs, in the selection of sources of supply, and in the marketing of their products. But the progress was much too slow and there were too many obstacles for enterprises to exercise those rights, primarily due to the existing institutional relationships. Sik pointed to the proliferated network of state control and administrative agencies and organs as built-in institutional barriers to reform implementation.[121]

> The enterprise is under the supervision of the branch directorate, which, in turn, is supervised by the ministry. These two agencies have their own ideas about what is necessary and what the individual enterprises ought to produce. It is only natural for these agencies to endeavor to have these ideas translated into action at the enterprise level.[122]

Moreover, the extent of decision-making by superiors was greater and that by enterprises more restricted than envisaged in the written regulations. It was officially explained as necessitated by the general state of economic disequilibrium, by the gradual process of reform implementation, by the _à tâtonnement_ introduction of economic instruments, by the slackness of economic pressures, and by the largely nonoperative market in many branches.[123]

Because of the shoddy reputation of directive indexes, their place was taken by various guiding indicators and informative indexes, recommendations, and suggestions. The phenomenon of "latent imperative planning" was discovered. The results of investigations conducted in the second half of 1967 disclosed that the guiding indicators were circumvented in many ways to make them _de facto_ obligatory. One device was to make the premiums of the top management dependent on fulfillment of informative indexes. Other methods included the breaking down of informative indexes, with the same practical consequences as if they were obligatory, a large number of operational interventions, etc.[124] There remained a persistent belief in the infallibility of upper echelons, for they alone could protect "social interests." Therefore, the recommendations of superiors carried the weight of binding indexes.

> A director who objected would risk placing himself into the position of a man who could not grasp the wider implications of social interest and who defended and fought for narrow, egoistic, local, anti-social interests. Obviously, he would hesitate to do this, since his job depended on his superiors.[125]

The minister's role in appointing and discharging the director of the branch directorate who then proceeds similarly toward the director of the enterprise has forged a chain of dependence and has enabled the central directive interference to remain well-entrenched in the system, notwithstanding the reform's devolution of decision-making to the enterprise. It was officially acknowledged that many EPU's have continued their practice of interfering in operative management, even where such activity was totally at loggerheads with the spirit of the reform. At the same time, they were not fulfilling the functions of long-term planning entrusted to them.[126]

The branch directorate was a typical remnant of imperative planning. It imposed too great impediments on adjustments to change and stifled managerial actions by confining enterprises to limits which they were not allowed to overstep. Eugene Loebl maintained that the impact of the branch directorate was even more adverse in Slovakia than in the Czech lands. The branch directorates that controlled most of Slovak enterprises were situated usually in the Czech lands which made them even more physically and psychologically remote from the needs of their Slovak wards. The latter felt that they were underprivileged when it came to allocations of investment and other resources and to operational decisions.[127] In order to safeguard the principles of the reform, it was advocated that the hierarchical relationship between central organs, EPU's, and enterprises be removed and that the centrally created EPU's be replaced by voluntary associations of enterprises entitled to decide on either vertical or horizontal integration and on patterns of development.[128]

RESULTS AND PROSPECTS

The May, 1967, CC Plenum called attention to the grave economic situation, including the under-utilization of productive resources, redundant stocks, an excessive volume of unfinished construction, deplorable housing, acute difficulties in foreign trade, and failure to advance the restructuring of the economy and to improve qualitative performance. The plenum's resolution called for a "slight reduction" in the share of investment in national income for the remainder of 1967 in comparison to the draft of the Fourth FYP. The declared policy was to stabilize investments. Industrial investments were to be reduced by 1 billion kcs. in 1967; special priority was to be accorded to investments in chemistry, consumer goods industry, the building materials industry, and investments that would produce the highest and quickest returns to alleviate the strained balance of payments. Additional investment resources were to be channeled to housing, transportation, communications, and urban construction in Prague and other cities. The size of investments in productive branches should not materially exceed the volume envisaged in the Fourth FYP, while it was anticipated that their relative share should significantly decline by 1970.[129]

In 1967, investments were to increase at a slower pace than national income. The 1967 plan envisaged about 6 per cent rise in national income; at midyear the forecast was that it would record a moderate rate of growth of about 4 per cent, probably in view of the rather poor performance in the first half of 1967.[130] Total investment was planned to increase by about 4 per cent over 1966. Investment in machinery was planned to decrease by 1 per cent and investment in construction to rise by 9 per cent. It may be noted that total investment rose by about 14 per cent in 1964, by 8 per cent in 1965, and by 9 per cent in 1966. The corresponding increases in stocks of machinery were about 17 per cent, 12 per cent, and 12 per cent, and the respective increases in construction work were 8 per cent, 5 per cent, and 7 per cent.[131]

The completion of unfinished projects was to be accorded precedence over the commencement of new construction. Priority was also to be accorded to retooling and maintenance of the existing stock of capital. Compared to the Fourth FYP, the restructuring of the economy would be somewhat accelerated, particularly in the chemical, consumer goods, and building materials industries.[132]

During the first half of 1967 the growth of industrial output declined somewhat as compared with the same period of the preceding year. Thus, during the first six months of 1967, industrial output rose by 5.5 per cent. The greatest increases were recorded in the chemical industry, 8.4 per cent; machine-building, 10.1 per cent; building materials, 8.5 per cent; and glass and ceramics, 6.6 per cent. On the whole, a higher growth rate was reported in the processing industries (6.2 per cent) than in the basic branches (4.3 per cent). The total sales of principal industrial branches registered an increase of 4.4 per cent. The stocks of the principal branches of industry were 4.6 per cent (3.5 billion kcs.) higher at the end of June, 1967, than at the beginning of January, 1967, while turnover was reduced by 4.5 days. The largest increase (15 per cent) was recorded in stocks of finished products, with a decline of consumer goods inventories, implying an inordinate accumulation of producer goods and exportables.[133]

About 58 per cent of profits before taxes was siphoned off by the state budget and about 42 per cent was retained by the enterprises.

The increase of industrial employment was reported to have been considerably lower than during the same periods in the last few years. Of the total increase of employment, machine-building accounted for 58 per cent, chemistry for 16 per cent, and consumer goods for 15 per cent. Only 72 per cent of the increment in industrial output was attributed to higher productivity which fell short of the planned target. Average wages of industrial workers were reported to have risen by almost 5 per cent and average productivity by 4 per cent.

Retail prices were reported to have increased by 1.1 per cent. Only 26,387 apartments were constructed, whereas the 1967 plan envisaged the completion of 81,000 apartments during the entire year.

Trade turnover with capitalist countries declined.

Investments declined by 2.2 per cent due to the decrease in the deliveries of machinery and equipment and to the adverse performance in housing construction. The share of investments in machinery in the state sector decreased from 42 per cent during the same period last year to 39.4 per cent. There was a marked increased in unfinished construction, freezing resources and aggravating inflationary pressures. In the state economic organizations 56.5 per cent of the cost of investment was financed by the investors' funds, 19.5 per cent by investment credit, and 24 per cent by state grants. The investment funds accumulated on the enterprises' accounts exceeded all expectations and amounted to 3 billion kcs.[134]

On July 7, 1967, the government reviewed the draft of the 1968 plan and assessed the Fourth FYP in the light of the new economic conditions. The targets for 1968-70 had not yet been finalized. One could surmise that the FYP remained "unbalanced" and that the unreconciled divergence of views persisted on the tempo and pattern of development. Jan Vintera, an economist of the SPC, published an assessment of the economic situation that seemed to underline the plan discussion and provided some information about the path envisaged. Admittedly, despite an over-all improvement in growth performance in the last two years, the same negative trends that had plagued the economy for a number of years persisted. The familiar listing again included: adverse trade balance with hard currency areas; persisting shortages of some consumer goods and industrial products; overcommitment of resources; capital unproductively frozen in protracted and widely dispersed construction projects; increase in redundant stocks; persistently widespread increase in employment, slack improvement in productivity; and an inordinate increase in enterprise financial resources without concommitant increase in the flow of required production. Whereas those negative trends abated somewhat in the first half of 1966, they continued or were intensified during the second half of 1966 and in the first half of 1967.[135]

A very broad indication of the growth and shifting priorities in investment allocations may be observed from Table 73. The combined share of total industrial investment channeled to consumer, chemical, and building industries was to increase from 31 per cent in 1966 to 35 per cent in 1967. In the 1967 plan industrial investments were reduced by 1 billion kcs. as compared to the envisaged allocation in the FYP, with a simultaneous increase of nonindustrial investments. There was structural redressing of industrial investment, with a faster growth of investments in chemistry, consumer goods, building materials, and decrease of investments in fuels and power, as indicated in Table 73.

In the main economic report delivered to the September, 1967, CC Plenum by Lubomir Strougal--who later, as we shall see, became Chairman of the Economic Council under Alexander Dubcek--certain positive developments were noted, such as improvement in the material input-output ratio and in the product mix. The 1967 recorded increase in employment was the lowest in a number of years, but it resulted from closing down some coal mines and was largely influenced by the sizable increases in

Table 73

INDEX OF THE GROWTH OF INVESTMENTS, 1955-67

	Index 1955-60	Index 1960-65	Index 1965-67
Industrial investments	216	118	99
including investments in:			
Chemical industry	143	205	125
Consumer goods	382	144	124
Building materials	380	45	187
Power	140	132	118
Fuel	230	117	88
Metallurgy	213	93	80
Machine-building	297	108	93

Sources: SR 1966, p. 125; and Jan Vintera, PH, No. 7, 1967, p. 8.

employment in 1966. Among the noted shortcomings were sharp increases of redundant stocks and unfinished construction. The most serious problems, aggravating existing imbalances, were evident in foreign trade, in the supply of goods to the domestic market to meet the population's purchasing power, and in the growing tensions in capital formation. Strougal attested to the imbalance of the economy, to the state of vagueness and hesitation, and to the confusion accompanying the changes.

> The main disparity lies in the considerable acceleration of created gross income, which in turn inflates financial resources of enterprises. The resulting higher income of the population is not accompanied by a corresponding quantity of goods on the market.

Whereas industrial output for the first six months of 1967 was reported to have increased by 5.6 per cent, final sales only increased by 2 per cent (the 1967 plan envisaged a 5.4 per cent increase of sales), attesting to the fact that there were insufficient pressures on the producers to adapt production to the requirements of the buyers.

The stabilization tax and investment credits were not operating effectively enough and there was no marked interest in the introduction of new technology. Wages rose out of proportion to productivity. With a rising income changes in income distribution, and alterations in the pattern of demand, the composition of consumer goods produced did not correspond to the needs of higher income brackets and was insufficient to cover some quite ordinary needs. Production for export increased faster than sales abroad. Producers favored sales to the less-demanding markets, but these markets were not ready sources of effective imports. Exports to hard currency areas were most disappointing. For the first seven months of 1967, exports amounted to 98 per cent of the corresponding volume in 1966, while they were planned to increase by 11 per cent. The large drop in the exports of machinery was particularly alarming. Further procrastinations in construction were observed. Unfinished construction "reached the greatest volume ever registered." The grave situation in housing construction continued. The tapping of resources allocated to housing for other needs and acute shortages of building materials were contributing factors. Profitability of construction varied markedly from 20-25 per cent in industrial construction to only 8-10 per cent in housing. Enterprises were warned that "they must respect the intentions of central organs and put an end to any overcautious approach with respect to the 1968 plan, otherwise it will again be necessary to intervene by means of supplementary measures and to tighten economic conditions still more.[136]

With greater reliance on intensive growth factors, national income increased by some 8 per cent in 1967, compared with the preceding year. In the report of the SSO,[137] the recorded increase in national income was attributed by about four fifths to higher labor productivity and the remainder to increase of employment. Productivity growth was

Table 74

VOLUME, STRUCTURE, AND INDEX OF PRODUCTION, 1966-67

Branches	Volume in million kcs. 1966	Volume in million kcs. 1967	Index 1966= 100	Structure in 1967 (in %)
Total gross industrial output	245,891.8	263,341.3	107.1	100.0
of which:				
Fuels and fuel products	18,253.8	18,736.6	102.6	7.1
Generation of electricity and power	7,910.3	8,584.7	108.5	3.3
Ferrous metallurgy and ore extraction	27,408.7	28,272.1	103.1	10.7
Nonferrous metallurgy and ore extraction	6,112.3	6,713.2	109.8	2.5
Chemicals, coke, rubber, and asbestos	14,545.5	16,162.7	111.1	6.1
Machine-building and metalworking	66,486.6	73,973.5	111.3	28.1
Building materials	7,352.2	7,955.6	108.2	3.0
Woodworking	8,875.2	9,570.6	107.8	3.6
Cellulose and paper	3,400.3	3,655.8	107.5	1.4
Glass, china, and ceramics	3,354.7	3,615.6	107.8	1.4
Textiles	15,090.2	15,715.6	104.1	6.0
Ready-to-wear clothing	5,507.9	5,878.9	106.7	2.2
Leather, footwear, and furs	6,400.0	6,729.2	105.1	2.6
Printing industry	1,590.5	1,778.9	111.8	0.7
Foodstuffs	46,932.4	48,846.4	104.1	18.5
Other industrial branches	6,671.4	7,151.9	107.2	2.7

Source: Statni Banka Ceskoslovenska, Bulletin, 1968, p. 37.

reported to have been predominantly responsible for the increment of industrial output.[138] Gross industrial output grew by 7.1 per cent (the increase was larger in the second half of 1967 than in the first half, but slightly lower than in 1966) and the volume of construction recorded an increase of 9.3 per cent.

In Slovakia gross industrial output increased by 10.1 per cent in comparison with 1966. Slovakia's contribution to state-wide industrial output increased further, reaching 22.2 per cent. Output of electricty and fuels was up by 27.2 per cent, of machine-building by 12.2 per cent, of chemistry by 13.2 per cent, and of building materials by 12 per cent. Output in processing industries grew slower than that in basic branches. The export plan to capitalist countries was exceeded by 2.2 per cent. The reported increase in productivity was 5.4 per cent and average income of industrial manpower rose by 5.3 per cent.[139]

The over-all results were considerably influenced by the rise of gross agricultural output by 3.5 per cent over the relatively high 1966 level. The grain harvest was the largest since the war. The planned delivery of crops was exceeded by 20,800 tons of grain (1.2 per cent), by 6,000 tons of rape-seed (8.1 per cent), and by 475,100 tons of sugar beet (7.0 per cent). The higher yields per hectare were attributed to favorable climatic conditions, application of more fertilizers (3.6 per cent more than in 1966), better agricultural implements, and more palpable material incentives. But the inadequate quality and variety of fertilizers remained serious problems, while the quantity of fodder was still insufficient. Livestock increased by 5.8 per cent over 1966. In spite of the need for mechanization, the stock of unwanted farm machinery filling central warehouses grew by 870 million kcs. in 1967. The over-all rate of decline of manpower in agriculture was somewhat arrested.[140]

There were essentially two schools of thought on the successes scored by agriculture in the last two years. One claimed that good weather in 1966 and in 1967 helped, but was not decisive. The increasing mechanization of agriculture, greater autonomy of agricultural enterprises enabling them to adapt output to local and natural conditions, and the use of synthetic fodders were said to have contributed most to the change in performance.[141] The other school maintained that the good agricultural performance was primarily due to good climatic conditions. Comparative analysis apparently showed that agricultural output in the advanced capitalist countries grew at a much more rapid rate than in Czechoslovakia. Moreover, the increase of animal output was made possible by the import of fodder. The main reasons for inefficiencies were blunders in the collectivization of agriculture. Preconditions for large-scale production were created, but farming suffered from the absence of economic pressures on agricultural producers. The reform devolved greater decision-making powers to agricultural producers, but the economic pressures of the market were still lacking. Expansion of output should be propelled not only by investments, but primarily by application of modern techniques and attraction of experts to agriculture.[142]

Over-all employment grew at a slower pace than in the previous year. The pace of increase of industrial employment abated, and the annual increase of 28,000 employees was considerably lower than the average increase in the last few years and was particularly affected by the manpower reduction (about 10,000 employees) in mining. Employment increases above the average persisted in the chemical industry (3.6 per cent), in machine-building (3 per cent), and in industrial enterprises under the Ministry of Construction (2.3 per cent)--hence in industries which reported the highest increases in gross output. On the whole, the number of manual workers registered a slower rate of increase (0.7 per cent) than the over-all average, but the rapid increase of engineers and technicians continued (3.8 per cent). Industrial labor productivity was reported to have grown by 6 per cent; 85 per cent of the increase in gross industrial output was attributed to the rise in productivity. The improvements in productivity were effected in the second half of the year. On the average the claimed productivity growth of 5.5 per cent in centrally managed industries was above the growth of wages of 4.8 per cent. Average wages in metallurgy and in the food industry grew faster than the claimed productivity.[143] In 1967 average wages increased by 4.2 per cent. Since the over-all index of retail price increases did not exceed the envisaged 1.5 per cent, it was claimed that real wages grew by 2.7 per cent.[144]

The volume of construction increased by 9.3 per cent, with 69 per cent of the increase attributed to higher productivity which registered an annual average increase of 6.2 per cent. The shortened working week in construction and the higher earnings (the average monthly wage grew by 5.9 per cent--by 8 per cent in regional building enterprises to arrest the outflow of labor--and reached 1,873 kcs., whereas the average wage in industry was about 1,690 kcs. in 1967) contributed to the stabilization of manpower in the building trade.

Total investments amounted to 70.4 billion kcs. --an increase of 2.6 per cent over 1966--representing 28.5 per cent of national income. Construction work accounted for 44.5 billion kcs. (7.6 per cent higher than in 1966) and investments in machinery and equipment accounted for 25.9 billion kcs. (5.1 per cent lower than in 1966). As envisaged, the share of investments in industry fell and that of investments in transportation rose. Investments in construction recorded a substantial rise of 34.7 per cent over 1966, in transportation they went up by 13.6 per cent, in the food industry by 6.2 per cent, and in the consumer goods industry by only 1.3 per cent. Investments in heavy industry declined by 3.1 per cent and in metallurgy investments decreased by 11.5 per cent. In mining investments decreased by 10.9 per cent.[145]

The situation in the investment field was again deplored at the end of the year. Pressures to invest persisted in spite of the restrictive policies.

The number of unfinished projects was not reduced to the planned niveau.[146] Some enterprises still found it more advantageous to invest rather than to use more effectively their existing stock of capital. The volume of investments in Slovakia amounted to some 23 billion kcs.--about 3.4 per cent more than in 1966. Slovakia's share in total investments reached about 33 per cent.[147]

Throughout the economy stocks increased by about 11-12 billion kcs., or some 9 billion kcs. more than envisaged in the plan. In 1967 the increase of inventories absorbed some 65 per cent of the increase of national income.[148] Final sales of industrial output increased by 6.2 per cent, including a 0.8 per cent increase of machinery and equipment, a 5.1 per cent increase of wares for domestic trade, and a 9.8 per cent increase of exports. In the course of 1967, stocks in the main branches of industry increased by 6.4 per cent (4.8 billion kcs.), with particularly pronounced increases in inventories of finished goods.[149]

Foreign trade turnover was reported to have risen by 2 per cent. Trade turnover with the socialist countries increased by 3.6 per cent. Exports to socialist countries recorded an increase of 6.9 per cent, mainly due to larger sales of machinery and consumer goods. Contrariwise, imports from the socialist countries remained roughly at the 1966 niveau. There was a drop in import of machines and consumer goods, with a rise in imports of raw materials for heavy industry, for the chemical industry, and for food-processing. Turnover with the capitalist countries was reported to have fallen by 1 per cent. There was little change in the imports of machinery, while imports of consumer goods were reported to have increased. Trade with the capitalist countries was said to have suffered from the continuing tensions in the balance of payments, slow adaptability of Czechoslovak producers to the requirements of demanding markets, and fluctuations in economic activity on capitalist markets. It was still difficult to compete with the capitalist producers, particularly due to the inferior technical standards of exported goods, to the poor quality of service, to inflexibility in the delivery of spare parts, and to bureaucratic rigidities.[150]

Obviously, food consumption cannot be covered by domestic production. The increasing gap could not be filled by higher imports from the socialist countries, thus aggravating the balance-of-payments difficulties with hard currency areas. The socialist countries were striving to meet the demand of their own populations to "a greater extent than was the case in the past" and, admittedly, "the assortment and quality of the manufactured consumer goods in the socialist countries were often described as unsatisfactory and the goods were not wanted."[151]

In 1967 food consumption accounted for 47 per cent of the total retail turnover and food turnover was 4.2 per cent higher than in 1966. Consumption of meat and dairy products increased. There was a shortage of pork, mainly due to insufficiency of grain fodder. Although supply of beef increased, beef consumption did not, due mainly to the peculiarities of Czechoslovak cuisine and to higher retail prices.[152]

In 1967 supplies of consumer goods for the domestic market were higher by 1.1 billion kcs. than in 1966.[153] Although total retail turnover was reported to have increased, the composition of the product mix was particularly deplored. There were many shortages and output of "wrong" industrial products persisted.[154] Only a little more than one third of consumer goods tested qualified for the first-class category.[155] Products that could not be exported to convertible currency areas or could not be disposed of on the domestic market were sent to "fraternal" socialist countries.[156]

There were persistent shortages of passenger automobiles. For example, in July, 1967, the waiting list for automobiles reached over 175,000 persons, some of whom had been waiting for several years. A prospective buyer was forced to deposit in a special account 20,000 kcs., undoubtedly to restrict effective demand.[157] Shortages were reported for various items of furniture, building materials and plumbing supplies, men's suits and shirts of synthetic fabrics, television sets, sporting equipment, fashion goods, novelties, glassware, bicycles, etc. Among food products there were special shortages of poultry, fresh-water fish, sausages, ham, certain kinds of cheese, and local shortages of beer, nonalcoholic beverages, and vegetables.[158]

Higher prices were charged for newly introduced consumer goods or those reclassified as such. "We cannot deny that prices are going up." Whereas it had been officially reported that in 1967 the cost of living index rose by 1.5 per cent, another estimate indicated the over-all increase to have been over 2 per cent. This includes such manipulations of assortments as shifts to more expensive goods, while the less expensive ones were disappearing; price increases "disproportionate" to the improvements in quality; "price increases based on the idea that the commodities are novelties when actually there is nothing new about them;" etc.[159]

A total of 78,294 new apartments were built in 1967; i.e., 96.9 per cent of the planned number. Of the new flats, 14,253 were built by the state-sponsored construction schemes, 44,095 were cooperative houses, 19,835 were built by private individuals, and 111 were built by enterprises.[160]

In 1967 the consumption fund grew at a slower rate than the accumulation fund. The consumption fund accounted for 76.4 per cent of national income and its share declined by 3.9 per cent in comparison with 1966.[161] Preliminary estimates showed personal consumption to have risen by about 4 per cent. The rise in nominal incomes by 7.3 per cent over 1966, and particularly the growth of income from agricultural activities (incomes of cooperative farmers rose by 8.8 per cent), were major factors in the claimed rise in living standards. Social consumption outlays rose by 8-9 per cent, partly as a result of increase in salaries in education and health services. The pace of increase of average wages in the nonfarm socialist sector was considerably faster than in the previous years. Average monthly wages increased by 83 kcs. over the 1966 level, to 1,586 kcs. Savings deposits increased by 5,620 million kcs. and the total amount of deposits in the savings banks reached 45,183 million kcs. The increase in the wage bill was attributed to the rise in average wages and only by 20 per cent to the increase in employment.

The over-all profitability (profit to costs) reached 12.3 per cent in 1967, i.e., 2.6 points more than in 1966. As observed throught the year, there was a considerable disparity in the profitability rates of different industrial branches, enterprises, and products. It was claimed that the interest of enterprises in the maximization of GY was apparent, inter alia, in the reduction of material inputs.[162]

Actual GY exceeded the planned figure by 6.4 billion kcs. Profit (GY less wages) was 5.4 billion kcs. higher than planned; 22 per cent of the increase was attributed to the overfulfillment of the output plan; 70 per cent to reduction of material inputs; and only 8 per cent to payroll savings. Out of the additional profit, the transfers to the state budget amounted to 2.7 billion; interest payments, insurance, fines, etc., absorbed 0.7 billion; and the remainder was retained by enterprises or was contributed to EPU's. The state budget receipts from enterprises were about 2 billion kcs. more than envisaged. The workers' fund was also 2 billion kcs. higher than planned. The largest share of additional financial resources was directed to the enterprises' reserve fund.[163]

Preliminary data for heavy industry indicated that GY and profit of metallurgy and machine-building enterprises were expected to exceed the 1967 plan. Proceeds of the state budget from heavy industry were to exceed 800 million kcs.--the amount planned for 1967. The exports of heavy industry products to the capitalist countries grew by over 7 per cent, and to convertible currency areas they grew by 25.8 per cent. The active balance of payments in heavy industry transactions with the capitalist countries grew by 1,300 million kcs. Deliveries of consumer durables for the domestic market increased by 15 per cent.[164]

During the preparation of the 1968 plan some serious divergencies were revealed between the government's targets and those envisaged by the lower level of management. The draft plans submitted by branch directorates to ministries approximately coincided with the central plan on production, on structural reconstruction, on profit and GY formation, and on slackened growth of wages. However, these plans departed seriously from the central estimates of inputs, of the use of financial resources, and of investments, and stipulated a faster growth of employment. On the whole, branch plans foresaw a rate of growth lower than that envisaged by the government. The branch directorates' plans fell short of the centrally established target for foreign trade, indicating no relief in sight to strains in the balance of payments. Draft plans also evinced a proclivity to excessive stockpiling and alarming cuts in deliveries of machines and equipment, threatening to impair the investment plan. The draft plans of branch directorates called for a 2 per cent increase in employment, whereas the central plan envisaged only a 0.7 per cent growth in employment.[165]

The December 19-20, 1967, CC Plenary session agreed on the plan for 1968 and revised the remaining portion of the current FYP. According to the national economic plan for 1968, national income was slated to grow by about 6-7 per cent, the volume of investment by 2 per cent, the number of employees in the socialist sector (excluding agricultural co-operatives) by 90,000-100,000, average wages by 5 per cent (or by an average of 75 kcs. per month), the population's total income by 10-11 billion kcs., and retail prices by 1.5 per cent. About 7 billion kcs.' worth of consumer goods over the original plan should be available.

The resolution called for larger imports from socialist countries and larger exports to capitalist countries in order to ease the strain on the balance of payments. The Minister of Foreign Trade stressed that foreign trade would continue to be directed mainly toward socialist countries, primarily CMEA members, with the U.S.S.R. as a major trading partner. In comparison to the volume of trade with the socialist countries in 1967, the trade turnover in 1968 was envisaged to increase by 8-10 per cent. Only such trade orientation would apparently ensure the required "stability" in the exchange of goods, the required "protection from fluctuations on capitalist markets and from the undesirable influence of the capitalist economy."[166]

Prices of imported raw materials were supposed to be boosted by 18 to 20 per cent as another measure to alleviate the disequilibrium in the balance of payments. Prices of coal used to generate power were supposed to be reduced by 9 per cent. On the whole, the wholesale price level was not to grow by more than 2 per cent. It was declared that while price subsidies were to be cut and prices were to be gradually adapted to those on the world market, such price adjustments would be made as to promote the branches of decisive importance for satisfying the domestic market and for increasing effective exports.[167]

The 1968 state budget envisaged revenues and expenditures of 144.8 billion kcs., i.e., according to the Minister of Finance, 5.8 per cent more than in 1967.[168] Bohumil Sucharda's frame of reference was probably the preliminary results for 1967, rather than the 1967 budget estimates which amounted to 142.5 billion kcs.[169] In 1968, 44.2 per cent of total expenditures was appropriated for economic development (as against 48 per cent in the 1967 budget and 58.1 per cent in 1966; the data were not quite comparable due to changes in financing methods and in prices). It was anticipated that enterprises would finance their expansion programs to a larger extent than heretofore from their own resources or from bank credits. For the first time the expenditures on combined cultural and social measures (44.6 per cent of total budget expenditures, whereas these expenditures in the 1967 and 1966 budgets had been 41.2 and 37.9 per cent, respectively) exceeded those for the development of the economy. Expenditures for cultural and social measures were to be 9.1 per cent higher than in 1967, including a rise of expenditures on culture by 10.6 per cent, on public health by 8.2 per cent, and also on education by 8.2 per cent. Contributions to social security and health insurance schemes were to increase by 7.6 per cent over 1967.[170]

Out of total outlays 8.9 per cent was appropriated for defense (as against 8.6 per cent in the 1967 budget and 7.1 per cent in the 1966 budget), reported to be 6.8 per cent higher than in 1967. State administration was to account for 2.3 per cent of planned expenditures as against the shares of 2.2 and 1.9 per cent in the 1967 and 1966 budgets, respectively. The budget for 1968 anticipated state expenditures on research and development to be 7.6 per cent higher than in 1967. It was envisaged that agriculture would receive in 1968 about 12 billion kcs. from the treasury. Agricultural output was to assist in reducing the 7 billion kcs. deficit in the balance of payments.

In 1968, state support of retail prices of foodstuffs was estimated to require subsidies of about 1.8 billion kcs.[171] Noninvestment subsidies (those to support current activity) to economic organizations were estimated at 20.3 billion kcs., investment subsidies at 10.16 billion kcs., non-investment subsidies to national committees at about 16.5 billion kcs., and subsidies for investment construction were anticipated to amount to 13.1 billion kcs.[172]

Transfers of GY of enterprises to the treasury were expected to increase by 7.4 per cent over 1967, turnover tax revenue was to go up by 6.6 per cent, and revenue from income and other direct taxes was to rise by 6.3 per cent. It may be noted that the total of budget revenues accruing from the transfers of GY was expected to amount to over 33 per cent (31 per cent in 1967). In 1968 the state revenue from turnover taxes was to amount to about 28 per cent of total receipts (27 per cent in 1967). Little change was anticipated in the share (over 12 per cent) of income and other direct taxes in the budgetary estimates.

Of the budgetary revenue, 67 per cent was to be derived from enterprises. Similarly, as in 1967, the 1968 state budget could not have been based on the submitted plans of branch directorates and national committees, as it would then, by all accounts, have resulted in high budgetary deficits. In drafting the budget the MF, together with other state bodies, envisaged the growth of the GY in 1968 to be 7.1 per cent. On this assumption, the total enterprise funds, net of payments into the treasury were slated to grow by 9.3 per cent, investment to increase by 7.1 per cent, and inventories to rise by 3.1 per cent. As mentioned, it was envisaged that in 1968, prices of imported raw materials would be raised. But instead of automatically projecting the higher prices of imports into the prices of import-using products, the enterprises would be expected to cover about 80 per cent of the increase from their own funds--an overt attempt to reduce "excessive" liquidity.[173]

It is noteworthy that at the September, 1967, Plenum, Dubcek--then still First Secretary of the Communist Party of Slovakia--called for intensification of the development of Slovakia; creation of a central fund for ensuring restructuring of the economy and for regional development. Investments were not distributed so as to utilize fully Slovak natural resources. The existence of an untapped labor reservoir in Slovakia would be no cause for alarm if capital formation were equitably distributed. The shifting of capital to underdeveloped areas should also result in saving huge social expenditures required for housing, health, education, and cultural facilities for relocated labor. Dubcek complained that whereas plan directives envisaged the share of Slovakia in total state investments to be 28 per cent, the results of the first six months of 1967 indicated that only 21.9 per cent of state-wide investment was channeled to Slovakia.[174]

In 1968 the national income of Slovakia was planned to increase by 9.1 per cent and industrial production to grow by 9.6 per cent (with a state-wide average of 5.5 per cent). In a number of branches of Slovak industry the 1968 growth rate was envisaged to be still higher: e.g., in metallurgy (19.5 per cent), in chemistry (13.19 per cent). The GY in Slovakia was anticipated to rise by 13.3 per cent as compared to 1967. Employment was to increase by 40,000 workers, or 2.9 per cent. According to Sucharda's budget speech, investment in Slovakia in 1968 was expected to amount to 22.6 billion, or to about one third of total investment. Noninvestment expenditures of budgetary organizations in Slovakia were expected to increase by 10.1 per cent. Expenditures would be concentrated on education, public health, social, and welfare measures.

Sucharda anticipated that the national committees' budget for the country as a whole would amount to a total of 47.4 billion kcs., i.e., a 10.7 per cent increase over 1967. Of this amount, 13.1 billion kcs. would be expanded on investments which were to increase by 18.4 per cent. The bulk of national committees' investments would be directed to housing, education, health, welfare, and transportation. The major share of total expenditures (over 26.5 billion kcs., or 2 billion more than in 1967) would be noninvestment outlays of budgetary organizations, of which 8.7 billion kcs. would be spent on education, 7.9 billion kcs. on public health, 3.5 billion kcs. on transportation, and over 4.1 billion kcs. was appropriated for (non-investment) grants to enterprises operated by the national committees.[175]

In 1968, the over-all volume of capital construction was to be 5.4 per cent higher than in 1967, while the rise of investments in the nonproductive sphere was to be more rapid (12 per cent). After many years of channeling investment to heavy industry, it was decided to ameliorate the situation, but, admittedly, not to rectify it. Significantly, in 1968 the chief beneficiaries of investment grants were to be transport and communications, forestry, water resources, agriculture, tourist trade, and services in general. Efforts were made to curtail investments. Some investment projects (totaling 2.7 billion kcs.) were conditionally accepted only if budgetary revenue would be exceeded or if budgetary expenditures would be curtailed in the course of 1968. Investment priority would be accorded to housing construction. Investments in transportation and for welfare and social measures would also be higher in 1968.[176]

The state budget bill for 1968 included an amendment to the tax shares of GY from domestic trade organizations, an amendment to the basis and rate of the income tax of cooperatives, and an amendment to provisions on the motor vehicles tax to be paid into the Road Fund. The rate of tax contribution from GY of centrally managed organizations of domestic trade (Cedok enterprise excluded) was reduced from 30 to 18 per cent. In developed industrial areas, to be determined by the government, the government was empowered to increase the surtax added to the stabilization tax prescribed by regional national committees to a maximum of 2 per cent of total payroll disbursed. Some branches could be exempt from the surtax. The government could reduce the rates payable on fixed assets engaged in the production and distribution of electricity. It could also prescribe temporary reduction of various taxes on enterprises slated for liquidation.[177]

In what proved to be his last New Year's day message, Antonin Novotny once again reiterated his commitment to economic reform, while borrowing a whole sheaf of leaves from his opponents' book. He attempted to swim with the tide and tried to conciliate the Slovaks. In 1968, "we shall begin with the gradual removal of disproportions between wholesale and retail prices." In eliminating these deformations, adjustments of retail prices cannot be avoided. Some prices may have to be increased to terminate state subsidies and some retail prices would have to be cut. But reduction of the standard of living was not envisaged, particularly of low-income groups and large families. While improving the variety and quality of consumer goods, only a minimal increase in the level of retail prices was envisaged to be more than counterbalanced by an increase in average wages. Expenditures from social welfare funds were also to be augmented.

A further industrial development was anticipated, with the main stress placed on modernization and reconstruction. The over-all economic development "must not override priority accorded to the development of Slovakia" which had not yet attained the economic level of Czech lands. Slovakia was not fully using its manpower and other resources, particularly since the rate of growth of the population in Slovakia was faster than that in the Czech lands. If the opportunities offered by Slovakia should be exploited, its economic development must be accelerated. These guarantees to Slovakia were not empty promises, as some said, but specific measures already formulated.

In view of the international tensions "we must go on expanding a considerable share of our national income on our armed forces." Novotny did not miss the mark when he said: "We are entering a year" in which much work and "many important political events await us. It will be a year whose results will undoubtedly influence the entire future course of the country."[178]

Frantisek Vlasak--who, as we shall see, was later to become the Minister of Economic Planning--contended that "during the current FYP the rate of investment should not be increased, but stabilized as much as possible." With the gathering of greater momentum by inflationary forces, Vlasak maintained that the 1968 plan must not permit an increase in investment, but must substantially reduce new investment undertakings. A revision of investments "should be only in the downward direction." All decisions on new capital formation were taken under strong, often political, pressures.[179]

The Fourth FYP was "adapted" to reflect the latest economic performance and to allow for shifts in policy. Growth rates of those branches that have a direct bearing on the increase of personal consumption were boosted. As compared to the recorded performance during the last quinquennium (1960-65) when the chemical industry grew by 54 per cent, it was envisaged to increase it by 63 per cent during 1966-70 (including manifold increases of output of synthetic fibers and plastics to meet the requirements of the textile and footwear industries). The building materials industry's growth rate was expected to be 44 per cent compared to 25 per cent in 1960-65. Consumer goods industry, which in the 1960-65 period grew by 20 per cent, was to register an increment of over 30 per cent.[180] These revised figures for the Fourth FYP indicate a growing concern with these industries when compared to the expected growth rates by 1970 in the earlier version of the FYP reported in Chapter 5.

Confident in the economy's continued upswing, the leaders again reverted to the well-known stepping up of growth rates. For the remaining years 1968-70, the rate of growth of national income was raised from 22-24 per cent to 31-32 per cent.[181] With an annual retail price increase of 1.5 per cent, and an average wage rise of 3.8 per cent, average real wages were supposed to grow by 2.3 per cent annually.[182] It is worth noting that the annual industrial average wage was to rise by only 2.7 to 2.9 per cent, indicating a faster growth of wages in the nonindustrial sectors. Priority was to be accorded to individual rewards for effective performance rather than to the use of collective funds. Fulfillment of housing construction targets was a paramount task; the intent was to increase housing construction from the annual 80,000 apartments originally stipulated to 100,000.[183]

As in the earlier version of the Fourth FYP, the structural changes were primarily to center on decreasing the consumption of solid fuels and power, while increasing that of liquid and gaseous fuels. The chemical industry was to be expanded. Machine-building would remain one of the mainstays of industry, with a reshuffle of its assortment in favor of technically advanced products. The resolution called for a deceleration of investments in heavy industry and a pumping of its profits into investment in nonproductive sectors. Faster expansion of the consumer sector and more investments for chemistry, construction and consumer industries were promised.

In 1968 preparations would be made to reduce the work week to five days--42.5 hours in 1969. Paid maternity leave would be extended from 22 to 26 weeks and benefits would be raised. Family allowances would be increased. The lowest pensions were to be raised by a total of 600 million kcs. in 1968, and the pension system was to be revamped in 1969 at an additional cost of 1.2 billion kcs. The underfulfillment of the targets for housing in 1966-67 was to be made good during the 1968-70 period to meet the target of 460,000 new flats in the quinquennium. More, and a greater variety of, consumer goods should become available and tourism to both socialist and capitalist countries should grow.

The main stress was on shedding the shackles of bureaucracy, on overcoming the "obsolete conservative" attitudes, and on allowing greater freedom of action to the "progressive, creative, and enterprising people." The Slovaks also scored a victory by forcing the issue of larger investment subsidies for the underdeveloped areas. State subsidies for up to 40 per cent of investment costs in certain areas were approved.[184]

In conformity with the announced policy of improving the lot of the consumer, investments in domestic trade in 1968-70 were to be higher by 1,455 million kcs. compared to the sum originally planned. This increase should make it possible to build 21 modern department stores, three large shops, five shopping centers, three hotels, and to complete the network of stores in new residential areas. Average wages of store personnel were to rise by 4 per cent per annum and were to reach by 1970, 87.2 per cent of the average wages in industry--a measure designed to attract or retain higher caliber personnel and thus to improve the very poor service in retail trade.[185]

It was expected that the market supply (mainly of consumer goods) envisaged in the Fourth FYP would have to be augmented by about 7-9 billion kcs. to absorb the planned wage increases. Particular stress was to be placed on producing the goods in short supply. In 1970 some 90,000 automobiles were to be available (80 per cent more than in 1966), 1.2 million tons of cement (50 per cent more than in 1966), 1,500 million bricks (a five-fold increase over 1966), 2.9 billion kcs.' worth of furniture (about 12 per cent more than in 1966). Imports of consumer goods were to increase substantially.[186]

According to the revised targets for the 1968-70 balance of the Fourth FYP, the planned rate of growth of national income in Slovakia was slated to grow by 50-52 per cent as against the originally envisaged 42.5 per cent for the entire FYP. Industrial output in Slovakia was scheduled to increase in the course of the FYP by 67 per cent as against the originally planned 58 per cent (by 36.4 per cent in 1968-70 as against 32 per cent originally planned). In the period 1968-70, investments were to exceed the original plan by more than 7 billion kcs. and the volume of construction was to increase by 3.5 billion kcs. In comparison to the original version of the plan, employment in Slovakia was to increase by 206,000 people (as against 136,000 originally planned). The nominal wages were to grow faster (3.8 per cent) than originally envisaged (2.2 per cent). Slovakia's share in the state-wide increase of employment was envisaged to rise from 42 to 48 per cent in 1968-70.[187] The Slovak population's nominal income (including that from increases in employment) was anticipated to increase by 6.4 per cent in 1968 and to reach by 1970 an increase of 18 per cent over 1967, as compared to 17.3 per cent originally planned.[188]

Table 75

ORIGINAL AND REVISED PLAN TARGETS OF GROWTH FOR SLOVAKIA, 1968-70
(Annual growth rates in percentages)

	Gross industrial output	Volume of construction	Gross agricultural output
1968 original plan	8.8	5.0	1.2
revised plan	9.6	3.0	3.7
1969 original plan	10.7	4.6	2.6
revised plan	11.8	4.8	2.6
1970 original plan	10.2	4.4	3.3
revised plan	11.3	4.6	3.4
1968-70 original plan	32.8	14.7	7.2
revised plan	36.4	13.0	10.1

Source: V. Komarek, RP, February 8, 1968.

In planning the economic development of Slovakia the hitherto untapped endowment of Slovakia in human and natural resources, the existing capacities, the proximity to the U.S.S.R. and to the other East European countries were to be taken into account and best use made of them. It was envisaged that in Slovakia a relatively large increase of manpower would take place which would supply over three quarters of the national manpower increment within the next ten years.[189]

Although sobriety must mark over-all investment policy, it was claimed in official quarters that, in view of the special importance of Slovakia's contribution to the country's economy, the proportion of investments channeled to Slovakia would continue to increase.[190]

Cernik declared that over the next two to three

years the cardinal task would be elimination of structural disproportions between production, consumption, investment, domestic market, and foreign trade. In comparison with the ill-fated Third FYP, the tempo of growth of national income should be twice as great.[191] A very high planned tempo of economic growth embodies the danger of an exaggerated pace, tensions, and strains; of excessive investments and stockpiles; of increase of unfinished investments; and of a rising foreign trade barrier. Thus, the reversion to administrative methods for coping expediently with the imbalances cannot be ruled out.

But, returning to the evaluation of performance, so far the record indicated that some changes in the structure of the economy were noticeable only in two areas: 1) Attempts were made to change the structure of the fuel and power industry. Imported oil and gas were competing with solid fuels. As a result of this, more rigid criteria were applied to the procurement and use of solid fuels, bringing about a limitation of extraction and use of ineffective fuels. The changes in the composition of the fuel-power balance resulted, as we indicated, in the release of manpower which was either not promptly reabsorbed or was not given the same earning opportunity, with the ensuing political pressures and perplexing problems.[192] Apparently, with all the talk about closing ineffective plants, only 41 ineffective plants in the mining sector were shut down.[193] The hard coal mines in the Plzen region of West Bohemia were slated for gradual closing down to be completed by 1974. The first of the pits were to be closed in March, 1968. Most of the miners would then be transferred to other pits, without any financial sacrifice.[194] 2) In 1967 there was a largely unplanned, moderate predominance of the rate of growth of output in the processing branches over that of the basic production branches and of heavy industry. One explanation advanced was that, despite the preponderance of the sellers' market, some producers were beginning to find difficulties in selling their output, as we have previously outlined. The slower rate of growth of the basic branches was probably also due to shortages of imported raw materials. The increase of output in food-processing was explained as due largely to the increase in agricultural output which helped in the last two years to alleviate the balance-of-payments strains by allowing greater exports of consumer goods.[195]

Cernik evaluated economic advancement in the 1966-67 period "as predominantly successful compared with that of the preceding years." In contradistinction to previous years, it was claimed that intensive factors of growth gained momentum and in 1967 accounted for the "overwhelming share of the total increase in national income." Notwithstanding the important steps forward, structural dislocations persisted; tensions between the availability of and the requirements for resources continued in the principal branches of the economy; and the main causes of imbalances were not eliminated or significantly reduced.[196] The exorbitant investments in inventories and unfinished construction were among the main sources of imbalances. The increase in stocks of inventories and in unfinished construction absorbed the share of the increment of national income which might have been allocated to the increase of consumption and/or to bringing new capacities into operation. A reduction of inventories and unfinished construction might have created supplementary sources of higher consumption and/or an expansion of productive capacity.[197]

Reporting on the "true state of the economy," Zdenek Vergner confirmed that the increase in national income was largely translated into incomplete investment projects and growing inventories. The substantial share of ineffective production in the aggregate industrial output was among the principal causes for the state of imbalance in the economy. Effective enterprises were subsidizing the ineffective ones. Consequently, the effect of the increment of national income on consumption and on effective capital formation was thus smaller than the reported rate of increase. Two good successive harvests were instrumental in preventing further deterioration. The foreign trade barrier would probably have been much higher than it was without the relatively successful agricultural performance. Short-term foreign debts in convertible currencies reportedly slightly diminished for the first time in 1967, but it was yet difficult to determine whether a new trend was being established.[198]

Contrary to official claims, many economists reported that during 1966-67 growth was still being achieved largely by extensive factors.[199] Growth was still being propelled by the methods and forces of the traditional system which were supposed to have been of a transitional and temporary nature: "One cannot expect that in the years to come the sharp increase in the volume of new production capacities which became operative will continue, particularly in the basic branches of industry."[200] Although the changing planning system was probably a factor in the stepped-up growth rates, economic development continued to be hampered by persisting growth-impeding barriers and escape channels. The 1966-67 economic recovery must be cautiously assessed. Should the new system fail to operate fully and consistently in the near future, a new decline in growth rates would in all probability follow. Without consistent reform measures and their unswerving implementation, reforms would become ever more mandatory in a few years' time. And, as a counterpart to the theory of quasi-cyclical development under socialism, one could envisage a theory of quasi-cyclical economic reforms.

A prudent choice of a growth rate must be considered to be a fundamental precondition for an effective application of the new system. The Goldmann argument was eloquently echoed by Vlasak at the September Plenum. He pointed to the evidence that after the attainment of "some maximum" rate in 1967, "we are at present finding ourselves in a situation where certain signs of a recession are again beginning to appear, as they always appeared under similar conditions in the past."[201] One of the key measures to reduce tensions must be a reduction of investments:

> We have gotten into a situation where we have the largest share of gross investment in national income in the whole postwar period. This gives rise to the justified concern lest this chief cause of the gap between resources and requirements should become an obstacle barring the required, relatively rapid, application of the price mechanism.[202]

One of the chief aims of the reform was to enhance dramatically the economic efficiency of the system as a powerful source of additional growth by restoring the market mechanism. This, as we know, has not yet been accomplished.[203] Notwithstanding some attempts to inject flexibility and to make the choice coefficients more meaningful, the preponderant share of prices still remained centrally fixed, rigid, and arbitrary. There was still a largely unbridged separation of the producer from the buyer of his products. The differentiated turnover tax was still among the factors which significantly contributed to the violation of consumer sovereignty.[204] There was still no economic mechanism to ensure that alterations in consumers' demand would invariably elicit from producers alterations of output in the "right" quantity and composition.[205]

Improvements in productivity were still disappointing. There seemed to have been some reduction in visible waste, particularly a relative decrease of material inputs, but the available evidence does not unequivocally point to pronounced improvements in the efficiency of the system. Neither, it seems, was the pace of technical progress sufficiently rapid to counteract or to substantially reduce the impact of economic inefficiency through significant shifts in parameters of the production function.

> Our economy can be compared to a machine with a large capacity, but technically obsolete, which consumes inordinate quantities of materials, which requires excessive

> operating manpower, but which does not function under conditions of effective management.[206]

By and large, with some notable exceptions, technical advancement was unsatisfactory; the gap between advanced technology and Czechoslovak standards was growing wider. The tenor of complaints about quality, technical standards, variety, service, etc., of goods produced for domestic and foreign markets was as strong as ever, as we have seen. Some "fraternal" socialist countries still provided ready markets for substandard goods and protected the producers from the pressures to improve production.

There is more than a grain of truth in Leobl's argument that the kind of evaluation that stresses positive features like growth of industrial output, reduction of material inputs, etc., serves little purpose. Even with a moderately impressive or encouraging statistical record, the paramount question is whether the results were achieved effectively,[207] or whether spurious results were hidden behind the reported magnitudes. Efficiency criteria are difficult to apply since, inter alia, neither the value frame (measurement requires efficiency prices) nor all required information is available. The only available information on the growth of inventories is in terms of prices assigned to stocks, but the real unknowns are whether such inventories can at all be disposed of and, if so, at what loss in terms of their opportunity costs. Similarly, the growing volume of construction in progress is reported almost exclusively in terms of cost considerations alone, but "we do not know what values they represent."[208] It may be argued that the production cost of a given product cannot be said to be price determining since its cost elements are determined by prices. But prices cannot be set rationally unless productive agents were beforehand allocated efficiently to their various uses.[209]

GY was increasing, but, aside from the effects of price revision, the magnitude, it should be remembered, is calculated on the basis of output sold plus inventories (including work in process). The latter account for some 20 per cent, so it is not certain whether the measured performance is anything to rejoice about.

Whereas the record of the index of growth of gross industrial output was respectable, final deliveries were on a very "unsatisfactory level." Final sales (including the deliveries of machinery and equipment for export and for domestic capital formation) were increased at the cost of a rise in manpower and of the preceding years' investment expenditures which were higher than the benefits accrued. All this shows, Loebl argued, that the increment of final sales "was actually very small. Moreover, a confrontation with foreign trade offers a convincing picture of the ineffectiveness of our economy." The more rapid growth of gross output--a questionable sign of improved performance--requires an even more rapid growth of imports. To pay for these imports, there is need for more exports at virtually any price, regardless of the cost accruing to the economy. Hence, great tensions in the adverse balance of payments persist.[210]

A permanent rectification of economic imbalances and the alleviation of suppressed inflation can hardly be accomplished by reverting to the imperative planning system.[211] Drahomir Kolder argued that in the "present stage" a combination of directive measures and economic levers was required to improve the structure of the economy and to enforce the national economic plan.[212] The moot questions were: What was the "optimum" combination of these factors? When and under what conditions would the planner revert to administrative methods to correct the situation, when disappointments with the more slowly operating economic levers under conditions of a taut plan were likely to occur? The allegedly new role of the plan is subjected to a conclusive trial whenever and wherever "unplanned" development occurs. So far, evidence seems to bear out that planners still considered it necessary to intervene and to take corrective measures (either by direct intervention or by economic devices) to ensure the fulfillment of the centrally conceived plan. Deviations from the plan were still considered as untolerable breakages of planned discipline and as violations of the supremacy and of the wisdom of the plan, rather than as signals that the plan needed correction; that the spontaneous and uncharted actions of enterprises might have been well-founded and legitimate; and that they are prerequisites of an integrated planning process and of plan verification. The planning system remains virtually unchanged as long as the central planner retains the ultimate discretionary power to determine what is a tolerable or an undesirable deviation from the plan and what correctives are to be used; and as long as the central planner passes the ultimate judgment on what is an erroneous and what is a correct signal and passes the final verdict to outlaw "harmful" spontaneity.

The center did not transfer its powers to intervene whenever and wherever it chose to do so. Neither can much confidence be had in the significant progress to learn and to understand the delicate tools of fiscal and monetary policy and the ability to tune the economy by market-type instruments. This is not to say that such lessons were learned fully in the West; but rather that while much is to be learned by doing, it is doubtful that after initial discouragement, an opportunity to do so would be looked upon with much favor.

Cernik emphasized that restrictive price control would prove to be ineffective unless coupled with consistent anti-inflationary policies. The pressing problems were 1) to adopt measures against excessive growth of liquidity in enterprises to arrest the conversion of funds into capital formation and accumulation of stocks and 2) to forestall an excessive rise of imports and of foreign credits to finance current domestic consumption. There was also a need for effective income and taxation policies designed to avert wage inflation, to cope with the acute problems resulting from the attempts to reconcile rising incomes with price stability. Furthermore, a consistent policy required a curtailment of budgetary expenditures and a limitation and control of investment and of operational credits.[213] But credit restrictions alone could not suffice to combat, for example, excessive accumulation of inventories and unfinished construction. Such a restrictive policy is doomed to failure unless coupled with other measures, including effective stabilization and counter-cyclical policies. Goldmann and Kouba touched the crux of the matter when they stated that what was required as a precondition was to curtail regulated--as contrasted with spontaneous--slowing down of the growth rate.[214]

Some of the key internal and external factors responsible for the state of imbalance of the economy were: 1) the population's forced savings, amounting roughly from 8 to 10 billion kcs., constituting an inflationary gap on the consumer goods market;[215] 2) forced savings of national committees (roughly 2 to 3 billion kcs.) resulting in inflationary pressures on investments; 3) forced savings of enterprises and excess demand for investment credits, difficult to estimate, but amounting to "much more than 10 billion kcs."; 4) "multibillion" price subsidies for imported raw materials and for a large number of consumer goods and services domestically produced; 5) redundant inventories and protracted construction; 6) spurious foreign exchange rates in terms of acquiring foreign currency through exports--at least as compared with the tourist or black market rates; and 7) frozen resources in exports to socialist and developing countries without a timely and commensurate flow of imports.[216]

According to Ota Sik's rather general pronouncement, to ensure a successful implementation of the reform there should be an accompanying policy aiming at a more rapid growth of aggregate supply and at gradually creating a moderate excess of supply over demand (a buyer's market). The central authorities should arrest the rise of effective demand by a "constant and determined" relative reduction in some or all major components of effective demand, classified as: 1) wages and premiums paid by enterprises; 2) enterprises' investment expenditures;

3) the enterprises' income, siphoned off by the state budget, and expended by the state on the non-productive sphere; and 4) the enterprises' income, siphoned off by the budget, and redistributed among enterprises. He concentrated on measures for constraining the various components of effective demand. It is "out of the question" to decrease wages and premiums paid by enterprises; contrariwise earnings should grow "much more rapidly" than in the past in order to raise productivity. Average wages of "nonproductive" employees should grow even more rapidly in conformity with the process of widening wage differentials. It is likely that "nonproductive" activity will increasingly claim a larger share of resources. To arrest excessive growth of purchasing power--apart from stopping wage payments for producing superfluous goods and from siphoning off income through taxation--two major measures could be taken: 1) to relatively slow down the rate of growth of employment in heavy industry, with an accompanying relatively higher export of producer goods and higher import of consumer goods and 2) to increase the propensity to save.

To curb the demand for producer goods a determined reduction of Items 2 and 4 above is required. Sik believed that the investment activity of enterprises can be restrained by tightening the terms of credit and by raising the interest rate, while inducing nonspending by higher interest rates on bank balances of enterprises.[217] He admitted that, mainly as a result of the 1967 price reform, various industries accumulated adequate investment funds and essentially did not have to rely on credits. Should the higher interest rates prove impotent, investments of enterprises could be restrained by requiring the enterprise to have on hand a given share of the investment costs (say 50 per cent) prior to starting the project. Enterprise liquidity can only be reduced by "active" salesmanship of state bonds, transfer of funds among enterprises, etc. Item 4 above should be severely restricted, since redistribution of income not only undermines incentives to improve efficiency, but also constantly inflates the demand for investments.

Sik rejected controlled inflation as a solution for overcoming a sellers' market and an extensive growth tendency, for this "would only stimulate demand and reduce the pressure on the effectiveness of production." An inflationary trend would have an income redistribution effect. If the necessary increase in average wages (by 3 to 4 per cent annually) is not accompanied by higher productivity or by accelerated imports of consumer goods (resulting from larger exports of producer goods), it will be necessary to revert to a moderate "rise of consumers' prices." However, such a policy cannot be pursued at the expense of the lower income groups. Although a rise in consumers' prices should not be allowed to deteriorate living standards of any broad segment of the population, some of the most striking price "disproportions" should be eliminated, with the aim of compensating price increases of some goods by lowering the prices of others. The need for central adjustments of various groups of retail prices is particularly urgent where wholesale prices exceed retail prices.[218] However, such or similar adjustments can hardly come to grips with the problem since nothing like a mechanism for approaching clearing levels is provided. What is needed is a countervailing force to eradicate or mitigate inflationary pressures by the output adjustment of the producer to the signals of the market, supported, of course, by an adequate monetary policy.

An accelerated rate of increase of nominal wages of highly skilled workers must be accompanied by a larger supply and a better selection of consumer goods.

Sik contended that the share of investment (particularly industrial investment) in national income should diminish, and that the changes in the structure of investment should considerably boost its effectiveness. Investments in mining, metallurgy, heavy machine-building, power, etc., to which the largest state grants are directed--

making them largely independent of credits--should be curtailed. At the present juncture these branches could better utilize the huge investments that were poured into them in the past. By shortening the credit repayment period, preference would be given to investments of shorter periods of gestation, hence favoring the processing industries, especially consumer goods. Sik assigned a decisive role to foreign trade in improving the efficiency of producers of capital goods who, in response to the expected reduced domestic demand for their goods, will have to seek foreign markets. He pleaded for the marginal rate of exchange obtained for exports to be also consistently applied to imports. The reduction of the share of investment in national income should be instrumental in reducing the import of raw materials used, particularly in heavy industry.

The subjection of enterprises to potent market pressures and, particularly, a relative decrease in the demand for investments would focus attention on ineffective production, so that whenever corrective measures do not suffice, it would be necessary to resort to liquidation. Sik was hopeful that the decision to liquidate an enterprise would not be an administrative one, but simply that under pressures of market forces it would be driven out of business and that no one would come to its rescue.[218]

In conclusion, he reiterated that the policy directed at restricting demand for investments in heavy industry is only a temporary measure, to be reversed with the birth of a buyers' market. Though the economic reform brought some good results, from the very beginning it was half-heartedly and inconsistently implemented. While the new system was hesitantly introduced, in the form of an unintegrated set of measures, it had little impact. The legacies of the old system were still largely felt and the tide of opposition against the reform had far from subsided.[219]

Definite tensions and mistrust were created in

relations between central agencies and enterprises. Central bodies often complained of the "antisocial" conduct of enterprises; of speculative manipulations; of concealment of reserves; and of a growth of liquidity and real assets unwarranted by performance, with a relative drop in central resources. Enterprises, for their part, complained about the frequent changes, with resulting uncertainty, in conditions under which they operated; about the distrust and suspicion of central agencies toward them; about their superiors' increasing reliance on directives; etc. Appeals to enterprises to "look after social interests," to adapt to the needs of the consumers, to uncover hidden reserves, to ensure implementation of technical progress, etc., reverberated from every corner. But, at the same time, not much was being done to create conditions for enterprises to conduct their affairs in such a way that, while striving to maximize their own benefits, they would automatically "look after social interests."[220]

Those responsible for economic decision-making did not seem to grasp fully the requirements of economic efficiency. One of the fundamental failures of the reformed system was an absence of integrated and consistent measures to link the macroeconomic plan and policy with the activities of the micro-units.

One of the reform's most significant weaknesses was the failure to get rid of the traditional methods and criteria for constructing the national economic plan--therefore, limiting the means of its implementation. The Czechoslovaks often convey the impression that their plans will be optimal. In fact, there is every indication that at present there have been no fundamental changes in the techniques of plan construction, that the material balances technique is used, and that, although a much greater degree of consistency is achieved with the aid of computers and although a larger number of variants is considered, there is still no economic verification of production processes. New planning methods refer largely to plan implementation and skirt the issues of plan construction.

The plan constructed at the center continued to be of a directive nature and was emphatically stressed by the central planner as the fundamental tool of management. Guideline indexes were treated as mandatory; assignments in foreign trade were repeatedly boosted; and lip service was paid to competition and the market. The reform did not permeate foreign trade. Domestic prices and the producer continued to be divorced from world market prices. Whatever influence the foreign market might have exerted was weakened by the system of surcharges and deductions. Little was done to effectively weaken the monopoly of foreign trade. In fact, monopolies were being strengthened in many sectors. Economic instruments were mistrusted by the central planner who feared a loss of control. No wonder that enterprises did not feel that the reformed system departed from previous practice. They considered it a manifestation of yet another tinkering with the system and a continuation of the past half-measure alterations of traditional imperative planning.[221]

One of the most outspoken and reformist of economists, Eugene Loebl, assailed the lack of comprehension of the interdependence between the macroeconomic plan and the activity of micro-units.[222] His criticism, particularly of what he considered the major flaw of the reform, although it is interesting, is couched in very general terms; it skims the surface of the techniques of plan construction; and his description of the interaction between all the players of the unfolding drama in the process of economic activity is vague. His discussion of the rationality of macro- and micro-units leaves much to be desired, for he does not spell out what are the maximization goals, particularly at the macro-sphere, and he only implies that profit should be the quantity to be maximized at the micro-level.

Loebl claimed that whereas the traditional system had functioned as if the entire economy was one mammoth enterprise, the reform had introduced two planes of activity, hence two planes of rational behavior: the center and the enterprise--the macro- and the micro-spheres.

> The new system does not imply a reorganization of the old system. But it is also not a transfer of the center's authority; i.e., decentralization. Also it would be incorrect to believe it to be only a means for enhancing the authority of the micro-sphere and of materially reducing the number of directive indexes.

The crucial point of such a system is the relationship and interaction between the macro- and micro-spheres: an interaction between the two so as to arrive at a self-adjusting system; a servo-mechanism which, through feedback action, automatically eradicates disequilibrium forces. It is precisely the lack of understanding of this primordial sine qua non that had, according to Loebl, undermined the first two years of the reform's existence.

Even though both the enterprises and the center seemingly acted rationally (in that they pursued their own interests and acted so as to achieve them), on the whole the results pointed to the irrationality of the system, for the relationship between the two planes was ill-conceived. For example, it is not irrational in a lasting sellers' market to accumulate supplies and to pay interest rather than to be faced with production stoppages.

Whereas in the traditional system the motor of the economy was the center whence the directives originated, the reformed system requires as its integral part a mechanism of microeconomic processes and adjustments. The pattern of behavior of micro-units is constrained by the pressure to act rationally (probably to choose between alternatives so as to maximize their benefits on the basis of rational choice coefficients--efficiency prices), by the ability of the economic subjects (enterprise managers) to act rationally, and by the scope allowed the micro-units for rational activity. The essential source of pressure to act rationally is competition: the kind of competition that would provide the spoils of victory for the victorious enterprise and its personnel (meaning that the enterprise can dispose at will of its net profits) and that would drive the losing enterprise into bankruptcy. Such a pressure would also provide criteria for evaluating the caliber of managers and for selecting them as well as stimuli to managers for improving their qualifications for the best posts. The scope for competition can be materially enlarged simply by removing administrative barriers that hamper managerial activity.

There is still too little recognition that the micro-sphere is capable of solving economic problems by itself. The prevailing conviction at the center is that the micro-sphere has to be tutored, hence the continuing proclivity to expand arbitrarily macroeconomic decisions into the micro-sphere. The short-circuit between the macroeconomy and the microeconomy which can result from viewing the plan only from the macro-sphere and attempting to regulate the market from there is perhaps most vividly illustrated by the price reform.

The two approaches that could have been chosen, according to Loebl, were: 1) the view that in the past the fallacious price system had resulted from a wrong approach and that, due to improved theoretical grounding and to modern computer techniques, the center was now able to set economically sound prices, and 2) the view that pricing is a microeconomic problem to be left largely to the forces which exert pressure on rational economic behavior and, hence, pressure to approach economically sound prices. The first alternative was chosen, resulting in the well-known and inherent shortcomings. It was considered inadmissible to leave price-setting up to the micro-sphere, yet it was advocated that Czechoslovak price relations should approximate those in the West; i.e., prices formed in the micro-sphere in capitalist countries. Loebl's critique of the price reform does not embrace those who conducted the reform, for, to him, somewhat in the Hayek vein, no central planner has yet been able--or for that matter will ever be--to create an economically rational price system.

The revised prices are usually taken to task for having created a situation where some enterprises earn unjustified profits and others suffer unjustified losses. To counteract this situation, a number of policy measures (e.g., changes in interest rates, taxes, supplementary levies, etc.) are being refurbished. The rationality behind these measures stems from the need to counteract the irrationality resulting from the center's actions. In fact, central price-setting impairs the rationality of the system, for it does not proceed from the acceptance of the micro-sphere as one of rational economic behavior.

Even though the micro-sphere possesses an extraordinary ability to regulate itself, to forecast, etc., it is not devoid of deficiencies. However, these cannot be eliminated by taking over micro-functions at the macro-sphere, but only by regulating the relationship of both planes.

The macro-sphere can actively engage in structural reconstruction through such measures as the issue of earmarked credits. It can subsidize infant industries that have not yet become profitable. It can sponsor research and development institutes. But more importantly, it is responsible for policies aiming at currency stability; for the correct relations to foreign currency; for stabilizing rules and regulations in the economy and the obligations of enterprises to the center; and for promoting measures ensuring growth of the living standard. Thus, the macro-sphere should have its own plan--a plan which would have no direct connection with the market, but whose measures will have a strong influence on both the plan and the market at the micro-sphere. Such a plan should enhance the efficiency of the system, for it would eliminate some of the uncertainty which hampers decision-making in the micro-sphere.

Although it is not clear what exactly would be the nature of the central plan in such a scheme, Loebl seems to lean toward indicative planning and he goes so far as to say that the plans prepared by large Western firms have proven more viable and less prone to disproportions than those of Soviet-type economies.

Opposition to the reform seemed to come from every corner. Voices were raised claiming that the reform was just another variant of past reorganizations. Reportedly, a state of confusion prevailed. To some, it all seemed incomprehensible in contrast to the clarity of past targets and quotas. There prevailed a general mistrust that central organs would increase contributions from GY to the budget.[223]

In the fall of 1967 the old Party stalwarts were overtly voicing their displeasure with the reform, something that they had only been covertly hinting at in the past two years. On the other hand, the radical reformers stressed that an end must be put to half-measures and that the whole gamut of reform measures must be consistently and uncompromisingly introduced, notwithstanding opposition and political unpopularity.

One of the more serious warning signs was the fatigue and virtual apathy of some enterprise managers, even including those who two or three years before had unreservedly supported the new system.[224]

In an on-the-spot study, provided with access to the best-informed sources, a delegation of leading Italian Communist Party officials affirmed that "there is still strong resistance within the very entities entrusted with carrying out the reform."[225] On the whole, they found little support for the reform. Aside from the agricultural sector, the two main walls of opposition were the bureaucracy and the workers. The bulk of industrial and government bureaucrats and Party <u>aparatchiks</u> were hostile to the reform.

A determined opposition was found among some of the 12,000 bureaucrats in the ministries, lead by 132 deputy-ministers and "a batallion of general directors" who feared not only the diminution of their powers, but also the threat to their ability to maintain their jobs or even to find new ones due to their lack of qualifications. Opposition was rife among the local organs of government. For example, the local organs of the Ministry of Agriculture were in the process of being transformed from supervisors into subordinates of local elective bodies. Hostility was displayed by some aparatchiks who "are experts in applying the old administrative methods." There are essentially inimical elements among those bureaucrats who enjoyed the position of plant directors and who were being removed by the reform from the "tranquil role of operators" and were being plunged into the "risky role of businessmen."[226]

Since about the mid-1960's there was a discernible trend to replace incompetent, but politically loyal, managers by experts. The big problem was to find managers who were not only endowed with technical skills (usually engineers), but who also had training and understanding of modern management techniques. Some start was made when an Institute of Management was opened in Prague in 1966 to expose engineers to business subjects. Early in 1968 it was proposed that some 20,000 officials from all levels of the hierarchical ladder attend special study groups organized by the Institute of Management affiliated with the economics faculties in Prague, Brno, and Bratislava.[227] Clearly an improvement of the qualifications of managers is a conditio sine qua non for the reform to come to fruition. But one wonders whether many traditional bureaucrats, after tasting a few courses and "purifying their souls," will not be able to use their attendance at these courses as a vehicle for survival without essentially changing either their outlook or working habits.

The human factor and the inadequate qualities of management are obviously stressed as a great stumbling block in the path of the reform. After a protracted period of "passing the buck," the faculty of independent decision-making, initiative, and entrepreneurial spirit may have withered away. It is not at all improbable that the damage done by the modus operandi of the traditional system to the human factor is much greater than is commonly realized.[228]

As far as the workers generally are concerned, their immediate self-interest dictates retention of the old system or, at worst, they are, together with the other "enthusiastic" reformers, for a snail-paced reform implementation. Surely a reform that assumes a premium for higher skill, exertion of effort, better performance, and the shutting down of inefficient plants cannot be accepted as a blessing in a country where wages have been "secure" and only some 10 per cent of the take-home pay varied with the degree of qualification and productivity. By all accounts the performance of the Czechoslovak worker has been generally poor and absenteeism and other "plagues" of overemployment have prevailed. The Italian Communists reported that a Neapolitan worker who had observed the performance of his Czechoslovak colleagues was "amused, amazed, and at the same time scandalized and troubled" by the little effort exerted by the Czechoslovaks.[229] A popular quip in Czechoslovakia represented the tragedy and irony of the situation in the worker's statement that "socialism is preferable to working." The workers' displeasure was provoked by the threat of closing down inefficient plants (such as the coal mines of the Ostrava basin) and of reshuffling the resultant unemployed to other posts. Such an event might often involve a cut in wages and retraining or other inconveniences, such as relocation to another area--no mean task in view of the scarcity of housing. The workers' resentment was also aroused by their fear and the spreading rumors that the reformers would work their "miracle" at the cost of a "temporary" cut in real wages. In addition, it should be noted that the workers', indeed even managers', enmity toward the reform was kindled by their proverbial distrust of the intellectuals. For example, the manager of

Tos-Hastivar, a leading machine-tool factory, voiced the widespread animosity toward the "reformer-professors" when he said: "Ota Sik needs us more than we need him."[230]

The group that later became known as the Novotny coterie propagated the views that economic reforms were enforced to the detriment of the workers, the pensioners, and the socially weak. On the contrary, acting as the spokesman for the economic revisionists, the "reformer-professor" considered the accusations of conservatives to be fallacious, abusive distortions of the stand taken by the radicals; indeed, the latter denied any intention to embark on the revitalization of the newly refurbished system at the expense of living standards of the population as a whole. Those public officials who claim that the new economic system is not paying sufficient attention to the workers' interests are guilty of "cheap and tricky politicking." The half-hearted and inconsistent measures taken by the center prevented the reformed system from achieving palpable improvements in living standards. A contributing factor to the disenchantment with the reformed system was the fact that the man on the street "has not felt much improvement so far." A particularly aggravating factor was the lack of substantial betterment in retail trade and in services.[231]

Precisely because the reformed system was prevented from penetrating into intra-enterprise units, it has been misunderstood by workers. Whereas redistribution among enterprises undermined initiative and incentives, the redistribution of earnings among employees had even more adverse effects. Workers failed to comprehend what the new system was all about. They complained that in some branches no premiums, or only nominal ones, were paid, but "elsewhere workers claimed that the managers distributed everything among themselves." Moreover, there was sudden clamoring from many sides about excessive wage hikes and the ministerial officials, "quite in keeping with the old administrative methods," drew their conclusions.

Authoritative practices were immediately applied to wage regulation, resulting in the imposition of, _de facto_, wage norms and wage ceilings. It is not surprising that the workers have not taken all this too kindly. They saw that the old wage ceilings remained in force. They did not receive the promised premiums or shares in profits in the expected amount and, on the other hand, prices were rising.[232]

Strong pressures were evinced both from above and from below to preserve some of the most damaging attributes of the traditional system (such as price distortions, widespread protectionism, and redistribution of profits and of earnings) in order to make it possible for the existing structure of ineffective production to survive.[233] The intent was not to expose flagrant inefficiencies at all levels and to shield the producers from the competitive forces and pressures of the domestic and world markets. It was pointedly remarked that "we have introduced only those measures that did not hurt anyone, but none of those that could have injured someone."[234]

From the inception of the reformed system the necessary political prerequisites and fundamental institutional changes at all levels of the hierarchy were lacking. There was no reshuffling of the entire cumbersome bureaucratic and costly planning apparatus; the vertical structure was not toppled in conformity with the requirements of the new system. The leadership was constantly pushing aside proposals of economists to reshape the institutional strata and this considerably weakened the reformed system. The regime was not overtly opposed to alterations in the forms of management, but it vehemently resisted the slightest attempt which might loosen the tightly knit administrative monopoly.

In no uncertain terms did Sik attribute the grave problems to the prevailing political situation. A certain power constellation in the central bodies--an immense concentration of power particularly at the highest Party levels--represented the main deterring factors. For many years the ultra-conservative forces and stalwarts of the old regime prevailed in the central Party and government bodies. Many of the political leaders and functionaries of the state apparatus in charge of reform implementation harbored traditional views, had vested interests in preserving imperative planning, and feared loss of control. Thus, they expressed their reservations and imposed restrictions on the new system and forestalled or watered-down its implementation. It was increasingly difficult to criticize failures of the reform's implementation, let alone to rectify the situation. A prerequisite for the successful implementation of the reform--drastic changes in personnel and in personnel policy--was not met. Political considerations (power politics) played a decisive role in the selection of senior management. The system of filling positions and of promotions was not conducive to the appointment of qualified and enterprising persons.[235]

In the fall of 1967, economic reform was facing a serious crisis. Unless its strong proponents were supported by mounting disenchantment in other areas to precipitate a political crisis which would be resolved in a leadership and a government more favorably disposed to radical reform in the full meaning of the term, there was little likelihood of survival of the reform.

CHAPTER **8** EPILOGUE

A BACKGROUND OF THE STRUGGLE FOR POLITICAL AND SOCIAL REFORM

The recent history of relaxation of controls over the cultural life in Eastern Europe has been characterized by advances followed by setbacks. It may perhaps be best described as two steps forward, one step backward--to borrow Lenin's phrase--so that at each stage a little more freedom was gained and a few more shackles were shed. This process has been vividly illustrated by the battles fought by Czechoslovak intellectuals since about 1963.

As we have seen in Chapter 3, some concessions were made to the belligerent Slovaks with the appointment of slightly more "liberal" men to key posts in the fall of 1963. Toward the end of that year, Novotny claimed at a speech in Moscow that de-Stalinization had been fully accomplished in Czechoslovakia by the Twelfth Congress of the CPC in 1962, and that continued delving into the past was unhealthy.[1] At the year-end Party CC Plenary Session, Vladimir Koucky denounced both "dogmatism" and "revisionism."[2] Interestingly enough, a report on the re-examination of the charges against the so-called Slovak bourgeois nationalists was discussed but not published. The Plenary Session's resolution on this report was not published either but was supposed to have been "debated" within Party circles.[3]

On February 29, 1964, word came of the resolution of the CC's Plenary Session on the bourgeois nationalists, which gave full rehabilitation to Gustav Husak, Laco Novomesky, Karol Smidke, and

Vlado Clementis and undermined the whole issue of bourgeois nationalism. The article further implied Novotny's demurring participation in the de-Stalinization process.[4] Indeed, Novotny seemed to have remained backstage during the CC meetings, giving rise to speculation in the West that he may have been on his way out.

Curiously enough, literature has had a long history of progressive torchbearing in Eastern Europe. In the previous century, writers grappled with a variety of moral, social, and political issues. They were the fomenters of liberal tendencies which could find no legal outlet in an opposition political party. This tradition was broken during the Stalin years. But as his successors saw fit to relax this stringent control over cultural life--without, however, being able to define the limits of the permissible--the more articulate broadsides against the regime came again from the cultural magazines; no other outlet existed. As long as open political debate is impossible, the written word will always be politically explosive.

The Slovak periodical Kulturny zivot continued to publish articles challenging Marxist orthodoxy, with rebuttals appearing in Rude pravo. Early in 1964, after a meeting between the Czech and Slovak writers and Novotny, Jiri Sotola, editor of Literarni noviny, reported that the hard line of 1963 had softened, but he conveyed the impression that Novotny exhorted the writers to be spokesmen of the CC's policies rather than active participants in policy-making.[5]

Early in March, Novotny once again showed himself intransigent and intractable and repudiated the demands for liberty.[6] This was followed by castigation of the editors of and contributors to Literarni noviny, Kulturni zivot, and Plemen for their revisionism, liberal tendencies, and deviations from the Party line.[7] The writers seemed to have been subdued by the severity of the attack, at least for the time being.[8] But the spirit of contrition did not permeate to Slovakia. The editors of Kulturny zivot expressed their full backing of their contributors and asserted that the journal was not only cultural in nature but political as well.[9] Notwithstanding continued vituperations by Party officials against the revisionists, a slight concession was indicated by the award of literary prizes to Laco Novomesky and to Ladislav Mnacko, two leading revisionists--the former a victim of the Slovak bourgeois nationalist trials.[10]

The intellectual upsurge which had begun in the spring of 1963 seemed almost to have disappeared by June, 1964, when the Party appeared to have won control of the situation.[11] This was perhaps a compromise for giving in nolens volens to the oncoming wave of economic revisionism. But the repression of the intellectuals was not altogether successful, especially in Slovakia where the revisionists refused to remain silent. As was pointed out, Novotny's two most irksome problems were the writers and the Slovaks, and Slovak writers were the most intractable of all.[12]

Nevertheless, on November 12, Novotny was "reelected" President of the Republic and held fast to his vital role as First Secretary of the Party. Rumors in 1964 that he might be on his way out proved to be just that--rumors, at least for the next couple of years. But friction between the gradually emerging two factions (the progressives and the stalwarts of the ancien regime) was slowly gathering momentum.

By mid-1965 the replacement of Vladimir Koucky by Jiri Hendrych as Chairman of the CC's Ideological Commission was interpreted as a strengthening of the ideological hard line. A paralyzing weariness seemed to have set in among the restive writers. Their national meeting in June, 1965, and the meeting in Slovakia were uninspiring and anticlimactic.[13] Early in 1966 the Party fired another broadside at the dissident writers and specifically attacked those writers who apparently were paying only lip service to the line laid out for the cultural periodicals in March, 1964.[14] This was seen as a further attempt to counteract the process of unshackling Marxist dogma which the Czechoslovak literature was promoting. It was a move dictated by the fear of the liberal tendencies, implicit in economic reform, and permeating to other levels of cultural and social life. But the growing unrest was not easily subdued. A reorganization of the editorial board of Literarni noviny was nothing more than another compromise. Jiri Hajek, editor of Plemen, analyzed the "basic differences" between "liberalization" and "democratization," underlining the need for greater diversity in cultural expression, but stressing that democratization does not mean that the Party should forgo the right of intervening in cultural affairs and of favoring works that it considers "most propitious for its social practices." This, however, should not mean that literary works could be written according to directives or that writers could be prevailed upon by force and required to "repeat the catechism."[15] Further inroads of the liberal trend were revealed in an article in an organ of the Law Institute of the Slovak Academy of Science, where a startling call for free elections was sounded to prevent the manipulation of the ruled by the ruling.[16]

At the Thirteenth Congress of the CPC, Novotny reiterated criticisms against the cultural periodicals which allegedly imparted "destructive attitudes toward the values of our society." He also reprimanded the teaching profession for allowing students to imbibe these "negative influences."[17] At the same congress, Alexander Dubcek firmly pledged his support to the Novotny policies. At the Congress of the Slovak Party a month earlier, the Party line on culture was somewhat dispiritedly supported by Vasil Bilak, whereas the spirit of the intellectuals was staunchly defended by the First Secretary of the Slovak Writers Union (SWU). Dubcek praised the rehabilitation of the bourgeois nationalists but condemned the "nihilism, skepticism, and discursiveness" that followed in the wake of de-Stalinization. He assured his audience that the Slovak Party had recovered from its negative tendencies and was able to uplift the morale of the people.[18] The winds of change seemingly blew stronger in the Slovak Party. This became strikingly noticeable from the array of revisionist articles which appeared in the fall of 1966 in its official daily organ Pravda.

Meanwhile, Novotny continued to be ideologically as recalcitrant as ever. Early in October, 1966, at the CC Plenary Session he vituperated against the revisionist outlook which had permeated almost all media of cultural and intellectual activity and complained that the Party's propaganda machine was not doing enough to counter this barrage. He attacked a Radio Bratislava commentator for daring to draw a parallel between the Chinese Cultural Revolution and the excesses in Czechoslovakia in the years following the inception of the Communist rule. Understandably such an allusion drove straight home to Novotny's tinted past. Finally he promised that the Party would devote greater attention to ideological education.[19]

A further attempt to tighten the Party's grip over the intellectuals was the initiation of a series of indoctrination seminars for leading personnel of the CAS and of the academic institutions.[20] In addition there were more changes on the editorial board of Literarni noviny in the second half of 1966 and the game of musical chairs continued into the new year.

At face value, the new press law which became effective on January 1, 1967, seemed to have been an important gain for the progressives. It provided for "freedom of expression, speech, and press" and for protection against any act which might obstruct such freedom. But this was immediately followed by outlining the task of the public press to promote "socialist awareness" and to uphold the Party's policy as the major force in the state and in society. A special board was set up to see to it that state, economic, and military secrets were not divulged in the press.

The splitting of the Ministry of Education and

Culture into the Ministry of Education (ME) and the Ministry of Culture and Information (MCI), with Jiri Hajek remaining at the head of the former and the appointment of Karel Hoffman to head the latter, could be interpreted as one of the moves by which Novotny hoped to control the intellectuals and to force them to adhere to the Party line.

Early in 1967, at a CC meeting devoted to ideological questions, Hendrych denounced those artists who expounded the absurdity of life. According to him "creative freedom should not be interpreted as license for nebulousness of views or anarchism." He struck out at those who allegedly propagated nonsocialist opinions and foreign ideology in the cultural magazines and he condemned those Communists who failed to implement the cultural line mapped out by the Party at the Thirteenth Congress.[21] The most vivid demonstration of the revolt of Czechoslovak intellectuals was yet to come in June, 1967, at the Fourth Congress of the Czechoslovak Writers Union (CWU), begun with a one-day conference of the SWU on May 11, which was surprisingly tame. The preamble of this conference called, _inter alia_, for a consistent widening of the scope for free exchange of opinions, for a defense of creative work "engaged in criticizing violations and distortions of men's humanistic ideals," for closer contact with _émigrés_ of all shades of opinion, and for no regimentation in literature.[22]

Before examining the bitter clash at the June, 1967, conference, it might be instructive to digress and to note briefly some inroads of unorthodoxy. There was a cultural rehabilitation of most prewar artists and even of the exiles, although their works were only republished on a selective basis. The ties with Western artistic life were strengthened. Articles praising the constructive activities of Edward Benes and Thomas Masaryk cropped up here and there. Czechoslovak writers protested to Moscow against the Sinyavski-Daniel sentences. Interest in sociology was growing, with pressures applied for republication of works by the most important Western sociologists. Old myths slowly faded away:

Josef Smrkovsky admitted that the Americans did not come to the aid of the Prague uprising in May, 1945, not because of unwillingness, but because General Patton stipulated that the request would have to come from leaders in Prague since it was in the area conceded to Soviet operations by agreement at the highest level between the U.S. and the U.S.S.R. Prague leaders refrained from asking the U.S. to intervene, for such a liberation of Prague would not have been politically advisable.[23]

There were even hints that another political party should be allowed. Moreover, there appeared strong intimations at federalism in the relationship between Slovakia and the Czech lands.[24] Another foray into the political *status quo* was an article by Zdenek Mlynar, then Secretary of the CC's Legal Commission, in which he contended that in order to afford the people a larger scope in decision-making, the representative bodies and the mass organizations must be allowed more responsibilities. In order for representative bodies to be more than mere transmission belts, they should become centers for conflicting views. He implied that the electoral system needed revising and that different interest groups of the population should be represented.[25] Mlynar's position is particularly worthy of notice because he was so closely associated with the Party hierarchy and especially because it was a forerunner of many of the liberal proposals that were later advocated during the Dubcek regime.

Much work was done on the ideological reassessment of Marxism. Several provocative contributions appeared. In one, a prominent philosopher expounded his views of the "dictatorship of leaders and cliques" reminiscent in many ways of Milovan Djilas' thesis.[26] Vaclav Kotyk, of the Institute of International Politics and Economics, challenged the alleged harmony among Communist states. Contrariwise, he called for a recognition of distinctness and championed the idea of various roads to socialism. The various Communist parties--according to Kotyk--should be independent not only organizationally and in domestic policy-making, but also ideologically and in their foreign policy. Countries judged by others as having forsaken Marxism should not be excluded from the Communist fraternity, and no pressures or embargoes should be waged against them.[27] Kotyk's theory is particularly interesting in view of the disquietude that Dubcek aroused among his East European and Soviet confreres in the spring of 1968.

THE WRITERS' REVOLT

The Fourth Congress of the CWU convened on June 27-29, 1967. If the Party had hoped that the Congress would endorse the Party's line on cultural affairs, it was to be bitterly disappointed. But such hopes were dispelled even earlier by the pre-Congress discussion papers. Hendrych was present throughout the meeting and warned the writers in the usual tone which had become so stereotyped in the Party's admonishments to intellectuals in the last few years.

In his report of the CWU's activities between congresses, Sotola reviewed the fundamental changes that had taken place and stressed the influence of external factors on the CWU's activities. He pointed to the influx of youth into the union and its regenerative influence on the membership. He deplored the banning of the young writers' periodical Tvar in December, 1965, but praised the manner in which the writers had conducted themselves and had debated the issues raised.[28]

One of the pre-eminent moments of the Congress came at Pavel Kahout's reading of the Soviet writer Aleksandr Solzhenitsyn's circular letter appealing for an end to literary censorship in the U.S.S.R.,[29] but it was almost anticlimactic in light of the speech by Ludvik Vaculik, a young Communist writer. He did not limit himself to criticizing the Party's attitude toward the arts but indicted the whole system.[30]

Vaculik's opening remarks dealt with the rulers' abuse of power over the ruled. He spoke of the mechanism of democracy which is neither socialist nor capitalist in nature but which is designed to protect not only the ruled from the rulers but also to safeguard the rulers from "being shot when their government is toppled." He charged that the Congress was not convened after its members had decided to meet but only after the rulers had "graciously consented." In return, they expected reverence. He exhorted his fellow writers in these words:

> I suggest that we do not show them reverence. Let us play this game as if we were citizens, as if we had permission to use this playground; and for three whole days let us act as if we were adult and had come of age.

He sternly criticized the fusion of the Party and government affairs to the point where a Communist was not able to discuss anything in public, since everything had become a Party matter to be debated in camera. He questioned the premises which had made it possible only for the meek and obedient to rise to posts of eminence and he abhorred the forces within the regime which had either broken or shifted to the background those who queried, those who in a way represented the public conscience. No wonder that most Czechoslovaks felt that their superiors were actually their inferiors!

Vaculik praised the material well-being which the writers enjoyed. "But when I stand here and speak, I do not in the least have the feeling a free man should have when he speaks his mind freely..." He spoke of the constant threat of reprisals; of the menace that the writers would be deprived of their periodical, of their publishing house, or even of their union; and of personal intimidation.

> But are they really the lords of everything? And what remains of us in the hands of others? Nothing? Then we need not exist. But they should say so. Then it would be perfectly clear that basically a handful of people decide on our existence or nonexistence.

What we should do, think, and feel.

Vaculik then touched upon the sore point of rehabilitations. He asked why the unjustly sentenced and rehabilitated people were not automatically granted their original rights; why they were not given back their dwellings; why there were no proper apologies made to these people; etc. He affirmed that he saw no guarantees of rights of citizens, even from the courts of justice, and went so far as to question whether the rulers possessed such guarantees of their own civil rights. He touched on the annoyance of the regime with those who speak of freedom:

> It does not understand that freedom exists only in places where one does not need to speak about it. The regime is annoyed because people talk about what they see. But instead of changing what people see, the regime wants to change their eyes.

Vaculik exploded the myth which has been so liberally spun all over Eastern Europe of the necessity of the Stalinist period. He deplored the shortage of housing and schools and the lack of prosperity. He denounced the regime for being unable to cope with those problems which cannot be solved by the undemocratic systems. Finally, he warned that he did not yearn to restore the First Republic:

> When I criticize the regime, I do not criticize socialism because I am not convinced that what happened here was necessary and because I do not identify the regime with socialism, in the way it tries to identify itself.

In his closing address to the Congress, Jan Prochazka upheld the perseverance of the writers for freedom of expression and their refusal to submit to dogma. He expressed his allegiance to the fighters against oppression, persecution, racism, anti-Semitism, chauvinism, etc.[31] Although it significantly toned down the aplomb and the gusto of the individual speeches, the resolution adopted at the end of the Congress was no mean achievement.[32] One of its novelties was the recognition of the prewar Czechoslovak democratic tradition. It condemned the propagandist function which degraded Czechoslovak literature after the war.

> Nowadays nobody dares to expound and defend any more the discredited thesis which foolishly identified ideology with culture, thus strangling spiritual and artistic creativity. Perhaps there might be no need to recollect such a primitive attitude were it not for its continued appearance in cultural policy; in editorial activities; in the application of the press law; and its hindrance of the free exchange of ideas, literature, and cultural development.

The resolution called for cultural tolerance, for abandonment of parochial attitudes, and for freer contacts with the West. It urged the restoration of certain periods and personalities of history to consciousness. A telling line was the call on the CC to take an active part in elaborating a new model for socialist culture along the lines of that worked out for the economy. The resolution also appealed for a limitation of censorship to state security matters and for a reform of the press law so that those writers accused of having violated it should be permitted to defend themselves instead of having to rely on editorial boards and publishing houses to do so.

The Party's wrath was aroused and voiced during and after the Congress. Hendrych spoke at the end, condemning in no uncertain terms the liberal tendencies of addresses.[33] An aftermath of the Congress was a letter to the CC wherein the writers proclaimed their allegiance to socialism, but their protest against subservience to Party dictates which they saw as vestiges of the "personality cult."[34] Novotny promptly replied that the Party would not tolerate the accusations against it.[35] Vaingloriously several contributions of the "loyal" Party writers were published.[36] Novotny's wrath at the revolt of the intellectuals was in sharp contrast to the benign disposition he demonstrated in an interview accorded to The Times earlier in the month. He went so far as to say that the elan and criticism of the young was vital in preventing the entrenchment of conservative habits of thought.[37]

Before examining the repercussions and reorganizations which followed the Congress, it might be interesting to note some of the issues and undercurrents which accompanied it. One dispute had to do with the writers' opposition to the official pro-Arab and anti-Israeli position adopted by Czechoslovakia during the June, 1967, Arab-Israeli war.[38] Ladislav Mnacko left for an unauthorized visit to Israel. He denounced the Party's stand as a seal of approval of anti-Semitism, which, he said, stemmed from the Slansky trial. He noted that Czechoslovakia's crisis was moral rather than economic. Since those responsible for the Slansky trial had left the political arena, "except one" (implying Novotny), Mnacko contended that Novotny sought in anti-Semitism a justification for past crimes. He represented his visit to Israel as a personal act of political protest.[39] A few days afterward it was announced that Mnacko was not only expelled from the Party, but was also deprived of Czechoslovak citizenship. Prochazka, who had been elected to head the CWU and was a candidate member of the CC, apparently also took strong exception to the Party's Middle East policy. The Party spokesmen defended their position as best they could. They denied claims of anti-Semitism and once again lashed out against the liberals who "preached capitalist morals and bourgeois ideology."[40]

The trial of Jan Benes, a writer, Karel Zamecnik, a film and television employee and student, and Pavel Tigrid, an émigré journalist residing in Paris, was considered to be yet another act in the drama of Czechoslovak intellectuals played out in the summer of 1967. The charges ranged from high treason to violation of national interests abroad, through the entire gamut of espionage, subversive activities, fraud, and even speculation, probably thrown in for good measure. Tigrid was sentenced in absentia to 14 years' imprisonment, Benes to five years, and Zamecnik was acquitted.[41] As an aftermath of the CWU's Congress, the trial was a warning to the intellectuals who, according to the Party, had opened their doors too wide to Western ideas and who generally thrived on contact with the West.

On September 15, 1967, there appeared an article by Prochazka commemorating the 30th Anniversary of the death of Thomas Masaryk in which he praised Masaryk for his dedication and tolerance and acknowledged that contemporary socialists could learn much from his wisdom.[42]

A fortnight earlier a mild sensation was provoked when The Sunday Times published on September 3 an appeal which apparently originated from about 450 Czechoslovak intellectuals, seeking world opinion in support of the struggle being waged by the writers and crying out against the "witch hunt" that the Czechoslovak Party leaders were waging to penalize the more liberal and outspoken who had taken a stand at the Congress. It was noted that although the authors of the document claimed to be faithful Marxists, some discrepancies pointed to the contrary. The consensus in the West was that the document did indeed originate in Prague but that its authorship could not be attributed to so large a group. Moreover, it was unthinkable that such a group could have come together in a city like Prague, without the authorities' knowledge.[43] Writing in a West German daily, Kohout pointed to some of the manifesto's inconsistencies. He doubted that Czechoslovakia's intellectual elite would have chosen to remain anonymous, for what is the value of a manifesto without signatures?[44] The remark seems quite plausible, for if the signatories were in the number claimed, they would not have had to fear repercussions, because the regime would have understandably recoiled from mass reprisals. The CWU promptly disassociated itself from the document and the authorities denied any knowledge that Czechoslovak writers had authored the document. Later it was suggested that the views expressed therein might be those of a small group of writers but certainly did not reflect the position of the vast majority.[45]

About two months later it was announced that "Dr. I. P." (Ivan Pfaff), a free-lance historian, was arrested on the charge of having written the manifesto. He had allegedly confessed to being its sole author.[46] It should be noted as a postscript that Pfaff was released from prison by mid-March, 1968. In an interview a few days later he did not deny authorship of the manifesto. Although he regretted the form and manner of the presentation, he reiterated his complete agreement with what he had said therein. His justification was the oppressive atmosphere of autumn, 1967. His outcry for freedom and justice was a wholly personal one, but he contended that the claim of several hundred possible signatories was not far-fetched, for he believed that at least such a number of intellectuals felt exactly as he did.[47]

One of the factors contributing to the lack of success of the summer, 1967, revolt of the intellectuals was the degree of divisiveness among the Czechs and the Slovaks--deriving from the renewed Slovak insistance on Slovakia as a separate political, social, and economic entity within the state. The fervor for federalism was gaining momentum. Indifference to national issues and preoccupation with purely Slovak problems was apparent from the scant attendance of Slovaks at the Congress. Although they basically espoused the sentiments expressed by the dissident Czech writers, the Slovaks as a group remained <u>en coulisses</u> and preferred to resort to their own arrangements with the Party leaders in Bratislava. It appears that the aspiration goals of the Czech intelligentsia which had shown itself so profoundly divorced from the past, alienated from current Party policies, and striving for broader and more humanitarian goals, have run against the more parochial goals of the Slovak intellectuals who were striving first and foremost for independence from oppressive centralism.[48]

Throughout that fateful summer the air over Prague was heavy with repercussions and reprisals which followed in the wake of the Congress. One of the main bones of contention was once again the editorial board of Literarni noviny. Early in July, Jiri Sotola was replaced by Dusan Hamsik to head the editorial board. Within a fortnight Sotola was reinstated. But by the end of September at a Plenary Session of the CC it was decided to divorce Literarni noviny from the CWU and to entrust its editorship to the MCI. As a first step the MCI discharged almost the entire editorial board and those who were retained resigned in protest. Literarni noviny became jestingly known as The Tales of Hoffman. Vaculik, Ivan Klima, and Antonin Liehm--three liberal intellectuals--were expelled from the Party by the CC and, as expected, Prochazka was relieved of his post as candidate member of the CC. These actions were made unequivocally clear as reprisals against the "negative" stand these writers had taken at the Congress. But it was claimed that critics were in minority and that most writers supported the Party.[49] The most articulate condemnation of the writers came from Hendrych:

> Our democracy is of a socialist and class content. It cannot be confused with liberalism and anarchy... We cannot identify literature and its creators with the writers' organization--and especially less so with those who at the congress attempted to come up with an opposition political platform.[50]

Although Hendrych's wrath at the liberals was echoed by the faithful, not all speakers at the meeting used the same harsh tones. The torch of freedom was notably upheld by Vladimir Minac, a Slovak writer, and Jaroslav Kladiva, the dean of the faculty of philosophy, Charles University. Minac demanded freedom for all, not just for intellectuals. He denounced reprisals against the restive writers as expediency measures which solved nothing. He pointed out that not only were the writers prone to hysteria but that a hysterical atmosphere had been created around them. Kladiva underlined the Party's willingness to readmit the expelled writers if their future political attitudes were acceptable, and its assurances that they would not be deprived of work along the line of their specialization.[51] It was reported that in the alignment of Party factions, those Presidium members actively participating in the economic changeover (for example, Jaromir Dolansky, Oldrich Cernik, and Drahomir Kolder) seemed to be aligned with the moderates rather than with the stalwarts of the old regime.[52]

The CWU's leadership suffered many vicissitudes. Prochazka's proposed chairmanship angered the authorities. After much wrangling, finally in September a six-man temporary council was appointed, which included Prochazka. It was reported that the main officers of the CWU were elected early in October. The Presidium of the CWU was composed of four staunch Party supporters, eleven moderates, and only one revisionist.

The Fifth Congress of Czechoslovak Journalists, held in Prague on October, 19-20, 1967, was exceedingly tame in comparison to the tumultuous events of that summer, although the abuse of the press law by censors came in for its share of criticism. However, Adolph Hradecky, General Secretary of the Association of Czechoslovak Journalists, went on record in defense of the press law and in true opportunistic fashion he blamed the writers for the difficulties in which they and their journals had found themselves. The writers were not easily silenced. Their voices now reverberated in the Western press. Writing in a West German newpaper, Kohout was quite blunt in claiming that the responsibility for "negative acts" did not fall on the Communist Party but on certain "specific people."[53] The same tone was overheard in mid-October at a Slovak writers' conference where apparently it was made quite clear that the arrow was directed at Novotny and his coterie.[54]

A further sign of erosion of totalitarianism in Czechoslovakia was evident from the nolens volens official condemnation of police brutality evinced during the clash between the police and Prague students in the demonstrations of November, 1967. What began as a protest against wretched living conditions was soon spearheaded into a full-fledged political confrontation. The students' exasperation was aroused by the violence with which the police attempted to suppress the demonstration.

In the meantime, the calls for democratization did not subside. One of the more interesting reports was that of a roundtable discussion on the prospects of democracy, organized by the Slovak Party daily.[55] The chief speaker was Mlynar and his views could be directly related to those he expressed a year earlier in an article that we have previously mentioned. In his opening statement he stressed that democratization of the Czechoslovak body politic could not be an empty slogan, for without it, it will become increasingly difficult to verify whether decisions made were in the interest of society. He suggested that the representative organs of government were not really representative, for to be so they would have to stand for the interests of the people whom they represented. He spoke of offering a slate of candidates in elections, of the need for the Party not to identify itself directly with government agencies, and of the "undesirability of certain functions being exercised by a single center of power." Some of the problems solved by "bourgeois democracies" were rejected or ignored in Czechoslovakia--to its detriment. Some guarantees of democracy were lost. Mlynar also raised the vital subject of workers' autonomy within the context of the economic reform and of the desirability for workers to control managerial activity. He raised the issue of social organizations formed on a voluntary basis which would exert pressure and safeguard special interests in forming the political line--providing a feedback to the government and the Party. What was involved--he said--was the entire concept of the political regime; the free expression of opinions and its pressure on policy. The point is not that everything should be subject to debate, but that when a real issue arose, there should be "a real possibility of discussion." The limiting of democracy begins when certain questions become taboo and may not even be raised, although society more or less clearly feels that something is amiss.

In the discussion that ensued, Andrej Lantay, a deputy director of the Economics Institute of the Slovak Academy of Sciences, underlined the need for democratization which has been brought to the fore by the economic reform. He was supported in this view by Jan Uher, of the Philosophical Institute, who bluntly pointed to the "conflict" between political and economic management. He called for setting up a "system of guarantees" to ensure that the democratic principles develop on the basis of their own legalities which could not be overturned by any individuals or institutions.

A POWER STRUGGLE

At the end of October, 1967, the CC met in another Plenary Session devoted, according to official press releases, mainly to ideological problems. The meeting was shrouded in secrecy and only a brief report appeared in the press.

According to reports circulating in the West, the question of Novotny's replacement had already been raised at the October Plenary Session. The disenchantment of the intellectuals and the stepping up of their critical efforts; the wrangles between the authorities and the restive writers; the disapproval of the existing state of affairs expressed by the frustrated students; and the rocking of the boat by the Slovak nationalists--all these were warning signals of the growing popular discontent with Novotny's policies. An increasing number of CC members had a change of heart or realized that the winds were blowing from a different direction. Their critical voices became more numerous, their tone of criticism was sharper, and above all they demonstrated a willingness to act. The situation was a remarkable demonstration of the changing face of the totalitarian Communist regime, where the previously impotent public opinion exerted an influence on the leadership's attitudes.

In a report on Bavarian State Radio on January 5, 1968, Heinz Hofmann described a tussle between Novotny and Dubcek at the October Plenum, wherein the latter was supposed to have objected in vigorous terms against the thesis presented toward the end of the Plenum which, according to Dubcek, emphasized the Party's negative role toward the economic reform. Novotny apparently took Dubcek's criticism personally and retorted by hurling at him the epithet of bourgeois nationalist. But this had the effect of rallying the Slovak members of the Presidium and of the CC behind Dubcek. The following day the session was held in camera and a formal demand for Novotny's dismissal as First Secretary of the Party was lodged. Voices were also reportedly raised to relieve Novotny of his post as President of the Republic. The session was suspended to allow Novotny and his retinue to attend the Soviet Fiftieth Anniversary celebrations. But Dubcek was not included in the delegation--a tactical error on Novotny's part--allowing him to muster forces for Novotny's ouster. Another meeting of the CC was planned for December 13, ostensibly to discuss the economic situation which was given press coverage, while the power struggle going on at the Presidium, which had been in session almost continually since the beginning of December, remained secret. Apparently, at the last vote taken before December 8, Novotny was supported only by Otakar Simunek, the Czechoslovak representative to CMEA.

The unheralded visit on December 8, 1967, by Leonid Brezhnev strengthened speculations in the West that some top-level changes were imminent. But not much credit was attached to them, for Novotny had proven to be a master at weathering the storms which had assailed him and at imperturbably surviving a number of such rumors. Brezhnev's visit was interpreted as meant to lend support to

Novotny. A fortnight earlier an editorial in Rude pravo commemorated the tenth anniversary of Novotny's accession to the Presidency by mildly extolling his rule.[56] It was a weak effort to bolster a rapidly failing popularity--if that term could ever have been applied to Novotny.

Brezhnev's visit was officially announced as having been in response to an invitation from the CC, but unofficially it came probably in response to Novotny's distressed call to Moscow. Brezhnev urged his Czechoslovak comrades to proceed with circumspection and to desist from fanfare and rash decisions. This had the effect of realigning the votes from the previous 8:2 to a deadlock of 5:5 which made it impossible for the Presidium to suggest a clear-cut line of action to the CC. The second plenary session of the power struggle was thus postponed until December 19.

According to all published material, this session dealt with the state of the economy and with a revision of plans for 1968 and for the remainder of the current FYP, as we have seen in Chapter 7. But the Western press, including the Communist papers,[57] reported that the crucial issue of the session was the changing of the guard. The session was apparently conducted in an unusually democratic manner. An exhaustive and outspoken debate took place where as many as twenty-two CC members were given the floor. It was apparent that an overwhelming majority was demanding Novotny's resignation, at least from his Party post. Reportedly, for the first time since 1945, the CC fully exercised its prerogatives. The undaunted and untrammeled discussion was reminiscent of Western democratic procedure and may yet prove to be an unhappy precedent for many a minor local functionary. But apparently difficulties were encountered in agreeing on a successor to Novotny. To this end, a commission, comprising the Presidium members and representatives of the eleven regions, was appointed. The Plenum was then adjourned until the beginning of January, 1968.

The final CC Plenary Session that was to resolve

the power struggle reconvened on January 3, 1968. The first speaker was Premier Josef Lenart, who upheld Novotny's policies with special emphasis on his salutary policy in the economic sphere and in the implementation of the reform. Again a remarkable number of speakers were heard; views clashed sharply and a confrontation of the strength of various power groups took place. Novotny's dwindling group of supporters was not to go down without a fight in this last stage of the scramble for power. Finally, at 8 P.M. on January 5, 1968, Czechoslovak Radio announced that Novotny had resigned as First Secretary of the Party (retaining the post of President) and that the CC had unanimously elected Dubcek as his successor. Furthermore, the CC had decided to expand the Presidium by adding four new members. This was interpreted as a move at re-alignment of Presidium members. On the whole, the four new members were considered to be progressives, strengthening Dubcek's hand.

But, as it was later disclosed, Novotny was not to relinquish his grip on power without a fight. Apparently he had engineered a coup in which the highest military figures were implicated, including General Jan Sejna who later defected to the U.S. (Paradoxically, Sejna is the first Communist conservative to have sought asylum in the West, escaping a liberalizing trend in his country. The opposite has usually been the case.) The attempt was successfully thwarted. These revelations were made later by the newly appointed army chiefs. It was also confirmed that a list enumerating the people who were to be arrested after a successful coup had been found. Naturally, the prime target on the list was the new First Secretary.[58]

With Dubcek at the helm of the Party, Czechoslovakia was entering a new era. For one thing, this was a new generation taking over from the old. Dubcek's hands were not tinted by the purges and he would have no need to justify his behavior in the past. For another, his performance as First Secretary of the Slovak Party, in establishing a modus vivendi and, more than that, a rapport with the Slovak intellectual community, augured well for the progressive trend. And then, his being the first Slovak to hold this high post was an indication that Slovakia might at last come into its own as an equal partner with the Czech lands. Just a few days before his accession to power in a New Year's day address in Slovakia, Dubcek emphasized the important role that the Party was called upon to play in this period of "transition toward a new quality of socialist society." In words somewhat reminiscent of Lincoln's Gettysburg Address, he said: "The Party exists for the working people. It serves the working people, and it is the leading political force of the working people."[59] By all accounts, it was expected that the new leadership would lead Czechoslovakia on to firmer grounds for political, social, and economic liberalization. The new regime was expected to make a serious attempt at democratizing and humanizing the socialist system. But the real meaning, scope, content, and timetable of the changes remained moot questions.

One of the major reasons for Novotny's ouster was probably the notorious procrastinations and ill will he had shown toward the economic reform. As we have seen, 1967, the first year of full-scale implementation of the reform, was marked by all sorts of impediments created by the bureaucracy and by Party functionaries. It was also a time when attempts were made to counteract revealed maladjustments by the old administrative methods or by economic devices manipulated so as to enforce the planners' arbitrary decisions. It was the year when most reformers were forced to greatly compromise. It was the year when, by all accounts, the economic reform seemed to be slowly dying. Another Novotny blunder was his failure to placate the dissident intelligentsia and to strike a truce. Moreover, his training, experience, and disposition ran counter to the rising call for democratization in all other domains. These three main shortcomings of the regime, together with the nationality problem, had given birth to the movement which had deposed Novotny, and, at the same time, they were the issues that Dubcek would have to solve if he were to remain at the center of power.

THE CHANGING OF THE GUARD

Obviously the personnel problem was crucial to the entire situation. With the separation of the Party and state function at the apex, a similar process had to be continued down the hierarchical ladder. Many of the diehard stalwarts of the Novotny regime, whether close to the center of power or only entrenched in posts of local Party functionaries, would have to be swept away by the new winds, in order to ensure that the changes which the new regime would seek to implement would not be frustrated at every stage. Some of the more important personality changes effected in the first half of 1968 were: The post of First Secretary of the Slovak Party, left vacant by Dubcek, was filled on January 23, by Vasil Bilak, who had served under Dubcek as the Chairman of the CC's Ideological Commission. The other personnel changes were slow in coming on the grounds that it would have been unwise to initiate from the start full-scale dismissals and replacements which might have recalled the onerous methods of the previous leadership. By mid-February there was a reshuffle of the CC's Ideological Commission, although Henrych still remained its Chairman. Concurrently new appointments were made to the posts of Head of the CC's Department of State Administration and Chief of the Army Political Headquarters. Vaclav Prchlik, who held the latter job since 1956 and in which he was replaced by his deputy, was apparently a protagonist in the power struggle and had helped squash the military coup which Novotny was preparing with the help of Bohumir Lomsky, the Defense Minister. As such, Prchlik was a reliable ally whom Dubcek entrusted with the important function of heading the CC's Department of State Administration--a vital link between the Party and the government. On March 5, it was announced that Hendrych had been replaced as Chief Party Ideologist by Josef Spacek, a staunch radical, former Party secretary of the Brno region who had exhibited a significant degree of tolerance in cultural affairs and who had aligned himself against Novotny early during the power struggle. Within the next ten days Michal Chudik, Chairman of the Slovak National Council, resigned. An avowed conservative and a puppet of Prague, he was particularly mistrusted by the Slovaks. Mid-March saw the dismissal of the Minister of Interior and Prosecutor General (both tinted by their participation in the purges and in various other unsavory acts).

Then, on March 20, it was learned that the NA Presidium was considering a nonconfidence motion tabled against President Novotny. He had once again demonstrated a remarkable proclivity to hold on to his post in the face of rising pressures throughout the first three months of 1968. Constitutional means were invoked to force his hand. However, Novotny anticipated the NA's decision and resigned on March 22. On March 29, the first day of the CC Plenum, Novotny was forced to resign from the Presidium. Thus, an important rallying point for conservative forces, personified by Novotny, was removed, and the forces obstructing the reform were considerably weakened. Concurrently a considerable number of functionaries both at the national and regional levels were removed from office. On March 30, the 73-year-old General Ludvik Svoboda was elected President of the Republic by the NA. By all accounts, the popular choice was Cestmir Cisar who was probably considered too radical for the post and who was vastly disliked in the Soviet Union. Svoboda was thought of as a middle-of-the-roader, who had been discredited and then rehabilitated by the *ancien regime.* His appointment was well received by the Soviet press and was interpreted as a nod toward the Soviet leadership which was growing decidedly hostile to the Prague reformists, as we shall discuss presently. Be that as it may, although Svoboda was not considered to be a staunch reformer, he was not expected to apply any appreciable brakes to the forward march of the *nouveau regime*; he is probably more sympathetic to the new regime's aims than the Soviets have bargained for.

After a prolonged six-day Plenum, the CC emerged

with a face lift of the major Party bodies. Only three members of the Presidium of the ancien regime retained their seats: Dubcek, Cernik, and Kolder. Among the more important deposed members were: Novotny, Lenart, Hendrych, Simunek, and Dolansky. Notwithstanding the presence of some very active reformists (Josef Smrkovsky and Spacek), it would seem that the Presidium membership is rather centrist--at least as judged by past performance, which is a far from adequate yardstick in the present Czechoslovak turmoil.

Contrary to the past, spheres of responsibility were delineated for the CC secretaries by the Presidium on April 16, 1968. Dubcek took over the areas of Party organization, defense, and security. Cisar was made responsible for science, education, culture, and mass information media. The conservative former Chairman of the SPC and thereafter Minister of Transport, Alois Indra, was to be answerable for Communist activities in the National Front (NF) and in mass organizations in state bodies. Kolder was entrusted with watching over the Party's economic policy and heavy industry. Kolder may probably be classified as a conservative in politics and as a moderate liberal in economic matters. Lenart, who was rather a moderate in Novotny's regime, but aligned himself with the forces of retrogression during the changeover, perhaps, inter alia, because he feared the loss of his post, was placed in charge of international relations and Party education. Stefan Sadovsky was to report on agriculture, food, light industry, and the Party's financial affairs.

Again, if such an epithet as centrist could at all be applied, then it would probably fit the majority (with the exception of some very resolute reformers) of the members of the new government formed early in April, 1968. Cernik, probably strongly committed to reform, replaced Lenart as premier. He is the only Party Presidium member to hold an exalted government post. Although he might have been partly responsible for the fumbling of the economic reform in 1967 as Chairman of the SPC, his utterances have often implied that he had to contend with strong reactionary forces and that he was acting under duress. His present appointment would indicate a renewed foremost attention to economic reform. This is also borne out by the appointment of Ota Sik--who needs no introduction to the readers of this book and whose dedication to economic reform and uncompromising fighting spirit are exemplary--as one of the five deputy premiers. We might mention here parenthetically that the omission of Academician Sik from the Party Presidium disillusioned many reformers. Another controversial and colorful figure among the deputy premiers is Gustav Husak, a prewar Communist and erstwhile Slovak bourgeois nationalist sentenced to a life term, released only in 1960, rehabilitated in 1963, but not readmitted to the political limelight by the Novotny regime. Another Slovak deputy premier is Peter Colotka, a liberal and a specialist in jurisprudence. One of the foremost Party critics of the manner with which the economic reform had been implemented in 1967, Lubomir Strougal, was also appointed deputy premier. Finally, Frantisek Hamouz, the former Minister of Foreign Trade, whose record was not particularly untarnished, was promoted to the post of deputy premier. Specific duties of the premier and of his deputies were also outlined as follows: Cernik - defense, security, and foreign affairs; Colotka - legislation; Sik - elaboration and implementation of economic reform; Hamouz - foreign trade and CMEA; Husak - constitution, social organs, and church affairs; and Strougal - Chairman of the Economic Council.

Josef Smrkovsky, a decided reformist, was named Chairman of the NA. Jiri Hajek, the former Education Minister, replaced the discredited Vaclav David as Minister of Foreign Affairs. Vladimir Kadlec, the rector of the Prague School of Economics, took over the post of Education Minister. Miroslav Galuska, a moderate reformer, replaced Karel Hoffman as Minister of Culture and Information. Josef Pavel, the new Minister of Interior, has had some experience along this line. In 1948 he was at the head of the people's militia. In 1951, while he was

Deputy Minister of Interior, he was arrested and given a life sentence. Rehabilitated in 1955, he was kept at a distance from politics. The new Defense Minister, Martin Dzur, had also been a victim of the purges. But he had been fully rehabilitated and since 1961 had served as Deputy Defense Minister. In this capacity he opposed the military coup.

Before examining more concretely the program mapped out by the new leadership, let us consider the period immediately following the changing of the guard and let us glance at some of the immediate solutions which clearly indicated the direction to be pursued and at some of the demands emanating from all spheres.

DEMOCRACY IN THE CZECHOSLOVAK SETTING

First, what attitude was taken in the cultural sphere and what was done to redress the relationship with the writers? Early in January, a substantially softened cultural policy was in the offing. The political editor of the Party daily rapped the knuckles of the MCI for its administrative interference, intimidation, and intolerance in cultural affairs. A policy of tolerance for cultural expression was the keynote for this article.[60]

On January 24, 1968, the CC of the CWU elected its officers: Professor Eduard Goldstuecker as Chairman and Miroslav Valek and Jan Prochazka as Deputy Chairmen, indicating the progressive course. Goldstuecker, who in the past was a somewhat moderate promoter of progressive ideas, has proven to be particularly intent on curtailing censorship. Valek is Chairman of the SWU and could be assessed as a moderate progressive. The real asset for the revisionists was the appointment of Prochazka. Milan Kundera, a revisionist, was also named to the CWU's Presidium. Literarni listy (edited by Hamsik and the editorial board of the old Literarni noviny) would become the new periodical of the CWU. Goldstuecker outlined the aims of the new weekly:

to support anything progressive and enlightening and to serve as a political forum.[61] At the same time Literarni noviny announced its rechristening into Kulturni noviny. In promulgating its editorial policy, it declared that it had no intention of serving as the mouthpiece of the MCI, nor of serving as a platform for conservative views, nor, for that matter, of acting for any group interest. It invited writers and journalists of all shades of opinion to contribute their polemics.[62]

Goldstuecker made it public that the CWU would appeal to the President of the Republic for clemency in Jan Benes' case, who, incidentally, was released from prison in March. On February 3, Goldstuecker communicated that the writers were undaunted in their determination to play a key role in political life. The CWU had, according to him, gone on record in requesting the Party's re-examination of the expulsion of Vaculik, Klima, and Liehm. Furthermore, he was reported to have claimed that the CWU intends to meet at a special congress in the fall of 1968 and that one of the key items on the agenda would be the selection of five candidates to the NA who would represent the CWU's platform at the November, 1968, elections.[63]

On February 16, the Ideological Commission of the Party's CC pledged itself to fight against bigotry and denounced administrative measures as ineffectual in resolving ideological polemics. The Commission was directed by the CC's secretariat to re-evaluate the entire approach to the June, 1967, Congress of Writers.

On February 14, at a meeting of the Czech section of the CWU, it was decided to appeal to the Party CC and the NA for help in resolving the difficulties encountered with the MCI in negotiating the practical issues for the new publication. The meeting also recommended that the CWU appeal for the full revision of all political trials.

The appointment of Spacek early in March as the Party's chief ideologist was another victory for the writers. Concurrently the Party Presidium charged the Premier to appoint another member of government, instead of the Minister of Interior, responsible for censorship. The MCI, in conjunction with the Union of Journalists, was charged to submit suggestions for amending the press law. The Presidium rescinded its own resolution (1966) which gave the censors powers exceeding those delineated in the press law. The trend was definitely for censorship to be confined to only military and state secrets which were to be kept at the source. Notwithstanding the curtailment of censorship on March 6, it was reported only a few days later that familiar abuses of the censors' powers had again cropped up, this time in relation to the Slovak newspaper Praca.[64] The reformers' spirit was well caught by Cisar when he said: "We regard preliminary censorship as an undignified institution in the conditions of socialism; it must be definitely cancelled."[65]

On April 5, the CC Plenary session revoked the measures that the Party had taken in the fall of 1967 against Vaculik, Klima, Kohout, Liehm, and Kundera, and proposed a re-evaluation of Prochazka's case. Yet another victory was scored by the revisionist writers in the dismissal of the notorious Stalinist Ladislav Stoll from his post as Director of the Institute of Czech Literature at the CAS and his replacement by Felix Vodicka, a progressive scholar. An enlarged scope for cultural expression became apparent from the decision of the CC of the CWU to publish a daily, Lidove noviny, which has a history dating back to the 19th century as a tribune for the liberal Czech intelligentsia. Literarni listy was to become its Sunday supplement. Moreover, Tvar, the ill-fated young writers' periodical, was to be resuscitated.

Meanwhile, some of the controversial issues raised in the cultural magazines in the past few years, which had so angered the ancien regime, were being more freely and forcefully aired in a variety of media, ranging from the Party press to radio and television--a veritable flood of soul-searching.

Among the issues most frequently raised was that of democratization.

In a most outspoken and rather prophetic article, written before Novotny's deposition and published the day of the announcement, Milan Huebl--a former prorector of the Party School of Politics, dismissed in 1964 from that post on Novotny's orders, and then promoted to rector by Dubcek on April 2, 1968--accentuated demands for institutional guarantees for the ruled to be able to exercise control over the rulers and to possess the power to change them. He called for the need to verify the skills and make-up of the leadership before entrusting it with the guidance of society.

> In order to avoid fresh disappointments and unrealized hopes and dreams, there must be an examination of what was lacking in the concept behind the activity of the previous unsuccessful leaders.

He emphasized that new policies and concepts cannot be expected to come to fruition unless the leadership is changed, for the <u>ancien regime</u> has far too deep roots in its previous ways. But more:

> If the changing of the guard is restricted to those at the apex, without adopting fresh work concepts and without setting up an entire network of effective checks and institutional guarantees, it is conceivable that the new leadership might slide into the old rut, leading it into a dead end.

Concurrently, Huebl demanded a separation of the executive, legislative, and judicial functions, which would enable society, at least to a certain extent, to exercise control over its mechanisms.[66] He also warned of the harm that comes of combining the various powers within <u>one agency</u>, and even worse, of entrusting them in the hands of a <u>single person</u>.[67] A week later, Husak, who was soon to be appointed deputy premier, fully backed Huebl's call for guarantees, lauded Dubcek's accession to the

Party leadership, and expressed the hope that the expectations aroused in 1968 will not prove illusory:

> Today's European wants to know what is going on in his state, he wants to participate in the decisions about his future and living conditions, he wants to elect his leadership, and then, depending on the leadership's actions, he wants to be able to praise or criticize it, or to replace it; in short he wants the constitutional principles--which affirmed that "the people are the source of all power"--to be reflected in daily and concrete practice.[68]

The call for democratization was echoed in a Rude pravo editorial, even if the reverberation was much less intense. Oldrich Svestka declared that essentially the "class conflict" had been resolved and that it was now time to devote all energies to solving the manifold issues of "micro-relations"--the daily concerns of the individuals.[69] A few days later the echo of democratization was picked up in an appeal for a wider participation of workers in management, without, however, offering specific suggestions as to just how this could be implemented.[70]

Coming back to the fray, Mlynar expounded on the historical development of the ancien regime and its raison d'être.[71] It came into being at a time when its hold over the population had to be maintained by strength and the centralist command over the economy had to be consolidated. The political system was conceived to ensure that a single interest, expressed in central command, should prevail without opposition. "Thus the logic of the whole system rested on the requirement that directives be executed, rather than that decisions be made in a democratic way." Hence, the people's participation was reduced to participation in execution rather than in decision-making. In these circumstances, control meant the verification of the directives' execution, rather than the control over the correctness of directives.

Such a situation was obviously conducive to tendencies for concentrating power in the hands of an ever-growing minority, nay, virtually in the hands of a single individual. Therefore, these tendencies cannot be explained away by blaming the individuals alone and remedy cannot be sought in simply replacing them. Such a solution would only skim the surface of the problem and would not reach its roots.

In attacking the roots, Mlynar raised many of the paramount problems to which a number of reformists had addressed themselves and to which we shall return throughout. As such, his contribution can serve as a guidepost in assessing the development of progressive political thought during these turbulent months.

Not only should "society as a whole" be granted the status of an independent political agent, but social groups, common interest groups, and the individual should attain this status. The status should be safeguarded so that no group or individual should be able to subjugate the others and to consider them as "levers of transmission" and as "objects of government." The rights of groups and individuals must be guaranteed so "these rights of citizens can really be exercised." Recognition of the independent identity of the various elements in the political system is a first step to creating guarantees against concentration of power. These elements and various people's interests, if threatened by a monopoly of power, should be permitted to resist concentration of decision-making. This principle is to be infused into all strata of relationships: people and organizations, organization and government, politics and public opinion, etc. There was more than a hint of the need for an organized voice representing minority interests--a loyal opposition:

> Guarantees must be provided, assuring within each political organ (be it party, social organizations, the state's representative bodies, etc.) recognition not only of the "whole" as the only agent, but a possibility for the minority to express its opinions,

> interests, and proposals, so that the minority (down to the individual) also possesses its own identity... Guarantees must be provided assuring that though bound to execute the majority's decisions, there can be no license to suppress, eliminate, or liquidate the minority as an agent of political activity.

Further, Mlynar insisted on mutual control of the various components of the governing systems within every component of the political system; i.e., the state, the Party, and every social organization. The division of power and responsibility affords the real possibility of control of one component by another of the same organization (say, control of the executive by the elective body). He was adamant about the harm of concentrating all kinds of security agencies and of enforcement agencies within a single body. Especially in this sector there was urgent need for a system of mutual controls, "a system where independent courts, subject to no one but the law, would play the decisive role."

Yet, the recurring question was whether personnel changes were sufficient assurances that the political system will be regenerated. As such, the changes were accepted as a first step, but definitely not as the final solution. According to Michal Lakatos, a political scientist at the CAS, to prevent domination of one group or one individual over others, policy-making must be channeled to other levels: i.e., the direct organizations of citizenry or the community of citizens. There is no democracy without such a community of citizens and without democracy the community is doomed. Without democracy socialism cannot accomplish what it proclaims, opening up an unbridgeable gap between word and deed.

The question posed by Lakatos was: Wherein are the guarantees to be found? In his opinion democratic government cannot be guaranteed by the state, but must rest within the community of citizens. These guarantees would find expression in the political power wielded by the interest groups and political parties functioning as independent agents whose line of thought or action is not mapped out in advance by some supra-power. Such organizations must be founded on freedom of the individuals to organize and they must be allowed freedom to form and sway public opinion.

This would also be the basic premise for an unfettered functioning of the government's representative bodies. People must be afforded free choice of their representatives from among candidates who cannot be appointed by organizations outside the community of citizens. Such representatives cannot be fed a preconceived political line, but must convey that line derived from the community of citizens.

And what about the Party's role in such a scheme of things? Lakatos endows the Party with the role of vanguard, but only if it does not thereby emasculate the other organizations and other political parties:

> To start with, the Party would have to realize its leading role vis-à-vis the organizations of the community of citizens not by the administrative means adopted by a superior organization vis-à-vis all the subordinate organizations, but as one of our society's political organizations...[72]

In a rather retrospective article wherein she decried the abuses, illegalities, and callousness of the Czechoslovak regime since 1948, Zora Jesenska, a prewar Communist and distinguished author, described democracy as a state wherein, notwithstanding the rule of the majority, there are built-in safeguards to shield the weaker from the stronger. And it is the weaker who are competent to judge whether democracy really exists. As she herself pointed out, she was calling for an introduction of democracy <u>tout court</u>; a democracy under conditions of socialism, i.e., without "any privileges due to property ownership," but also without necessarily implying, as others were wont to, that it would afford more freedom than the classical democracies. Her stand on this issue is particularly noteworthy in view of the official pressures to recognize that the socialist democracy that Czechoslovakia was adopting was infinitely superior to the more crass variety of "bourgeois democracy."

Like Lakatos, she would not trust the constitutional, legal, institutional, and other guarantees alone. They could be altogether too easily subverted by shrewd rulers. She placed her trust in the political maturity of the ruled and in their determination to remain free and to control their destiny. Such guarantees were lacking and their realization could not be foreseen overnight, for dictatorship had altogether too successfully extirpated the required qualities. But there was hope. Jesenska could not foresee a return to the old regime; it was only possible for the new regime to either halt the trend and to be complacent about a pseudo-democracy or to go all out and instate a genuine democracy.[73]

The Lakatos-Jesenska theme was picked up by Vladimir Manak, a Slovak journalist. He posed the crucial question whether the ruling circles were aware that the call for democratization was born in the midst of the progressive citizens, regardless of Party allegiance, that the Party had grasped it as a social force, and that it was then simply doing the unavoidable if it wanted to remain at the forefront. Because, if the Party would not admit that the present process of democratization was a direct result of social pressures, then the process would continue at the grass roots in spite of the Party. All the other reasons for the democratization process--such as its being a maneuver in order to get the economy moving again, or its being simply a power struggle exchanging an old set of rulers for a new set--can only further undermine the people's trust in the Party. For, after all, is it not the same Party that has been responsible for all the abuses and ills of the past twenty years which are now being vented?

> What reason is there for trusting the Communists--a Party which, within the last twenty years, made itself responsible for everything done in this country and which has conceded that it has fulfilled its leading role very ineffectively? Should people have confidence in the Party because it inaugurates democratization again by itself, of its own initiative, without any outside pressures?[74]

One of the main issues that preoccupied many commentators was the role of the Party. It was often heard that the Party would retain its leading role in society, but the interpretation of just such a role ranged over an entire gamut of opinions. For example, if the Party is to lead effectively it must divorce itself from daily interference, and its apparatus, instead of being a network of tentacles, reaching into every center of activity, should be transformed into a well-trained board of experts and advisors to the elected Party organs.[75] The Party's leading role should not be confused with the idea that it represents all citizens and is their mouthpiece. It cannot have a monopoly on criticism.[76] Another radical comment was that the leading role must be granted to the Party by the non-Communists--a sort of vote of confidence. This role cannot be taken as something immutable. On the contrary, the Party should strive daily to win the people's confidence.[77] However, not even all progressives agreed on the essence of this role and it was not uncommon to meet with basically the idea that, while with social organizations the Party should merely guide by good example, in the relation to government, political, and economic organs, it is a power factor.[78] On the other hand, for those who adhered to the orthodox supremacy of the Communist Party, the crucial issue was how the Party could retain a monopoly of effective political control and simultaneously change the political style of its work so that it would rule to a larger extent by persuasion and consent, rather than by sheer coercion and dictatorship.

A point of attack was the lack of democracy within the Party: the deceptive monolithic unity that it always presented to the people. For a short time in January, 1968, the curtain lifted and it became evident that Party members were thrashing out diametrically opposed views. But the curtain was again slowly coming down on a new unity--true, of a more progressive variety--threatening to stifle free thought and expression once again. Was this altogether advisable?[79]

Just as it was being echoed in all commentaries that the Party cannot wield a monopoly of power and that the role of government should be invigorated, the relationship of the highest organs within the Party was also being questioned. Smrkovsky, who emerged as one of the more outspoken proponents of the liberalization trend, warned that the Presidium can no longer behave as the supreme policy-maker, that it is merely an executive organ, and that it is the CC that is the highest organ between congresses.[80]

Now, what about this popular subject of division of power between Party and state and the strengthening of the latter's bodies? It first started when publicly the reasons given for Novotny's demotion in the Party revolved around the pressing need for a separation of state and Party organs. The idea caught on immediately and calls were sounded for further separation. Some of the government agencies which had been entirely under the Party's aegis should be liberated.[81] The resounding call was for letting the government govern and for a separation of the executive, legislative, and judiciary. The government agencies should be responsible to the NA and if the NA should find fault with the government's or individual minister's activity, a vote of nonconfidence could take care of that.[82]

Obviously, such a trend revived the sore question of elections. Sharp attacks were launched from all corners against the fixing of quotas, the selection of candidates from narrow circles of functionaries, the nomination of candidates, etc.[83] One of the major issues was that of reviving the population from its apathy toward the entire process of choosing representatives.[84] People interviewed on the street for the Public Affairs program which appeared on Czechoslovak Television on February 29, 1968, exhibited a remarkable disillusionment with the right to vote. One of the more seething indictments of the election practices was found in a reader's letter to the editor of Kulturni noviny, clearly indicating what was to be done. In the first place there was a feeling that all had been decided already. The candidates were part of a coterie of "little Caesars." Secondly, candidates were not known beforehand by their electorate:

> I am just a pawn which is supposed to nod in assent, throw a piece of paper in a ballot box and go--everything proceeds without me, no one pays attention to me anyway--why should I bother?[85]

Pleas were heard for allowing free pre-election debates and campaigning so that the result should be a true endorsement of the candidate by his electorate. Moreover, a representative government would require the candidates' responsibility to the electorate and not to the small circle that had nominated them. This, of course, is closely linked with the idea of a wider choice of candidates and of their representing particular interest groups and even different platforms--a point to which we shall return later.

The critics were quite articulate about the preposterous lack of information which had created a credibility gap resulting, in a sense, in an alienation of the population from the liberalization movement--a disbelief of the regime's total commitment to the trend. For one thing, the insecurity stemmed from what was in many quarters considered to be only a turtle-paced liberalization. Few things had yet changed. Even the personnel changes were not taking place fast enough.[86] "Somewhere deep in our minds there is still the fear that there might be a reversal again. Only deeds can dispel this fear."[87] There were half-expressed fears that the trend might be halted, that the half-measures might become calcified, and that the system would fail to regenerate itself by injecting that necessary degree of flexibility which would permit bringing it to its logical conclusion in the future.[88] In addition, the promised democracy and freedom were doubted by some on the grounds that the conservatives were not being allowed to have their say. Once again only the ideas of the winning side in the power struggle were being propagandized. Would this not lead the system to be ensconced in another ideological strait jacket?[89]

The information gap was being deplored on all sides. Aside from criticism of the <u>ancien regime's</u> policy of secretiveness, a sore spot was the lack of disclosures on what had actually happened at the three plenary sessions which resolved the power struggle. Aside from the outcome and from what leaked out through a variety of unofficial channels, scant information on the discussions and attitudes of various CC members had been offered for public consumption. "We knew precious little about what actually happened at the Central Committee sessions and we had to rely on our instinct."[90] And worse, much of the information provided to local Party members was twisted and interpreted according to the stand taken by the local CC members.[91] The demands for opening up the clogged information channels emphasized the need for a dialogue--for information also flowing upward providing a sort of feedback to the upper echelons, enabling them to keep their finger on the pulse at the lower levels.[92]

Apparently there was yet a wide division among CC members as to the extent of information that should be allowed to permeate the lower echelons. The reticence evinced by some officials was interpreted as an attempt to keep the rank and file in the dark, thus inarticulate, and unable to exercise its right of recalling its representatives.[93] Conceivably, the conservative elements would be on the losing side with a wider dissemination of information. Concurrently, such dissemination would strengthen the hand of the progressives and would allow the new regime to get rid of the Novotny supporters who were thwarting the progressive moves. On the other hand, the disclosures of sharp divergence of positions at the higher Party level would tend to undermine the impression of a new united front within the Party which the new leaders were striving to present.

Be that as it may, throughout this fateful Czechoslovak spring in mid-winter there were recurring demands for literally "purging" the Party, government agencies, and other organizations at all levels of the old stalwarts. Smrkovsky called for a thoroughgoing reassessment of people occupying important posts from top to bottom of the Party and of the state hierarchical ladders, applying the criterion "who is right and who is not, who is progressive and who is not." He insisted on a veritable removal of the "layers of the past."[94] With his usual verve, Radoslav Selucky fired a broadside at the _nomenclatura_ system--a system which had vested in certain Party agencies the power of determining the suitability of individuals for government or business posts and even of those to be elected to the committees of common interest groups and social organizations. This sectarian cadre policy had prevented well-qualified people from ascending to certain posts. How could such people who had determined the fate of others be allowed to remain in their posts? Moreover, he asserted that those who do not have faith in what they are doing would bungle the job. Hence, the turncoats would undermine the new policy and, what is worse, the population would tend to lose confidence in the new policy if the names of the turncoats are associated with it. Those people should be transferred to less influential positions and thereby prevented from thwarting the new policies.[95]

Yet such dismissals presented an important dilemma for the new leadership. How could it smugly denounce the past excesses of the _ancien_ *regime*, the indiscriminate purges of people who dared to oppose its policies, and the *nomenclatura* system, and in the same breath demand the resignation of all those who did not support it? How could it then lay claim to democratization?[96] Indeed, the slow-paced process of personnel changes might be attributed to the distaste of applying hastily the methods of the discredited regime and thus of undermining the confidence of the rank and file. And yet it is not altogether inconceivable that the conservatives were attempting to turn the new regime's slogans against it, thus trying to remain in their well-entrenched bastions.

Dramatic last-minute loyalty switching was yet another way chosen by the conservatives to protect their positions. The clamor for resignations was not heeded. And how could it be when so many of those in executive posts all down the line did not have sufficient professional qualifications to find other jobs?

> The nation... does not recognize the supersonic speed with which those who always want to lead and to be at the forefront manage to transform themselves. Apparently yesterday's dogmatists, opportunists, and frauds were nothing but disguised illegal democrats.[97]

The bitter and derisive attacks on the turncoats became more personal, with many of the better-known dogmatists, who were suddenly preaching democracy, pointed at personally.[98] Or was it perhaps a gibe at the regime for letting turncoats be the spokesmen of new policies while those who (like the outspoken writers of the Fourth Congress) had been at the vanguard of reformism were receding into the background?

PRESSURE GROUPS AND LOYAL OPPOSITION

Meanwhile, demands were increasing for letting pressure groups (so-called common interest groups) become an effective countervailing power to the Party. Such interest groups would be a first step in the creation of a democratic political mechanism.[99] Even though the Party would rely on its members to defend ideology in these groups, it should desist from appointing its hand-picked men to lead these groups.[100] And what about the emergence of such groups?

One of the earliest stirrings could be detected among the Prague students. They demanded the right to withdraw from the Youth Federation and to organize an independent group, reviving the former University Students' Union, on the grounds that the federation was hostile in its present position toward the students' interests. At first, the CC of the Youth Federation conceded that such a new organization could only be in the nature of an academic club, but definitely not an independent union. Demands for federalization of the student movement were also heard.[101]

Another interesting development was the ferment, although cautious, that was taking place in the trade unions. Calls were heard to revitalize the trade unions, to reinvest them in reality with the powers with which they were endowed on paper, and to extricate them from their subservient position.[102] The contradictory dual function of trade unions--1) to protect the workers' interests and 2) to be answerable to the state for implementing its economic policy in enterprises and for the enterprises' performance--was debunked.[103] Even though wider powers for trade unions in striving for improved working conditions, higher wages, etc., were invoked,[104] it is surprising that little was said at the early stages of discussion about the possibilities of revitalizing the trade unions to participate effectively in management--something along the lines of the role played by the workers' councils in Yugoslavia. But the trade unions were called upon to become an important factor of public control over those in power. Moreover, the gap between the views and aspirations of the rank and file and of the leadership of trade unions was pointed to, with an appeal to effect some personnel changes.[105]

As with other groups, the trade union leadership should not be imposed from outside, with a wider participation of non-Communists that can no longer be controlled by some artificial ceilings.[106] Obviously, here too the progressives collided with the conservatives. On March 12, the Chairman and two secretaries of the CCTU resigned, thus removing a major opposition block to the progressive forces. Ten days later, the Plenary Session of the CCTU opened with a strong attack on the old leadership; at the centralistic, bureaucratic, and autocratic methods used; at the over-all disregard for members' interests; and at the lack of support for the progressive forces of the new regime. Karel Polacek was elected Chairman. However, speakers the following day denounced this election both because it was carried out by acclamation and because they claimed that Polacek was not qualified for the post. They had support among workers, for about 70,000 workers in Prague threatened to strike in opposition to Polacek's election. On the whole, the session did not resolve the future position of trade unions, which presumably would come to a head at the nationwide conference of trade unions. However, one of the more promising moves in trade unions occurred at the metalworkers' union which, according to Radio Bratislava of March 27, 1968, has demanded autonomy in management, underlining that it would resort to strike in its fight for its members' interests. Similarly, on the basis of freedom of association proclaimed in the Action Program, as we shall see later, there were further intimations of independent unions. Thus, it was announced that an independent federation of locomotive crews might be formed outside the CCTU.[107]

Aside from the convulsions that were shaking the existing groups, new pressure groups were mushrooming. Thus, for example, in mid-March a meeting of the former members of the Czechoslovak Army abroad during World War II was held. Presumably the meeting was illegal, for it violated the provisions of the statutes of the League of Fascist Fighters.[108] Then, on March 31, the non-Communist victims of the postwar purges combined in an association called Club 231 (after the number of the Penal Code's paragraph under which they had been sentenced). The purpose of the association was to seek a prompt and honorable redress of the hardships its members had endured. Club 231 has been under fire from many sides. Rude pravo has claimed on a number of occasions that it was infiltrated by many people who had been justly sentenced and who were yearning for a return to capitalism. This and similar clubs added to the Soviet disquietude with the political situation and was probably used as a pretext by the Soviets in their propaganda about a Czechoslovak counterrevolution.

Early in April, it was announced that an informal meeting was held in Prague to discuss the establishment of a Club of Engaged Nonpartisan People and an application for registration was filed with the Prague municipal committee. The organization was based on support for democratic socialism. One of its aims was to run its own candidates for election to national committees and to the NA. The precedent of a nonpartisan organization was set when a Circle of Independent Writers was set up within the CWU as a counterpart to the union's Communist Party cell.

The logical conclusion of the demands for invigorating common interest groups and investing them with wider powers to stand up for their members was the shifting of that call on to a political plane; i.e., for the emergence of demands for one or more political parties. True enough, ever since February, 1948, a NF had existed which, besides incorporating groups like the Youth Federation, included the People's Party and the Socialist Party and towering above them was the supreme commander of the NF--the Communist Party. However, these parties were mere puppets of the Communist regime.[109] "Their public activity was usually restricted to welcoming various decisions and resolutions of the Communist Party." Moreover, the Communists themselves had always brushed off these phantom parties lightly. True, of late these parties have been active in the general regenerative spirit. There too some of the old guard has been replaced and some rather outspoken articles have appeared in their official organs. But once again they have been following in the footsteps of the Communist Party and have been faithfully conforming to the line. They still do not have a platform of their own on which they could firmly stand, nor, it is claimed, have they the people who can work out such a program in the near future.[110] Such parties are "incapable of assuming the role of an opposing partner, abstracting from the honorable role of opposition to his majesty--socialism."[111]

The rising call for an opposition party among the more progressive and vocal elements in Czechoslovakia should obviously not be interpreted as unanimous. Even among those clamoring loudest for democracy there was some reservation as to the necessity and feasibility of organized political opposition. They were leaning rather to a solution of a single party which allows outside criticism.[112] Among those who raised their voices in support of some sort of loyal opposition the common bond--aside from the recognition that democracy would be best served if some sort of organized mouthpiece for criticism existed--was their acknowledgment that the opposition would remain within the socialist context; i.e., that it would not uphold any class interest nor would it question the public ownership of the means of production. On the whole, the divergence of views could be compartmentalized into three more or less distinct positions. The first, which seems to be rather favored by the Party officials (like Mlynar) who have advocated an opposition, would confine the opposition within the existing framework of the NF and/or would see it arise spontaneously among independent individuals. The second, whose representative spokesmen were Jesenska and Lakatos, would still confine the opposition to the NF, but a resurrected, regenerated, and refurbished NF, with equal partners, where the other parties would not be pushed into subservience and where the Communist Party would play the role of a _primus inter pares_.[113]

The third, on the other hand, assumed the position that democratic guarantees would be totally absent without a fully fledged opposition party. Among them was the playwright Vaclav Havel, a founder of the Circle of Independent Writers within the CWU.

Havel opened his arguments by stressing that the Communist Party cannot be relied upon to be the instigator for the formation of an opposition party, for such a concept has always been anathema to the Communists. He argued that such a party would have to be a strong countervailing force willing and able to contend with the Communists for the helm of government. He went on to discredit the positions taken by the other advocates of an opposition. He rejected the idea that internal party democratization would offer a sufficient guarantee for democracy, mainly because the internal control pressures would become ossified if they were not fed from the outside. Opposition which relies on individuals without an organization is doomed to failure, for it would necessarily fail to capture popular support. Common interest groups, though a step in the right direction, would still be too weak, for, even assuming that their leadership would no longer be appointed by the Communist Party, they would still be infiltrated by Communists. Even though the existing organizations and press of the NF parties would offer a starting point nucleus, these "mummified remnants" are so discredited that to start with them might amount to political suicide. No, what Havel appealed for was a party of equal strength to its Communist counterpart. What he seemed to suggest was the creation (or resurrection) of a party along social democratic lines that would stress the humanistic, individualistic approach which he intimated would appeal to the Czechoslovak youth of today.[114]

It was disclosed that the CC of the CPC had been approached by five members of the preparatory committee for a resurrection of the Social Democratic Party of Czechoslovakia, with a rejection of the 1948 merger with the Communist Party. The CC expressed its opposition on principle to such a revival, for it would lead to a renewal of political strife and to the creation of parties outside the NF.[115]

PURGES AND REHABILITATIONS

The recurring theme throughout these discussions was that of the need to redress, if at all possible, the injustice of the purges--an almost compulsive collective urge to atone. The new regime's attitude toward rehabilitations had also a political underpinning, for the raking over of past inequities was strengthening the new leaders' popularity, simply by finally discrediting the old rulers.

Early in February an editorial in the official Party daily stressed that in order to dispel public incertitude about the new regime's good faith, it was necessary to speedily make amends for the injustices perpetrated in the past not only against the Communists but also against all other citizens.[116] Here and there appeared articles describing the atrocities and bestial treatment of the victims.[117] Much was written about the need to indemnify the victims and appeals were made to use the talents of these people.[118] And what about justice for those who had been forced to interrupt their studies, for those who had not been allowed to enter schools of higher learning because of "ideological deviationism," and finally for those who have been forced into exile? --asked Havel.[119] Eugene Loebl, a former victim, who, as we have seen, had become in recent years one of the most forceful critics of the Novotny regime, emphasized that one of the main issues was to broadcast far and wide the truth of these persecutions so that such monstrosities could never again happen in Czechoslovakia.[120] Justice for the victims was very noble, but should not retribution be meted out to the prosecutors, the judges, the defense attorneys, to all those who knew the truth about this astounding hoax and who kept silent?[121]

To a certain extent the reponsibility for these crimes lies heavily on the shoulders of all Communists who tacitly kept silent.[122] It was not long before Novotny was pointed to as a chief culprit, and that demands were raised for the CC to conduct a full investigation into Novotny's share in the persecutions.[123] At first only allusions were made to the participation of Beria's henchmen in the purges,[124] but they were shortly followed with more specific accusations. Karol Bacilek, the former First Secretary of the Slovak Party, replaced by Dubcek in 1963, and former Minister of National Security, revealed that Anastas Mikoyan had been sent to Prague in 1951 by Stalin to order Klement Gottwald to stage the show trials, bringing with him a sheaf of documents for the frame-up.[125] This revelation was not of a kind to help the already strained Czechoslovak-Soviet relations.

Meanwhile, a Party Rehabilitation Commission was set up to look into the cases of those prosecuted during 1949-54. The later miscarriages of justice were still left in abeyance. None of the members of this Commission was directly involved in the excesses of that era. Both judicial rehabilitation and indemnification were to be carried out later by state bodies. But protests were lodged against the procrastinations on the new law on indemnifications.[126]

Early in June, it was reported that the NA was working on the first of several rehabilitation laws aimed at about 35,000 cases of individuals illegally convicted of sabotage, conspiracy, and treason from 1948 to 1956. Victor Knapp, Chairman of the Constitutional and Legal Committee, predicted that it would take about two years to complete this undertaking. The MF suggested an equivalent of a maximum of $1,250 per annum for indemnification, rejected by the Committee. Obviously, the compensation of the nonjudicial victims, i.e., those dismissed from their posts or prevented from studying, etc., was a much more intricate matter. The Union of Fascist Fighters and the CWU have set up rehabilitation commissions to apply pressure on the Party.[127] Also during the first week of June, the government recommended that special senates be elected by the NA to look into the individual cases. Moreover, it is worth noting that for the first time in twenty years the Minister of Interior reported on the activities of his ministry to the NA's Armed Forces and Security Committee. He mentioned that the Ministry's personnel was being screened for involvement in purges and about 250 officials had left the Ministry in the past few years.[128]

ON FEDERATION

Another gnawing issue, much entangled with the period of purges, has been what to do about the Slovak problem. The postwar solution to the coexistence of the Czech and Slovak nations resulted in the 1945 Kosice Government Program which recognized the Slovak National Council as the representative of state authority in Slovakia and the Slovak Board of Commissioners as an autonomous government. While recognized by many as still affording too little self-government to Slovakia, the Kosice Program was being consistently violated by the regime until it was totally abolished by the 1960 Constitution and the Board of Commissioners was disbanded. The 1960 Constitution legalized the restrictive centralistic approach to Slovak autonomy of Novotny's regime.

As we have previously mentioned, the tide of Slovak dissatisfaction has been consistently rising and has often been interpreted as one of the major causes which spearheaded the power struggle. For example, in the economic field alone, among the many grievances were such economic inequities as the speed and pattern of industrialization, the earmarked and *de facto* investments and other resources, the striking divergencies in the standard of living, outright discrimination, etc. While the industrialization of Slovakia was rapid, it was understood primarily as assistance that a more wealthy relative gives to a poorer one. At the threshold of the 1950's a campaign was initiated by Viliam Siroky, then Deputy Premier, to transfer old industrial equipment from the Czech lands to Slovakia. The Slovaks were apprehensive of getting obsolete equipment and the Czechs were dissatisfied about the closure of factories to be relocated in Slovakia. The process was understood primarily as a Czech subsidy of the development of Slovakia, rather than as a "Slovak contribution to the Czechoslovak national economy."[129]

Dubcek's accession to power elicited considerable uneasiness among the Czechs that the Slovaks were "taking over"--an apprehension which was easily kindled by the complacency and patronizing attitude evinced by many Czechs toward their Slovak compatriots.[130]

There was more than a hint at the advisability of a federative arrangement when Anton Tazky, the Slovak Commissioner for National Committees, suggested that it might be desirable to have corresponding national organs in Slovakia and in the Czech lands.[131] The dismissal of Michal Chudik, a former Prague puppet, from his post as Chairman of the Slovak National Council could be interpreted as making room for a less hampered operation of this body. Just a few days earlier the official daily of the Slovak Party unequivocally demanded full-fledged federation, or what it termed a "symmetric model." The federal system should be set up by reckoning with two national integrated economies. In both constitutionally equal entities corresponding systems should be established of the chief national legislative and executive organs.[132] Then, on March 14, the Presidium of the Slovak National Council determined that a federative arrangement along the lines proposed in _Pravda_ should be established. It further proposed that this resolution be incorporated in the Party's new program and be constitutionally implemented. However, it seemed that the idea of federation hung in a precarious balance for a while, for this declaration was unilateral in that it did not provoke a definitive and unambiguous pronouncement on this matter from the center.[133] The ambiguity of this situation was further underlined when Huebl reported an inverview he had conducted with Frantisek Kriegel, a new member of the Party Presidium, who allegedly answered his probings about the center's attitude to federation by the cavalier advice that the Slovaks should "federalize themselves" if they wanted to, but that the Czechs would certainly not set up parallel organs, thus discounting genuine federation.[134] Simultaneously, veiled warnings were issued to the center that the Slovaks would have to take "some steps" in view of the center's intractable attitude.[135] This was rapidly followed by a direct threat of Slovakia seceding from the Republic and setting itself up as an independent socialist state unless its demands for a federation were met.[136] Possibly these threats were taken seriously for further steps were taken to implement the idea of genuine federation.

Meanwhile the idea of federation was quickly picked up in Moravia where, if not an equal status, a recognition of specific Moravian interests was demanded, without clarifying the specific arrangements sought. But on April 17, the South Moravian regional national committee resolved that Moravia should be constituted as an equal entity in a tripartite federation of Bohemia, Moravia, and Slovakia.[137] However, that idea did not seem to have a fighting chance.

Generally, the Slovak proposals stressed a loose federation, with strong powers vested in the national bodies, whereas the Czechs, understandably, were in favor of a close federation, with strong power vested in the federal bodies. The Slovaks were favoring redistribution of resources and expected from the federal government economic assistance up to 1980. They stipulated equal voting rights on the allocation of central funds for economic development. The Czechs considered 1980 as an unrealistic deadline and parity decision-making as unacceptable. The Slovaks emphasized parity in the composition of key federal organs as a safeguard against the rule of Czechs over the Slovaks. The Czechs promulgated the principle: "one citizen--one vote," stressing that the numerical strength of the Czechs must also be numerically reflected in the central organs. Should the Czech demands be adopted, it would virtually amount to the previous asymmetric relationship as the federal government and the NA would be controlled by the Czech majority and would be stronger than their Czech and Slovak counterparts.

A draft proposal jointly prepared by Czech and Slovak economists attending a conference organized in Bratislava in April by the Ideological Departments of Czechoslovak and Slovak Communist Parties adopted the premises that the Czech and Slovak national organs would be vested with the primary authority and sovereign power. The prerogatives of the federal organs would be derived from and limited by the powers that the original state-creating authority of the national bodies delegated to them. The Czechoslovak economy was viewed as an "integrated synthesis of the two national economies" and uniform principles of planned management were to be applied. Economic unity was to be preserved with a common market, single currency, uniform rate of foreign exchange, free movements of goods and productive agents, identical prime principles of labor law and social welfare, uniform wage and price policies, etc. A nondiscriminatory policy of economic integration and equalization would be followed.[138]

The competence of federal organs in economic matters would entail over-all planning of development and of restructuring of the integrated economy. Foreign economic relations would remain within the purview of the federal organs. The system of plans would include a federal plan and the national plans of the Czech lands and of Slovakia. The budgetary system would be comprised of three independent budgets: the federal, Czech, and Slovak budgets, which would be approved by respective legislative organs.[139]

While it was feared in some quarters that federation might lead to the disintegration of the Slovak and Czech economies, Sik emphasized that the federal arrangements should facilitate the solution of certain specific economic problems and should accelerate the development of Slovakia.[140]

THE ACTION PROGRAM

At the outset of the Action Program (AP), a warning was sounded that it is not a precisely mapped-out plan of action, that it only offers guidelines, and that these guidelines are far from rigid and unalterable. The document in itself is quite remarkable in the sincere and uncompromising commitment to reform, even though a good number of people with various shades of opinion obviously had a hand in drafting it. It offers a distinct counterpart to the Soviet-type brand of Communism, emerging with a specific "Czechoslovak road to socialism." From the radicals' vantage point the AP is a minimum acceptable program. It was seen as a maximum compromise program under the conditions under which it was adopted, with the conservatives still strongly entrenched in positions of power. However, the radicals were hopeful that a more progressive blueprint of action would emerge after the extraordinary fall 1968 Party Congress--about which later.

The program consists of four main divisions: 1) a preamble outlining the aims and nature of the program; 2) by far the most explicit section defining the social and political structure; 3) an economic program resembling in broad lines the new economic model, with some significant amendments; and 4) a rather fluidly defined foreign policy.

1) The AP characterizes the contemporary stage of the transformation of society to socialism where there are no antagonistic classes and where the process of rapprochement of all social groups becomes the main feature of internal development. The planning system hitherto operating has become obsolete. There is an urgent call for changes in the economic system capable of bringing about a transition to intensive growth and to restructuring of the economy. The integration of Czechoslovakia into the world scientific and technical revolution will require broad cooperation among workers, farmers, and the intelligentsia. The prerequisites are a wide scope of public initiative, a frank

exchange of opinions, and democratization of the whole political, social, and economic structure. The opening of old wounds and exposing of past deformations were necessary in order to clear the path for reform.

The program stresses the Party's reliance on the working class, while also underlining the importance of the farmers and the intelligentsia. An equal coexistence of Czechs and Slovaks, with national self-assertion for other minorities, is pointed to as the foundation of a Czechoslovak state. Individuals will be judged by their contribution to the development of the community. Expert qualifications will be commensurately rewarded and the differentiation of incomes is stressed. This should not be interpreted, however, as a new stratification of society.

In a delicate section of the AP, where every effort is made not to convey the impression that there is a hazard of slipping into some variant of a "bourgeois parliamentary democracy," the leading role of the Communist Party is reaffirmed, but with the significant reservation that such a role hinges on the quality of the Party's service to the people and of the people's voluntary support. Instead of wielding its power over the people, the Party must consistently strive to attract them by its actions. As the leading political force, which alone can guarantee the correct development of socialist society, the Party must also exercise corresponding weight and influence in the entire society and in its institutions and organizations. The Party must occupy functions in state, economic, and social organizations, but this cannot be at cross purposes with the principles that the people at large, or various groups, choose their representatives who are responsible to all the people or all the members of the group. Non-Communists must not be given the impression that their rights and freedom are limited by the Party. Contrariwise, they must see in the activity of the Party a guarantee of their rights, freedom, and interests. The Party will promote "down-to-earth" discussions and confrontations of views and be sensitive to the currents of public opinion. Discrimination against non-Party members and the practice of nomenclatura can no longer be tolerated. Decision-making in collective organs must rely on discussion and frank exchange of opinion.

2) The political system must, above all, provide guarantees which would prevent the recurrence of subjectivism and arbitrariness. The program then promised a new constitution and called for replacement of opportunists, nincompoops, and little Caesars, by those who are not power-grabbers, and for a clear delineation of duties, jurisdiction, and responsibilities.

The NF would henceforth participate in state policy-making. The political parties included therein are partners and they act in accordance with the NF's joint political program. However, shattering the expectations of the advocates of loyal opposition, the AP states that the Communist Party considers the NF as a political platform without distinguishing the parties therein as government and opposition from the standpoint of opposition to the government's policy and from that of a power struggle. Hence, the other parties of the NF were once again reduced to subservience, with the significant distinction that they could be more vocal in the future--not a mean achievement in itself.

Social organization (common interest groups) and political parties are not interchangeable. Legal guarantees must be provided for the freedom of assembly and association, so that these organizations can be constituted on a purely voluntary basis without any bureaucratic constraints. Only the law will be the judge as to what is antisocial, forbidden, and punishable. Similar freedoms should apply to the different religious communities. Public opinion on Party policy cannot be elicited and attempts at suppressing popular initiative and criticism cannot be combatted unless freedom of expression and of political and personal rights of citizens is legally guaranteed. The AP also promised a new press law within a short period which would delimit precisely when a state organ can suppress information in the mass media and which would abolish preliminary censorship. Legal guarantees should also provide for freedom of movement, trips and residence abroad, while preventing a braindrain. More legal protection is required for the population's personal and property rights. The rehabilitation of both Communist and non-Communist victims of the purges should be completed.

While upholding the advantages of a federal arrangement, the AP is more than ambiguous for it does not provide for Czech counterparts of the following organs which it proposes should be set up in Slovakia: Slovak National Council as the legislature and the Council of Ministers as the executive authority. This ought to be set up by a constitutional act that would provide a symmetric pattern. State secretaries would be appointed to the central ministries, particularly to the Ministries of Foreign Affairs, of Foreign Trade, and of National Defense.

Two security organs, state security to protect the country from espionage and subversive activity and public security to fight crime and to maintain public order, should be set up to be controlled by the government and the NA. This should guarantee that people who have not engaged in espionage should not have their political views investigated by the state security apparatus.

The Party renounces direct supervision and control of the Youth Federation, but reserves the right to ideological guidance.

3) The economic program was not worked out in detail. Much space was devoted to the acknowledgment of economic dislocations, of the retrogressive effects of the traditional system, and of the need for a radical and consistent application of economic reforms. The transition to intensive development "cannot be achieved by the traditional methods or by partial improvements of imperative planning, but by a basic change of the mechanism of the functioning of the

socialist economy." From the main line it could be gathered that the new regime intends to continue along the principles of the new economic model, but by backing more forcefully its main progressive ideas which have succumbed to the compromises inflicted on it in the practical implementation of 1966 and 1967, and simultaneously by abandoning some of the restrictions imposed in 1966 and in 1967 which had threatened to invalidate the main concepts.

> We are placing great hope into reviving the positive functions of the market as a necessary mechanism of the functioning of socialist economy and for verifying whether the work in enterprises has been expended in a socially useful way. However, we have in mind not the capitalist, but the socialist market, and not its uncontrolled but its regulated utilization. The plan and the national economic policy must appear as a positive force contributing to the normalization of the market and directed against tendencies of economic imbalance and against monopolistic control of the market.

One of the most significant novel points of the program is the advocacy of voluntary association of enterprises. The AP quite unequivocally asserts that each enterprise should be empowered to decide <u>its own</u> integration into higher units. This obviously is a step toward solving the problem of injecting competition into the Czechoslovak industrial system, for, as we have time and again pointed out, such competition could not be expected in the former arrangement when EPU's were being built up into mammoth monopolistic producers. A further step in paving the way for competition is the appeal to facilitate the existence and encourage small- and medium-scale producers and distributors especially of consumer goods and foodstuffs.

The AP is critical of the past growth strategy, but recognizes that the restructuring of the economy cannot be accomplished overnight.

The state's economic policy and decisions on the plan should result from a multifaceted interaction and coordination of diverse interests and from short- and long-run prospects. Consumers should be protected from monopolistic abuses of producers and distributors. The plan and economic policy should be effectively controlled by the NA, subjected to expert verification by the various scientific insitutions, and promoted by the government.

The AP condemns the policy of subsidizing those who work poorly by those who work well, which could be interpreted as an oblique thrust at the egalitarian wage policy, but could also significantly mean the abandonment of redistribution between enterprises. As we have seen, this could mean the removal of an important roadblock in the path of economic reform. It advocates freedom for enterprises in deciding all matters pertaining to their management and their flexible adaptation to market demand.

Concurrently the program deplores the isolation from world markets which has retarded technical advance, depressed product quality, and created balance-of-payments tensions. Czechoslovakia must be fully integrated into the international division of labor in order to prepare itself for the scientific and technical revolution. The stress on economic cooperation with the U.S.S.R. and with other socialist countries (especially CMEA members), as a basis for foreign economic relations, was perhaps a degree weaker than in the past. Economic relations with other countries on the basis of mutual advantage and equality should be actively and indiscriminately encouraged. It is necessary to formulate the conditions under which the producers and trading enterprises would be entitled to act independently on foreign markets. If world market pressures are to be felt, the foreign trade monopoly should disentangle itself from its administrative concepts and methods and should forgo direct interference in foreign trade transactions. But the AP does not specify what would be the function, if any, of this monopoly. The ultimate aim is to achieve convertibility of the Czechoslovak currency, but to avoid in the process the piling up of too many social problems and to preclude adverse effects on the living standard.

It is necessary to bring the domestic and world market prices gradually closer together. This practically means a policy of "more energetic elimination of various surcharges." Enterprises must realize that the protection is only temporary and they must work out a program of such changes in production which will enable them in the next few years to do without subventions.

The growth of wages is bound up with that of labor productivity. A five-day week was forecast for the end of 1968. The program singled out housing construction as one of the chief problems that could be tackled by employing foreign building contractors and construction workers and should be concentrated primarily where housing shortage is most acute.

Slovakia should develop at a faster rate than the rest of the country, permitting it to reach the economic level of the rest of the country by 1980. But Slovakia should rapidly shift to an intensive pattern of growth.

"The Party considers the development of agriculture in the collective and state farms to be the decisive form of large-scale agricultural production." The Party upholds the right of agricultural producers to form a statewide organization of cooperative farmers, the right of the unified agricultural cooperatives to engage in business outside of agriculture, and the possibility of selling part of the farm products directly to the consumers. Even though they are greatly outnumbered, private farmers should be afforded every facility for their work. The poor performance and shortage of services were deplored and the high cost of the bureaucratic apparatus in this area was condemned. Costs should be cut by splitting up the concerns into individual workshops. Moreover, legislation is to provide for encouraging the emergence of small-scale enterprises in this area.

4) Foreign policy is the least explicit portion of the AP. In its opening statement, it envisages that the complex international situation might bear on the implementation of some of the program's crucial tenets. It reaffirms that Czechoslovakia would side with the forces of "progress, democracy, and socialism" against those of "reaction and aggressive imperialism"--whatever that is supposed to mean. Perhaps the purport is clearer in the affirmation that the foreign policy would remain fundamentally oriented to the alliance with the U.S.S.R. and with other socialist states on the basis of equality, sovereignty, mutual respect, and solidarity, applying also the Czechoslovak participation in CMEA and the Warsaw Pact. It is difficult to distinguish between this statement and others of a similar nature in the past; the crux probably lies in the extent to which Czechoslovakia intends to impart meaning to each of these attributes and to insist on consistent adherence to them.

Czechoslovakia proposes to follow an active policy of peaceful coexistence with the advanced capitalist countries and to pursue a more active European policy aiming at mutually advantageous relations with all countries and international organizations and at establishing a collective European security system. A vital point is the upholding of the existence of two German states and the readiness to support the "realistic forces" in West Germany. Such an attitude, aside from many others of the AP, could easily embroil Czechoslovakia with its Communist allies, especially with Poland and East Germany whose policy has been consistently aimed at discrediting any rapprochement with West Germany.

In closing, the Party explains that the proposed measures were not decided upon as a retreat from Party ideals or as a defeat at the hands of adversaries. Contrariwise, the intention is to rid the system of past shackles which had made it so unpalatable to countries with a democratic tradition.

ASPECTS OF NEW ECONOMIC ARRANGEMENTS

Some significant rearrangements were effected in the state economic agencies as a step toward remodeling the machinery of implementing the new working arrangements. Thus, an Economic Council (EC) was established as the supreme economic organ of the government to direct over-all economic policy and to coordinate the work of economic ministries. (The Economic Council somewhat resembles the National Economic Council in existence from 1945 to 1951.) It was a serious blow to the reformist forces that Strougal and not Sik was named its Chairman. This was seen as an indication of a possible tussle between Sik and Cernik on the content, extent, and rapidity of the economic reform, with Cernik's more moderate views prevailing. Be that as it may, Sik has obtained a seat on the Council together with the Ministers of National Economic Planning, of Finance, of Foreign Trade, of the State Price Board, of Labor and Social Affairs, and of Technology; the Director General of the CSB; and the Chairman of the Slovak Planning body. Valtr Komarek was named Secretary General of the EC. The SPC was transformed into the Ministry of National Economic Planning, headed by Frantisek Vlasak, who previously was Chairman of the SCT and has been a backer of the reform. This might indicate the significance attached to invigorating the role of technology. The SCT was renamed the Ministry of Technology, headed by Miloslav Hruskovic, a technical expert hailing from Slovakia and a member of the Slovak CC Presidium. A State Price Board was established under Minister Vaclav Hula, a former Deputy Chairman of the SCFPW. The latter agency was abolished, but Bohumil Sucharda retained his post of Finance Minister. A new Ministry of Labor and Social Affairs was established. Michal Stancel, a Slovak expert and former Chairman of the State Office of Social Welfare, was named Minister. The State Office of Social Welfare and the State Commission for Management and Organization were dissolved. The Ministry of Heavy Industry was changed into the Ministry of Metallurgy and Machine-Building and Josef Krejci has retained his post.

An appointment which augurs well for agricultural progress is that of Josef Boruvka as Minister of Agriculture and Nutrition. A farmer by profession, he is supposed to be a reformist.

The manifold functions of the EC include the preparation of variants of perspective, long- and short-term development, analysis of the state budget, studies and assessment of economic processes, design of measures to implement current economic policy, etc. The EC is to intervene so as to "reconcile the interests and activities of economic units and those of the center." It should coordinate all measures of economic policy, particularly if such measures are beyond the authority of the individual central organs.[141]

Evidently, in order to enthrone the EC as the central and sole macroeconomic policy-coordinating body, a number of government agencies had to be degraded to the ministerial level. Somewhat paradoxically, the creation of another powerful central organ (EC) was envisaged not as a strengthening of centralism, but rather as a device for its weakening so as to curtail the powers of ministries and to free industry from their tutelage and interference. The reformers identified the ministries primarily as bastions of the traditional system, hampering the invigoration of the role of enterprises and representing the interests of branch directorates. The EC was envisaged as an organ that could restrain and frustrate the powerful ministries. Naturally, it was also decided to reduce the number of ministries.

The traditional ministry was seen as one of the pillars of the protectionist system. As long as a ministry is responsible for the development of a certain branch of production, it will always attempt to protect and look after the interests of enterprises under its aegis; to strive to obtain for them more investments and greater material and human resources; and generally to make life easier for its wards.[142] The ministries are spokesmen for and protectors of the "monopolistic interests of the branch directorates." All the administratively formed monopolies forcing on the buyers the sellers' market must be resolutely broken up. If they are not dismantled, the center will not be able to exercise effective control and to subordinate them.[143]

There was stress on removing the enterprise from its subjection to the ministry. One of the key legal measures was to be that defining the status of the enterprise, expected by the fall of 1968.[144] There were demands to break up some enterprises and grant this status to those that had been reduced to the status of plants by past amalgamations.[145] There seems to be some danger that adverse effects on efficiency (economies of scale) might accompany the exaggerated zest to break up monopolies.

The foreign trade monopoly was particularly politically untouchable. Even here institutional changes were mandatory to permit multifarious organizational forms to emerge and to give producers more opportunity to enter foreign markets both as buyers and sellers. Every enterprise should be forced to sell its wares at prices which can be earned on foreign markets. Enterprises may apply for assistance, but a time limit must be placed on the subsidy.[146]

According to Vaclav Vales, the new Minister of Foreign Trade, an active foreign trade policy requires learning how to behave according to the rules of the world market, how to avail oneself of its opportunities, and how to make use of its advantages; producing a sufficient quantity of high-quality and widely convertible products; and being able to realize them on demanding markets. The existence of monopoly in foreign trade has its advantages, but the institutional arrangements, content, forms, and methods must be substantially altered. There must be a relaxation of present conditions of isolation of production from the currents of the world market. In the future, the Ministry of Foreign Trade should use economic devices to promote and to support effective products and not to carry out a policy of protecting producers who live off the state purse and who are isolated from the competitive pressures of the world market.[147] About a month later Vales announced that production organizations and cooperative enterprises would be given the chance to market their wares independently on foreign markets. According to the new measures, which were then being worked out, the monopoly of the existing foreign trade organizations would be abolished, though the state would still retain "some control." State permits would be granted to producers to export their goods directly, but at their own risk; possible failures would not be compensated from the state purse.[148]

The government announced that in the near future 20,000 business licenses would be issued, mainly to improve the ill-operating services. Craftsmen would get business licenses, private individuals would be able to rent small restaurants or shops. They would merely pay rent and tax to the state. New cooperatives would be formed, but the nationalized enterprises "would never become private property again!"[149] The MF disclosed that conditions for small-scale private enterprise would be set by law, probably before the end of 1968. Private enterprises would be operated by individuals, sometimes with their families. The fixed assets in private workshops would belong to owners or might be borrowed. The proprietors would probably be given the opportunity to train one apprentice. Up to the end of 1967, national committees had issued over 20,000 permits to private craftsmen to work independently.[150]

As to the performance of the economy in those turbulent months, it was reported that a state of imbalance persists; there are "disproportionate" demands for investments, failures in housing construction, and a preponderance of demand over supply in the consumer goods market. Performance of foreign trade further aggravates the state of imbalance. Exports to socialist countries continue to outpace imports, resulting in a continuing rise of "frozen assets."[151] The growth rate recorded in the first three months of 1968 was higher than in the same period of 1967, but it was lower than in the last three months of 1967. Moreover, Cernik reported that in April and May there had been some further slackening of the growth rate.[152] Gross industrial output rose by 6.2 per cent in the first quarter of 1968 over the first quarter of 1967. Reportedly, over 80 per cent of the increase was attributed to the improvement in productivity, while employment went up by only 0.8 per cent (industrial employment in Slovakia grew by 3.7 per cent and a decline was registered in Bohemia and Moravia). Housing construction again did not fare well. Only 8,242 dwellings were completed, i.e., 576 less than in the same period in 1967 (the results were particularly adverse in Slovakia).[153]

Exports increased by 7 per cent and imports by 4 per cent during the first quarter of 1968 over the same period in 1967. Exports to capitalist countries increased by 10 per cent and to socialist countries by 5 per cent. Imports from socialist countries increased by 9 per cent and imports from capitalist countries dropped by 5 per cent. The statistics are deceiving. It should be kept in mind that the results for the first quarter of 1967 were very unfavorable--constituting merely 20.5 per cent of the annual volume of exports. In spite of this year's respectable increase in exports to capitalist countries, they did not reach the average quarterly amount of 1967 annual exports. Reportedly, the situation is even worse for there are not enough orders from capitalist countries for the rest of the year (including orders for equipment).[154]

On June 6, 1968, the CSB reported that no pronounced improvement of the economy has been registered. The continuing tendency is for high, "ill-distributed," and "unwarranted" formation of GY, with an accelerated growth of the population's income. Enterprise incomes are growing, but the state does not have a "sufficient" share in the rise of income. Demands for investment, for imports from convertible currency areas, and for appropriations from the state purse continue to grow.[155]

In January and February, 1968, personal income considerably exceeded the envisaged development, without corresponding augmentation of the supply of goods for the domestic market. The total nominal income of the population in the first quarter of 1968 was 10.4 per cent higher than in the same period of 1967, due, inter alia, to payments of profit-sharing. Wages grew by 9.5 per cent, farmers' income rose by 23.6 per cent (including supplementary income for last year), and old age pensions and other social payments went up by 7.2 per cent. Wages in industry and construction were 8.1 per cent higher in January and February, 1968, than in the corresponding period of last year. Wages in the nonproductive sector rose more rapidly than in industry and construction.[156] Average wages in the nonfarm sectors of the economy increased in the first quarter of 1968 by 119 kcs. monthly (from 1,563 to 1,682 kcs.). In 1964 and in 1965, the increase in the first quarter was about 50 kcs., in 1966 it was 21 kcs., and in 1967 it was 78 kcs. Average wages in Slovakia grew by 136 kcs. in the first quarter of 1968, while in the Czech lands they grew by 114 kcs.[157] The index of the cost of living in the nonagricultural sectors rose by 5.4 per cent and by 5.2 per cent in agriculture.[158] The trend toward wage equalization continued and Cernik disclosed that in April and May, 1968, the relationship between the growth of average wages and productivity further deteriorated.[159]

Sucharda disclosed in April that demands for additional wages had become more vocal and amounted to 20 billion kcs. There was an increasing number of demands for higher wages and improvement in working conditions originating at factories, with threats of strikes unless those demands were met.[160] The regime recognized the workers' right to strike, but considered it only as an ultimate weapon, to be used exclusively after all concerned had failed to reach agreement by negotiation.

Reportedly, the government was determined to tackle the most urgent wage problems (particularly of sectors and branches which had lagged behind in wage increases over the past years) within the next two years or so and has issued instructions for some wage increases during the course of 1968. The government did not wish to announce a policy of belt-tightening, but enterprises and employees are apparently unrealistic about the feasibility of meeting all demands. Cernik stressed that the government does not demand that the trade unions should identify themselves with the government's policy. But it is unreasonable to expect that the government and its institutions should bear only the responsibility and that the trade unions should only submit demands.

Wages are to be increased, *inter alia*, in consumer-oriented industries in order to attract more and better manpower which is badly needed to augment promptly the flow of consumer goods and services, to improve quality, to alleviate flagrant wage inequities, and to foster an exodus of labor from heavy industry. Simultaneously, more versatile plants of heavy industry are to be adapted to the production of consumer goods, but problems in such desirable reorientation of production are immense. The Minister of Consumer Goods Industry demanded more investment to enlarge and renovate capacities and has accused the government of not having effected a radical change in the allocation of investments.

The government apparently regards the present allocation of national income to investment as the maximum limit, for otherwise "one would be investing at the expense of living standards." It was envisaged that in 1968 a total of 70 billion kcs. would be invested (i.e., lower than planned), out of which health, education, housing, transport, etc., would get about 35 billion kcs. The share of investments to be made in the heavy, mining, and power industries was reduced to 18 per cent.[161]

Premier Cernik disclosed that by 1980 steel production would be 13 million tons (24 million tons previously planned), that power output would be 90 million MWh (154 million previously planned), and that, consequently, the previously envisaged coal production would also be lowered by about 35 per cent.[162] Obviously, in 1968 more drastic steps were envisaged to redress past misallocations by curbing the expansion of heavy industry and by shifting more resources to consumer goods and foodstuffs production. A commitment to accelerated rectification of what Sik calls "an erroneous investment policy and an unsuitable macrostructure of production" are reiterated and some preliminary steps taken point in this direction. But more evidence is required to determine the real extent of the actual shift in policy.

FOREIGN RELATIONS

Besides the forces of opposition with which the new regime had to contend at home, as we shall see later, there were those of the international arena--or, more precisely, those of the "fraternal" socialist (especially Warsaw Pact) countries. In broad outlines, two distinct attitudes could be seen: 1) how these countries reported the events in Czechoslovakia and 2) what their attitude was to Czechoslovakia in immediate relations. Obviously, these attitudes are interdependent. However, it should be noted that in the second case these countries were more apt to wait and see what the attitude of the U.S.S.R. would be, whereas in the first their response was rather conditioned by their domestic situation. On the whole, as was expected, their attitudes varied with the degree of independence they had lately evinced. Thus, once again, with distinct intergroup variations, two groups of countries came into being: 1) countries rather hostile to the developments in Czechoslovakia: the U.S.S.R., Poland, East Germany, and Bulgaria; and 2) countries well-predisposed to the new regime: Rumania and Hungary (with some hesitations), with the intense moral support of Yugoslavia.

At the outset there was reluctant and more than reticent reportage of the Czechoslovak political scene in the first group. As a matter of fact, the Czechoslovak mass media did not fail to remark how pointedly uninterested its immediate allies were in Czechoslovak news. The U.S.S.R. and Poland were particularly singled out for their inadequate coverage of the momentous events in Prague, and East Germany was even criticized for distorting these events.

After a rather warm and congratulatory article on the changing of the guard,[163] the Soviet coverage of Czechoslovak events was very scant until mid-March, when some favorable extracts from Rude pravo were reprinted,[164] but still without original Soviet comments. Actually the first Soviet analysis came at the end of April from the pen of Pravda's Prague correspondent in the guise of a very moderate commentary, stressing the positive in the present leadership and its program and warning against the fringe elements, against the liberality of mass media, and against too many personnel changes.[165] A few days later, Cernik and Svoboda were allowed to present their case to the Soviet people.[166] Although stressing the nefarious effects of Novotny's policy, especially on the economy, the articles were clearly designed to allay Soviet fears as to the Party's many-faceted hold over the situation. Yet, this was followed by a mordant attack on Party noninterference in state and economic affairs and on some demands in Czechoslovakia for an opposition party--a clear warning to some of the Soviet intellectuals who would be ready to be swayed by the Prague breezes.[167] Aside from a seething attack on Prochazka, which amounted to a denial of Czechoslovakia's right to choose its own road to socialism,[168] the Soviet press also delved into history and denigrated Thomas Masaryk as an "imperialist hireling"--an extremely untactful move in view of the recent full-scale rehabilitation of its first President in Czechoslovakia as a national hero.[169]

Even though there appeared here and there a few well-disposed commentaries, the Polish press has been matter-of-fact about Czechoslovak events from the start.[170] It has tended to report on matters which had no particular bearing on affairs in Poland. Since the intensification of the clamp-down on Polish revisionists, there has been more apparent hostility toward the liberalization trend in Czechoslovakia, presumably in order to shield Polish readers from the dangerous winds blowing across the border.

The scant and selective reports in East Germany were distinctly cool from the start and intimated how objectionable, distasteful, and politically dangerous the Czechoslovak events were to the Ulbricht regime, which probably felt that the slightest wind across the border might produce stirrings in East Germany that would serious threaten the present regime's survival. It should be remembered that Ulbricht is effectively the only surviving Stalinist in power in Eastern Europe and as such his position might become somewhat precarious.

Bulgaria is in this context a case apart. About two months of an almost condemning silence followed the rather cordial reception of Dubcek's access to power. Then by mid-March the ice was broken by a well-disposed article stressing the positive steps taken to regenerate the economy and concluding with a mention of the democratization trends.[171] This was followed by a variety of undistorted, even if at times still selective, news from Prague.

As for the second group of countries, their more benevolent attitudes were by no means of equal intensity. At one end of this range was Hungary, where, although ample and well-informed, the reportage still tended to be somewhat discriminatory. Although the Kadar regime is itself in a liberalizing mood, especially in the economy, it was probably taken aback by what it considered to be a policy of "too much too soon" on Dubcek's part. The freedom of expression might also be rather unpalatable to the Hungarian regime which, so far, has not been particularly generous in that direction. Hence, the ambivalent Hungarian attitude. However, it seems that on the whole Hungary has opted for neutrality.

Rumania, on the other hand, probably shares Hungary's misgivings about the strength of the Czechoslovak democratization drive and even of its economic reform, although it is embarking on a cautious one of its own, but its regime is obviously delighted over the foreign relations implications of Czechoslovak developments. Its coverage of these events has been fairly adequate, even if rather noncommittal. This, one might presume to be caused by a tactical maneuver not to embroil Czechoslovakia, or for that matter itself, any further with the other CMEA and Warsaw Pact signatories.

As could be expected, the Czechoslovak events found their most ample coverage in Yugoslavia. In a way they are nothing but a vindication of the road that Yugoslavia has covered since Tito's rift with Stalin. All aspects of the Czechoslovak ferment have been receiving thorough treatment from on-the-spot reporters. On the whole, the Yugoslav response has been one of jubilation and unambiguous support for every socialist country's right to self-determination and to the choice of its own road to socialism. But a note of jealousy could be detected in some Yugoslav writings of Czechoslovakia's usurpation of their limelight as the Communist heretic. The new Czechoslovak political leadership was described as the most progressive within the Party.[172] Toward the end of April, Tito visited Moscow and it is perhaps a coincidence that the Yugoslav press coverage of the Czechoslovak scene abated somewhat in volume and enthusiasm. There was a sharp reproof of some "antisocialist" tendencies in Czechoslovakia, namely, of the demands for re-establishing relations with Israel and of those for an opposition party.[173] But clearly this did not constitute a trend.[174]

China's attitude has remained somewhat of an enigma due to the lack of coverage of Czechoslovak events. Albania's disdainful silence was broken in March with a barrage against the evils of revisionism. On the other hand, the West European Communist Parties have assumed a rather cordial attitude, although here again the opinions canvassed were far from unanimous, especially between the two most powerful Parties--the Italian and the French. The Italian Party was from the start strongly sympathetic to the new regime. Engaged in a pre-election campaign, the Italian Party was eager to materialize on the voter appeal of the liberalizing movement. The Czechoslovak process of democratization was right along the lines of what the Italians had been advocating for many years. Czechoslovak developments afforded stronger backing for the Italian Party's incessant battling for the independence of Communist Parties and their right to choose their own road. The French Party, on the other hand, refrained for some time from commenting on the events. However, once started the commentaries proved to be well-disposed, even if they were lacking the note of enthusiasm that permeated the writings of the Italians. The French Party's stronger ties with Moscow obviously influenced its behavior, notwithstanding its demonstrated desire to appeal to the non-Communist left by exhibiting a liberal appreciation of the Czechoslovak scene.

As to the thorny problems of relations, especially with the allies in the Warsaw Pact, the Dubcek regime attempted from the start to win them over to its side. With that end in view, a series of personal top-level visits was initiated. At the end of January, Dubcek went to Moscow. Several days later he met with Janos Kadar at the Slovak-Hungarian border. Then on February 7, Wladyslaw Gomulka visited Ostrava where he too met with Dubcek. On February 10, Vladimir Koucky, CC secretary for international Party affairs, went to Bucharest. On February 24, the Czechoslovak delegation to the Budapest meeting, headed by Koucky, left Prague. Koucky spoke on March 1, condemning Rumania's walk-out and disassociating himself from the anti-Yugoslav stand taken in Moscow in 1957 and in 1960. He also called for an early convocation of the world Communist conference--a move which no doubt pleased the U.S.S.R. On March 5, Dubcek and his retinue arrived in Sofia for the meeting of the Political Advisory Council of the Warsaw Pact. Later in the month Cernik visited Moscow for consultative meetings on 1971-75 plan coordination and Pepich was visiting with high Soviet military officials.

A milestone in these early meetings is certainly the unheralded top-level meeting held in Dresden on March 23. It was attended by the Party leaders and top government officials of the U.S.S.R., Poland, Hungary, Bulgaria, East Germany, and Czechoslovakia. Since it was unabashedly called hastily together to discuss internal Czechoslovak affairs, Rumania refused to participate on the grounds that it does not subscribe to interference in another country's internal affairs. In short, the purpose of the meeting appears to have been to exert pressure on and seek reassurance from Dubcek that he intends to support the Warsaw Pact policies and that he would put a damper on the liberalization movement to prevent it from spreading like an infectious disease. Further developments indicated that the Dresden meeting was not a resounding success. An interesting sideline topic of the meeting was that of economic cooperation for the 1971-75 period. The call issued for a top-level meeting devoted exclusively to that question suggested that all was not smooth in that domain either.

The tension generated between Czechoslovakia and Poland and East Germany resulted even in some minor skirmishes. Thus, for example, Polish border guards apparently created difficulties for Czechoslovak tourists, especially students.[175] Two Czechoslovak journalists were evicted from Warsaw. On April 18, Jiri Lederer reported over Radio Prague that Professors Leszek Kolakowski and Zygmunt Bauman had not received the invitation to lecture proffered by Charles University. The Czechoslovak government protested through diplomatic channels the March 26 statement of an East German politbureau member that Czechoslovak developments were occasioned by West German interventionalism to split the allegiances of socialist countries and his derogatory references to Smrkovsky. Sometime later Czechoslovakia again resorted to diplomatic channels to protest East German allegations that U.S. and West German tanks were on Czechoslovak soil.[176] This was all the more serious because of the ostensibly increasingly strained Czechoslovak relations with the U.S.S.R.

Soviet-Czechoslovak tensions mounted on two different planes: present and historic. Perhaps a subsidiary, but nonetheless irritating, element was the delving into the past. The two main causes célèbres were the Slansky and Jan Masaryk cases. As we have previously outlined, evidence incriminating Soviet officials as having a large share in precipitating the Slansky purges and in rigging evidence for the trials was unearthed. The case of the non-Communist postwar Foreign Minister, Jan Masaryk, was even more delicate. On March 27, Professor Frantisek Blaha implied over Radio Prague that "foreign elements" were involved in what had been thus far accepted as Masaryk's suicide on March 10, 1948. It was reported a few days later,[177] that Jan Masaryk's case was being investigated, prompted by demands by Ivan Svitak who, basing himself on some Western fact-finding, alleged that Masaryk had been murdered and implied Soviet involvement. The Soviets, on the other hand, vehemently retorted that these allegations were a figment of fiction from beginning to end and were used to drive a wedge between Soviet-Czechoslovak friendship. Nevertheless the investigation has assumed serious proportions and investigators were being sent to the West to obtain information. It was expected that it would continue at least until the end of 1968.[178]

The frictions that developed about present policies were both at the official and at the unofficial levels. Thus, the Czechoslovak press reacted rather vehemently against the implications in a speech made by V. V. Grishin, First Secretary of the Moscow City Party Committee, over Radio Moscow on April 22, 1968, wherein he blamed "revisionists" and "nationalists" for trying to cause a rift among socialist countries.[179]

On the official level it was reported in the West that Dubcek lodged a protest with the Soviet ambassador to Prague, expressing his indignation at the latter's contact with the deposed President Novotny.[180] However, these allegations were denounced the following day by Radio Prague. Then came Dubcek's unheralded visit to Moscow on May 4, accompanied by Cernik, Smrkovsky, and Bilak. Upon his return, Dubcek admitted that this brief visit had not been conclusive and that another Czechoslovak delegation would visit Moscow shortly. He implied that one of the purposes of the visit was to report to the Soviet leaders on Czechoslovakia's scene and to reassure them that the process of democratization was not aimed against socialism. In this connection he interposed that on several occasions since his assuming the reins of power the Party was forced to repudiate "anti-socialist excesses," and that such a stand is wholly concordant with the Party's policy.[181] Obviously, there is much ambiguity in this statement, for it hinges wholly on a precise definition of socialism which was not supplied and, for all we know, might not yet have been completely agreed upon by the Czechoslovak leadership. Dubcek also pointed out that the problem of how the U.S.S.R. could best aid Czechoslovakia in restructuring its economy had not been resolved.

It was officially confirmed that the government would look for a foreign loan to partly finance restructuring of the economy, to alleviate imbalances, and to assist in achieving the convertibility of currency. A loan of about $500 million would, according to Sik, greatly facilitate overcoming the technical backwardness of industry. Two conditions would have to be satisfied: 1) that no political strings be attached and 2) that the loan be used to facilitate "an effective creation of means of its repayment." Czechoslovakia submitted a loan proposal to the Soviet government which was supposed to study it and reply at its convenience.[182] A report was circulated in the West, with the information seemingly originating with Mlynar, that the U.S.S.R. had offered a $400 million hard currency loan if Czechoslovakia would agree to deliver to the U.S.S.R. goods which the latter usually buys on the hard currency markets.[183] Obviously, the arrangement was not found quite acceptable.
On the other hand, official sources disclosed that Czechoslovakia is asking the U.S.S.R. for a 400 to 500 million loan in gold rubles (rather than in

raw materials) so as to be able to buy advanced equipment and patents on the world market. Contrary to rumors, no reply from the U.S.S.R. was officially acknowledged.[184]

The Soviets are in an awkward position. Of course, the Czechoslovaks have compelling reasons to demand such a loan, mainly as a compensation for the services they have rendered in industrializing the CMEA members, and as an "investment" to keep Czechoslovakia under Soviet economic dominance. Political reasons probably dictated approaching the U.S.S.R. first. Since it is problematic that the Soviets would seize the opportunity by extending such a sizable loan in the stipulated form (this would, *inter alia*, significantly reduce Soviet gold reserves), Czechoslovakia could not be accused later of looking elsewhere. But it cannot be entirely ruled out that the U.S.S.R. would extend the credits demanded, but largely on its own terms and only if no such credits would be sought in the West. Apart from political repercussions, a Soviet refusal *in toto* is unlikely, for it might, *inter alia*, endanger Soviet long-term plan fulfillment.

The Minister of Foreign Trade confirmed that unofficial contacts have been established with foreign capitalist countries and trade partners concerning the possibility of loans. The government was also urged to look into the question of a possible loan from the International Monetary Fund.[185] For obvious reasons, there was mixed reaction in the West. We cannot delve here into the involved political implications of such loans. But it is interesting to note that, contrary to some Western reports, Czechoslovak sources disclosed that France, the U.S., West Germany, and some smaller West European countries expressed their willingness to grant such a loan to Czechoslovakia without political strings attached. Apparently a similar willingness to assist Czechoslovakia was expressed by spokesmen for both the International Bank for Reconstruction and Development and the International Monetary Fund. However, Czechoslovakia would have to become a member of these organizations and would have to comply with their rules.[186] This might prove to be a difficult task that would definitely embroil Czechoslovakia with its CMEA partners, for it would have to disclose a lot of hitherto secret economic information (particularly trade statistics with CMEA). Furthermore, it would involve, inter alia, outside dictates on steps to be taken toward currency convertibility.

It was suggested that a most effective approach would be to secure a combination of loans from different sources. The crucial point was not of securing the means of payment for imports (or partly for refinancing short-term credit obligations to the West by long-term ones), but of undertaking commitments which would force the Czechoslovak industry to repay the loans by exports to the most competitive markets. Should the loan ensure the import requirements only, without concomitant export obligations to a demanding market, the danger is that there would be no palpable and sustained pressures to rejuvenate the economy.[187]

The political situation was becoming increasingly strained and serious enough for the U.S.S.R. to have considered it advisable to call a top-level meeting of the Warsaw Pact signatories, excluding Rumania and Czechoslovakia. The leaders of Poland, East Germany, Bulgaria, and Hungary met with the Soviets in Moscow on May 9, ostensibly to discuss the case of Czechoslovakia, but little information leaked out whether an agreement had been reached on the measures to be adopted to preserve the status quo of the Warsaw Pact and to prevent the Czechoslovak fever from contaminating its neighbors.

One of the more serious incidents in the Soviet-Czechoslovak relations of spring, 1968, was the Western report that General Yepishev, Chief of Political Administration in the Soviet Armed Forces, had intimated military intervention to subdue Czechoslovakia.[188] Even if the statement was not altogether correct, there must have been a grain of truth to it for it came too close to reports of Soviet troop concentration on the Czechoslovak border and to the crucial period of the Soviet-Czechoslovak controversy about the Warsaw Pact troop maneuvers on Czechoslovak soil. The resolution of this issue into one of maneuvers eased the tensions created by the fears of the possibility of another Hungary. How imminent such a possibility had been we may never know, but much credit goes to the undaunted spirit of the Czechoslovaks, noticeable in Dubcek's speech at Rip Hill on May 10, and obvious from the mass media. For example, the Czech trade union daily appealed to the U.S.S.R. to forcefully abjure the rumors of a possible Soviet military intervention. It condemned the statements or actions (such as Soviet troop maneuvers in Southern Poland) which might have given rise to such speculations. Finally, it warned the U.S.S.R. that further pressure on Czechoslovakia would only incite "antisocialist forces."[189] In a broadcast on May 9, Petr Pithart, who replaced Mlynar as head of the scientific group elaborating a new "political model," besought Czechoslovakia's socialist allies to desist from measures similar to Yugoslavia's excommunication in 1948 and to the repressive measures toward Hungary in 1956. He entreated them to allow Czechoslovakia to choose its own road and to make its own mistakes. But his supplication for tolerance was untinted by any weakening under the strain of applied pressures.

Some of the major differences between the spring, 1968, state of affairs in Czechoslovakia and that of Hungary in 1956 might have been instrumental in softening the Soviet approach. Whereas the Party's control of this situation in Hungary was obviously slipping, Dubcek was probably able to convince some of the Soviet leaders that the Party was in control of events in Czechoslovakia. Violence was obviously absent from the Czechoslovak scene. The population was on the whole more sympathetic to Communism. The Communists continued in all crucial posts. And last, but not least, Soviet troops were not on hand on Czechoslovak soil.

Another round of the controversy was played out a few days later when a delegation of the highest military brass, headed by the U.S.S.R.'s Defense Minister, Marshall Andrej Grechko, arrived in Prague on May 17, followed within a few hours by Alexei Kosygin's impromptu visit--officially labeled as a ten-day cure at Karlove Vary. Czechoslovak officials (e.g., Smrkovsky on Radio Prague, May 19, 1968) were hopeful that the visit would clear the air and prove helpful in concretizing the state loan. Smrkovsky also asserted that Czechoslovakia was gradually appeasing the fears and doubts of her allies.[190]

Yet, the West German Foreign Minister, Willy Brandt, went on record on May 22 that he had proof that Czechoslovakia was being pressured to accept a contingent of 10,000-12,000 Warsaw Pact troops for permanent stationing there, quite apart from the agreement which had been extricated to hold maneuvers on Czechoslovak soil.[191] If so, this was only a slightly veiled attempt at having on the spot a nucleus of armed forces to quell any possible Czechoslovak developments which might be unsavory to the other Warsaw Pact countries or to intimidate the Czechoslovak leadership to tone down the liberalizing trend. It could not be satisfactorily explained as a defensive measure, because since the early 1960's the Warsaw Pact European defense has relied increasingly on massive nuclear retaliation rather than on the use of conventional forces. Be that as it may, Czechoslovakia announced on May 24 that maneuvers of Warsaw Pact troops would be held on its soil in June, 1968, under Marshal Ivan Yakubovsky--the Soviet Warsaw Pact Commander-in-Chief. These were to be limited staff exercises, but Western reports suggested that the deployment of communication vans, signal corps units, supporting troops, and Soviet tanks was seemingly assuming larger proportions early in June.[192] In an interview, Major General Josef Cepicky assured the Czechoslovaks that the maneuvers planned for mid-June were scheduled exercises. He was not particularly explicit as to their nature, but mentioned that they would consist of motorized infantry armed with light weapons and possibly the use of tanks on a limited scale. Interestingly enough he was asked whether in view of rumors in the West about Soviet armed intervention, it might not have been more advisable to postpone these maneuvers or at best to use only Czechoslovak troops. His answer to that was rather evasive.[193] On another occasion Cepicky also denied Western rumors that a permanent stationing of Warsaw Pact troops in Czechoslovakia was in the offing.[194]

On his arrival in Prague, Marshal Yakubovsky reassured the Czechoslovaks that the maneuvers were to be of a limited scope, involving mainly command staffs, without the participation of a large number of troops.[195] However, the maneuvers finally proved to be on a much grander scale, involving not only an undisclosed number of tanks and aircraft, but also more than 9,000 (and some reports listed 20,000) troops. In a way this controversial development was likened to a slowly unfolding drama where in the first act the possibility of maneuvers was flatly denied; in the second act it was admitted that a small-scale routine exercise was being prepared; and in the third act the entire case in full regalia was on stage. This commentary also implied that the director of the play was not a Czechoslovak and that it was precisely steered in that direction in order to create a confidence gap between the Czechoslovak leadership and the population.[196] It is quite plausible that the Dubcek leadership was kept in the dark as to the proportions that the maneuvers were going to assume and that the entire process was a show of strength to drive home to the Czechoslovaks that they had not entirely escaped Soviet tutelage. Be that as it may, the units that had acted as marker troops and signal and logistics units were preparing to leave at the end of June, 1968, but the staffs were to remain apparently to evaluate the results of the maneuvers. At the end of a Czechoslovak-Soviet friendship rally Dubcek, reportedly, said: "The units that participated are leaving. We heartily salute them." Even if he had no intention of being sarcastic, these words probably well described the attitude of the Czechoslovak people who were more predisposed to hail the Soviet troops on their departure than on their arrival.[197]

By all accounts Kosygin's visit seemed to have won another breathing spell, if not an outright vote of confidence, for the Dubcek regime. For obvious reasons, one can only conjecture as to the nature of the bargain struck by Kosygin on his departure from Prague. One can only surmise what demands the U.S.S.R. put forward, but, by all accounts, it seems that it was not in a position to exact them, barring the risky alternatives whose looming specter could never be entirely disregarded. There was then not much choice left for Kosygin but to take at face value the reassurances that the Prague leaders were disposed and interested in offering. From the immediate developments one may safely assume that the Soviets found it inadvisable (even had they wished) to pressure the Czechoslovaks into restoring the pre-January, 1968, status quo. At the bargaining table Kosygin probably did not deny the Czechoslovaks their right to their own road to socialism, but attempted to prevent that road from swerving into directions which would seem intolerable from the U.S.S.R.'s standpoint. The main three points on which the Soviets probably sought assurance were: 1) that Czechoslovakia would remain an active participant in the Warsaw Pact, that it would honor its commitments to its CMEA partners, and that it would not make objectionable overtures to the West; 2) that the tenor of the liberalization trend would be toned down and that there would be effective resistance to the more revisionist ideas, such as the demands for a full-fledged opposition party; and 3) that the Party would not let the democratization process escape from its tutelage, that it would retain control over the communications media, that Party officials would remain in the important posts, that generally the Party would remain committed to directing the country's political, economic, and social life, and that it would retain effective control over the process of transformation.

The assurances involved in those three points are intertwined. Those in point 3 would maintain not only Communist rule over Czechoslovakia, but also the kind of strong rule which the Soviets could trust to wield sufficient power to enable the

Party to enforce the assurances in points 1 and 2. The assurances under point 1 would preserve Czechoslovakia in the Soviet sphere of influence both politically and from a defense point of view. They would also safeguard Soviet influence over the Czechoslovak economy due to the U.S.S.R.'s major share in Czechoslovak foreign trade, thus allowing the U.S.S.R. a more direct control over Czechoslovak domestic affairs. The assurances under point 2 are mostly designed to facilitate implementation of those under 3, but they also intend to prevent the spreading of the liberalizing trend and its infection of neighboring countries by putting a damper on the elan, thus lessening the trend's popular appeal.

A secondary issue that was probably worrying the Soviets was that of the severe attacks that were hurled at the U.S.S.R. in the Czechoslovak press, especially the unearthing of unsavory Soviet participation in the Slansky and Masaryk affairs--so damaging to the Soviet image in Czechoslovakia. As the tensions between Moscow and Prague were growing, the Soviets were accusing the new regime of nationalism, revisionism, and other "deviations"; of undermining the unity of the socialist camp; of anti-Communist hysteria; etc. Although on May 15 some of the conservative deputies to the NA asked for definite government measures to prevent information media from spreading dissent among Czechoslovakia and its socialist neighbors, the result was nothing more than an admonition from the NA's Foreign Affairs Committee to the information media that they should contribute to the strengthening of friendship among the socialist countries while retaining freedom of expression. Similarly, during Kosygin's visit--on May 23, to be exact--Cisar asked the press to refrain from undignified polemics against friendly socialist countries. Such exhortations have not proven to be overly effective.[193] But then it seems as if the Czechoslovaks had enough provocation, for the barrage of invectives, such as references to the Czechoslovak counterrevolution, originating in East Germany, Poland, and the U.S.S.R. did not abate. Significantly a number of workers' committees sprung up in several industrial enterprises to protect freedom of the press and obviously in response to the Party's demands for restraints. It remains to be seen whether the new press law and that regulating radio and television will in fact allow the government some sort of inconspicuous censorship when they finally come into effect. The Czechoslovaks might well be well-advised to demonstrate restraint in taking advantage of their newly won freedom of expression if they want to preserve it in an unadulterated form, and not to provoke their touchy neighbors to regrettable acts.

In the same vein, to show Kosygin Czechoslovakia's resolution to carry out its assurances, the Party Presidium condemned independent political groups and denounced social democratic torch-bearers for yearning to return to the pre-1948 state of affairs. The Ministry of Interior went as far as to announce that any new political parties (i.e., outside the NF) were illegal. How this would affect the various clubs formed to promote a political platform, such as the Club of Engaged Nonpartisan People, was not altogether clear. Yet it was explained by a legal expert that there was actually no law banning political parties and as such what is not explicitly prohibited must be permitted.[199] The Presidium also proposed a unified federated youth organization and opposed the formation of youth groups by political parties within the NF.

For the time being, it would seem that the U.S.S.R. adopted a sort of dual policy toward Czechoslovakia. On the one hand, the official relations have been relatively unruffled since Kosygin's visit. Smrkovsky's parliamentary twelve-day visit to the U.S.S.R. at the beginning of June ended with the usual protestations of "cordiality" and "warm friendship" on both sides. Josef Zednik, Deputy Speaker of the NA, on his return described Brezhnev's contrition and repeated assurances that the U.S.S.R. had no intention of invading Czechoslovakia and that it was prepared to go in front of an international tribunal to justify its actions which had given rise to unjust accusations. At the same time, Brezhnev emotionally deplored the Czechoslovak press unfriendliness to the U.S.S.R.[200] On the other hand, however, Czechoslovakia's democratization policy continued to be vilified in the Soviet press. For example, Cisar, Czechoslovakia's chief ideologist, was taken to task by Academician Fyodor V. Konstantinov, who came into the limelight during Stalin's regime, for his allegations that Leninism is only a onesided and monopolistic interpretation of Marxism. Konstantinov equated Cisar's views with those of Father Joseph Bochensky, to whom Konstantinov contemptuously referred as "the Jesuit philosopher."[201] This was the first time that a high Czechoslovak official was publicly accused of deviationism. It was another mark of the domestic problems faced by the Soviets in their current ideological vigilance campaign distinguished by a painstaking unearthing of heretics at home and in the "fraternal" parties.

Further insight into the prevailing state of affairs between the U.S.S.R. and Czechoslovakia could be gained from Dubcek's speech at the CC Plenum which convened on May 30. The gist of Dubcek's speech was a rebuke to his allies for interfering in Czechoslovakia's internal affairs. He reiterated the thesis that due to the specific conditions in various countries and due to the differenc in the atmosphere in which the Communist Parties work, it would not be possible to "reach any ideal and complete unity on all questions of development in respective socialist countries." He asserted Czechoslovakia's right to put its house in order as it sees fit and he assured others that Czechoslovakia would not meddle in their domestic problems. "Let us not do to others what we would not want them to do to us," he adjoined. Dubcek then went on to reiterate the Party's friendly predisposition to West Germany and assured his audience that Czechoslovakia's membership in the Warsaw Pact does not prevent it from actively and flexibly developing its cooperation and relations with other countries in accordance with its political and economic interests.[202] All this was accompanied by an outwardly reverent lip service to the U.S.S.R. which has come to constitute the formal liturgy of such meetings.

Aside from these ritual invocations, it was transparent that the new leadership meant to free itself largely from cramping Soviet guardianship in as elegant and as dignified a manner as possible. At the same time, the leadership seemed fully aware that one of the crucial prerequisites for meaningful progress of the Czechoslovak reforms is to obviate Soviet indignation and animosity.

ANOTHER STEP FORWARD

On the home front, the May 29-June 1, 1968, CC Plenary Session was marked by many currents. On the whole, the tenor was one of impatience to pursue in concrete terms the line mapped out by the AP. On several occasions the meeting was reassured that the Party had no intention of retreating from the road it had traced for socialism in Czechoslovakia and that a return to the pre-January, 1968, state of affairs was unthinkable.[203] Concurrently, there was a warning that the return to the state of affairs prevailing before 1948 or before 1939 was out of the question. The Party called for support from all quarters. It warned against those "discredited political forces" which are attempting to exploit the liberalization trend and to stage a comeback.[204]

Here and there there were admonitions that the accomplishments of the past twenty years should not be treated lightly. Some speakers also blamed the information media for taking too much liberty with delicate issues and evinced fears that "anarchism and liberalism" were being propagated.[205] Dubcek charged that hostile _émigrés_, foreign espionage services, hostile news agencies, internal anti-Communist forces, etc., were increasingly taking interest in Czechoslovak developments, spreading false reports, and trying to gradually advance by disrupting Party unity and the unity of socialist countries.[206]

But the attacks on the _ancien regime_ were infinitely more forceful. Deputy Premier Sik rallied to the defense of the press. He pointed out that unless a full and public official criticism and "profound analysis" of the excesses of the former undemocratic system were made, there could be no guarantees against similar abuses of personal power in the future and the Party might not gain the population's and especially the intellectuals' confidence. He delivered a seething attack on the oldtime "demagogues" who were still holding to their positions and, what is more, who were presuming to speak for and to represent the Party. He denounced Novotny's position as "a mockery of the whole Party rather than self-criticism and help to the Party." Sik unabashedly demanded not only the dismissal of those responsible for past distortions from the Party's CC, but also their punishment, for otherwise the entire Party would have to continue under the opprobrium of past misdeeds.[207]

Two important steps were taken at the Plenum to cleanse the highest Party organs of conservative opposition. Novotny and the hard core of his supporters (including Karol Bacilek, Viliam Siroky, Bruno Kohler) were dismissed from the CC and their Party memberships were suspended. The latter action was taken on the grounds of their involvement in the infamous purges. The suspension of Party membership also affected some of the participants in the legal machinery involved in the purges, such as chief prosecutor Jiri Urvalek. Depending on the results of investigations into this gloomy past, these Party members would either be expelled or fully reinstated. Such was the ultimate disgrace of Czechoslovakia's "mini-Stalin," accomplished by compromise, for there had been demands for Novotny's outright expulsion from the Party. Although there were some resignations of Novotny's supporters from the CC, such as those of General Lomsky and Martin Vaculik, the CC still remained with about forty out of the one hundred and ten members committed to the old-line policies. Such an opposition constituted too strong a barricade against the policies of the new leadership. However, concerned as the new leadership showed itself about legal niceties, it could not very well revert to a wholesale purge to rid itself of that significant opposition block. Therefore, an emergency session of the Fourteenth Congress of the CPC (due to meet only in 1969) was convoked for September 9, 1968. It was expected that the composition of the CC to be elected at the Congress would be more propitious to pushing through the slated reforms. As Sik pointed out, "the major demand of the program of the extraordinary Fourteenth Congress is an exchange of the cadres in the supreme Party bodies."[208] In order to ensure that the delegates to the Congress be predisposed to electing a progressive CC, the key figures of the new leadership fanned out throughout the country immediately after the Plenum to acquaint the Party rank and file with the decisions and to explain the undertakings of the Plenary Session.

Apart from these steps, some significant points were brought out by several speakers and some important items registered in the resolution. One of the key issues was that of federalization which was particularly stressed by Smrkovsky. He pressed for rapid conclusion of the preparations for this new step which would afford "institutional guarantees of the equalities of our two nations" and which would mean "a new definition of national self-determination not only for Slovaks but also for Czechs." While rejecting tripartite federation, he urged the setting up of an interim Czech National Council to act as the supreme national body in Czech lands.[209] As pointed out by Viliam Plevza, the Secretary of the Commission of Experts preparing the legislation on Czechoslovakia's federalization, the main problem was that there were no Czech counterparts to the Slovak National Council.[210] The CC's resolution foresaw that federalization would be legally enacted and introduced by the beginning of 1969 and then elections would be held.[211] The CC also recommended to the government that a commission to prepare the setting up of Czech national bodies in a federal system be set up under the Chairmanship of Spacek--significantly a Moravian. At the same time, the formation of a Party federalization commission to look into the problems of arranging a federal Party system was approved by the CC.[212]

Once again, the creation of an opposition political party outside the NF was categorically rejected. Cooperation and "joint government" with the NF was reiterated. The inclusion of existing common interest groups and those being formed into the NF was urged so that the NF could also represent the interests of people who are not affiliated with any political party. However, these organizations should have binding political statutes to prevent their infiltration by antisocialist elements.

One of the more significant notes struck in Dubcek's speech and again expounded by Mlynar was the necessity of setting up some sort of formally organized participation of workers in the management of their enterprises. The resolution also noted that the workers cannot be denied the right to strike, but added that such a right is not the main factor guaranteeing the workers' freedom. It upheld the establishment of "democratic organs of management" in enterprises.[213] A few days later the government approved provisional outlines for the establishment and testing of "collective bodies of democratic management" in enterprises, which should be discussed at the national conference of trade unions.[214] Although these utterances were far from explicit as to the nature, scope, and form of such workers' self-management, the idea was probably to create organizations similar in their aim to the Yugoslav workers' councils and to the ill-fated Polish workers' councils when they were spontaneously formed in 1956.

After the June Conference of the CCTU, provisional regulations were issued on the workers' councils. They were to be set up in three stages: on July 1, 1968, on October 1, 1968, and on January 1, 1969. The intent was to test the workability of councils before officially legalizing them, probably at the end of 1968.[215] The provisional regulations prescribed a ten- to thirty-person composition of the workers' council (depending on the size of the enterprise), elected by secret ballot. From 10 to 30 per cent of the council's members should be independent outside experts. Its membership would also include representatives from suppliers, customers, the CSB, and the state, if the enterprise is one of key importance. The workers' council was charged with appointing and discharging the enterprise's director and his deputies, with deciding managerial salaries and premiums, with elaborating the basic questions of the enterprise's development, with participating in investment policy and the apportionment of GY, and with reviewing final accounting reports. The enterprise's management would be required to carry out the council's decisions, but all executive powers would be vested with management. The workers council was admonished that it could not duplicate the functions of management, nor could it bypass management's authority.[216]

Without indulging in speculation, one may question the extent of workers' participation in management that could be allowed in the complex industrial structure of Czechoslovakia. Would not the sheer size of most Czechoslovak industrial enterprises preclude any meaningful partnership between workers and management in decision-making? At a time when Czechoslovak industry badly needs invigoration of managerial functions, a new businesslike style of work, and the entrepreneurial spirit, the thought comes to mind whether the timing of the introduction of workers' councils was properly chosen and whether it may not hinder the process of managers learning their new roles.

INTERNAL OPPOSITION

To what extent the new leadership rests on the firm foundations of popular approval is still largely unknown. An indication of the support for the new regime may perhaps be gauged from the results of some of the flourishing public opinion polls, but the evidence, of course, is inconclusive and sometimes contradictory.

According to an opinion poll of a representative sample of 300 people, conducted from May 24 to 26, 1968, by the Institute of Public Opinion Research of CAS, 53 per cent of those interviewed thought the present democratization trend to be of benefit to all; 21 per cent considered it did not much benefit the ordinary man; and the rest thought it essentially produced little change. Of those questioned, 47 per cent felt there was too much talk in the communications media about the failures of the past and too little said about what to do next. About 35 per cent thought the balance of coverage between past and future to be fairly adequate. About two thirds of those questioned, who are not associated with a politically oriented organization, did not intend to join any such organization, while one tenth wished to do so. In judging the post-January political events, 26 per cent of those questioned declared that their confidence in the Party had increased, 40 per cent confided no change in their attitude, while one fifth registered a decline in their confidence.[217]

According to 67 per cent of the 1,476 persons questioned in another public opinion poll carried out by the same Institute, the changes being made in political life were permanent, while 14 per cent believed that in time everything would revert to what it had been before. Asked for suggestions for improving political conditions in the country, 46 per cent called for further advancement of democracy (civil liberties, free elections, public criticism of shortcomings); 28 per cent were in favor of more political parties (22 per cent of them expressly demanding an opposition party); and 26 per cent demanded equality for nations; 91 per cent in Slovakia considered the demand for equality as uppermost, compared with 5 per cent in the Czech lands. Of those questioned, about 1.5 per cent were reported to favor the restoration of private enterprise and 1.9 per cent demanded a greater independence from the U.S.S.R.

The results of the opinion poll carried out by <u>Rude pravo</u> indicated that over 90 per cent of non-Party members, over 85 per cent of Party members, and 87 per cent of leading secretaries of district and regional Party organizations expressed themselves in favor of the new political regime.

Arguments were heard that the changes were introduced too slowly and there were ominous warnings of the inherent dangers of a counteroffensive by the diehard conservatives if the regime would allow too much time for the "flow of words" before taking action. The conservatives were reported to be lining up and trying hard to turn the clock back. An organized opposition of the conservative forces was noted. Leaflets and various resolutions signed and unsigned were distributed in which demands for a return to the pre-January, 1968, regime were spelled out. In some enterprises, Party cells called for an end to the present chaotic situation, for a recognition of the leading role of the working class, and for the prevention of a return to capitalism. Workers' councils were denounced. Demands were made for the resignation of the Dubcek group and for the surrender of the leadership to "proven Communists."[218]

The hubs of opposition were mainly the professional <u>apparatchiks</u> who, in the light of the new regime's platform, foresaw a gradual, if not complete, withering away of the <u>apparat</u> and of the bureaucracy; with the ominous meaning of potential erosion of power, of loss of positions, and downfall from the Communist room at the top. Various tactics were used to stir the workers against the new regime. The conservatives banked on the workers' fear that they would have to exert greater effort and would have to subject themselves to the discipline of the competitive economy, of the reduction of the standard of living, and of the specter of unemployment. The workers resented the "proverbial" widening of wage differentials and were afraid that they would receive a smaller distributed share of the wage fund.

One of the more obvious means used to incite the workers against the new regime was the distortion of information which filtered through the <u>apparat</u>. Another was the appeal to the workers' material interest by claiming that their well-being was being undermined by a radical economic program. The

Novotnyites were telling workers that they stood to lose from the new economic adventurism, that the socialist system would eventually wither away under Dubcek's leadership, and that the conservatives were not getting a fair deal from the communications media and from the Dubcek clique. Yet another tactic was to claim that the intelligentsia had taken over the reins of power, thus appealing to the prejudices against the intellectuals. Other prejudices, such as anti-Slovak feeling in the Czech lands or anti-Semitism, were also exploited.[219]

These appeals were not without success. For example, Novotny was loudly cheered after a speech he made on February 17 at the CKD enterprise in Prague. Workers from the Tesla plant near Prague, although expressing tacit support for the new regime, protested against the liberalization trend by condemning what they considered to be harmful freedom of the press.[220] But the successes scored by the Novotny coterie were counteracted by the reawakening of mass media, by the help of the intellectuals in propagandizing the attributes of political reform, and by the leaders' personal appearances and denial of any workers-intelligentsia antinomy. Moreover, night after night the "high and mighty" were obliged to present themselves on television and to expose their views. The authorities encouraged these probings. Awkward questions (particularly about the past) were being asked and even the darkest cupboards were investigated. Obviously, the unmasking of the conservatives was a powerful weapon for the new leaders in maintaining and consolidating power. Another successful tactic used by Dubcek was the stress laid on political, rather than economic reform, thus dispelling the workers' mistrust of the new economic model. Furthermore, the <u>apparat's</u> attempt at subverting the elections by fixing slates so as to ensure the least possible changes, failed due to the postponement of elections. Finally, the new regime sought to discredit Novotny by revealing the attempted military coup he had engineered. In this case the defection of General Sejna also played into Dubcek's hands.

But attacks upon the <u>nouveau regime</u> were not only to be found in the reactionary circles. There was something more than a veiled allusion to Dubcek and his regime when Ludvik Vaculik denigrated tolerance and liberty emanating from the "ruler's court," for he feared the ruler's prerogative in doling out these precious commodities and questioned whether they would be meted out to all people.[221] Vladimir Manak was still more forthright when he questioned the allegation that there was greater democracy in Slovakia than in the Czech lands in the past, since "the most progressive individuals were at the head of the Party and in high office there since 1963." He vehemently condemned Dubcek's delaying tactics, placating of Prague regime, and sacrificing moral standards for the sake of biding his time. Manak posed the question:

> How could we distinguish today between those who are qualified to regenerate our political situation from those who, motivated by opportunism and utilitarianism, have now jumped on the band wagon of the movement for democracy?[222]

Many were apprehensive that the democratization process was too slow and that the translation of words into deeds was not forthcoming. Many were impatient and wondered whether there were any guarantees against retrogression and whether the democratization process would be concluded.[223]

For better or for worse, the radicals now had to rely on Dubcek for pushing through the liberal reform program. But such a program and its degree of progressiveness relied heavily on the alignment of the responsible leaders in Party and government on the crucial issues. The progressives rallied around Dubcek to fight off the intransigent Novotny forces, but amongst themselves various shades of opinion prevailed and the reform had a variegated meaning. It seems that here again one could discern a radical and a moderate group, with Dubcek seemingly threading the middle of the road holding on as it were to a most precarious balance.

Smrkovsky, Spacek, Sik, Cisar, and Kriegel have emerged as probably the eminent radicals in the leadership, with Cernik professing more moderate views. Kolder, Indra, and Bilak would be found in the conservative circles.

The radical changes may abate when the new power elite gradually begins to feel secure in its seat of power and becomes understandably reluctant to see its powers curbed, criticized, or threatened. Also pressures for change might abate as soon as those who were the underprivileged become the new elite. There might be many disappointments and frustrations among the more radical reformists. While learning by doing, the new leadership might find that it is easier to moderate the course than to keep under control the ferment and passion aroused in the population. The real test for the regime will come when it is faced with searching and offensive criticism rather than when its opponents' actions are under the fire of criticism. Also, it is questionable to what extent those in power will be enthusiastic about setting into motion a machinery of government that might yet prove to be for their own undoing.

The supreme test of success of the broad program of political reforms finally rests on the ability to successfully alleviate economic ills, nay, to remove the causes of economic dislocations. Not surprisingly what the rank and file wants is immediate marked improvement in living standards. It does not want to bear the burden of rejuvenating the economy. An austerity program would be vastly resisted. While the political advancement and dialogue were taking place, the concentration on economic issues abated. There was very little progress made on the economic front. There was still much rhetoric and verbosity on economic reform, but in a sense, it was quietly postponed to more opportune times. Whereas the condition for the implementation of the new economics was political recasting, the condition for survival of the reformed political system is a consistent and prompt implementation of economic reform.

There is a passionate desire, at least on the part of the intelligentsia, to ensure that retrogression cannot take place, but, of course, the intellectuals cannot be treated as a homogeneous group or force. The relentless petitions of the intransigent economists, under the leadership of Deputy Premier Sik, seem to provide the necessary, at least for the time being, force to steer the leadership toward preservation of the new course. To the extent that such pressures produce palpable results in the overall complex, the prospects for sweeping changes in the economy's working arrangements are encouraging.

But the supreme task facing the political leadership is to propitiate the Soviets without essentially departing from the new course. The possibility that the U.S.S.R. may try to use military force to impose its will cannot be ruled out. Indeed, to intervene or not to intervene--that is the question! It cannot be inferred, however, that the Soviets are committed to this type of intervention. Some division and hesitation among Soviet rulers could be detected. What the final shift of the balance of power will be remains an open question. But should the U.S.S.R. revert to the use of force, it seems that the gains would not offset the over-all losses for the Soviets. The U.S.S.R. may exert surreptitious economic pressures to compel Czechoslovakia to moderate its course, but by doing so, it may act as advocatus diaboli. Economic pressures are dangerous to pursue for they might push the Czechoslovaks into closer ties with the Western economies and ultimately with the Western capitalist democracies. While the new regime is strengthening its relations with Yugoslavia, Rumania, and Hungary, and is undoubtedly looking with one eye to the West, the Czechoslovaks have good historical and geographical reasons to preserve voluntarily good relations with the Soviet-dominated orbit of power. If for no other reasons, geography alone dictates that the Yugoslav solution may not be entirely politically acceptable for Czechoslovakia. The problems are indeed formidable. It remains to be seen to what extent Czechoslovakia succeeds in casting away the Soviet shield and in instituting a new variety of democratic socialism.

The momentous transformation on which the new leadership is about to embark, if the "friends'" intervention should prove to be only a threat and if domestic opposition is successfuly overcome, might yet develop into one of the most interesting experiments in modern politics and economics. Here, I can do no more than to wish Mr. Dubcek and the other ardent Czechoslovak reformers success in their endeavors, and to relegate to another study a more detailed account of the 1968 saga and the analysis of the accomplishments.

POSTSCRIPT

As this book was about to appear, the advancement of liberalization in Czechoslovakia was brutally interrupted by the invasion by troops of the U.S.S.R. and of the other "fraternal" countries, members of the Warsaw Pact.

It is gratifying to see that my rather cautious assessment of the state of popular support that the Dubcek regime enjoyed has proven to be too pessimistic. During the times of crisis not only did the church bells ring and were prayers offered in support of the reformist Communist regime, but the Czechoslovaks have proven to the world the best of their national characteristics and spirit: an astonishing discipline and a stubborn determination to remain free. Above all the frustrated and compromised invaders were dismayed by the unexpected and extraordinary popular defiance and by the unity of the nation at large against the forces of aggression and oppression. The "liberators" may yet come home contaminated by the ideas they were sent in to suppress.

By all accounts, the Soviet leaders, or the power group that pressed for the invasion, have committed a political blunder of incredible proportions and dimensions. However, whether the Czechoslovaks will be so united in striving to resist the dilution of reforms or to maintain some of the crucial gains, is another question. Much depends on the strength of their newly evinced unity, for the invader might effectively attempt to divide and conquer. Yet there are some indications that in the last analysis the Czechoslovaks might emerge victorious from their defeat. Although such an interpretation is gratifying, a good deal more evidence is needed to make it plausible. What the future has in store for Czechoslovakia is still very nebulous. The situation is fluid. Almost any assumption is conceivable. To repeat what has become a cliché--almost anything can happen in 1968. It is doubtful whether even the Soviet leaders are quite clear about their intentions and about the policies they are going to pursue on this issue.

Economic reform was not among the revisionist heresies of the Dubcek regime that worried the Soviets most. Quite true, economic reform has probably not gone far enough in practice to become a real threat and to have visible and immediate political repercussions. It is reasonable to assume, but by no means certain, that, greatly constrained on the political front, yet desirous of showing that they remain faithful to the relatively modest AP, and compelled by a deteriorating economic situation, the Czechoslovak leaders will act on the economic front. But such a restrained reform could probably, at least in the near future, remain only a half-measure--a further tinkering with the system. There would be new pronouncements on the requirements of a transitional period which would be steadily extended. We would probably again witness much of the give-and-take and inconsistencies of 1967. If this should unfortunately prove to be so, the stop-gap measures might aggravate, rather than rectify, the situation. Like in the case of the ill-fated 1958-59 decentralization reform, pressures to revert to the proven and expedient methods of the traditional system might again gather momentum.

It is not beyond the realm of possibility that such a situation might be especially engineered by the dialecticians in the Kremlin in order to discredit the Dubcek regime. Although I do not subscribe to the doctrine of economic determinism, I have faith in the demonstrated applicability of the theory of cyclical fluctuations to conditions prevailing in Czechoslovakia under the traditional variant of a socialist economy. But this is a protracted process, and the rulers are most concerned about maintaining power today and in the immediate future. John Maynard Keynes used to say that "in the long run we are all dead." But the "long run" might be sooner than they bargained for.

To the extent that individual and group action acts as a catalyst of events, it is a disquieting thought, as I write these lines, to have learned that the reform movement has been impoverished by the resignation, or forced resignation, of one of its most courageous leaders--the energetic, vocal, devoted, and uncompromising Academician Ota Sik. It is only a few months ago that in reply to my congratulatory note on his elevation to the post of Deputy Premier, Sik answered that he will now be able to help to a much greater extent in implementing the necessary economic changes. Of course, the reform may be carried out without its originator and most ardent defender. Sik was not the only architect of the reform. But his removal from the power group is a setback to the entire reform movement. Sik's stress on the interdependence of the political and economic changes is as timely as ever.

Another disquieting thought is that the Soviets will probably be forced to render economic assistance to Czechoslovakia to alleviate some of the economic dislocations, to compensate for the disruptions caused by the invasion, and above all to strengthen their economic hold over the regime. Such assistance will impose a considerable burden on the Soviet economy. Yet the U.S.S.R. must reckon with the repercussions that Czechoslovak economic disruptions must have on its own plan fulfillment and on that of the other CMEA countries. Assuming that the Soviet assistance will not be in the form of a loan in gold rubles--as originally requested--no matter how great may be the benefits of such aid to Czechoslovakia and notwithstanding other adverse consequences, it would have the effect of further separating the Czechoslovak economy from the competitive forces of foreign markets, of further strengthening Czechoslovak economic dependence on the U.S.S.R. (CMEA), and, above all, of shielding industry by providing it with a secure, protected, and relatively undemanding market.

It is difficult to conceive that in the unfolding drama only the forces of retrogression will win and that the system will slowly retrograde to a version of what it was before--a Stalin-Novotny system without Stalin and Novotny (by itself no mean achievement). Something must have been learned during the momentous eight months. We have seen evidence of it during the difficult moments of trial. The final and crucial chapter is yet to be written.

ABBREVIATIONS USED IN NOTES

AER	*American Economic Review*
CCH	*Ceskoslovensky casopis historicky*
CEP	*Czechoslovak Economic Papers*
CFT	*Czechoslovak Foreign Trade*
CTK	*Ceskoslovenska Tiskova Kancelar*
EBE	United Nations, *Economic Bulletin for Europe*
EC	*Ekonomicky casopis*
EF	*Ekonomie a finance*
EJ	*Economic Journal*
EMM	*Ekonomika i matematicheskie metody*
EP	*Economics of Planning*
ER	*Ekonomicka revue*
ESE	United Nations, *Economic Survey of Europe*
FU	*Finance a uver*
GP	*Gospodarka planowa*
HN	*Hospodarske noviny*
IV	*Investicini vystavba*
JPE	*Journal of Political Economy*

KN	Kulturni noviny
KT	Kulturni tvorba
KZ	Kulturni zivot
LD	Lidova demokracie
LL	Literarni listy
LN	Literarni noviny
MF	Mlada fronta
MR	Modern rizeni
MV	Mezinarodni vztahy
NM	Nova mysl
NS	Nova svoboda
NTCE	New Trends in Czechoslovak Economics
NZO	Noviny zahranicniho obchodu
OMF	Otazki marxistickej filozofie
PE	Politicka ekonomie
PH	Planovane hospodarstvi
PM	Prace a mzda
PO	Podnikova organizace
PS	Pozemni stavby
RaPr.	Radio Prague
RESt.	Review of Economics and Statistics
RN	Rolnicke noviny
RP	Rude pravo

SA	Statistical Abstract
Sbirka	Sbirka zakonu Ceskoslovenske Socialisticke Republiky
SK	Statistika a kontrola
Sl.P	Slovensky prehled
Sl. Rev.	Slavic Review
SP	Statisticke prehledy
SR	Statisticka rocenka Ceskoslovenske Socialisticke Republiky
SS	Svobodne slovo
SZ	Statisticke zpravy
VZ	Veda a zivot
WES	United Nations, World Economic Survey
WMR	World Marxist Review
ZE	Zemedelska ekonomika
ZG	Zycie gospodarcze
ZN	Zemedelske noviny
ZO	Zahranicni obchod
ZS	Zivot strany

Notes: 1. In all cases diacritical marks have been omitted.

2. References to Pravda pertain to the daily organ of the CC of the Slovak Communist Party (Bratislava) unless otherwise indicated.

NOTES

NOTES TO CHAPTER 1

1. Leo Pasvolsky, Economic Nationalism in the Danubian States (New York: The Macmillan Company, 1928), pp. 35-37.

2. Besides Czechs and Slovaks, there were large groups of Germans, Hungarians, and Ruthenians living within the Czechoslovak borders.

3. In 1937, for every 100 inhabitants of the Czech lands, 10.9 were employed in industry; whereas in Slovakia, only 3 per cent were so employed.

4. For data on prewar concentration in industry see M. Svantner, J. Slama, and M. Borak, Odvetvova struktura ceskoslovenskeho prumyslu (Prague: 1959), p. 88.

5. See Harriet Grace Wanklyn, Czechoslovakia (London: George Philip and Son Limited, 1954), pp. 280-81; and William Diamond, Czechoslovakia Between East and West (London: Stevens and Sons Ltd., 1947), pp. 33-34.

6. Wanklyn, op. cit., p. 280. But according to Ingvar Svennilson, exports in 1938 accounted for 23 per cent of total commodity production and imports for 19 per cent of total commodities available. Svennilson, Growth and Stagnation in the European Economy (Geneva: United Nations, 1954), p. 214.

7. Vratislav Busek and Nicolas Spulber (eds.), Czechoslovakia (New York: Frederick A. Praeger, Inc., 1956), pp. 348-52.

8. Cf. Wanklyn, op. cit., p. 277.

9. Wieslaw Iskra, PRL--CSRS, poziom uprzemyslowienia, wspolpraca gospodarcza (Warsaw: 1964), pp. 25-27.

10. Diamond, op. cit., pp. 135-49.

11. Cf. Ibid., pp. 126-34; Josef Goldmann et al., Planned Economy in Czechoslovakia (Prague: 1949), pp. 11-13.

12. Goldmann et al., op. cit., p. 142.

13. For details about the instructive experiment with the Two-Year Plan, see Goldmann, Czechoslovakia: Test Case of Nationalization (Prague: 1947); Goldmann et al., op. cit.; Karel Kaplan, CCH, No. 6, 1966, pp. 844-61; and D. Fiser, Teoriticke otazky vrchlonych planovacich organu (Prague: 1965).

14. WES 1955, Part I, p. 88; ESE 1956, Chapter I, p. 24; ESE 1958, Chapter I, p. 20; ESE 1959, Chapter II, p. 12; and ESE 1960, Chapter IV, p. 4.

15. Cf. Albert O. Hirschman, The Strategy of Economic Development (New Haven: Yale University Press, 1958), Chapter 4.

16. Cf. Karel Kouba, Miroslav Sokol, and Otakar Turek, PH, No. 1, 1966, p. 14.

17. Benedikt Korda, PH, No. 7, 1963, p. 74.

18. Goldmann et al., op. cit., pp. 64-67.

19. Ibid., p. 142.

20. Ibid., pp. 41-43 and 53-57.

21. The shift away from Western markets was due not only to Soviet pressures but also was significantly affected by the Western trade embargo. Cf. Nicolas Spulber, The Economics of Communist Eastern Europe (New York: John Wiley and Sons, 1957), pp. 446 ff.;

and Frederic L. Pryor, The Communist Foreign Trade System (Cambridge, Mass.: The M.I.T. Press, 1963), pp. 166-70.

22. Goldmann et al., op. cit., p. 142.

23. Artur Bodnar, Gospodarka europejskich krajow socjalistycznych (Warsaw: 1962), p. 320.

24. Alfred Zauberman, Industrial Progress in Poland, Czechoslovakia, and East Germany 1937-1962 (New York: Oxford University Press, 1964), p. 59. Zauberman's "recomputation (to be published separately), [was] based broadly on methodology and conventions applied in the West and on pre-war pricing." Ibid., p. 58. For a discussion of the difficulties of estimating the contributions of craftsmen, see also Boris P. Pesek, Gross National Product of Czechoslovakia in Monetary and Real Terms, 1946-58 (Chicago: The University of Chicago Press, 1965), pp. 18-19.

25. Thad P. Alton assumes that the size of GNP expressed in current prices is the same whether reckoned at current transaction (market) prices or at factor costs, and within this total the returns of labor to the services roughly correspond to differences in marginal productivity of labor in various occupations as depicted in the recorded market prices, with the residual entirely attributable to nonlabor productive agents. To arrive at GNP (Western definition) by sector of production at factor cost, Alton's adjustment consisted in aggregating to each sector of origin the return to labor and to nonlabor factors. For labor, actual data were virtually accepted; for nonlabor factors, they were derived by allocating the aggregate nonlabor returns among the various sectors, according to net replacement costs of fixed and working capital. The findings are contingent on the size and "rationality" of the numerator, on reliability of capital valuation, on the rates of turnover of capital, on estimates of depreciation, and on the adopted uniform rate of return to capital in all sectors. Cf. George R. Feiwel, AER, December, 1966,

pp. 1300-302.

26. In assigning sectoral weights, "to avoid making housing services an unreasonably large share of GNP," Maurice Ernst adjusted Alton's estimates "to give housing a rate of return one-half as high as that of the economy as a whole." Ernst, in U.S. Congress, Joint Economic Committee, New Directions for the Soviet Economy (Washington: GPO, 1966), pp. 882-83 and 878 and 913.

27. For detailed official statistics, see Ekonomicheskoye razvitie Chekhoslovakii (translated from the Czech) (Moscow: 1959), Chapter 1.

28. Cf. G. Warren Nutter, Growth of Industrial Production in the Soviet Union (Princeton: Princeton University Press, 1962), p. 154; and Alexander Gerschenkron, Economic Backwardness in Historical Perspective (New York: Frederick A. Praeger, Inc., 1965), p. 236.

29. Milan Cizkovasky, CEP, No. 7, 1966, p. 188.

30. Zauberman, op. cit., p. 121. For an evaluation, see Jan Michal's contribution in Miroslav Rechcigl Jr. (ed.), The Czechoslovak Contribution to World Culture (The Hague: Mouton & Co., 1964), p. 376.

31. Zauberman provides two alternative indexes. Set I shows 289 for 1961 and Set II, 301. These indexes were obtained through an alternative assessment of the contribution of machine-building. Zauberman, op. cit., p. 120; cf. Michal, Central Planning in Czechoslovakia (Stanford: Stanford University Press, 1960), Chapter 2.

32. George J. Staller, AER, June, 1962, pp. 391 and 398.

33. Using 1955 as 100, the official index is 166 for 1960, 199 for 1964, and 215 for 1965. SR 1966, p. 194.

34. Ernst, op. cit., p. 883.

35. WES 1959, Chapter III, p. 112. For comparative data see Bodnar, op. cit., p. 11. The fluctuations in the annual rate of growth of national income and investment can be discerned from SR 1966, pp. 24-25.

36. Cf. WES 1959, Chapter III, pp. 116 ff.; Zauberman, op. cit., p. 40; and Feiwel, The Economics of a Socialist Enterprise (New York: Frederick A. Praeger, Inc., 1965), Chapter 2.

37. Cf. Vladimir Nachtigal, CEP, No. 5, 1965, p. 167; Michal, Central Planning in Czechoslovakia, Chapter 10; and Jaroslav Havelka, PE, No. 6, pp. 503-14.

38. As Pesek pointed out, the data for the year 1953 are of particularly dubious validity, because the Czechoslovak monetary reform and the changes connected with the reform so complicated the work of the state's and enterprises' accountants that even basic data are unavailable. Pesek, op. cit., p. 27.

39. WES 1959, Chapter III, p. 118.

40. Zauberman, op. cit., p. 40.

41. Thad P. Alton et al., Czechoslovak National Income and Product 1947-1948 and 1955-1956 (New York: Columbia University Press, 1962), p. 234. For market price valuations in relation to factor cost and method of adjustment see ibid., pp. 48 ff.

42. Pesek, op. cit., p. 6. Computed in constant 1948 kcs. the shares of investment were about 20 per cent in 1955 and about 22 per cent in 1956. Ibid., p. 44. Pesek pointed out that Alton's and his results "are not exactly comparable," due to fundamentally different approaches. Whereas Alton decided to concentrate on a few selected years and for those he reconstructed exceptionally comprehensive accounts, Pesek concentrated "on major

items likely to reflect general trends." Imputed incomes are responsible for most of the major differences between those two estimates. Whereas Pesek eliminated all imputed items, Alton estimated all major imputed incomes like farmers' and home-owners' and some minor ones. Ibid., pp. 5-6.

43. Staller, op. cit., p. 398.

44. Alexej Balek, Statistika, No. 4, 1965, p. 147. For a summary of statistics on growth and allocation of investments in 1948-65 see SR 1966, pp. 26-7.

45. Ernst, op. cit., pp. 889-90. In Western Europe, the share of investment in GNP rose from about 20 per cent or less in the early 1950's to about 25 per cent in the early 1960's. The share of investment channeled to industry and construction was generally below the 40 per cent mark and services claimed about 60 per cent of investment. Cf. Nachtigal, CEP, No. 8, pp. 117-18; and Kouba, CEP, No. 4, 1964, p. 25.

46. Balek, op. cit., pp. 150-51.

47. Zdenek Srein and Zdenek Tlusty, PE, No. 3, 1963, p. 191.

48. Ibid. pp. 186 ff.

49. Balek, op. cit., p. 150.

50. Ota Sik, PE, No. 1, 1966, p. 11.

51. Miroslava Janderova and Jaroslav Volf, Statistika, No. 3, 1966, p. 127.

52. Cf. Srein and Tlusty, op. cit., p. 195.

53. SR 1966, pp. 34-5. The agricultural labor force decreased to 59 per cent of that employed in 1948. See the July issue of ZE, 1963, pp. 371-438, devoted to the manpower problems in Czechoslovak agriculture. See also the report of a seminar on

manpower problems in Czechoslovak agriculture in PE, No. 6, 1965, pp. 589-94.

54. Reportedly, only in Southern Slovakia and perhaps in Southern Moravia could agriculture be a source of increasing employment in other sectors of the economy. Jozef Mihalik, EC, No. 2, 1966, p. 139.

55. Janderova and Volf, op. cit., p. 128; and SR 1966, p. 112.

56. Balek, op. cit., pp. 151-52; Janderova and Volf, op. cit., p. 129; Vaclav Cap and Stanislav Dubsky, Statistika, No. 5, 1966, p. 199.

57. Milan Horalek, CEP, No. 7, 1966, p. 54.

58. Emil Moravec, PM, No. 6, 1967, p. 240.

59. Janderova and Volf, op. cit., p. 125.

60. According to the 1961 census 88,162 people were leaving Slovakia annually for work in Czech regions, whereas only 6,149 were migrating from the Czech lands to Slovakia. Jan Mihalik, EC, No. 2, 1966, pp. 130-42. This article also contains useful information on manpower in Slovakia.

61. Jiri Kanturek, KT, February 17, 1966; and Bernard Levcik and Jiri Kosta, NTCE, No. 8, 1968, pp. 53-61.

62. Antonin Straub, HN, August 18, 1967. Michal's estimate (admittedly, a very rough one) indicated that "in 1966 Czechoslovakia's ratio of visible exports to gross national product, in terms of approximate factor cost, was one fifth and the ratio of import to GNP only slightly less than one fifth." Sl. Rev., June, 1968, p. 212. On the marked difference among developed countries in the share of total foreign trade to national income see Simon Kuznets, op. cit., pp. 300 ff.

63. Zauberman, op. cit., p. 280.

64. Michal, Central Planning in Czechoslovakia, p. 98.

65. Ernst, op. cit., pp. 899-902.

66. Zauberman, op. cit. pp. 278-79; Cf. J. Budin, HN, May 3, 1968; and Straub, op. cit.

67. For the reasons and consequences of autarky see Abram Bergson, in Alan A. Brown and Egon Neuberger (eds.), International Trade and Central Planning (Berkeley: University of California Press, forthcoming); Michael Kaser, COMECON (London: Oxford University Press, 1967), pp. 16-21 and passim; John Michael Montias, Economic Development in Communist Rumania (Cambridge, Mass.: The M.I.T. Press, 1967), Chapter 4; and Pryor, op. cit., pp. 23-48.

68. Predvoj, November 24, 1966, p. 13.

69. Cf. Dusana Machova, CSSR v socialisticke mezinarodni delbe prace (Prague: 1962), p. 226; and Rudolf Olsovsky, CEP, No. 3, 1964, p. 188. On the high cost of defense see K. Rotter, Acta Universitatis Carolinea, Oeconomica, I, 1967; and Luciano Barca, Renascita, No. 47, 1967, p. 29.

70. For a brief review of the long-term trade agreements between Czechoslovakia and the U.S.S.R. see Josef Sebasta, NM, No. 16, 1967, pp. 12-13.

71. Anton Strucka, Pravda, November 22, 1967.

72. Sebasta, op. cit. p. 13.

73. Miroslav Stribrsky, PH, No. 12, 1967, pp. 1-12.

74. Ibid.

75. Zdenek Horeni, KT, No. 4, 1968; and Sebasta, op. cit., p. 15.

76. Horeni, op. cit.

77. Zdenek Sedivy, KT, November 2, 1967; and Jan Vintera, Prace, February 26, 1967.

78. Sebasta, op. cit., p. 15.

79. Sedivy, op. cit.

80. Radoslav Selucky in a Radio Prague interview, CTK, March 7, 1968.

81. NS, November 28, 1967.

82. Stribrsky, op. cit.

83. HN, March 10, 1967; and Frantisek Marek, CFT, No. 8, 1967.

84. Sebasta, op. cit.

85. Stribrsky, op. cit.

86. Miroslav Kolanda, PO, No. 12, 1967, p. 556. An estimate of the ratio of export price index to import price index (1964=100) showed 1937 as 102, 1950 as 109, 1955 as 95, and 1960 as 98. Ernst, op. cit., p. 902. Michal suggests that in 1948-54 the "terms of Czechoslovakia's foreign trade worsened more in relation to capitalist countries than in relation to Communist countries." This is not to suggest that trade with the latter "was more advantageous" as the index indicates only relative movements since the base year (1948). "Since 1954 the terms of trade tended to develop more favorably in relation to capitalist countries than in relation to Communist countries, especially in 1955, 1958 and 1961," the last year for which comparative data are available. Sl. Rev., June, 1968, pp. 220-22.

87. Sedivy, op. cit.; Vneshnaya torgovlia SSSR (Moscow: 1967), p. 83; and Vintera, ZN, December 16, 1966.

88. Jan Klacek and Jan Pleva, PE, No. 7-8, 1967, pp. 613-31 and references therein.

89. *Ibid.*, p. 615.

90. Kolanda, *op. cit.*, p. 555.

91. Klacek and Pleva, *op. cit.*

92. Straub, *op. cit.*; and Machova, *op. cit.*, p. 36.

93. Sebasta, *op. cit.*

94. Montias, *op. cit.*, pp. 159-60. Bulgaria and Rumania, two of the least industrialized countries of CMEA, could procure, by contrast to other countries, sizable quantities of machinery from the West since they had sufficient quantities of raw materials and foodstuffs to enjoy a surplus in these groups with the Soviet bloc and, on top of it, to pay for imports of machinery from Western markets. Moreover, after 1960 they benefited from the extension of credits from the West. *Ibid.*, p. 243.

95. Sebasta, *op. cit.*

96. Vitozslav Vinklarek, *PH*, No. 7-8, 1965, p. 162.

97. By 1962 trade with China was a mere 16 per cent of what it had been in 1960. Sedivy, *PE*, No. 7, 1963. p. 541.

98. Barca, *op. cit.*, p. 29.

99. On the questionable benefits of Czechoslovak trade with developing countries see *Pravda*, April 28, 1968; and Barca, *op. cit.*, p. 29. Aid to underdeveloped countries amounted to about $100 million in 1954-56 and reached $276 million in 1960-62. It was subsequently reduced in view of the adverse domestic situation. *MV*, No. 1, 1966.

100. Miroslav Maruska and Vladimir Novacek, *ZO*, No. 10, 1967, p. 1.

101. In addition to data in Tables 30 and 31 and SP, No. 4, 1967, p. 129, somewhat different figures were reported by other sources; e.g., Budin, op. cit.

102. On the failures to meet the capital investment plans in metallurgy and on the problems in development of metallurgy see E. Gajdosek and O. Mesaros, PH, No. 7, 1962.

103. Zdenek Vergner, PH, No. 11, 1964, pp. 2-4.

104. Kouba, CEP, No. 4, 1964, pp. 24-5.

105. Sik, op. cit., pp. 24-5; and Kouba, CEP, No. 6, 1966, pp. 18-20. On the Soviet experience see Alexander Erlich, in Max F. Millikan (ed.), National Economic Planning (New York: National Bureau of Economic Research and Columbia University Press, 1967), p. 260.

106. Cf. Simon Kuznets, op. cit., pp. 20-26, 374-84, and passim; Edward F. Denison, Why Growth Rates Differ (Washington: The Brookings Institution, 1967), pp. 11-12 and Chapter 2; and ESE 1961, Part II, Chapter 2.

107. The important findings of Staller's research on comparative fluctuations in economic activity (1950-60) were "that the planned economies of the Communist bloc were subject to fluctuations in economic activity equal to or greater than those experienced by the free-market economies of the OECD" (Organisation for European Cooperation and Development). Large variations in the amplitude of fluctuations occurred both within and between the groups. For example, Poland, the U.S.S.R., France, Italy, and Norway displayed relatively smooth growth paths, whereas in Bulgaria, Yugoslavia, Greece, Turkey, and the U.S.A. the tempo of economic activity fluctuated considerably. On the whole, "the free-market economies had fewer interruptions in positive growth of total output and, by a slight margin, in agriculture, while planned economies showed fewer lapses from positive growth in industry and construc-

tion." Staller, AER, June, 1964, pp. 388-92; cf. Staller, AER, September, 1967, pp. 879-86.

108. Angus Maddison, Economic Growth in the West (New York: The Twentieth Century Fund, 1964), p. 25. On Western Europe see Dennison, op. cit.; comparative growth rates for nine Western countries are summarized on p. 17; and M. M. Postan, An Economic History of Western Europe 1945-1964 (London: Metheum & Co., 1967; Simon Kuznets, op. cit., passim; and Bergson, Planning and Productivity Under Soviet Socialism (New York: Columbia University Press, 1968), Lecture 3 and the comparative data on productivity in the Appendix.

109. Ernst, op. cit., p. 881.

110. ESE 1961, Part II, Chapter II, pp. 9-10.

111. Estimates of the rate of decline vary from about 2 to 4 per cent.

112. Ernst, op. cit., pp. 882 and 886; cf. Pesek, op. cit., p. 44. For a comprehensive evaluation of personal consumption, see Vaclav Holesovsky, "Personal Consumption in Czechoslovakia, 1937, 1948-60" (Columbia University: Ph.D. dissertation, 1964). The official figures for the annual increment of individual and collective consumption are respectively: for 1950, 16.4 and 10.9 per cent; for 1951, 1.0 and 14.6 per cent; for 1952, 2.3 and 29.9 per cent; for 1953, -3.7 and 17.5 per cent; for 1954, 13.9 and 8.1 per cent; for 1955, 8.0 and -5.6 per cent; for 1956, 8.2 and 0.5 per cent; for 1957, 8.5 and 2.7 per cent; for 1958, 1.0 and 2.2 per cent; for 1959, 5.1 and 3.2 per cent; for 1960, 9.5 and 7.3 per cent; for 1961, 3.4 and 8.0 per cent; for 1962, 2.4 and 5.0 per cent; for 1963, 1.1 and 3.6 per cent; for 1964, 3.0 and 3.7 per cent; and for 1965, 5.1 and 5.2 per cent. ESE 1965, Part II, Chapter 7, p. 67.

113. Ernst, op. cit., pp. 886-7. Personal consumption per capita reportedly increased from 1948 to 1963 by 91 per cent, and real income per

capita doubled during that period. For a summary of official claims see Balek, op. cit., pp. 153-4 and B. Stibalova and Z. Urbanek, PH, No. 1, 1966, pp. 61-68. Selected indicators of prewar and postwar consumption are summarized in SR 1966, pp.454-60. It may be noted that the 1961 census revealed that as a statewide average there were 9.7 square meters of living area per capita and 1.3 persons per room (including kitchens). During the 1961-65 period 408,000 apartments were constructed, but the acute shortages and poor quality of housing prevail. Cf. Holesovsky and Gregor Lazarcik, "Trends in Czechoslovak Housing, Government, and Other Services, 1937-1962," Occasional Papers of the Research Project on National Income in East Central Europe, Columbia University, 1965. Shortages persist, particularly for automobiles, high-grade meats, nylon raincoats, fashion goods, technical novelties, residential construction, trips to foreign countries, etc. Vaclav Cap and Stanislav Dubsky, Statistika, No. 5, 1966, pp. 193-207.

114. Cf. Vladimir Nachtigal, CEP, No. 5, 1965, p. 173.

115. For the development of the Soviet model see Feiwel, The Soviet Quest for Economic Efficiency (New York: Frederick A. Praeger, Inc., 1967), Chapters 1-3.

116. This is not to condone the applicability of the Soviet growth strategy to a particular stage of development or endowment with natural resources--a view currently popular in Eastern Europe. See the contribution by Erlich and comment by Bergson in National Economic Planning. On the notion of extensive development see Sik, PE, No. 1, 1966, pp. 2 ff.; Gunther Kohlmey, CEP, No. 6, 1966, pp. 23-30; and Simon Kuznets, op. cit., pp. 72 ff.

117. Goldmann, PH, No. 11, 1964, pp. 11 ff.

118. For a summary of statistical evidence see Sik, PE, No. 1, 1966, pp. 13 ff.; and Nachtigal, CEP, No. 5, 1965, p. 171. For a criticism of the

measurement of labor productivity see Feiwel, Economics of a Socialist Enterprise, Chapter 5.

119. Ernst, op. cit., p. 892.

120. Cf. Maddison, op. cit., pp. 76 ff.; and Simon Kuznets, op. cit., passim.

121. WES 1959, Part I, Chapter III, pp. 112 and 128.

122. Obviously the results differ with the kind of price weights used and are not easily reconcilable. Cf. Sik, PE, No. 1, 1966, p. 13.

123. Oldrych Kyn, "The Process of Development of a Centralized Economic System in Czechoslovakia" (mimeographed, no date), p. 9. The incremental capital-output ratio for the economy at large was reported for the period 1950-55 as 2.61, for 1955-60 as 3.14, and for 1960-65 as 14.28. The incremental capital-output ratios related to productive investments were for the period 1950-55, 1.84; for 1955-60, 2.24; and for 1960-65, 10.83. The comparison of relative increases in the incremental capital-output ratios in Eastern Europe indicates that Czechoslovakia was holding the lead. EBE, Vol. 18, No. 1, p. 39.

124. When Czechoslovak economists speak of the optimum rate of growth of national income or the maximum rate (share) of investment in national income, their theoretical framework is derived from Michal Kalecki's work. See Kalecki, in Essays in Planning and Economic Development (Warsaw: 1963), pp. 11 ff; and Mojmir Hajek and Miroslav Toms, PE, No. 1, 1967, pp. 17-23; and PE, No. 3, 1963, pp. 191 ff. For discussion of the controversies surrounding this concept see, inter alia, Branko Horvat, Towards a Theory of Planned Economy (Belgrade: Yugoslav Institute of Economic Research, 1964); Benjamin Ward, AER, June, 1967, pp. 516-18; and Amartya Sen, EJ, September, 1961, pp. 479-96. The same terminology is often used in Czechoslovakia (Eastern Europe) to describe the empirically formed

notion of the maximum allowable growth rate or share of investment in national income. Generally attention is concentrated on the adverse repercussions that follow from the overcommitment of resources ensuing from the proclivity of political decision-makers to maximize the immediate rate of growth. For a further discussion see Feiwel, The Soviet Quest for Economic Efficiency, Chapter 1.

125. Srein and Tlusty, op. cit.

126. Supra, p. 21.

127. Srein and Tlusty stressed the importance of structural changes in the decline of effectiveness of investments. They pointed out that electric power, fuels, mining, and metallurgy's share in total fixed assets increased from 35 per cent in 1950 to 43 per cent in 1960, but these industries exhibited the lowest increases in effectiveness of investments. Apparently, structural changes in industrial output (measured by share in fixed capital) led to a shift of weight within industry to those sectors where increase of output was most capital intensive, manifesting itself in the increase of the over-all capital-output ratio. Op. cit., p. 191.

128. For the deviation of the "potential" growth rates see Hajek and Toms, in Ekonomicky Ustav, Ceskoslovenske Akademie Ved, Studie z teorie ekonomickeho rustu (Prague: 1966), pp. 108-12; and PE, No. 1, 1967, pp. 15-26. It may be noted that B. Mikhalevsky fitted a Cobb-Douglas production function to data on postwar Soviet economic growth. During the period 1951-53 he attributed 68.19 per cent of economic growth to extensive factors and 31.81 per cent to increase in efficiency (mainly due to technical progress). The respective figures for 1959-63 were 94.42 and 5.58 per cent and for the 1964-70 plan 81.18 and 18.82 per cent. EMM, No. 2, 1967, pp. 199-222; cf. Robert M. Solow, REStat., August, 1957, pp. 312-20.

129. Simon Kuznets, op. cit., pp. 80-81. It

would seem that Kuznets does not attribute a crucial role to improvements in allocative efficiency. See Benjamin Higgins, Economic Development (New York: W. W. Norton & Company, 1968), pp. 425-30; Everett E. Hagen, The Economics of Development (Homewood, Illinois: Richard D. Irwin, 1968), pp. 188-92; and Bergson, Planning and Productivity Under Soviet Socialism. On the decomposition of sources of economic growth see also Denison, op. cit., and The Sources of Economic Growth in the United States (New York: Committee for Economic Development, 1962).

130. Simon Kuznets, op. cit., p. 82.

131. Goldmann, PH, No. 9, 1964, pp. 1-14 ; and No. 11, 1964, pp. 11-27; Goldmann and Kouba, Hospodarsky rust v CSSR (Prague: 1967); and Goldmann and Josef Flek, PH, No. 9, 1967.

132. Cf. Kalecki, in Oskar Lange (ed.), Zagadnienia ekonomii politycznej socjalizmu, (Warsaw: 1959), pp. 145-75; Kalecki, Zarys teorii wzrostu gospodarki socjalistycznej (Warsaw: 1963); and Zauberman, Kyklos, No. 3, 1966.

133. The value of the total effect of non-investment factors of growth ($u_1 + u_2 - a$) on the growth rate was obtained by applying a linear trend to the observed rates of growth by using multiple correlation techniques, with the ratio I/D and time as independent variables and growth rates as dependent variables. The value of I/D was obtained from official statistics of national income, adjusted for depreciation; 1/m was calculated as equal to 0.48. The reciprocal value of the incremental fixed capital-output ratio (assumed constant) was m = 2.08. Having obtained ($u_1 + u_2 - a$) and ascertained the values of u_1 and a from published statistics (the value of u_1 was estimated on the basis of published indicators of the degree of utilization of basic types of machinery and equipment in the various branches of industry and transport and a was estimated on the basis of official statistics), the value of u_2 was found as a residual from the equation ($u_1 + u_2 - a$) = 1.3 +

$u_2 - 1.0 = -0.81$.

134. It is worth noting that as early as 1964, Benedikt Korda seriously questioned whether the imperative planning system had any positive effects at all, even during the early 1950's. PE, No. 4, 1964, pp. 86-7.

135. Goldmann and Kouba, Hospodarsky rust v CSSR, pp. 88-107; cf. HN, April 21, 1967.

136. Goldmann and Kouba, Hospodarsky rust v CSSR, p. 100.

137. Ibid., Chapter 6.

138. Aside from the inspiration Goldmann drew from Kalecki's work, he was also strongly influenced by Wlodzimierz Brus, Ogolne problemy funkcjonowania gospodarki socjalistycznej (Warsaw: 1961). For an exposition of Brus's views see Feiwel, The Economics of a Socialist Enterprise, Chapter 1. In addition to Western writings, Goldmann refers, inter alia, to the Soviet economists G. A. Feldmann and A. I. Notkin; to the Polish economists Oskar Lange, Jozef Pajestka, Bronislaw Minc, Wladyslaw Sadowski, Ryszard Chelinski, and Aleksander Lukasiewicz; and Yugoslav economists Radmila Stojanovich and Branko Horvat. Hospodarsky rust v CSSR, pp. 54 and passim.

139. Kalecki, in Essays in Planning and Economic Development, p. 12.

140. The designation "quasi" is used to denote the "fundamental" difference between cycles deemed inherent in the capitalistic economy, of which the planned economy is supposedly free, but which result only from "subjectivism and voluntarism." "Quasi-cycles in the rate of growth of the socialist economy are, to some degree, exogenous in character, as far as their origin is concerned. They are not inherent in our economy, and, hence, they are not inevitable. Because of this, we call them quasi-cycles." Goldmann and Flek, PH, No. 9, 1967, p. 10.

141. Often changes in the volume of unfinished construction are much smaller than the changes in inventories which are of decisive significance. It is admitted that it may be inappropriate to consider every increment in inventories and unfinished construction as growth-decelerating factors and that further investigation is required to study the behavior of various components of inventories during the cycle.

142. Cf. Kalecki, Zarys teorii wzrostu gospodarki socjalistycznej, Chapter 6.

143. Cf. Staller, AER, June, 1964, pp. 388-9; and T. V. Ryabushkin, Tempy i proportsii narodnovo khozyaistva sotsialisticheskikh stran (Moscow: 1966), p. 73.

144. See ESE 1962, Chapter I, p. 31.

145. Goldmann and Flek, PH, No. 11, 1967, p. 11.

146. In 1962 Zdenek Vergner maintained that the deteriorating performance was not of a temporary nature, but was due to structural dislocations, and reached far back to the pattern of development and allocation of investment in the First FYP--perpetuated thereafter. He implied that the situation could only be remedied by restructuring the economy, as discussed above; chiefly by reshuffling investment priorities. Neither the size nor the rate of investment was questioned, but only its pattern. PH, No. 11, 1962, p. 2.

147. Karel Soska, RP, March 9, 1966.

148. Goldmann and A. Suk, RP, January 18, 1966.

149. For support, reference was made to Western experience as assessed by Simon Kuznets, op. cit., pp. 76 ff.

150. Ladislav Jungling, RP, March 22, 1966; Goldmann, Jungling, and K. Janecek, NTCE, No. 5, 1966, pp. 77 ff.

151. *Ibid.*

152. Flek, Goldmann, and Kouba, *RP*, June 23, 1966; and Goldmann and Kouba, *HN*, April 24, 1967.

NOTES TO CHAPTER 2

1. For an illuminating discussion of the institutional changes see the excellent paper by John Michael Montias, _Survey_, April, 1964, pp. 63-76.

2. Cf. Radoslav Selucky, _VZ_, No. 3, 1964, p. 151.

3. Karel Kaplan, _CCH_, No. 6, 1966, pp. 858-59.

4. Cf. Karol Bacilek, _Tvorba_, December 20, 1951.

5. _RP_, January 29, 1953.

6. Jiri Tesar, _HN_, No. 29, 1964.

7. _ESE 1953_, Part II, p. 60. For a good assessment of the First FYP see Kaplan, _CCH_, No.3, 1965, pp. 350-69.

8. Cf. Viliam Siroky, _RP_, December 6, 1953.

9. _RP_, October 4, 1957; and Otakar Simunek, _PH_, No. 11, 1967.

10. _SS_, October 19, 1958.

11. _RP_, July 6, 1960.

12. _EF_, No. 8, 1952; and _FU_, No. 1, 1953.

13. Ladislav Veltrusky, _HN_, No. 22, 1966.

14. Wladyslaw Jaworski, _Systemy kredytowe europejskich krajow socjalistycznych_ (Warsaw: 1962), pp. 125-27.

15. _RP_, September 16, 1963.

16. ESE 1954, p. 40.

17. RP, August 12, 1955.

18. RP, January 14, 1954.

19. RP, October 17, 1953.

20. Siroky, RP, June 12, 1954; RP, June 14 and June 15, 1954.

21. Maurice H. Dobb, Papers on Capitalism, Development, and Planning (New York: International Publishers, 1967), p. 194; and my review in AER, June, 1968, pp. 592-95.

22. Ragnar Frisch, "An Implementation System for Optimal National Economic Planning Without Detailed Quantity Fixation From a Central Authority" (Oslo: Memorandum from the Institute of Economics, University of Oslo, September, 1963). For a general discussion of plan construction in Soviet-type economies see L. M. Dudkin, Optymalnyi materialnyi balans narodnovo khoziaystva (Moscow: 1966).

23. Cf. Alfred Zauberman, Aspects of Planometrics (New Haven: Yale University Press, 1967), p. 254; and Karel Kouba, CEP, No. 6, 1966, p. 17.

24. Cf. Otakar Turek, PE, No. 5, 1964, pp. 384-85.

25. Cf. Turek, HN, No. 33, 1964, p. 4.

26. "As soon as a plan was adopted, its fulfillment became the criterion for satisfying the goals of society; but it would have been more logical to regard the interest of society as the criterion by which to judge the expediency of fulfilling the plan." Oldrich Kyn, PH, No. 12, 1964, p. 24; cf. Selucky, KT, February 28, 1963.

27. Cf. Ota Sik, PE, No. 1, 1966, p. 26.

28. Cf. Bohumil Komenda and Cestmir Kozusnik,

PE, No. 3, 1964, pp. 220-21.

29. Sik, op. cit., p. 25.

30. Cf. Frantisek Bores and Ladislav Matejka, PE, No. 8, 1963, p. 639.

31. Sik, op. cit., p. 26.

32. Komenda and Kozusnik, op. cit., p. 221.

33. Sik, op. cit., p. 26.

34. Bores and Matejka, op. cit., p. 640.

35. Sik, op. cit., pp. 25-6.

36. Selucky, VZ, No. 12, 1962, p. 701.

37. Sik, op. cit., p. 27.

38. While prices remained unaltered, quality deteriorated; de facto the price stability was an illusion. Cf. Anton Klas, HN, No. 19, 1964.

39. Pavel Vlach, HN, No. 26, 1964.

40. For an exposition of the dual price system see George R. Feiwel, The Economics of a Socialist Enterprise (New York: Frederick A. Praeger, Inc., 1965), Chapter 2.

41. Kozusnik, Problemy teorie hodnoty a ceny za socializmu (Prague: 1964), pp. 224, 241, and 284.

42. Kozusnik, VZ, No. 7, 1964, p. 386.

43. Komenda and Kozusnik, op. cit., p. 230.

44. Sik, op. cit., p. 27.

45. Ibid. p. 28.

46. Leopold Ler, FU, No. 6, 1964, p. 324.

47. For a discussion of khozraschet see Feiwel, The Soviet Quest for Economic Efficiency (New York: Frederick A. Praeger, Inc., 1967), pp. 59 and 74-5.

48. Veltrusky, op. cit.

49. Jiri Tesar and Vladimir Siba, PH, No. 8-9, 1966, p. 32.

50. Turek, HN, No. 22, 1966.

51. Cf. Komenda and Kozusnik, op. cit., p. 222; and Sik, op. cit., p. 23.

52. Antonin Novotny, RP, June 12, 1956.

53. Siroky, RP, June 13, 1956. On the scope of increased autonomy for enterprises and on the new powers of the Slovak National Council to approve economic plans and budgets for Slovakia, within the limits set by the central government, and to nominate members to the Board of Commissioners see ESE 1956, Chapter I, pp. 40-1.

54. Cf. Sik, Prace, March 5, 1968.

55. Cf. Novotny, RP, December 8, 1956; on fulfillment of the 1956 plan see in particular RP, February 12 and 13, 1957.

56. RP, March 2 and 6, 1957.

57. RP, October 4, 1957.

58. Cf. RP, March 6 and 7, 1957.

59. Miroslav Rosicky, CEP, No.2, 1962, pp. 41-6.

60. Ibid., p. 44.

61. Prace, November 18, 1956, and November 25, 1956; RP, December 6, 1956.

62. RP, March 14, 1957; Prace, January 8, 1957; cf. RP, April 20, 1957; and RP, December 8 and 10,

1957.

63. Rosicky, *op. cit.*, p. 57.

64. *RP*, June 19, 1958; and *Prace*, July 23, 1958.

65. *RP*, May 21, 1958.

66. Cf. Jiri Kosta and A. Cervenkova, *LN*, May 27, 1967.

67. B. Kratochvil, *HN*, No. 25, 1962; and Miroslav Sokol, *PH*, No. 11, 1961.

68. *PE*, No. 3, 1964, p. 266.

69. Rosicky, *op. cit.*, pp. 50-54.

70. *PE*, No. 3, 1964, p. 265; and *ESE 1960*, Chapter II, p. 12.

71. *PH*, No. 2, 1960; cf. *RP*, February 16, 1960.

72. *RP*, September 13, 1959. For a graphical illustration of the planning procedure see Rosicky, *op. cit.*, pp. 66-7.

73. Adam Zwass, *GP*, No. 4, 1963, p. 34.

74. Rosicky, *op. cit.*, p. 48.

75. *RP*, November 28, 1962.

76. For an exposition of settlement prices see Feiwel, *Economics of a Socialist Enterprise*, pp. 91-2.

77. Vladimir Janza and Jiri Typolt, *Zagadnienia ksztaltowania cen w nowym systemie zarzadzania przemyslem Czechoslowacji* (Translated from the Czech) (Warsaw: 1960), pp. 20-83.

78. Miroslav Koudelka, *NM*, No. 4, 1961.

79. Jaworski, *op. cit.*, pp. 146-7.

80. Ibid., p. 147.

81. Cf. Komenda and Kozusnik, HN, No. 13, 1964; Sik, PE, No. 1, 1966, p. 28; and Sik, Prace, March 5, 1968.

82. Sokol, op. cit.

83. Bores and Matejka, op. cit., p. 640.

84. Sokol, op. cit.

85. J. Novak, HN, No. 34, 1964.

86. PH, No. 10, 1963, p. 63.

87. For a distinction between "earned" and "unearned" profits and a discussion of audits, manipulations, and confiscations see Koudelka, op. cit.

88. PE, No. 3, 1964, p. 266.

89. Bores and Matejka, op. cit., p. 639; cf. PH, No. 10, 1963, pp. 62-3; Sik, PE, No. 1, 1966, p. 28; and Sokol, op. cit.

90. PE, No. 3, 1964, p. 265.

91. Jaworski, op. cit., p. 133.

92. Milan Reh and Miroslav Zidicky, FU, No. 5, 1964, pp. 266-70.

93. Kosta and Cervenkova, op. cit.

94. Tesar, HN, No. 29, 1964.

95. Reh and Zidicky, op. cit., pp. 266-70.

96. ESE 1960, Chapter II, p. 12.

97. Tesar, HN, No. 29, 1964.

98. ESE 1961, Chapter II, p. 21.

99. Vladimir Jindra, FU, No. 4, 1964, p. 235; Florian Brousek, HN, No. 16, 1964.

100. Karel Johanovsky, PH, No. 4, 1963, p. 3.

101. Bohumil Vondracek, PS, No. 11, 1962, pp. 565-66.

102. Miroslav Belohlavek, PS, No. 12, 1963, pp. 629-31.

103. Zidicky, PH, No. 8, 1963, p. 78.

104. Belohlavek, *op. cit*. p. 630.

105. Reh and Zidicky, *op. cit*., p. 270.

106. ESE 1962, Part I, Chapter I, p. 33.

107. Jaworski, *op. cit*., p. 134.

108. *Basic Questions of the Financial Economy of the Czechoslovak Socialist Republic* (Prague: 1965), pp. 44-5.

109. Jiri Zanecek, FU, No. 7, 1964, p. 393.

110. Jaworski, *op. cit*., p. 132.

111. Bronislaw Blass, *Zagadnienia systemu finansowego przedsiebiorstw przemyslowych w panstwach socjalistycznych* (Warsaw: 1964), p. 180.

112. Zanecek, *op. cit*., p. 393.

113. Johanovsky, *op. cit*. pp. 3-4.

114. Blass, *op. cit*., p. 181.

115. Ler, *op. cit*., pp. 325-26.

116. Reh and Zidicky, *op. cit*., p. 272.

117. Milan Bouchal, FU, No. 6, 1964, p. 356.

118. Ler, *op. cit*., p. 328.

119. Zanecek, *op. cit*., p. 396.

120. *Ibid*., p. 386.

121. Bohumil Kotrc and Milos Vesely, *FU*, No. 3, 1964, pp. 129-38.

122. Komenda and Kozusnik, *PE*, No. 3, 1964, pp. 223-24.

123. Cf. Selucky, *VZ*, No. 3, 1964, pp. 152-53.

NOTES TO CHAPTER 3

1. Jiri Kosta and A. Cervenkova, LN, May 27, 1967.

2. There were marked differences between Slovakia and the Czech lands. The rate of over-all advancement was at a snail's pace in comparison to the postwar upsurge in living standards in Western Europe.

3. Karel Kaplan, CCH, No. 6, 1966, p. 845. See, however, the claims about Karel Englis' contributions by Jaroslav George Polach in Miroslav Rechcigl Jr. (ed.), The Czechoslovak Contribution to World Culture (The Hague: Mouton & Co., 1964), pp. 329-41.

4. Otakar Turek, HN, No. 43, 1967.

5. Oldrych Kyn, PE, No. 7, 1965, p. 695.

6. For samples of Czechoslovak writings on planometrics see CEP, Nos. 3 and 4, 1964; and the periodical Ekonomicko-matematicky obzor first published in 1965.

7. Benedikt Korda, PH, No. 7, 1963, pp. 79-80.

8. Cf. Ota Sik, PE, No. 1, 1966, p. 24; and Jozef Cibulka, OMF, No. 3, 1964, p. 238.

9. RP, December 27, 1961; RP, February 3, 1962; RP, July 6, 1962; Antonin Novotny, RP, January 2, 1962.

10. RP, March 30, 1962; PH, No. 3, 1962, pp. 5 ff.; and Zdenek Vergner, PH, No. 11, 1962, p. 2.

11. RP, May 25, 1962; The Economist, May 12,

1962, p. 546; cf. Vergner, _op. cit_., p. 4.

12. _SK_, No. 2, 1963, p. 2; _RP_, February 2, 1963.

13. _WES 1962_, Part II, p. 79; and _ESE 1962_, Chapter I, p. 24.

14. D. Scheibal and Jan Vintera, _PH_, No. 11, 1963, pp. 1-2; _RP_, January 9, 1963; and Vergner, _op. cit_., pp. 4-5.

15. _SK_, No. 2, 1963, pp. 9 ff.

16. _Ibid_., pp. 3 and 13.

17. _Ibid_., p. 13.

18. _RP_, January 9, 1963.

19. _ESE 1963_, Chapter I, pp. 4 ff.; and Scheibal and Vintera, _op. cit_., pp. 1-2.

20. _HN_, July 12, 1963; _SZ_, No. 3, 1963; _EBE_, August, 1963, p. 50; and Scheibal and Vintera, _op. cit_., pp. 2-4.

21. Drahomir Kolder, _RP_, January 26, 1964; _RP_, February 11, 1964; _HN_, No. 9, 1964; and _ESE 1963_, Chapter I, pp. 2-5, 30, 53, and 10.

22. _NS_, June 6, 1962.

23. Zbigniew K. Brzezinski, _The Soviet Bloc_ (Cambridge, Mass.: Harvard University Press, 1967), pp. 94-5; J. F. Brown, _The New Eastern Europe_ (New York: Frederick A. Praeger, Inc., 1966), pp. 22-6.

24. _RP_, August 14, 1962; and Novotny, _RP_, December 5, 1962.

25. Radoslav Selucky, _KT_, February 7, 1963; cf. Milan Plachky, _HN_, May 24, 1963.

26. Novotny, _RP_, March 24, 1963.

27. For a similar view see Barbara Wolfe Jancar, "The Twenty-second Congress and the All-people's State in Czechoslovakia" (Columbia University: Ph. D. Dissertation, 1965), p. 109.

28. See Karol Rosenbaum, KZ, May 4, 1963; Miro Hysko, Pravda, June 3, 1963; RP, June 15, 1963; Jiri Hendrych, RP, June 29, 1963.

29. RP, August 8, 1963; Pravda, July 18, 1963.

30. Josef Lenart, RP, September 26, 1963. On the reshuffle see The Economist, September 28, 1963, p. 1102.

31. Selucky, KZ, August 10, 1963.

32. Sik, Ekonomika, zajmy, polityka (Prague: 1962); NM, No. 9, 1963; and RP, November 22, 1963. For an expanded version of Sik's views see his Plan and Market Under Socialism (Prague: 1967).

33. RP, December 22, 1963.

34. HN, Nos. 45 and 46, 1963.

35. Vladimir Koucky, RP, December 24, 1963.

36. Kolder, RP, January 26, 1964.

37. RP, April 6, 1964.

38. RP, May 29 and 30, 1964.

39. RP, April 3, 1964; and The Economist, May 2, 1964, p. 478.

40. Novotny, RP, August 28, 1964.

41. Selucky, VZ, No. 3, 1964, p. 152.

42. RP, December 19, 1964.

43. RP, December 22, 1964.

44. Novotny, RP, January 3, 1965.

45. Lenart, RP, February 2, 1965; RP, February 3, 1965.

46. This entire section is based on "Draft Principles of a System for Improving the Economy's Planned Management," RP, October 17, 1964. It is worth noting that the economists' original proposal (so-called Yellow Paper) included a section on the political, social, and institutional alterations required to ensure the successful implementation of the economic reform. This entire section was apparently found unacceptable and was never included with the draft principles. Sik, Prace, March 5, 1968.

47. This is a concept borrowed and adapted from the Yugoslav brand of "market socialism." See Benjamin N. Ward, AER, September, 1958, pp. 566-89.

48. To place the Czechoslovak discussion in its proper perspective, one would have to revert to the interwar debate on the economic merit of socialism. The reader is strongly urged to consult Abram Bergson's illuminating article in JPE, October, 1967, pp. 655-73.

49. Sik, WMR, No. 3, 1965, p. 18.

50. Sik, in Charles H. Feinstein (ed.), Socialism, Capitalism, and Economic Growth (Cambridge: Cambridge University Press, 1967), pp. 154-57.

51. There were suggestions that annual national economic plans be dispensed with and that only "correctives" to long-term plans be announced to adjust for changing conditions.

52. Sik, NM, No. 9, 1964. The "unrealistic and abstract" premises of the indicative five-year plans were subjected to vehement criticism by the traditional imperative planners. See, for example, Kurt Rozsypal of the SPC in HN, No. 9, 1964; cf.

Otakar Turek, HN, No. 43, 1967.

53. Ladislav Matejka, PH, No. 2, 1964, pp. 32-4.

54. See George R. Feiwel, The Soviet Quest for Economic Efficiency (New York: Frederick A. Praeger, Inc., 1967), Chapter 1.

55. Turek, PE, No. 5, 1964, pp. 385-91.

56. Czechoslovak economists draw heavily on Kalecki's paper "Method of Constructing a Perspective Plan" in Essays on Planning and Economic Development (Warsaw: 1963). "The average annual rate of growth of the national income may be considered the most important parameter of a long-term plan. Thus the selection of the correct variant of the plan is really tantamount to a choice of the appropriate rate of growth of the national income." Ibid., p. 11.

57. Karel Kouba, CEP, No. 6, 1966, pp. 19-20.

58. Ibid., pp. 12-13.

59. Ibid., p. 12.

60. Oskar Lange, Political Economy, I (Translated from Polish by A. H. Walker) (New York: The Macmillan Company, 1963), p. 167.

61. Kouba, op. cit., p. 14.

62. Ibid., p. 15.

63. Kyn, PH, No. 12, 1964, pp. 23-30.

64. Bohumil Komenda and Cestmir Kozusnik, PE, No. 3, 1964, p. 224

65. Rudolf Kocanda, PH, No. 2, 1964, pp. 25 and 28-9.

66. Komenda, PH, No. 7, 1964, p. 30.

67. Komenda, PE, No. 9, 1966, pp. 771 and 773.

68. Sik, WMR, No. 3, 1965, p. 17; and Selucky, HN, No. 45, 1963.

69. Kocman, PE, No. 3, 1964, p. 259; Oldrych Truhlar, PE, No. 3, 1964, p. 263; and Truhlar, PE, No. 5, 1964, p. 429.

70. Bohumil Krejcar and Jiri Tesar, PH, No. 11, 1964, pp. 30-31 and 33-34.

71. See Truhlar, PE, No. 5, 1964, p. 427.

72. Sik, RP, November 22, 1963.

73. Sik, NM, No. 9, 1964.

74. Komenda and Kozusnik, *op. cit.*, pp. 226-8.

75. Miroslav Koudelka, FU, No. 8, 1964, p. 461.

76. Komenda and Kozusnik, *op. cit.*, p. 229.

77. Turek, HN, No. 33, 1964.

78. Jaroslav Libus, HN, No. 32, 1964.

79. Turek, HN, No. 33, 1964.

80. *Ibid.*

81. L. Machon, HN, No. 31, 1964.

82. Vaclav Filip, HN, No. 12, 1964.

83. Miroslav Tucek, FU, No. 9, 1964, pp. 529-34.

84. Zdenik Kodet, HN, No. 23, 1964.

85. Kozusnik, PH, No. 6, 1964, pp. 26-27.

86. Komenda and Kozusnik, *op. cit.*, pp. 231-32.

87. Sik, CEP, No. 5, 1965, pp. 29-30.

88. Kozusnik, PH, No. 6, 1964, p. 28.

89. Sik, WMR, No. 3, 1965, p. 20.

90. Vladimir Kadera, HN, No. 19, 1964.

91. Kozusnik, PH, No. 6, 1964, pp. 27 and 29.

92. Rolf Grunwald, FU, No. 10, 1966, pp. 620-22.

93. Kozusnik, PH, No. 6, 1964, p. 31; and Kozusnik, VZ, No. 7, 1964, pp. 388-90.

94. Kyn, PE, No. 3, 1964, p. 269.

95. Kozusnik, PH, No. 6, 1964, p. 32.

96. Komenda, PE, No. 9, 1966, p. 776.

97. *Ibid*., pp. 775-77.

98. Reported by Josef Valach, FU, No. 5, 1964, p. 319.

99. Julius Branik, HN, No. 23, 1964.

100. Karel Prochazka and Milos Ruzicka, HN, No. 20, 1964.

101. Tesar, HN, No. 29, 1964.

102. Matejka, *op. cit*., p. 35.

103. Turek, PE, No. 5, 1964, pp. 392-93.

104. Tesar, *op. cit*.

105. Matejka, *op. cit*., p. 35.

106. Koudelka, *op. cit*., p. 465.

107. Jan Pleva, PH, No. 12, 1964; and Viliam Cerniansky and Pleva, HN, No. 9, 1965.

108. Frantisek Hamouz, NM, No. 11, 1964.

109. For the various methods of calculating the coefficients see Bohumil Zajic and Ladislav Tokan, PH, No. 6, 1965.

110. Pleva, *op. cit.*; and Cerniansky and Pleva, *op. cit.*

111. Miroslav Sokol, PH, No. 5, 1964, pp. 31-44.

112. Truhlar, PE, No. 5, 1964, pp. 430-33.

113. Jaroslav Vejvoda, PE, No. 3, 1964, pp. 237-50.

114. PE, No. 3, 1964, p. 259.

115. In a report of a price conference organized by HN, Frantisek Nagy, HN, No. 44, 1964.

116. Cf. Vejvoda, EC, No. 10, 1966, pp. 919-30; Felix Oliva, EC, No. 10, 1966, pp. 904-18; and Sik's criticism of the above in EC, No. 5, 1967, pp. 434-48; and Oliva's reply in EC, No. 9, 1967, pp. 916-25.

NOTES TO CHAPTER 4

1. Miloslav Kohoutek, HN, No. 13, 1965.

2. HN, No. 20, 1965.

3. Ibid.; and Supplement to HN, No. 16, 1966.

4. Josef Goldmann and Josef Flek, in CESES International Seminar (Florence: September 15, 1966), Part II, p. 126.

5. HN, No. 20, 1965.

6. For a comprehensive description of the relationships between EPU's and the Ministry of Heavy Industry see Supplements to HN, Nos. 15 and 16, 1966; in the chemical industry see Supplement to HN, No. 30, 1965; in mining see Rudy, January 1, 1966; in consumer goods production see Supplement to HN, No. 31, 1965; in the food industry see Supplement to HN, No. 33, 1965; in construction see Supplement to HN, No. 21, 1965; and in domestic trade see Supplement to HN, No. 46, 1965.

7. Zdenek Valouch, NTCE, No. 5, 1967, pp. 57-66.

8. This is similar to the approach adopted in East Germany.

9. Interview with Kohoutek, HN, No. 6, 1965.

10. Karel Kotrbaty, KT, No. 16, 1965.

11. Ibid.

12. Slavomir Vosecky, HN, No. 20, 1965.

13. Kotrbaty, op. cit.; PO, No. 8, 1965, p. 341.

14. Interview with Kohoutek, op. cit.; PO, No. 8, 1965, p. 341.

15. Jan Helexa and Vladimir Trangos, HN, No. 37, 1965; reported by Frantisek Nagy, HN, No. 25, 1965; and Juraj Balaz et al., HN, No. 19, 1965.

16. Bohumil Krejcar, Karel Prochazka, and Jiri Tesar, PH, No. 1, 1965, p. 31.

17. PO, No. 8, 1965, p. 337.

18. Ibid.; Krejcar, Prochazka, and Tesar, op. cit., p. 31; and interview with Kohoutek, op. cit.

19. PO, No. 8, 1965, p. 340.

20. PO, No. 1, 1966, pp. 3-4. For examples of individual experiments with the inter-enterprise system see Karel Matous, Figyelo, July 28, 1965; and Nagy, op. cit.

21. PO, No. 8, 1965, p. 337.

22. For example in 1959 the ratio of wages of workers to that of engineers was 100:133 and by 1963 it was 100:126.

23. Ladislav Klinko, HN, No. 40, 1965.

24. Matous, op. cit.

25. Vladimir Marcon, HN, No. 38, 1965.

26. This is somewhat similar to the method adopted by the Soviets to convert their enterprises to the reformed system in 1966. See George R. Feiwel, The Soviet Quest for Economic Efficiency (New York: Frederick A. Praeger, Inc. 1967), pp. 292-304.

27. Jan Vitek, PM, No. 9, 1966, pp. 419-21.

28. *Ibid*., p. 422.

29. Bohumil Krejcar and Jiri Tesar, *HN*, No. 23, 1965.

30. Miroslav Pospisil, *HN*, No. 32, 1965. For the experience of the Trinec Iron Works see Rajmund Tesarcik, *FU*, No. 12, 1965, pp. 734-35. The experience of the Klement Gottwald New Metal Works in Kuncice which had been experimenting since 1963 served as a basis for tests in metallurgy. See Bohuslav Mestak, *PO*, No. 2, 1965, pp. 63-65.

31. Vladislav Jebavy and Josef Kepecky, *HN*, No. 38, 1965; *PO*, No. 1, 1966, p. 2.

32. Jebavy and Kepecky, *op. cit*.

33. *Ibid*.; and Kotrbaty, *op. cit*.

34. Jebavy and Kepecky, *op. cit*.

35. Kotrbaty, *op. cit*.

36. Vladimir Kadera and Karel Prochazka, *HN*, No. 39, 1965; and Krejcar and Tesar, *op. cit*.

37. Tesarcik, *op. cit*., p. 736.

38. Interview with Kohoutek, *op. cit*.

39. Krejcar, Prochazka, and Tesar, *op. cit*., p. 38; and Krejcar and Tesar, *op. cit*.

40. *PO*, No. 1, 1966, p. 2; *PO*, No. 8, 1965, p. 339; and Vosecky, *op. cit*.

41. Ladislav Hula, *PM*, No. 11, 1965, p. 505.

42. Krejcar and Tesar, *op. cit*.; and *PO*, No. 8, 1965, p. 338.

43. Numerous examples were cited in *PO*, No. 8, 1965, p. 338.

44. Krejcar, Prochazka, and Tesar, *op. cit.*, pp. 33-36.

45. *Ibid.*, pp. 37-38.

NOTES TO CHAPTER 5

1. Josef Goldmann, Josef Flek, and Karel Kouba, RP, June 23, 1966; and Ota Sik, PE, No. 1, 1966, p. 32.

2. Goldmann, EC, No. 4, 1966; SR 1967, p. 25; Goldmann, HN, April 21, 1967; and Sik, *op. cit*., p. 31.

3. RP, January 29, 1965; ESE 1964, Chapter I, pp. 2, 6, 8, 15-16, and 28; ESE 1966, Chapter II, p. 2.

4. RP, January 28, 1966; Supplement to HN, No. 5, 1966; ESE 1965, Part I, Chapter I, pp. 2, 6, 12, 16-17, 19, 35-36; and ESE 1966, Chapter II, pp. 2 and 30.

5. The following description of the Fourth FYP relies heavily on Vladimir Lukes and Vaclav Rendl, PH, No. 6, 1965, pp. 1-10; Eduard Pracko, PH, No. 9, 1965, pp. 27-38; interview with Zdenek Vergner and Miroslav Soucek, HN, No. 29, July 23, 1965; Antonin Novotny, RP, June 1, 1966; Oldrich Cernik, RP, October 28, 1966; Rendl, CEP, No. 9, 1967, pp. 7-21; Lukes, NTCE, No. 8, 1966, pp. 38-42; ESE 1966, Chapter II, pp. 42-52; Bohumil Sokol, HN, No. 17, 1966; and the article on the preparations for long-term forecasts of economic development by Soucek, Vergner, and J. Tauchman, PH, Nos. 9, 10, 11, 1965.

6. Miloslav Kohoutek, PH, No. 7-8, 1965, pp. 2-3.

7. Josef Lenart, NM, No. 1, 1966.

8. Sik, NTCE, No. 2, 1966, p. 65.

9. M. Kulich and Vl. Markvart, PH, No. 7-8, pp. 27-33.

10. Kohoutek, op. cit., pp. 4-5.

11. Karel Kouba, Miroslav Sokol, and Otakar Turek, PH, No. 1, 1966, pp. 17-18.

12. NTCE, No. 2, 1966, pp. 33-34.

13. Stanislav Sourek, FU, No. 7, 1965, pp. 396-97.

14. Leopold Ler, FU, No. 1, 1966, p. 4.

15. Sourek, op. cit., pp. 396-97.

16. Ler, op. cit., p. 4; cf. A. N. Kosygin, Pravda, September 28, 1965.

17. Ler, op. cit., p. 3.

18. Since these calculations were made in 1965, estimates had to be made on the expected results by the end of 1965 and adjusted for windfall gains and unusual losses.

19. Supplement to HN, No. 15-16, 1966.

20. Sourek, op. cit., pp. 397-400.

21. Cf. Vladimir Jindra, FU, No. 7, 1965, p. 407.

22. Cernik, RP, December 19, 1965.

23. Ler, op. cit., p. 6.

24. Sourek, op. cit., pp. 400-403.

25. Decree No. 8, issued by the SCFPW on January 24, 1966, in Sbirka, Part III, February 16, 1966, pp. 18-28.

26. Sik, NTCE, No. 2, 1966, p. 68.

27. Bohumil Komenda, PE, No. 9, 1966, p. 775; cf. HN, No. 39, 1966; J. Typolt and O. Novak, PH, No. 2, 1966, pp. 63-64; RP, April 4, 1967; ZN, March 11, 1966; RP, August 4, 1965; Lenart, op. cit.; and Sik, NTCE, No. 2, 1966, pp. 66 and 68.

28. Ler, op. cit., pp. 4-5.

29. Gustav Thomas, FU, No. 7, 1965, p. 394.

30. Supplement to HN, No. 6, 1966; and Richard Dvorak and Oldrych Cernik, RP, December 19, 1965.

31. Thomas, op. cit., p. 390.

32. Supplement to HN, No. 6, 1966.

33. Jindra, op. cit., p. 405.

34. Interview with Karel Snopek in Supplement to HN, No. 6, 1966.

35. Interview with Karel Podloha in Supplement to HN, No. 6, 1966.

36. Jindra, op. cit., p. 413.

37. Stanislav Musilek, FU, No. 7, 1966, p. 419.

38. Jindra, op. cit., p. 407.

39. Supplement to HN, No. 6, 1966.

40. Jan Jakubeczy, FU, No. 7, 1966, pp. 416 and 418.

41. Jaroslav Treska, FU, No. 7, 1966, pp. 423-24.

42. Interview with Snopek, op. cit.

43. Interview with Podloha, op. cit.

44. Data on 1966 plan fulfillment are mostly drawn from SP, No. 2, 1967; HN, No. 7, 1967; RP, February 7, 1967; and ESE 1966, Chapter II.

45. CFT, No. 4, 1967, p. 8.

46. Miroslav Sokol, ZG, No. 10, 1967.

47. Musilek, op. cit., p. 420.

48. Josef Vlcek, ZG, No. 19, 1967; and Miroslav Sokol, ZG, No. 10, 1967.

49. Dvorak, RP, December 19, 1965.

50. Law No. 52/66, Sbirka, July 13, 1966.

51. Data on foreign trade were primarily drawn from the report in SP, No. 2, 1967, pp. 62-67.

52. SA 1967, pp. 85-87.

53. Vlcek, op. cit.

54. SA 1967, p. 85; CFT, No. 4, 1967, p. 9; Interview with Lenart, NTCE, No. 2, 1967, pp. 3 ff.

55. Cf. Miroslav Maruska and Vladimir Novacek, ZO, No. 10, 1967, pp. 1-3; and Frantisek Stransky, CFT, No. 1, 1968, p. 3.

56. Vlcek, op. cit.

57. Goldmann and Flek, PH, No. 9, 1967.

58. Drahomir Kolder, HN, No. 41, 1966.

59. Miroslav Sokol, ZG, No. 10, 1967.

60. Emil Moravec, PM, No. 6, 1967, pp. 246-47.

61. Ibid., pp. 247-48.

62. SR 1966, pp. 142-43; and SP, No. 2, 1967, pp. 44-45.

63. Eugene Loebl, KZ, No. 2, 1967.

64. Ibid.

65. Jiri Kanturek, KT, May 26, 1966.

NOTES TO CHAPTER 6

1. J. Typolt and O. Novak, PH, No. 2, 1966, p. 63.

2. Ibid., pp. 65-7.

3. Vladimir Janza, FU, No. 1, 1967, p. 38; Josef Goldmann and Josef Flek, in CESES International Seminar (Florence: September 15, 1966), Part II, p. 122.

4. This section draws heavily on Lubos Hejl, Oldrych Kyn, and Bohuslav Sekerka, EC, No. 6, 1966; Hejl, Kyn, and Sekerka, PH, No. 11, 1965; Hejl, Kyn, and Sekerka, in Charles H. Feinstein (ed.), Socialism, Capitalism, and Economic Growth (Cambridge: Cambridge University Press, 1967); United Nations, Economic Advisers 1966/Conference 13, "The Price Model and its Use in Economic Practice in Czechoslovakia," (Mimeographed, March 24, 1966); and Typolt and Novak, op. cit.

5. Hejl, Kyn, and Sekerka, in Feinstein (ed.) op. cit., p. 102.

6. For an exposition and evaluation see George R. Feiwel, The Soviet Quest for Economic Efficiency (New York: Frederick A. Praeger, Inc., 1967), Chapter 4.

7. The calculations were conducted for a single level price system, without turnover tax. In this case surplus product is essentially equal to computed profit.

8. United Nations, op. cit., p. 7.

9. Supplement to HN, No. 30, 1966.

10. Typolt and Novak, *op. cit.*, pp. 64-65.

11. Vladislav Knobloch, PH, No. 1, 1967, pp. 60-61.

12. Typolt and Novak, *op. cit.*, p. 64; and Supplement to HN, No. 30, 1966.

13. Janza, *op. cit.*, p. 40.

14. Supplement to HN, No. 30, 1966.

15. *Ibid.*

16. Knobloch, *op. cit.*, p. 61; and Janza, *op. cit.*, pp. 41-42.

17. Supplement to HN, No. 30, 1966; and Knobloch, *op. cit.*, p. 64.

18. Supplement to HN, No. 30, 1966.

19. Janza, *op. cit.*, p. 43.

20. *Ibid.*, pp. 43-46.

21. Antonin Novotny, RP, December 21-23, 1966.

22. Supplement to HN, No. 30, 1966; Supplement to FU, No. 2, 1967; and Supplement to HN, No. 33, 1965.

23. *Sbirka*, No. 44, December 20, 1966, pp. 499-521.

24. This reduction of the stabilization tax was a relatively new proviso which was not included in government resolution No. 242 of July 15, 1966. See Supplement to HN, No. 30, 1966.

25. Cf. Supplement to HN, No. 30, 1966.

26. Similar conclusions were reached by Jan Michal, in George R. Feiwel (ed.), *New Currents*

in Soviet-Type Economies (Scranton, Pa.: International Textbook Co., 1968), pp. 492-93. Alexander Dubcek stressed the adverse effects of the stabilization tax on the utilization of the stock of capital and on the allocation of manpower. RP, September 29, 1967; cf. Jiri Danencek, PH, No. 3, 1968.

27. Cf. K. Vlachunsky, HN, No. 47, 1966.

28. Sbirka, December 20, 1966, pp. 522-28.

29. The section on investment is mainly based on Jiri Tesar and Vladimir Siba, PH, No. 8-9, 1966, p. 28; Supplement to HN, No. 15-16, 1966; Vaclav Zahalka, FU, No. 5, 1967, pp. 294-5; and Otakar Turek, HN, June 3, 1966.

30. The rates were only approximate because the budget levy was paid on the residue, bank interest charges were paid prior to commissioning the asset, bank interest was paid on the outstanding balance, etc.

31. Frantisek Hamouz, HN, No. 33, 1967; cf. Zbynek Sojak and Ladislav Riha, ZS, No. 1, 1968.

32. RP, December 21-23, 1966.

33. Josef Lenart, Predvoj, August 18, 1966; cf. Marcel Brozik, RP, August 31, 1966.

34. Novotny, ZS, No. 21, 1966.

35. Lenart, Predvoj, August 19, 1966.

36. Zahalka, op. cit., pp. 298-99.

NOTES TO CHAPTER 7

1. Interview with Josef Goldmann and Karel Kouba, HN, No. 16, 1967.

2. Vladimir Siba, PH, No. 10, 1967, p. 36.

3. A recalculation of wholesale prices alone involves more than 1.5 million items. Cf. Bohumil Sucharda, ZS, No. 12, 1967.

4. Ota Sik, NTCE, No. 5, 1967; cf. Zdenek Bednaryk, PE, No. 5, 1967, pp. 477-72.

5. Interview with Vladimir Janza, Reporter, No. 22, 1967. It was later reported as the increase in wholesale price level of 32 per cent instead of the planned 19 per cent. Karel Souska and Karel Spacek, HN, No. 11, 1968.

6. Oldrich Cernik, NTCE, No. 6, 1967, p. 10.

7. Oldrich Novotny, Supplement to FU, No. 8, 1967.

8. Ibid.

9. Milan Reh, FU, No. 10, 1967, pp. 663-65.

10. Bohumil Zbornik, Supplement to FU, No. 7, 1967.

11. Cernik, NTCE, No. 4, 1967, p. 54.

12. Zbornik, op. cit.; cf. Cernik, RP, January 11, 1968; and Vaclav Hula, KN, No. 17, 1968.

13. S. Hejduk and V. Janecek, HN, No. 4, 1967;

cf. HN, No. 5, 1967; RP, January 30, 1968; and Jindrich Uher, RP, September 27, 1967.

14. Uher, *op. cit*.

15. Cernik, NTCE, No. 4, 1967, pp. 62 and 50; Sucharda, RP, September 27, 1967. Miroslav Soucek advocated redistribution of national income in favor of capital formation to be accomplished mainly by inflationary measures. He was in favor of increases of retail prices that would outpace increases in nominal wages, resulting in temporary reduction of real wages as a means to finance investments and to propel economic growth. PH, No. 8-9, 1966. Soucek's views met with sharp criticism. See the account of the roundtable discussion, with the participation of Josef Adamicek, Julius Branik, Jaromir Cisar, Zdenek Kodet, Karel Kouba, Oldrich Kyn, Eugene Loebl, Miroslav Sokol, Miroslav Soucek, Jiri Typolt, and Augustin Zamecik, in ER, No. 4-5, 1967. The redistribution of national income in favor of investment would result, *inter alia*, in the disincentive effects of the reduction or slowdown in improvements of real consumption, with effects on workers' productivity, and would reinforce extensive development. As a result of overinvestment, the imbalances and hypertensions would be aggravated and existing barriers would be raised and/or new ones erected. Escape channels would be widened. The market mechanism would not operate effectively and inefficiency could not be eradicated. There would be no meaningful signals for allocating investments and other resources. In view of the impact of the flagrant inefficiencies, the final result is bound to be a decline in consumption, without palpable improvements in sustained growth. In a discussion on the "fear of inflation" and the effect of the market mechanism, Vaclav Klaus and Tomas Jezek stressed the necessity of moderate price increases (about 1 to 2 per cent), accompanied by an even faster rise of wages, as a general prerequisite for a balanced development of the entire economy. Such price increases would elicit an increased supply of goods, act as corrective for imbalances, equilibrate demand with supply, influence enterprises'

investment decisions, and expand capacity by directing the flow of investment resources to the excess-demand branches. KT, December 15, 1966. A faster growth of nominal wages should not only have a stimulating incentive role, but the relative increase in the price of labor should curb the demand for labor, arrest overemployment, induce introduction of labor-saving innovations, etc. Whereas price stability or declining retail prices may, under conditions of chronic excess demand under prevailing terms of exchange, aggravate the imbalances, the restoration of the market mechanism is tantamount, under existing conditions, to a visible hike of most prices. The latter is considered to have a stimulating effect on economic development as it would elicit the required and the desired output. Cf. Karel Soska, KT, February 23, 1967. The decentralization of price-setting seems to be equated with an over-all price increase. To what extent the central authorities would be capable of containing inflation is a moot question. There are definitely grounds for the financial authorities' fear of strong inflationary forces. They are incapable of dealing with such forces without the traditional weapons of discipline.

16. Emil Moravec, PM, No. 6, 1967, p. 241.

17. Interview with Janza, op. cit.

18. Oldrich Novotny, op. cit.; cf. Vladislav Knobloch, HN, No. 28, 1967, p. 9.

19. Moravec, op. cit., p. 241.

20. Reh, op. cit., p. 661.

21. Leopold Ler, FU, No. 10, 1967, p. 652.

22. Oldrich Novotny, op. cit.

23. Cernik, NTCE, No. 4, 1967, p. 60; and Lubomir Strougal, RP, September 27, 1967.

24. Sucharda, PO, No. 9, 1967; Frantisek Cihak,

HN, No. 28, 1967; and Josef Lenart, NTCE, No. 2, 1967, p. 4; cf. Antonin Novotny, NTCE, No. 1, 1967, p. 8.

25. Siba, *op. cit.*, p. 35.

26. Cernik, NTCE, No. 6, 1967, p. 9.

27. Ler, *op. cit.*, pp. 657-59.

28. Antonin Kapek, RP, September 29, 1967; cf. Jan Vintera, HN, No. 27, 1967; and Josef Kotrc, HN, No. 49, 1967.

29. J. Reznicek, RP, February 27, 1968.

30. Otakar Turek, HN, No. 43, 1967.

31. NTCE, No. 7, 1967, p. 4.

32. Cf. Strougal, *op. cit.*

33. Siba, *op. cit.*, p. 37; cf. Frantisek Vlasak, RP, September 27, 1967; and Vintera, *op. cit.*

34. Turek, *op. cit.*

35. Vintera, *op. cit.*

36. Ler, *op. cit.*, pp. 651-2.

37. Cernik, NTCE, No. 6, 1967, p. 5.

38. *Ibid.*, p. 8.

39. Ler, *op. cit.*, p. 655.

40. Reh, *op. cit.*, p. 661.

41. Miroslav Koudelka, HN, No. 28, 1967.

42. Reh, *op. cit.*, pp. 661-2.

43. Cihak, *op. cit.*

44. Vintera, *PH*, No. 7, 1967, p. 3. On the size and distribution of investment credits as of December 31, 1967, see Statni Banka Ceskoslovenska, *Bulletin*, 1968, p. 45.

45. Vlasak, *op. cit.*

46. Reh, *op. cit.*, p. 659.

47. For the statistics on the state of unfinished construction as at June 30, 1967, see *ibid.*, pp. 662-63; and Karel Johanovsky, *PH*, No. 4, 1968, pp. 41-51.

48. Otakar Pohl expected that the target of 8 billion kcs. reduction of unfinished construction in self-supporting units would be fulfilled by about 75 per cent, but the plan of reduction of unfinished projects undertaken by national committees "has been entirely without success." *RP*, September 27, 1967.

49. Vlasak, *op. cit.*

50. Pohl, *op. cit.*; Vlasak, *op. cit.*; and Jiri Vojtech, *HN*, No. 28, 1967.

51. Reh, *op. cit.*, p. 663.

52. *NTCE*, No. 4, 1967, p. 6.

53. Reh, *op. cit.*, p. 665.

54. J. Kosta and A. Cervenkova, *LN*, May 27, 1967.

55. Rudolf Rahlicek, *NM*, No. 9, 1967.

56. Siba, *op. cit.*, pp. 36-37; cf. Strougal, *op. cit.*; Milan Horalek *et al.* *HN*, No. 14, 1968; and Miroslav Sokol, *FU*, No. 5, 1968, pp. 299-306.

57. Reh, *op. cit.*, p. 662.

58. In 1968, still on an experimental basis, about one third of investment credit was to be

allocated by means of competitive bidding. Pohl, op. cit.; cf. Statni Banka Ceskoslovenska, Bulletin, 1968, p. 45.

59. Vojtech and Knobloch, HN, No. 28, 1967; Knobloch, HN, No. 28, 1967; and Jiri Hruska, HN, No. 28, 1967.

60. Reh, op. cit., pp. 659-60; cf. Vintera, HN, No. 27, 1967; and Pohl, op. cit.

61. Cernik, NTCE, No. 4, 1967, pp. 43-44.

62. Reh, op. cit., p. 662.

63. Pohl, HN, No. 28, 1967.

64. Siba, op. cit., p. 39.

65. Cf. Turek, op. cit.

66. Siba, op. cit., pp. 35-37.

67. Strougal, op. cit.

68. Sik, NTCE, No. 5, 1967.

69. Cestmir Kozusnik, Reporter, No. 21, 1967.

70. Rahlicek, op. cit.

71. Ervin Mikula, Lud, September 3, 1967.

72. Antonin Straub, HN, No. 33, 1967.

73. Rahlicek, op. cit.

74. See Jiri Slama, NM, No. 10, 1967, pp. 23-26.

75. The findings were summarized and reported by Zdenek Vergner, RP, October 27, 1967.

76. Mikula, op. cit.

77. A. Mechura, NTCE, No. 6, 1967, p. 53.

78. For example, the sales organization of farm machinery informed manufacturers that it would have to substantially reduce the contracts already concluded for 1968 and that the 1968 orders would be considerably below those of 1967. It was reported that orders for equipment of one manufacturer were cut in 1967 by 30.8 per cent in comparison to contracted deliveries and the order for 1968 would amount only to 33.8 per cent of the original orders for 1967.

79. Jan Tucek, HN, No. 31, 1967.

80. ZN, January 26, 1968.

81. Siba, op. cit., pp. 38-39. The 1967 changes in policy, such as increasing the interest rates, requiring that enterprises finance above-normative inventories from their own funds, the freezing of funds in reserve funds, and changing the base for computing budget levies from GY, had the effect of making enterprises feel "that they had been stabbed in the back by such a use of the operational instruments of the reformed planning system." Miroslav Vejnar, FU, No. 5, 1968, p. 335.

82. HN, No. 28, 1967.

83. Pohl, LD, January 4, 1968.

84. Turek, op. cit.

85. Vergner, op. cit.

86. Drahomir Kolder, RP, November 9, 1967.

87. Siba, op. cit., pp. 37-38.

88. Mikula, op. cit.; cf. Statni Banka Ceskoslovenska, Bulletin, 1968, p. 44.

89. For the first half of 1967, the reported increase of industrial labor productivity was 4 per cent, whereas industrial wages rose by almost 5 per cent in comparison with the first half of 1966. RP, August 1, 1967.

90. Moravec, op. cit., pp. 240-41.

91. Miroslav Pastyrik, RP, September 28, 1967; and A. Kaperk, RP, September 29, 1967.

92. Kolder, op. cit.

93. Kozusnik, op. cit.

94. Turek, op. cit.; Slama, NM, No. 43, 1967, p. 9. For the Western experience with income policy see, among others, George P. Shultz and Robert Z. Aliber (eds.), Guidelines (Chicago: University of Chicago Press, 1966); John Sheahan, The Wage-Price Guideposts (Washington: The Brookings Institute, 1967); and Andrew Shonfield, Modern Capitalism (New York: Oxford University Press, 1965).

95. Cernik, NTCE, No. 6, 1967, p. 14.

96. Turek, op. cit. On the wage ceiling as a "psychological barrier" see also Vladimir Bradik, RP, November 28, 1967.

97. Sucharda, RP, September 27, 1967.

98. Basic cost accounting data for individual cost centers or basic operation were not available. Sucharda, PO, No. 9, 1967.

99. SS, January 18, 1968.

100. Jaroslav Kux, HN, No. 20, 1968.

101. Bradik, op. cit.

102. Moravec, op. cit., pp. 241-43; cf. Strougal, op. cit.; and Sucharda, PO, No. 9, 1967.

103. Bradik, RP, November 30, 1967.

104. Rahlicek, op. cit.

105. Jaroslav Pokorny, PM, No. 5, 1968, p. 211.

106. Bradik, RP, November 30, 1967.

107. Kux, op. cit.

108. Pokorny, op. cit., pp. 209-10.

109. Arnost Frydrych, Reporter, No. 23, 1967; and Rahlicek, op. cit.

110. In his 1958 budget speech Sucharda reported that during preliminary investigation on the wholesale price manipulations, 750 million kcs. was uncovered of which enterprises paid into the treasury 538 million kcs. by the end of September, 1967. The investigation was supposed to have continued into 1968. RP, January 11, 1968.

111. Sucharda, RP, September 27, 1968.

112. Strougal, op. cit.

113. Strougal, op. cit.

114. Interview with Janza, op. cit.

115. Rahlicek, op. cit.

116. Ler, op. cit., p. 651.

117. Sucharda, RP, May 18, 1967.

118. Ler, op. cit., pp. 650 and 655-56; and Sucharda, RP, May 18, 1967. For a report on the budget intake and outlays see Karel Houska and Karel Spacek, HN, No. 11, 1968.

119. Vejner, FU, No. 7, 1967, pp. 473-74.

120. Josef Chalupa, HN, No. 28, 1967; cf. Slama, NM, No. 10, 1967, p. 25; Kolder, ZS, No. 10, 1967, p. 9; and Sokol, FU, No. 5, 1968, pp. 299-306.

121. Sik, NTCE, No. 5, 1967.

122. Kozusnik, op. cit.

123. Kolder, RP, November 10, 1967.

124. Sokol, FU, No. 5, 1968, p. 304.

125. Kozusnik, op. cit.

126. Kolder, RP, November 10, 1967.

127. Eugene Loebl, KZ, February 9, 1968.

128. Kozusnik, op. cit. Similar action was advocated by Loebl, KZ, January 13, 1967.

129. Cernik, NTCE, No. 4, 1967, pp. 33 ff.

130. Vintera, HN, No. 27, 1967.

131. Vintera, PH, No. 7, 1967, p. 8; cf. SA 1968, p. 43.

132. Cernik, NTCE, No. 4, 1967, p. 58.

133. RP, August 1, 1967.

134. Ibid.

135. Vintera, HN, No. 27, 1967.

136. Strougal, op. cit.

137. RP, January 30, 1968.

138. RP, January 22, 1968.

139. CTK, January 18, 1968.

140. RP, January 30, 1968.

141. Prace, January 5, 1968.

142. ZN, January 31, 1968.

143. RP, January 30, 1968.

144. R. Kostka, RP, January 4, 1968.

145. Statni Banka Ceskoslovenska, Bulletin, 1968, p. 5; RP, January 30, 1968.

146. Only 25 per cent of construction projects which were supposed to have been completed in 1967 were reported to have been completed. Pohl, RaPr., May 8, 1968. According to investigations of the Central Commission of People's Inspection the new system "has not yet brought improvement to the excessive volume of unfinished capital construction existing since 1958, and which, in 1967, exceeded the planned target by several billion kcs." RP, January 19, 1968. On the mounting investment pressures by investors in 1967 see, inter alia, Ljubomir Texl, IV, No. 1, 1968, pp. 11-13. Reportedly, it takes "twice to three times as long" in Czechoslovakia to complete constructions "as compared to countries where conditions are otherwise comparable." Interview with Vaclav Hula, KN, April 26, 1968.

147. RP, January 30, 1968; cf. Gustav Capko, RP, January 4, 1968.

148. RP, January 30, 1968; Sucharda, RaPr., April 10, 1968. According to Hula, the increase of inventories absorbed 40 per cent of the increase in national income. Interview with Hula, op. cit.

149. RP, January 30, 1968.

150. RP, January 14, 1968.

151. Frantisek Hamouz, RP, September 28, 1967.

152. ZN, February 22, 1968.

153. RP, January 12, 1968.

154. RP, January 30, 1968.

155. RP, January 31, 1968.

156. Vergner, March 28, 1968; and Sucharda, RaPr., June 26, 1968.

157. Cf. Vladimir Nachtigal, HN, No. 45, 1967.

158. RP, January 30, 1968.

159. Interview with Hula, op. cit.

160. Prace, February 4, 1968.

161. Statni Banka Ceskoslovenska, Bulletin, 1968, p. 4.

162. RP, January 30, 1968. It should be noted that since Slovakia's main industry is that of basic raw materials, whereas in the Czech lands the processing industry is prevalent, the recorded profitability is considerably lower in Slovakia (in 1967 it was only 9.5 per cent) than in the Czech lands (in 1967 it was 13 per cent). Hence the resulting "disproportionate " share for self-financing development in Slovakia. Jan Marcek, CTK, May 28, 1968.

163. Houska and Spacek, op. cit.

164. RP, December 29, 1967.

165. Kolder, RP, November 9, 1967.

166. The long-term agrements signed with Great Britain, the German Federal Republic, and the Benelux countries make it possible for Czechoslovak exports to have greater access to these markets. Hamouz, NZO, January 5, 1968.

167. RP, December 23, 1967; and Bohumil Simon, RP, December 29, 1967.

168. Sucharda, RP, January 11, 1968.

169. Houska and Spacek, op. cit. Sucharda disclosed that the 1967 budget ended with a deficit of 777 million kcs., consisting of a central budget deficit of 2,831 million kcs. and a surplus of the national committees' budgets totaling 2,054 million kcs. The national committees used their surpluses to strengthen their own reserves and development

funds. Their funds cannot be used to offset the deficit of the central budget. The planned quotas of state subsidies were exceeded by 2.5 billion (and reached 30.6 billion kcs., including about 10 billion kcs. to investment and about 20 billion kcs. to current activity). Sucharda underlined that should subsidies be removed immediately, prices of foodstuffs would increase by 20 per cent and rents would more than double. Subsidies were to be removed only gradually. The stated aim was to decrease their volume in 1968 by only 1.1 billion kcs. RP, June 14, 1968; and RaPr., June 26, 1968.

170. Sucharda, RP, January 11, 1968.

171. Among foodstuffs, subsidies are required mainly for milk, poultry, and canned goods. Subsidized industrial goods include fuels, building materials, children's clothing and footwear, glass, and porcelain. It was disclosed that losses amount to 60 per cent on rents, to 70 per cent on theatre admission tickets, to one third on milk, to more than a quarter on fuels. Hula reported that subsidies to support the excess of wholesale over retail prices for goods and services amounted to over 9 billion, of which almost 6 billion kcs. represents support to services and more than 2 billion kcs. to foodstuffs. In addition, other price subsidies proliferate. For example, subventions paid for procurement of milk amount to about 1.7 billion alone. Interview with Hula, op. cit.

172. Sucharda, FU, No. 1, 1968, p. 6.

173. Sucharda, RP, January 11, 1968.

174. Alexander Dubcek, RP, September 29, 1967; cf. Gustav Tomas, FU, No. 4, 1967, pp. 227 ff; and Michal Sabolchik, Pravda, June 10, 1967.

175. Sucharda, RP, January 11, 1968.

176. Ibid.

177. Sbirka, January 12, 1968, pp. 12-16.

178. Antonin Novotny, RP, January 2, 1968.

179. Vlasak, op. cit.

180. Cernik, HN, No. 1, 1968.

181. Much more ambitious variants were advocated. For example, it was proposed to step up the rate of growth of national income to 37-38 per cent. Simon, NM, No. 25, 1967.

182. The government assumed that in 1968-70 real wages per capita would rise on the average by 2.3 to 2.8 per cent annually. Cernik, RP, January 12, 1968. The 1968 plan envisages a 4.3 per cent increase of wages (economy-wide) on the assumption that national income would increase by about 5 per cent. Real wages should increase in the range of 2.3-2.8 per cent. PM, No. 2, 1968, p. 52.

183. During the discussion on the 1968 budget, Samuel Takac, the Minister of Construction, informed the NA that apparently measures were taken to ensure housing construction and availability of sufficient quantity of building materials for that purpose. Whereas the output of building materials was in 1967, 8 per cent higher than in 1966, in 1968 it was expected to increase by 13 per cent and by 1970 by 50 per cent. RP, January 12, 1968.

184. RP, December 23, 1967; and Simon, RP, December 29, 1967.

185. LD, January 16, 1968. An extensive plan of development of ultramodern department stores up to 1980 was disclosed. New department stores should be opened in 1968 in Bratislava, Pilsen, Kosice, and Komarno. Construction of department stores is envisaged for the period 1969-70, including a huge one in Prague. LD, December 29, 1967.

186. LD, February 3, 1968. During the discussion on the 1968 budget in the NA, deputy Lubomir Dohnal recommended "to increase the limit for the imports of consumer goods, which has been set at 9.3 per cent,

while in some advanced countries it is 25-30 per cent." _RP_, January 12, 1968.

187. _CTK_, January 6, 1968.

188. V. Komarek, _RP_, February 8, 1968.

189. _Ibid_.

190. Cernik, _RP_, January 11, 1968. The present process of rectifying inequities in the allocation of resources can give rise to still further inflationary pressures by accommodating various groups of society and by satisfying local interests (e.g., Slovakia) which would place additional demands on resources. There probably is a danger of the government authorizing "political investments"--which might prove to be ineffective. Vergner, _RP_, March 28, 1968.

191. Cernik, _RP_, January 11, 1968; and _RP_, February 8, 1968.

192. Josef Kotrc, _HN_, No. 49, 1967.

193. _The Economist_, October 14, 1967, p. 149.

194. _RP_, January 3, 1968.

195. Kotrc, _op. cit_.

196. Cernik, _RP_, January 11, 1968.

197. Josef Goldmann and Josef Flek, _PH_, No. 9, 1967.

198. Vergner, _RP_, March 28, 1968.

199. Loebl, _PH_, No. 11, 1967; cf. Nachtigal, _HN_, No. 45, 1967.

200. Flek, Goldmann, and Kouba, _RP_, June 23, 1966.

201. Vlasak, _op. cit_.

202. Kouba, HN, No. 16, 1967.

203. The work conducted on the second phase of the price reform "is lagging behind schedule, causing much uncertainty." The results of the first phase are "constantly being only explained and corrected, but a specific program for further action is not tabled." Strougal, op. cit.; cf. Hamouz, RP, September 27, 1968. The idea of competition was stifled and prices were not permitted to perform their economic functions. See the discussion by Sik, Prace, March 5, 1968, and the interview with Hula, op. cit.; cf. Horalek et al., op. cit.

204. Early in 1968 the turnover tax rates continued to be vastly "differentiated." The turnover tax rates, calculated in relation to wholesale prices, oscillated between -60 per cent and +1,900 per cent (in 1966 and 1967 the range of rates was even broader). Sucharda, RP, April 30, 1968. Taxes vary around 130 per cent for clothing, gasoline, and a number of durable consumer goods (such as automobiles, television sets, and refrigerators). Among foodstuffs, high taxes are levied on coffee, tea, alcoholic beverages and most of the products made of flour. Taxes amount to as much as 50 per cent on sugar, chocolate, and tropical fruits. Interview with Hula, op. cit. Even assuming that equilibrium should be achieved, it does not necessarily follow that market pressures would be correctly exerted on the producers. Various barriers may be preserved or erected, such as the prevailing widely differentiated turnover taxes and the surcharges and deductions in foreign trade. Other impediments to the faithful transmission of market pressures include the limitations imposed (or that might be imposed) on the producers regarding the choice of product mix and of production techniques; barriers to entry; real dependence of the enterprise's profit (profit-sharing) on market performance (redistribution).

205. See Oskar Lange's discussion of a market as a servo-mechanism based on the feedback principle, summarized in George R. Feiwel, The Soviet Quest for

Economic Efficiency (New York: Frederick A. Praeger, Inc., 1967), pp. 202-204; cf. Loebl, PH, No. 11, 1967.

206. Sucharda, RP, May 1, 1968.

207. Meaning that by reallocating resources, ceteris paribus, no improvement in the total value (satisfaction) can be achieved. Ineffective combination of productive agents diminishes output and ineffective combination of output lessens productive inputs, or the exchange value of products on foreign markets and diminishes the present satisfaction from the output composition obtained, or diminishes future consumption.

208. Loebl, PH, No. 11, 1967. On persisting flagrant inefficiencies see interview with Hula, op. cit.

209. Cf. George R. Feiwel, The Economics of a Socialist Enterprise (Frederick A. Praeger, Inc., 1965), Chapter 2.

210. Loebl, PH, No. 11, 1967.

211. Vergner, RP, October 26, 1967. It may be noted that an economist of the SPC complained that for the past two or three years the supply of foodstuffs was ameliorated and the shortages of consumer goods were reduced. But the reduction of imbalances was frequently accomplished by nonmarket methods--by suppressing a legitimate increase in wages and by regulating the sale of some goods by administrative measures. Vintera, HN, No. 27, 1967.

212. Kolder, ZS, No. 10, 1967, p. 9.

213. Cernik, NTCE, No. 4, 1967, pp. 54-58.

214. Goldmann and Kouba, HN, No. 16, 1967.

215. According to Simon, the forced savings amount to about 3 per cent of the total population's annual income. NM, No. 25, 1967; cf. interview with

the Deputy Minister of Domestic Trade, A. Mechura, NTCE, No. 6, 1967; Nachtigal's review of the 1967 Statistical Yearbook, HN, No. 45, 1967.

216. Miroslav Tucek, FU, No. 5, 1967, pp. 333-34. See the call for a reform of the kcs. exchange rate by Rudolf Zukal, PE, No. 6, 1967, pp. 539-52. See also Radoslav Selucky on the gradual transition to the convertibility of the kcs. in SS, December 31, 1967; and the survey of opinions on the exchange rate of the kcs. by Frantisek Fojtik, ER, No. 12, 1967, pp. 532-38. It is noteworthy that Czechoslovakia now received on the average $1.00 for about 30 to 32 kcs. of output and 1.00 r. for about 20 kcs. of output exported. Sucharda, Reporter, No. 13, 1968.

217. In switching over to market prices Jiri Danecek, *inter alia*, emphasized the necessity of a well-conceived policy of reallocating financial resources, of rewarding depositors, and of redistributing credit "on commercial principles both through the banking system and the whole money market." The commercial reallocation of funds through the banking system and the money market should be based primarily "on the market prices of money," on an effective interest rate, and on the principles of profitability. He added--"this is not being understood thus far, and everyone demands concessions and a reduction of interest charges." PH, No. 3, 1968.

218. Cf. Loebl, PH, No. 11, 1967.

219. Sik, NTCE, No. 5, 1967; and MF, February 21, 1968.

220. Reznicek, RP, February 27, 1968; and Danecek, *op. cit*.

221. Sik, MF, February 21, 1968; Sokol, FU, No. 5, 1968, pp. 299-306.

222. Loebl, PH, No. 11, 1967, pp. 10-22; cf. Kouba, PE, No. 9, 1967, pp. 773-83.

223. Frydrych, op. cit.; and Vejner, FU, No. 7, 1967, p. 473.

224. Kosta and Cervenkova, op. cit.

225. Luciano Barca, Rinascita, December 1, 1967, pp. 29-30.

226. Ibid.

227. ZN, January 22, 1968.

228. The varied managerial qualities required by the old and new systems were stressed by Milos Machac, Director of the Institute of Psychology, Charles University. MR, No. 10, 1967, pp. 5-13.

229. Barca, op. cit.

230. The Economist, August 13, 1966.

231. Horalek et al. op. cit.

232. Sik, Prace, March 5, 1968.

233. Sik claimed that should redistribution be abolished, at least half of the enterprises would go bankrupt. CTK, June 5, 1968.

234. Horalek et al., op. cit.

235. Sik, MF, February 21, 1968; and Horalek et al., op. cit.

NOTES TO CHAPTER 8

1. Antonin Novotny, RP, December 13, 1963.

2. Vladimir Koucky, RP, December 24, 1963.

3. RP, December 20, 1963.

4. RP, February 29, 1964.

5. Jiri Sotola, LN, February 1, 1964.

6. RP, March 5, 1964.

7. RP, April 3, 1964.

8. See Sotola, LN, April 11, 1964; and a report of Karol Rozenbaum's speech at a meeting of Slovak writers in RP, April 14, 1964.

9. KZ, May 1, 1964.

10. RP, April 30, and May 1, 1964.

11. See Koucky, RP, June 23, 1964.

12. The Economist, June 20, 1964, p. 1351.

13. See KZ, June 18, and June 25, 1965.

14. ZS, No. 1, 1966.

15. Jiri Hajek, RP, April 1, 1966.

16. Michal Lakatos, Pravny obzor, No. 3, 1966.

17. Novotny, RP, June 1, 1966.

18. See Pravda, May 13-15, 1966; and KZ, May 20, 1966.

19. ZS, No. 21, 1966.

20. RP, September 6, 13, and 20, 1966.

21. Jiri Hendrych, RP, February 10, 1967.

22. KZ, May 19, 1967; and LN, May 20, 1967.

23. Josef Smrkovsky, RP, May 4, 1965; and Student, June 20, 1967.

24. See Viktor Pavlenda, Pravda, October 19 and 26, 1966.

25. Zdenek Mlynar, RP, August 16, 1966.

26. Miroslav Kusy, Pravda, October 19, 1966.

27. Vaclav Kotyk, Sl.P, No. 5, 1965. For a similar view see Andrej Kopcok, Pravda, October 25, 1966.

28. LN, July 1, 1967.

29. See The New York Times, June 11 and July 6, 1967.

30. This speech was not published in Czechoslovakia but somehow found its way to the West. See Die Weltwoche, July 21, 1967, and excerpts in East Europe, September, 1967, pp. 18-20.

31. LN, July 29, 1967.

32. LN, July 8, 1967.

33. Hendrych, RP, June 30, 1967.

34. MF, July 5, 1967.

35. Novtony, RP, July 1, 1967.

36. See, inter alia, Alexander Matuska, RP, July 16, 1967; Ivan Skola, RP, July 21, 1967; and Hajek, RP, July 27, 1967.

37. The Times, June 2, 1967.

38. See The New York Times, July 3, 1967.

39. Ladislav Mnacko, Frankfurter Allgemeine Zeitung, August 11, 1967.

40. See in particular Novotny, RP, August 12 and September 2, 1967.

41. RP, July 16, 1967.

42. Jan Prochazka, LN, September 15, 1967.

43. Cf. The New York Times, September 17, 1967.

44. Pavel Kohout, Die Zeit, September 15, 1967.

45. LN, September 8, 1967; and RP, September 6 and 8, 1967.

46. Prace, November 11, 1967.

47. Interview with Ivan Pfaff, LD, March 21 and 27, 1968.

48. Cf. Jan Mlynarik, CCH, No. 5, 1967.

49. RP, September 28, 1967.

50. Hendrych, RP, September 30, 1967.

51. RP, October 3 and 4, 1967.

52. Michel Tatu, Le Monde, October 10, 1967.

53. Kohout, Die Zeit, November 10, 1967.

54. Neue Zuercher Zeitung, December 9, 1967.

55. Pravda, October 25, 1967.

56. RP, November 19, 1967.

57. L'Humanite, December 23, 1967.

58. See, inter alia, RN, March 21, 1968.

59. Alexander Dubcek, Pravda, December 31, 1967.

60. Milos Vacik, RP, January 14, 1968.

61. Prace, February 1, 1968.

62. LN, January 27, 1968.

63. Guiseppe Boffa, L'Unita, April 25, 1968.

64. Pavel Dvorak, KZ, March 22, 1968.

65. CTK, May 30, 1968.

66. See also Vladimir Kaigl on ensuring the supremacy of the NA over the government. KT, March 14, 1968.

67. Milan Huebl, KZ, January 5, 1968.

68. Gustav Husak, KZ, January 12, 1968.

69. Oldrich Svestka, RP, January 14, 1968.

70. Vaclav Savik, RP, January 30, 1968.

71. Mlynar, RP, February 13, 1968.

72. Lakatos, KN, February 24, 1968.

73. Zora Jesenska, KZ, April 5, 1968.

74. Vladimir Manak, KZ, April 26, 1968.

75. Jan Uher at a roundtable discussion in Pravda, February 2, 1968.

76. Josef Sabata, Radio Brno, February 7, 1968.

77. Public Affairs Program, Czechoslovak Television, February 29, 1968; Jiri Hanzelka, roundtable discussion, Reporter, No. 12, 1968.

78. Savik, Prace, February 7, 1968.

79. Manak, op. cit.

80. Smrkovsky, Prace, January 21, 1968.

81. Sabata, op. cit.

82. Smrkovsky, RaPr., February 2, 1968.

83. See Jaroslav Mesko, Pravda, February 28, 1968.

84. Discussion Forum, RaPr., February 28, 1968.

85. R. Dohnalova, KN, February 24, 1968.

86. See Ondrej Kolkoc, Pravda, April 2, 1968.

87. Vlastimil Dovera, RP, February 26, 1968.

88. Cf. Husak, KZ, February 2, 1968.

89. Vladimir Davis, KN, March 8, 1968.

90. Max Froman, RP, February 26, 1968.

91. Mlynar, roundtable discussion, Reporter, No. 12, 1967.

92. See Uher, roundtable discussion, Pravda, February 2, 1968; and Smrkovsky, RP, February 9, 1968.

93. Lumir Civrny, Prace, March 24, 1968.

94. Smrkovsky, Prace, January 21, 1968.

95. Radoslav Selucky, Prace, March 14, 1968.

96. Jaroslav Klofac, roundtable discussion, Reporter, No. 12, 1968.

97. Vladimir Ferko, Predvoj, March 28, 1968.

98. Cf. Helena Klimova, LL, March 14, 1968; Kohout, LL, March 7, 1968.

99. Jesenska, op. cit.

100. Smrkovsky, RaPr., February 2, 1968.

101. Student, January 31, 1968; Prace, February 29, 1968; MF, March 1, 1968; and Student, March 6, 1968.

102. See, for example, Vojtech Daubner, Praca, February 25, 1968.

103. Selucky, SS, February 18, 1968.

104. Ladislav Zajac, Praca, February 25, 1968.

105. Praca, February 29, 1968.

106. Discussion Forum, RaPr., February 28, 1968.

107. Karel Pasek, LL, April 18, 1968.

108. Cf. Filip Jansky, LL, March 28, 1968.

109. Cf. Frantisek Kriegel, RP, June 19, 1968.

110. Vaclav Havel, RaPr., May 8, 1968.

111. Jiri Lederer, LL, March 21, 1968.

112. Among others, Huebl expressed such leanings in a roundtable discussion on RaPr., February 20, 1968.

113. Jesenska, op. cit.; and Lakatos, KN, April 5, 1968.

114. Havel, LL, April 4, 1968. For somewhat similar views see, inter alia, Ivan Svitak, Filmove a televisni noviny, April 4, 1968; Milan Sutovec, KZ, March 29, 1968; Alexander Kliment, LL, March 14,

1968; Jaroslav Opat and Karel Kaplan, roundtable discussion, Reporter, No. 15, 1968; and Pavol Stevcek, KZ, April 12, 1968.

115. RaPr., June 7, 1968.

116. RP, February 8, 1968.

117. See particularly , Jansky, op. cit.

118. Vaclav Kraus, Prace, February 22, 1968.

119. Havel, LL, April 4, 1968.

120. Eugene Loebl, RaPr., February 20, 1968. See also excerpts of Loebl's book on his personal experiences during the show trials, LL, April 25, 1968; and Reporter, No. 20, 1968.

121. Student, March 6, 1968; RN, February 24, 1968.

122. Manak, op. cit.

123. RaPr., March 18, 1968; ZN, March 16, 1968.

124. Cf. LD, March 22, 1968.

125. Smena, April 28, 1968.

126. Karel Taus, LN, January 27, 1968.

127. Cf. The Washington Post, June 3, 1968.

128. RP, June 7, 1968.

129. Loebl, KZ, February 9, 1968.

130. For a seething denunciation of these attitudes see Huebl, Prace, January 28, 1968; and LL, March 14, 1968; Anton Hyskisch, Plemen, No. 1, 1968.

131. Anton Tazky, Predvoj, February 8, 1968.

132. Pravda, March 10, 1968.

133. Julius Strinka, KZ, April 5, 1968.

134. Huebl, Predvoj, April 18, 1968.

135. See Vojtech Mihalik, Predvoj, April 18, 1968; and Uher, KZ, April 12, 1968. It is worth noting here that Valek, Mihalik, and Novomesky resigned on April 18 from the editorial board of KZ, presumably on the grounds that the weekly had been stressing of late democratization before federation and Slovak national rights--a stand then favored by Prague.

136. Marian Sklenka, RN, April 20, 1968.

137. Prace, April 18, 1968.

138. RP, May 18, 1968.

139. CTK, June 7, 1968.

140. Ota Sik, RaPr., April 6, 1968.

141. Oldrich Cernik, RaPr., April 3, 1968.

142. Sik, Prace, March 5, 1968.

143. Selucky, SS, February 18, 1968; and LL, May 2, 1968.

144. Cernik, CTK, May 14, 1968.

145. Josef Kriz, RaPr., May 27, 1968.

146. Sik, Prace, March 5, 1968.

147. Interview with Vaclav Vales, CTK, April 17, 1968.

148. Vales, RaPr., May 24, 1968.

149. Vladimir Kadlec, CTK, May 22, 1968. It was suggested that the lessons to be learned from the NEP period are more instructive than those of any subsequent period of imperative planning. "Small

capitalist enterprises" are required in a socialist state as a complement of and a supplement to the socialist sector. They were needlessly eliminated "in too much of a hurry." The socialist state need not be apprehensive of "small capitalists" as long as it maintains the commanding posts. The fundamental question is the existence of "equivalent exchange" between the state, cooperative, and private sectors. But high discriminatory taxes should be levied on the private sector. It was also maintained that the cooperative sector in the socialist countries has often proven to be "more viable than the state sector." Josef Ceconik, Pravda, February 2, 1968.

150. CTK, May 15, 1968.

151. Vaclav Cap, RP, May 28, 1968.

152. Cernik, CTK, June 8, 1968.

153. CTK, April 29, 1968.

154. CTK, May 13, 1968.

155. CTK, June 6, 1968.

156. CTK, April 22, 1968.

157. CTK, June 2, 1968.

158. CTK, June 18, 1968.

159. CTK, June 8, 1968.

160. RaPr., April 16, 1968.

161. Cernik, RaPr., April 24, 1968.

162. CTK, May 24, 1968.

163. Pravda (Moscow), January 6, 1968.

164. Pravda (Moscow), March 14, 1968.

165. Pravda (Moscow), April 30, 1968.

166. *Pravda* (Moscow), May 9, 1968.

167. V. Stepanov, *Pravda* (Moscow), May 11, 1968.

168. *Literaturnaya gazeta*, May 8, 1968.

169. Cf. *Sovetskaya Rossia*, May 14, 1968.

170. *Trybuna ludu*, January 6 and 7, 1968.

171. Jirji Stano, *Robotnichesko delo*, March 12, 1968.

172. See, *inter alia*, Zivko Milic, *Ekonomska politika*, March 11-17, 1968; and Velimur Budimir, *Vjesnik*, March 17, 1968.

173. Melita Singer, *Vjesnik*, May 10, 1968.

174. See, for example, the very positive article by Milor Mica, *Politika*, May 12, 1968.

175. Cf. *Smena*, April 4, 1968.

176. *Berliner Zeitung*, May 9, 1968.

177. *CTK*, April 3, 1968.

178. *RP*, June 7, 1968.

179. See, for example, Milan Syrucek, *MF*, April 25, 1968; and Eugen Rosian, *Prace*, April 25, 1968.

180. *United Press International*, April 23, 1968.

181. Dubcek, *RP*, May 7, 1968.

182. Cernik, *RP*, April 24 and May 14, 1968; and Sik, *CTK*, April 29, 1968.

183. *The New York Times*, May 1, 1968.

184. Frantisek Kovril, *RaPr*., May 16, 1968.

185. Vales, *RaPr*., April 18, 1968; and *CTK*,

April 19, 1968.

186. Jaromir Vanek, Reporter, No. 22, 1968.

187. Ibid.

188. Le Monde, May 5, 1968.

189. Ervin Jiricek, Prace, May 13, 1968.

190. Smrkovsky, RP, May 19, 1968.

191. The Washington Post, May 23, 1968.

192. See, for example, The Times, June 7, 1968.

193. Interview with Major General Josef Cepicky, Prace, June 2, 1968.

194. RP, June 7, 1968.

195. RP, June 18, 1968.

196. KZ, June 28, 1968.

197. Cf. The New York Times, July 1, 1968.

198. For example, the U.S.S.R. has lodged its first formal protest through diplomatic channels against the reprinting in LD, June 5, 1968, of an article which appeared in The New York Times implicating a Soviet general in Sejna's defection. On June 5, the Czechoslovak Defense Ministry denied the allegations of The New York Times article. RP, June 6, 1968.

199. V. Pavlicek, LD, June 1, 1968.

200. LD, June 17, 1968.

201. Fyodor V. Konstantinov, Pravda (Moscow), June 14, 1968.

202. Dubcek, RP, June 4, 1968.

203. This point was particularly driven home in speeches by Dubcek, RP, June 4, 1968; Mlynar, RP, June 3, 1968; Cisar, RP, June 3, 1968; and Sik, RP, June 5, 1968.

204. RP, June 3, 1968.

205. See, *inter alia*, Emil Rigo, RP, June 6, 1968.

206. Dubcek, RaPr., June 4, 1968.

207. Sik, RP, June 6, 1968.

208. *Ibid*.

209. Smrkovsky, RP, June 6, 1968.

210. RP, June 7, 1968.

211. RP, June 3, 1968.

212. *Ibid*.

213. *Ibid*.

214. RP, June 7, 1968.

215. CTK, June 29, 1968.

216. RaPr., June 7, 1968; Cernik, CTK, June 20, 1968; and Tanyug (Yugoslav Telegraph Service), June 29, 1968.

217. CTK, May 29, 1968.

218. Radio Belgrade, dispatch from Prague, May 28, 1968.

219. See, for example, the excerpts of a "letter from old Communists" being circulated to the public and reprinted in KZ, March 22, 1968, with discrediting commentary. Smena, June 25, 1968, pointed to the slanderous campaign waged anonymously against some leading politicians of the progressive group. For instance, Goldstuecker received threatening anonymous

letters condemning him as a "Zionist hyena" and declaring war upon him. See his appeal to "be on guard against anti-Semitic elements with fascist leanings" in RP, June 23, 1968.

220. RP, March 10, 1968.

221. Ludvik Vaculik, LL, March 1, 1968.

222. Manak, *op. cit*.

223. SS, July 3, 1968.

ABOUT THE AUTHOR

George R. Feiwel is a Professor of Economics at the University of Tennessee. From 1962-66 he was an Associate Professor at the University of Alberta. He spent the Easter Term, 1965, as Visitor at the Faculty of Economics and Politics, University of Cambridge, and in the summers of 1966-67 he was an Associate of Harvard University's Russian Research Center.

Dr. Feiwel has conducted firsthand research on the efficiency of the plan and the market in Yugoslavia and the Scandinavian countries. His publications include _Cost: The Various Meanings of the Concept_ (Edmonton, Alberta: University of Alberta, 1964); _The Economics of a Socialist Enterprise_ (New York: Frederick A. Praeger, 1965); _The Soviet Quest for Economic Efficiency_ (New York: Frederick A. Praeger, 1967); and (ed.) _New Currents in Soviet-Type Economies_ (Scranton, Pa.: International Textbook Co., 1968).

Mr. Feiwel received his Ph.D. degree in economics from McGill University. He has done postgraduate study at the University of California in Berkeley.